FAITH IN THE CITY

Preaching
Radical Social Change
in Detroit

ANGELA D. DILLARD

With a Foreword by
Dr. Charles G. Adams

THE UNIVERSITY OF MICHIGAN PRESS
Ann Arbor

Copyright © by the University of Michigan 2007
Published in the United States of America by
The University of Michigan Press
Manufactured in the United States of America
⊗ Printed on acid-free paper

2010   2009   2008   2007   4   3   2   1

A CIP catalog record for this book is available from the British Library.

Library of Congress Cataloging-in-Publication Data

Dillard, Angela D., 1965–
    Faith in the city : preaching radical social change in Detroit /
Angela D. Dillard ; with a foreword by Charles G. Adams.
        p.   cm.
    Includes bibliographical references and index.
    ISBN-13: 978-0-472-11462-7 (cloth : alk. paper)
    ISBN-10: 0-472-11462-x (cloth : alk. paper)
    ISBN-13: 978-0-472-03207-5 (pbk. : alk. paper)
    ISBN-10: 0-472-03207-0 (pbk. : alk. paper)
        1. African Americans—Civil rights—Michigan—Detroit—History—
20th century.   2. African Americans—Michigan—Detroit—Social
conditions—20th century.   3. Civil rights movements—Michigan—
Detroit—20th century.   4. Detroit (Mich.)—Social conditions—20th
century.   5. Hill, Charles Andrew, 1893–1970.   6. Cleage, Albert B.
7. Clergy—Michigan—Detroit—Political activity—History—20th
century.   8. Civil rights—Religious aspects—Christianity—History—
20th century.   I. Title.

F574.D49N437   2007
323.1196'073077434090904—dc22   2006039829

Grateful acknowledgment is given for permission to reprint "Goodbye Christ" and "Christ
in Alabama," from The Collected Poems of Langston Hughes, by Langston Hughes, copyright
© 1994 by The Estate of Langston Hughes. Used by permission of Alfred A. Knopf, a
division of Random House, Inc.

TO THE EXTENDED DILLARD CLAN

to all those who keep faith with Detroit

ACKNOWLEDGMENTS

U ltimately, this book is about connections: between religion and politics, between two of Detroit's leading Black political ministers, and between the city's two distinct phases of the civil rights struggle. The following chapters represent one way to explore the complexity of movements for civil rights and social justice in a local setting. Although Detroit is in some ways unique, I hope the implications of this narrative will extend beyond the city's limits and speak to the experiences of generations of activists whose stories have yet to be recorded. Fortunately, much of Detroit's history has been preserved in the manuscript collections of individuals and organizations and in the oral histories and audiovisual materials housed in the Archives of Labor History and Urban Affairs at Wayne State University (ALHUA). This remarkable assortment of primary materials, including a 1967 oral history conducted with the Reverend Charles A. Hill and recordings of Reverend Albert B. Cleage Jr.'s sermons, has been invaluable for my understanding of political radicalism in Detroit.

Thanks to the generosity of the Hill family, I was also given access to the "Red Squad" file kept on Hill by the Detroit Police Department and to many of Hill's personal papers. These materials now form the bulk of the Hill Family Papers at the University of Michigan's Bentley Historical Library, which also houses an impressive segment of the city's religious history, including the records of C. L. Franklin, Bethel AME, and Gerald L. K. Smith.

During the winter of 2005, I had the good fortune to be awarded a Public Goods Fellowship to teach classes at the University of Michigan based on the Bentley's archival holdings. My interaction with colleagues and students at Michigan shaped this manuscript in myriad ways. This terrific group of students influenced my understanding of issues ranging from the mural of the Black Madonna and Child, which still hangs in the sanctuary of the Shrine of the Black Madonna, to what Robert F. Williams learned from one generation of militant Black Detroiters and taught another. I wish to thank them all. Thanks, too, to the archivists, especially Karen Jania, and the staff for putting up with me. My visiting appointment in Michigan's History Department as a Public Goods Fellow allowed me the time and space necessary to complete this manuscript, and I am equally grateful to my home institution, the Gallatin School of Individualized Study at New York University, for granting me an academic leave, as well as a research grant from the Stephen Golden Enrichment Fund.

Many of the connections I trace in the subsequent chapters were first suggested to me years ago during my childhood in Detroit. It was my good fortune to be in a position to hear many of the stories told at holiday parties (at "Uncle" Ernie and "Aunt" Jessie Dillard's and at Dolores and Oscar Paskal's) and other casual gatherings by those who had been active in local political struggles. Their memories have influenced this book in ways too numerous to decipher or fully acknowledge. While not all of them would agree with all the arguments and analyses I put forth, I owe them a debt of gratitude I can never repay. Special thanks to the extended Hill clan, especially the late Bermecia (Hill) Morrow McCoy, Charles A. Hill Jr., and Lantz Hill for sharing their memories of their father. Many other individuals also allowed me to interview them, including Christopher Alston, James and Grace Lee Boggs, Ernest C. Dillard, Arthur McPhaul, Hodges Mason, David Morrow, Oscar and Dolores Paskal, B. J. Widick, Dorothy Johnson, the Rev. Nicholas Hood Sr., DeVon Cunningham, Barbara (Cleage) Martin, Mark Solomon, Margaret Dade, Malcolm G. Dade Jr., and Jaramogi Menelik Kimathi (Cardinal Demosthene Nelson), Holy Patriarch and Presiding Bishop of the Shrines of the Black Madonna of the Pan African Orthodox Christian Church. Another member of the shrine community, Paul Lee, was equally helpful. A thoughtful and thorough local historian, he was kind enough to share numerous resources (and e-mails) on the early days of the shrine and Reverend Cleage.

The Reverend Charles G. Adams was kind enough to talk with me about "growing up under" Reverend Hill. A "son" of Hartford, Adams took over the pastorate of the church upon Hill's retirement and has guided the congregation for the past three decades. He is a remarkable man in his own right and a figure about whom an entire book could (and should!) be written. I also "grew up" in Hartford (my grandparents joined the church in the 1920s), and years of listening to Pastor Adams's voice booming from the pulpit schooled me in an understanding of the power of language and the meaning of a passionate devotion to a living and politically engaged faith.

One last person who also granted me an interview needs to be thanked: my mother, Marilynn (Adams) Dillard. She was the first secretary at the Trade Union Leadership Council and was involved in civil rights work in the city in the 1950s and 1960s. Moreover, along with my father, Paul Anthony Dillard Sr., she has provided me with a constant source of love and support—and great stories!—over the years. I could not have lived this life or written this book without them. My late brother, the Rev. Paul Anthony Dillard Jr., who at the time of his premature, AIDS-related death served as dean of the Cathedral of the Imani Temple, an African American Catholic Congregation headquartered in Washington, DC, and led by Bishop George Stallings, also influenced my perspective on the interrelationship between politics and religion in both word and deed.

A number of friends read and commented on parts of this manuscript over the years. It began as a doctoral dissertation at the University of Michigan and was stewarded by a remarkable dissertation committee: Earl Lewis, Robin Kelley, David Scobey, Roger Rouse, and Don Herzog—each of whom gave me a wealth of advice, even when I was too stubborn to take it. I also benefited greatly from the feedback of former colleagues at the University of Minnesota, especially David Roediger, Sara Evans, and Rose Brewer, as well as present colleagues at New York University, including George Shulman, Kim Philips-Fein, Stephen Duncombe, and the entire faculty of the Gallatin School of Individualized Study, along with the members of the Social Movements Workshop. I would also like to thank Jeanne Theoharris and the rest of the contributors to the *Freedom North* volume for deepening my knowledge of and appreciation for the history of civil rights struggles outside the South. My own contribution to that collection (which forms the basis of chap. 6) benefited from the feedback and editorial suggestions made by Jeanne and her coeditor, Komozi Woodard.

A host of others read sections of the manuscript or shared thoughts on how to understand the religious and political history of Detroit, including Thomas Klug, Professor of History and Director of Marygrove College's Institute of Detroit Studies, whose reader's report for the press is a model of scholarly commitment and professional graciousness; Kevin Mumford, who imported insights from his own work on political movements in Newark; Nick Salvatore, most recently the diligent biographer of Detroit's Reverend C. L. Franklin; Evelyn Brooks Higginbotham; and Charlie Bright.

My editor at the University of Michigan Press, James Reische, has made the process of revising this manuscript not only tolerable but enjoyable. Many thanks, too, to his boss, the ever-charming Phil Pochoda, for whom there will always be a place around my dinner table. That table would also have to include several friends who offered their support along the way: Richard and Miriam Miesler; Allison Miller; Brad Lewis, Jo and Benny, margies and burritos all around; Malcolm Duncan; Heather Hendershot, who totally shakes the world for Jesus; Christopher Dyson; Karen Brown; Judge Bruce Morrow, one of Reverend Hill's many grandchildren, his wife Beth, and their children; Norma Chanerl, who served (again) as my unofficial copy editor. Finally, the intellectual fingerprints of Alan M. Wald are scattered across the pages of this book. He has been an intellectual sounding board, a careful editor, and a loving companion. I cannot imagine what life would be like without him. I have lived and struggled with the project off and on for over ten years. Any mistakes that remain, even after the wealth of generous advice and support I have received, are my own.

CONTENTS

FOREWORD

"By Their Institutions
Shall You Know Them"

For the better part of my life I have been a preacher and pastor; there-fore, I am intrigued, gratified, and most delighted by the subject, sub-stance, and excellence of Dr. Angela Dillard's *Faith in the City: Preaching Radical Social Change in Detroit*. It is a refreshing and resourceful presen-tation of how private faith can serve effectively to create public institu-tions that act valiantly, impartially, and noncoercively to bring about pos-itive and universal social change. Such religious activism as is described by Doctor Dillard as being responsible for the birth and rearing of orga-nized labor unions, civil rights groups, and human rights institutions does not portray religion as loving and serving religion but religion that is willing to pour out its life and energy into institutions and associations that serve the common good. In most instances of human progress in art, science, politics, and economics, there is the presence of the hidden, unselfish, altruistic, affirmative, loving, lifting, life-giving, freedom-directed hand of faith at work in the world to redeem and advance the interests of all humankind.

James Luther Adams, late Harvard professor of Christian social ethics, used to say of churches, "By their institutions you shall know them." Professor Adams was paraphrasing a favorite Bible reference that was constantly quoted in every one of his sermons by the salient protag-onist of this book, the late Rev. Dr. Charles Andrew Hill Sr.: "Beware of false prophets who come to you in sheep's clothing but inwardly are ravenous wolves. You will know them by their fruits. Are grapes gathered from thorns, or figs from thistles? In the same way, every good tree bears good fruit, but the bad tree bears bad fruit. A good tree cannot bear bad fruit, nor can a bad tree bear good fruit. Every tree that does not bear good fruit is cut down and thrown into the fire. Thus, you will know them by their fruits" (Matt. 7:15–20).

If labor unions have served and still serve the public good, if such associations stem inordinate corporate greed and foster the reasonable and fair redistribution of wealth, if democracy is still being advanced, if the inclusive masses of people are benefited and sustained in a society that provides opportunity for all, requires responsibility from all, and builds a just community of all, Angela Dillard's book demonstrates and documents the "good fruit" that has been harvested from the social institutions that were spawned in, by, and through the churches in Detroit that encouraged, backed, and supported the birth of labor unions "way back in the day" when it was not popular, safe, or easy to do so.

Sixty-five or seventy years ago, three black pastors turned their backs on the rich automobile-manufacturing companies that opposed the organization of labor unions and threw the weight of their faith and influence behind the movement to organize factory workers to protect their material interests by using the power and tools of collective bargaining. Corporate power resisted and violently opposed such a movement. There were rich corporate rewards for the pastors and churches that would discourage their laboring members from organizing. The majority of the pastors in Detroit, white and black, backed the owners and managers of the corporations and discouraged unionization. Charles A. Hill of Hartford Baptist Church, Malcolm Dade of St. Cyprian's Episcopal, Horace White of Plymouth Congregational (now Plymouth United Church of Christ), Henry Hitt Crane of Central United Methodist, and several others took an oppositional stance against corporate power and in favor of the laborers who, without unionization, had no power to protect themselves, advance themselves, or sustain their communities. Citing the evidence presented in this book, it can be brilliantly and successfully argued that without the life and work of religious faith common people could not have organized themselves into effective institutions.

How sweet it is that this book has arrived at such a critical time for religious institutions, particularly those that are located in the inner city. I look at my own city, and it is very evident that the downsizing of the automotive industry, the automation of manufacturing processes, the globalization of production and sales, the undermining of the labor

movement, and the flight of jobs and the middle class from the city, coupled with the intensification of urban social problems, have created an
economic crisis. Detroit is begging for economic development and an
enlarged tax base to pay for public services and police protection. Our
newest hotels are in trouble, as the occupancy rate is 50 percent or less.
Cobo Hall, our newly expanded convention center, has been sparsely
occupied. If massive numbers of new jobs are not created here, our
future will soon be bleak. But Detroit does not stand alone; we see dete-
rioration, decay, hopelessness, and despair all across the face of the
United States. And I would venture to say that urban life worldwide is in
crisis. Paris, London, and Rome are not the cities they used to be. And
the church is being called upon to act as an instrument of transformation and hope.

Two of the most precious hours of a sabbatical Merrill Fellowship
that I had at Harvard Divinity School were spent in the company of my
old and then very feeble, retired professor, James Luther Adams, no relation to me, who wrote the book on being human religiously. I asked him,
"Dr. Adams, will you please tell me what in your opinion is the hope of
the world today?" And that sagacious, white-skinned, white-haired octo-
genarian looked me straight in the eye and said, "The hope of the world
today is the African American preacher." Now, I want to change that to
"African American church" because I think that is what he meant to say.
But can you imagine a white Harvard scholar who spent all his life, more
than ninety years, in celebrated white institutions, in a white academic
world of power and privilege, a man who has never wanted for any honor
or distinction, saying to me that the hope of the world is not white
wealth, not white culture, not white America, not white academic institutions, not the white Republican Party, not white corporate America,
not General Motors, not IBM, not Harvard University with its multi-bil-
lion-dollar endowment? According to him, the hope of the world is none
of these things that we respect and adore. He said that the hope of the
world is the black church. It is a shocking statement both because of its
source and because of its substance.

As to its source, I would not have been surprised if these words came
from a black demagogue, charlatan, or perennial presidential candidate.
Wouldn't you expect people like me to make such a cavalier and offhand
assertion? Black preachers like me are often given to hyperbole, overkill,
and media hype. All demagogues, politicians, and propagandists claim
that they and their ethnic groups are the hope of the world, the source
of a new world order. But this man is not a demagogue; he is too feeble.
He is a seasoned, sober, reasonable Harvard scholar. And he said with no

uncertain tone and no unexamined sense that the American African church is the hope of the world today. Now, I know that means all colors because the color black includes all color and excludes none. But it's still a startling statement.

Second, I am startled by the substance of the statement. How can we who have received the least be expected, even required, to give the most? Are we who are crucified by the world now to become is saviors? Are we who have been left out of the structures of power and privilege now to be the key that unlocks the door to freedom and power and liberty and justice for all? It seems absurd, doesn't it? Yet perhaps the victims of society's injustice and indifference are the inevitable redeemers of the society that has rejected them. For when God was ready to build a new people to be the instruments of divine salvation, God chose not a yuppie or a buppie, but God chose those who were underprivileged, a hundred-year-old Abraham and a ninety-year-old, shriveled up Sarah. God made *them* the mother and father of a holy nation. Then, when God was ready to draw Israel out of bondage in Egypt, God chose an eighty-year-old, tongue-tied fugitive from justice named Moses and made him the first international leader and liberator in human history. As Gardner C. Taylor says, "Moses left Egypt as a fugitive from justice, and Moses returned to Egypt as the prosecuting attorney." When God was ready to break the back of the British Empire, God chose not the armies and generals of Europe but a thin, gaunt, brown, praying man of peace named Mahatma Gandhi, who crushed the largest, most far-flung, most impressive empire in the world not by military might but by prayer and fasting.

When God was ready to desegregate America, God chose as the leader not a privileged, preferred, pampered, and honored person but a hated, rejected, despised, exploited, excluded, segregated, dishonored man named Martin Luther King Jr. and made him the greatest moral and spiritual leader of the twentieth century. Does it take an exiled Moses to humanize and save a whole society? Does is take a blind Milton to see an invisible Paradise? Does it take a deafened Beethoven to hear a humanly inaudible symphony of brotherhood and peace and write it down on paper? Does it take a once-excluded Maynard Jackson and Andrew Young to re-create the urban vitality of Atlanta? Does it take a Shirley Franklin to claim for Atlanta the written documentation of Martin King's legacy? Does it take a once rejected Coleman Young to raise Detroit from pronounced social and economic death? Does it take an excoriated and vilified Harold Washington to transform Chicago politics? Does it take a crucified savior, a wounded healer, to redeem the world? And will it take ebony and ivory people of intelligence and spirituality and integrity to lift all of humanity to the light and life and love that should belong to all people?

Since African Americans are in the intensive care ward of the U.S. economy, there is a tremendous opportunity for churches in general, and the African American church in particular, to initiate and demonstrate a better use of human and financial capital. White churches, like the Episcopal Diocese of Michigan and its McGee fund for Urban Development, are stepping up to the plate and seeking to raise and invest much more in the inner cities as both a moral obligation and an economic opportunity.

Likewise, black churches must continue to merge across denominational lines, to work in tandem with theological schools, universities, and business schools, to conceive, implement, and complete an economic development plan not only for African Americans but for all of urban America. The Clinton economic stimulus plan went the way of all flesh. Republicans are in power but seem to be distracted by wars and rumors of wars. Corporate America is running away from the problem, but African Americans, working in tandem with other faith communities, could make a difference. African Americans grossed eight hundred billion dollars last year. That is more than the gross national product of Canada and fifteen other nations. A united church community could seek to garner 5 percent of that gross, not as gifts from individuals but as investments made by individuals through an envisioned African American church community development fund. Expertly managed, such a fund could build factories, finance institutions, employ the indigent, solve social problems, educate youth, multiply and strengthen community-based banks, liberate and dignify the human race, and save and deliver children from drugs, crime, guns, gangs, violence, teenage pregnancy, and high school attrition to the end that the entire urban environment would be transformed. The church could take the lead because the church already has the human capital, the moral credibility, and the organizational skills to get things done. Is it not true that the African American church has given African Americans everything they have?

An African American lawyer once told me, "I don't go to church because I think it has kept African Americans down." I said, "How ignorant can an intelligent man be? You need to read Carter G. Woodson's *History of the Negro Church*, E. Franklin Frazier's *Negro Church in America*, Gayraud Wilmore's *Black Religion and Black Radicalism*, Eric Lincoln's *African American Churches*, Albert Raboteau's *Slave Religion*, Cornell West's *Prophesy Deliverance*, or Aldon Morris's *The Origins of the Civil Rights Movement*. They all agree that everything we possess was mothered and nurtured by African American churches. Let me cite a few lines from *Black Theology and Documentary History,* edited by Gayraud Wilmore and James H. Cone.

> The black church of the 19th Century, despite its client relationship to white churches, was clearer about its identity than many of us are today. It knew itself to be God's judgment upon the inhumanity of racism. Its blackness was therefore an expression of its sense of cultural vocation. . . . By every measure, it was an amazing institution, led, for the most part, by illiterate preachers, many of whom were slaves or recently freed men. Poverty stricken and repressed by custom and law, this church converted thousands, stabilized family life, established insurance and burial societies, founded schools and colleges, commissioned missionaries to the far corners of the world and at the same time, agitated for the abolition of slavery, supported illegal actions on behalf of refugees, organized the underground railroad, fulminated slave uprisings, promoted the Civil War, developed community, political, education and action on behalf of civil rights and provided the social, economic, political and cultural base for the entire black community in the United States.

Everyone should know that the African Methodist Episcopal Church created and supported the first African American university, Wilberforce, in 1858, predating emancipation. Everyone should know that black Presbyterians, along with the white philanthropic response to their initiatives, created Johnson C. Smith University, which once had its own medical school, and also Knoxville College. Everyone should know the black United Methodists created Gammon Theological Seminary, Houston Tillotson College, and many others. For their part, African American Baptists, working in tandem with the American Baptist Home Mission Society and Black Baptist State Conventions, established a black college or university in every southern state. In Alabama, it was Selma University; in Florida, it was Florida Memorial College; in North Carolina, it was Shaw University; in South Carolina, it was Benedict and Morris; in Virginia, it was Virginia Union; in West Virginia, it was Storer College; in Arkansas, it was Arkansas Baptist College; in Mississippi, it was what has now become Jackson State College; in Kentucky, it was Simmons University; in Tennessee, it was Roger Williams College now LeMoyne-Owen College; in Texas, it was Bishop College; in Louisiana, it was Leland College; and in Georgia it was Morehouse and Spelman.

Can't the churches do for economic development today what they did for educational opportunity 150 years ago? The African American church is all that African Americans have. It sits in the midst of our urban, ghettoized situation. Everyone in the ghetto does not belong to the church, but the church belongs to everybody in the ghetto.

It is a preserver of our culture. It is a producer of our genius. It is the power base for political ascendancy. It is the parent of our music and art. It is the sponsor of our creativity, versatility, and ingenuity. It is the incubator of our leadership. It is the storehouse for the disinherited. It is the power base for the disfranchised, and it is a hospital for wounded souls. It is a love tabernacle for the hated and exploited. It is an open door to the least, the last, the lost, the little, the lowest, the unlucky, and the left out. It is the biggest enemy of the status quo. It is a central agency for antisegregation and antidefamation. It is a rock in a weary land of oppression. It is a shelter from the story blast of bigotry; it faces a frowning world and shouts and shows that we shall overcome. Let's join it, engage it, and use it to encourage African Americans and others to be partners, movers, and shakers in the vast underdeveloped vistas of economic possibility and social responsibility. Above all, churches must continually create new public services, voluntary associations, and advocacy institutions in order to fight to preserve affirmative action, labor unions, civil rights, and civil liberties. The Rev. Charles A. Hill admonished his church and the surrounding community to work tirelessly to build a better world and a just society. The institutions spawned by churches can serve the public good better and promote the general welfare best when they remain open to all, practically and religiously impartial.

As Hill's prodigy and Dillard's pastor, I'm intrigued, gratified, and delighted by this book. It is a scholarly, well-documented, and thoroughly substantiated historical account of how the preaching and practice of faith in God served to create active, voluntary, inclusive, secular associations of people who were motivated by their religious experiences, spiritual feelings, and doctrinal convictions to work hard in order to generate nonviolent, affirmative, socially inclusive changes in the city of Detroit and its suburbs. This book demonstrates and validates the power of the pulpit in public affairs. For many decades, the pulpits in Detroit have sounded forth the trumpet that has never known retreat, retrenchment, or retraction. White and black, Jew and gentile, Protestant and Catholic pastors of conservative or liberal inclinations have made all the difference in the formation of Detroit's unique character, diverse culture, and undying hope. Saint Anselm used to say, *Fides quaerens intellectum,* "faith seeks intelligence." But intelligence is not all that faith seeks. Faith also seeks radical change, collective righteousness, social equality, the unfettered opportunity to rise higher (both collectively and individually), and the courage to transform old systems of exclusion into open doors of opportunity.

Faith perpetuates hope.

Faith generates love.

Faith actuates justice.

Faith elucidates freedom as it lights the way for humankind to become a Beloved Community of all races, nations, and religions.

It was a Harvard philosophy professor, Josiah Royce, who coined the phrase, "Beloved Community" and inspired the intellectual consciousness of Martin Luther King Jr., who found in Royce's writings a powerful social commentary conceived from those Bible scriptures that articulate the demand of God for justice as a religious priority. The God of the Hebrew Bible and the Greek New Testament made justice, not personal piety, the ultimate priority. That God is love does not denigrate justice but necessitates it. Justice is the inevitable fruit, offspring, issue, and consequence of love. M. Scott Peck, of blessed memory, used to say that love is the active and determined and diligent search for, and dedication to, the total fulfillment and ultimate satisfaction of the beloved. To love is to be profoundly and indefatigably committed to the best interests of the beloved's life, liberty, justice, empowerment, and fulfillment. It is only puppy love, hound dog love, or purely undisciplined love that would deny justice for the sake of "love." Such love that obstructs and violates and denies justice is not authentic love but an imposter posing as something that is called love but falls far short of true love.

It is because Angela Dillard unearthed the words and works of several Detroit activist pastors who truly understood the real nature of love as the basis of justice that her book presents compelling documentation that can fill out our historical comprehension and appreciation of dynamic faith in the life of the city. The author, her brilliant late brother, Father Paul Anthony Dillard, dean of the Cathedral, Imani Temple, African American Catholic Congregation, and I were blessed beyond measure to have been born and reared on the near west side of Detroit, whose earliest and most distinctive, dynamic, religious, cultural, and political center was Hartford Church, the birthplace of Ford's United Auto Workers Local 600. It was Charles Andrew Hill Sr. who delivered the baby union into the life of the world. Charles Andrew Hill was born in Detroit on April 28, 1893. He was educated at Cleary Business College in Michigan and Lincoln University and Seminary in Pennsylvania. Having finished his social gospel studies and standard seminary work at Lincoln, Hill was elected by the congregation of Hartford

Avenue Baptist Church to serve as its pastor. The congregation was composed of thirty-five intrepid souls. Pastor Hill assumed the pulpit in November 1920, and the church grew rapidly into one of the city's largest.

Pastor Hill retired on his seventy-fifth birthday, on April 28, 1968, with a huge celebratory banquet that lauded our beloved pastor for his unequaled contribution to the advancement of his race, the uplift of humankind, and the enhancement of his native city. Talk about a profile of courage and imagination, Hill was Detroit's greatest. Angela Dillard raises Reverend Hill from dusty death and immortalizes his personality and power. Like the Apostle Paul, Hill did not preach about himself; he preached Christ, community, courage, and change. Before the present publication, we knew very few of the biographical details of Hill's birth, parentage, and rearing. We were unable to catalog his childhood experiences, choice of church, and call to ministry or understand how he happened to be so radical, progressive, universal, relentless, and fearless in his pursuit of justice. He never cringed in the face of threats or the massive opposition of and intimidation by the local, state, and federal governments. He loved his God, his church, his community, and his country. He loved America too much to leave it as he found it in 1893. I never met a human being so persistent and yet so cheerful, so Christ-like and nonviolent in his fearless fight for peace, equality, and universal inclusivity.

In 1953, I saw what the government of the United States did to my pastor and mentor, the Rev. Charles A. Hill, how they hauled him in to testify before the House Committee on Un-American Activities, how he was condemned by the clergy, smeared in the media, and abandoned by many members of the church who feared the loss of jobs and fortunes. I sat in church that Sunday morning after seeing the televised hearings, which were meant to discredit and destroy this powerful, wonderful man, this organic intellectual and community leader. We wondered what Reverend Hill would say now.

Would he continue the debate?

Would he denounce the media?

Would he castigate the government?

Would he condemn his enemies by using the sword of the spirit, which is the word of God?

No. His text that day was Matthew 5:43, "You have heard that it was said, 'You shall love your neighbor and hate your enemy.' But I say to you, Love your enemies and pray for those who persecute you, so that you may be children of your Father in heaven; for he makes his sun rise on the evil and on the good, and sends rain on the righteous and the unrighteous." Obviously, Reverend Hill was inherently strong but totally nonhostile and nonviolent, slow to anger, and incapable of hate. He demonstrated a peaceful calm and confidence. He showed to the whole world the power of the love of God to change the world. The focus and joy of our religion is not brute power but unconquerable love! 1 John 4:20 says, "If a man say I love God and hateth his brother or sister, he is a liar: for he that loveth not his brother or sister whom he hath seen, how can he love God whom he hath not seen?" The world needs the religious roots and social fruits of the spirit of Charles A. Hill Sr.

There is an old black spiritual that asks the question, "Is You Got Good Religion?" Not just "Is you got religion?" but is it good religion? There's a whole lot of dangerous, bad, sick religion in the world; bad religion can make you hard, cold, mean, and insensitive. Bad religion is worse than no religion. I once heard the New Testament scholar Krister Stendahl say, "There's not an evil cause in the world that has not been sponsored by somebody's sick, perverted, bad, hateful religion." Bad religion spawned the medieval military crusades. Bad religion grabbed the enforcement of the state to destroy freedom of conscience. Bad religion set up the inquisitions to enforce religious conformity. Bad religion murdered the anabaptists, burned Joan of Arc at the stake, executed John Huss and Hans Denck, and persecuted and banished Roger Williams. Bad religion killed William Tyndale for translating the Bible into the vernacular of the people. Bad religion took apartheid to South Africa; brought slavery to America; fostered segregation, bigotry, and exploitation; organized the Ku Klux Klan; generated the Nazi Party; created the immoral majority; and produced Jim Jones, Jimmy Baker, Jimmy Swaggert, Jerry Falwell, and David Koresh.

Bad religion assassinated Mahatma Gandhi, murdered Anwar Sadat, slew Indira Gandhi, cut up Lebanon, destroyed Iran, devastated Iraq, oppressed the poor, made September 11, 2001, a day of infamy, crucified Jesus, killed Martin Luther King Jr., and devastated Yugoslavia.

That's why grandma wanted to know, "Is you got good religion?"

Bad religion takes life.

Good religion gives life.

Bad religion castigates folks.

Good religion liberates folks.

Bad religion talks about national defense.

Good religion talks about national purpose.

Bad religion divides folks.

Good religion unites folks.

Bad religion makes you hate folks.

Good religion makes you love everybody.

Bad religion segregates.

Good religion integrates.

Bad religion stays in the church.

Good religion breaks loose in the world.

Bad religion hangs around the altar.

Good religion walks down the Jericho Road with healing in its hands.

Bad religion is shaped like a spurious pole, trying to reach up to God without reaching out to anybody.

Good religion is shaped like a cross, the vertical beam reaching up to God for power, and the horizontal beam reaching out to people and sharing love, power, peace, joy, hope, life, freedom, jobs, education, and opportunity all around. Is you got good religion? When we get good religion, true religion, strong religion, inclusive religion we will not be discouraged by anyone, defeated by anything, destroyed by any evil. I believe that Angela Dillard's book promotes good religion and authentic faith, and for that I am both grateful and very proud.

Dr. Charles G. Adams, Pastor
Hartford Memorial Baptist Church
Detroit, Michigan

ABBREVIATIONS

ACLU	American Civil Liberties Union
ACTU	Association of Catholic Trade Unionists
ADA	Americans for Democratic Action
ADC	Aid to Dependent Children
AFL	American Federation of Labor
AIWA	Automotive Industrial Workers Association
AME	African Methodist Episcopal Church
AOC	African Orthodox Church
AWU	Auto Workers Union
BCN	Black Christian Nationalism
BTWTA	Booker T. Washington Trade Association
CFPCR	Conference for the Protection of Civil Rights
CIO	Congress of Industrial Organizations
CIO-PAC	CIO Political Action Committee
COINTELPRO	Counter-Intelligence Program
CORE	Congress of Racial Equality
CP	Communist Party
CRC	Civil Rights Congress
CRF	Civil Rights Federation
DCC	Detroit Council of Churches
DCCR	Detroit Commission on Community Relations
DCHR	Detroit Council for Human Relations
Detroit NLC	Detroit chapter of the National Negro Labor Council
DHC	Detroit Housing Commission
DRUM	Dodge Revolutionary Union Movement
DUL	Detroit Urban League
FBI	Federal Bureau of Investigation
FEPC	Fair Employment Practice Commission

FHA	Federal Housing Administration
FNP	Freedom Now Party
FOR	Fellowship of Reconciliation
GCL	Good Citizenship League
GM	General Motors
GOAL	Group on Advanced Leadership
HUAC	House Committee on Un-American Activities
HUD	Housing and Urban Development
ICOC	Inner-City Organizing Committee
IFCO	Interreligious Foundation for Community Organization
ILD	International Labor Defense
IWO	International Workers Order
JCC	Jewish Community Council
KKK	Ku Klux Klan
LRBW	League of Revolutionary Black Workers
LSNR	League of Struggle for Negro Rights
MCCR	Michigan Committee on Civil Rights
MDCFEP	Metropolitan Detroit Council on Fair Employment Practice
MDCP	Michigan Division of the Communist Party
MFSA	Methodist Federation for Social Action
MOWM	March on Washington movement
NAACP	National Association for the Advancement of Colored People
NALC	Negro American Labor Council
NCLC	Northern Christian Leadership Conference
NNC	National Negro Congress
NNLC	National Negro Labor Council
NOI	Nation of Islam
PAOCC	Pan African Orthodox Christian Church
PIAR	People's Institute of Applied Religion
RAM	Revolutionary Action Movement
RUM	Revolutionary Union Movement
SACB	Subversive Activities Control Board
SCLC	Southern Christian Leadership Conference
SNCC	Student Nonviolent Coordinating Committee
STFU	Southern Tenant Farmers Union
SWP	Socialist Workers Party
TAP	Total Action against Poverty
TULC	Trade Union Leadership Council
UAW	United Auto Workers
UNIA	Universal Negro Improvement Association
WCO	West Central Organization
YMCA	Young Men's Christian Organization
YWCA	Young Women's Christian Organization

INTRODUCTION

In 1963 the *Michigan Chronicle,* Detroit's major African American weekly paper, invited its readers to pause in the midst of the city's ongoing civil rights struggles to take stock of the past and reflect on the contributions of an earlier generation. In a multipart series, the paper considered the contributions of labor organizers and union members, especially those within the United Auto Workers, Congress of Industrial Organizations (UAW-CIO), and of the heads of race improvement organizations such as the National Association for the Advancement of Colored People (NAACP) and the Urban League. Last, the *Chronicle* dedicated one installment of the series to three ministers: the Rev. Horace A. White, pastor of Plymouth Congregational (now UCC) Church; Fr. Malcolm C. Dade of St. Cyprian's Episcopal; and the Rev. Charles A. Hill of Hartford Avenue (now Memorial) Baptist. Accentuating the experiences of this ecumenical trio, all of whom were early supporters of industrial unionism, the article positioned them as part of a generation that laid the foundations for protests in later periods. "Present Negro leadership in Detroit," the article proclaimed, "is a direct descendant, an offspring of Negro leadership that was born of necessity during the foggy gloom of the depression years and that later matured into a formidable and militant vanguard of Negro progress. There are many grandparents who insist that Detroit is ahead of other northern cities in race relations because of 'the dedicated and sterling leadership' of Negroes a quarter century ago."[1]

This volume helps construct a narrative about what activism in the 1960s owed to that of the 1930s. In myriad ways, activists in places such as Detroit (i.e., northern, urban, and industrial) managed to sustain a record of progressive political activism over the course of three decades. Like other studies of what social movement theorist Aldon Morris calls "local movement centers"—interlocking networks of resources, strategically placed activists, effective tactics, and strategies of protest developed out of indigenous traditions on a local, as opposed to national, level— *Faith in the City* seeks to account for patterns of change and continuity from the 1930s to the 1960s.[2] Detroit's range of strong indigenous traditions linking civil rights and labor makes it a particularly rich site in which to situate such a study. The early labor-based struggles in which Hill, White, and Dade played a role do not constitute merely a "prehistory" of the modern (and national) post–World War II movement. Rather, as the *Michigan Chronicle* article suggests, those struggles in defense of the rights of labor were an integral influence on the contours of political protest in later periods.[3]

Moreover, the labor movement provided Detroit's Black activists, both inside and outside the unions, with organizational power and experience that was virtually unmatched by any other African American urban community. The 1963 *Chronicle* article acknowledges that Reverends Hill and White, along with Father Dade, first came to the attention of a broader public via their support of industrial unionism, especially during the 1941 Ford Motor Company strike: "The trio marched with other union leaders in front of the plant on Schaefer Road; they appeared at the plant gates to talk with workers, and they were threatened at public meetings for espousing 'radical views.' " In assisting in the cause of labor, community and religious activists learned lessons about organizing both within the Black community and across racial and ethnic lines. So, too, did Black workers. As union activist Robert "Buddy" Battle expressed his sense of the connection between labor and the Black freedom struggle after World War II, "Having been union leaders for many years we thought we had the know-how to change the situation. And after twenty years of existence, we didn't feel we had to wait any longer."[4]

Some have argued that the postwar movement in the South was so unique that it is best viewed as a discrete phenomenon. In *Civil Rights and the Idea of Freedom,* for instance, Richard H. King insists that the "recent emphasis on the movement's ideological and institutional continuity with the past tends, wrongly, I think, to minimize what was different, even unique about the civil rights movement of the 1954–68 period."[5] I do not believe that the movement should be so bounded, either temporally or, for that matter, geographically.

In arguing for a certain continuity from the 1930s to the 1960s I also hope to highlight the importance of the "middle period" (roughly 1954 to 1963), which historians and social scientists have traditionally analyzed almost exclusively with reference to the South. (It is not until the "long hot summers" beginning with the Watts rebellion of 1964 that the urban North regains the limelight.)

In a sense, then, this book could be read alongside the work of scholars such as Martha Biondi, Robert O. Self, Jeanne Theoharis, Komozi Woodard, and Beth Bates, who have recently begun piecing together the history of movements outside the South and before 1955.[6] In Detroit, it was during this still understudied period that Buddy Battle, Horace Sheffield, and other seasoned veterans of union struggles created groups such as the Trade Union Leadership Council (TULC) and joined with ministers such as the Rev. Nicholas Hood, the local NAACP, and others to create a liberal coalition that fought on the Detroit front of the northern struggle. Reverend Hood replaced Reverend White at Plymouth Congregational in 1958. Although he was born and raised in Terre Haute, Indiana, he came to Detroit from New Orleans, where he had been involved in the founding of the Southern Christian Leadership Conference (SCLC). Consequently, he personifies the North-South connection.[7]

An appreciation for the intimate relationship between the rights of labor and the rights of African Americans and other minorities provided Detroit's militant activist communities with a sense of continuity from decade to decade. Another thread was Detroit's well-defined tradition of religious radicalism. Indeed, in profiling the political work of "a Baptist, a Congregationalist, and an Episcopalian," the *Michigan Chronicle* article reminds us of the importance of religious activists and their churches in the struggles that gave meaning and form to the city's protest movements. The *Chronicle* author, however, fails to explore the broader political and cultural significance of religion—a topic that has garnered much more sustained attention in studies of the American South, especially during the civil rights movement of the 1950s and early 1960s. Unfortunately, this discrepancy has led to the labeling of southern movements as religious and northern ones as secular. Yet, as numerous histories of Detroit have suggested, politically engaged ministers were in the forefront of every major movement for social change throughout the city's distinctive history, from industrial unionism in the 1930s to civil rights and civil liberties in the 1940s and 1950s and the rise of Black power and Black Christian nationalism (BCN) in the 1960s.[8]

THE RELIGIOUS DIMENSION OF "SECULAR" MOVEMENTS

The Rev. C. L. Franklin, pastor of Detroit's New Bethel Baptist Church for nearly three decades and a leading voice in the city's post–World War II civil rights community, once opined that Detroit "has a reputation as a city of good preachers."[9] By the time the Mississippi-born Franklin relocated to Detroit from Buffalo, New York, in 1945, the city's clergy had a formidable record of progressive political activism. Religious leaders and their congregants—from a variety of racial and ethnic backgrounds—joined the sit-ins and sit-downs, the strikes and marches and organizing campaigns. They led angry confrontations in the streets and pursued quieter moments of personal reflection and collective solace in the pews of their churches.

Religion and politics were fused in this unique northern industrial city on the banks of the Detroit River. Known as the Motor City, the home of Motown and the UAW, Detroit is also a city in which faith has sustained the population, where activists found a little soul to match the beat of industrial production. One of the major aims of this book is to highlight religion's place within Detroit's protest communities from the 1930s to the 1960s.

Men of the cloth such as Hill, Dade, White, and Franklin frequently placed the power of their moral authority in the service of progressive causes. At the same time, they remained ever mindful of their duty to minister to the spiritual needs of their flocks and the communities of protest in which they lived and worked and struggled and prayed. Maintaining this delicate balance among the personal, political, and pastoral was doubtless not an easy task, yet there were times when the world of politics and the world of faith merged to such a degree that they must have seemed merely different aspects of a single life. While this is surely true of politically engaged ministers and priests and rabbis overall, I want to suggest that it was (and is) particularly so among African American clergy and within the Black freedom struggle.

The seminal role of the Black church in sustaining communities and fostering protests on behalf of civil rights, social justice, and human dignity is by now well known. From the often clandestine and "invisible" institutions of the slavery era to the massive brick-and-mortar structures that dot the present-day urban landscape, the Black church has been heralded as the most important institution built and maintained by African Americans for African Americans.[10] It has also been the locus of social and political activism for Black women. Ministers' wives, in particular, often played a role as "first ladies" of their respective congregations:

they joined forces with other churchwomen to organize ladies' aid and missionary societies and participated, externally, in the Black women's club movement, which dedicated itself to racial uplift. As a crucial part of the Black public sphere, the church also provided women with an avenue of engagement in the broader social, political, economic, and cultural debates that shaped African American political culture from the late nineteenth century onward.[11]

The much-vaunted independence of the Black church, however, has never been automatically assured and has often been secured at a painfully high price. In point of fact, the Black church might best be seen as a contested space in which ministers, congregants, activists, and other interested parties have battled for control and influence. For instance, in the late 1930s, as the fledgling UAW-CIO waged its protracted battle to unionize the massive automotive industry, the Rev. Horace White—surely one of the "good preachers" Franklin had in mind—asked, rhetorically, "Who Owns the Negro Church?"

Writing in the *Christian Century*, White charged that in Detroit

> people interested to see to it that the Negro stays anti-labor start with the preachers. . . . The one organization through which the Negro ought to feel free to express his hopes and to work out his economic salvation cannot help him because the Negro does not own it—it belongs to the same people who own factories. . . .The leadership of the Negro people is still in the hands of the clergymen and will be for years to come, and these clergymen are at the moment leading for the industrialists rather than for the welfare of the Negro people.[12]

White was speaking about African American ministers who had aligned themselves with the automotive industry, especially the Ford Motor Company—clergymen who relied heavily on Ford's patronage to secure their own personal power and jobs and other benefits for their congregants. Ford's persistent influence was one of the major reasons why Hill, among others, saw the automaker's plants as "the battleground for the civil rights movement whether you worked for it or not."[13]

By 1938, when White penned his attack, it was already clear that powerful ministers and their churches were going to be a major roadblock to union efforts. This was also true to some extent within white ethnoreligious enclaves. Although the local Catholic hierarchy was generally sympathetic to industrial unionism, Polish workers and organizers were frequently confronted with the accommodationist attitudes of local parish priests. Some, such as Fr. Charles Coughlin, actively worked against CIO-affiliated unions, believing them to be "communist dominated." And the majority of white Protestant clergymen were equally troublesome. As a young minister straight out of Yale's divinity school and committed to "social justice versions of modern Protestantism," theologian Reinhold Niebuhr remembered being "particularly disconcerted" by the "sub-servience of the Detroit churches to the myths of justice in the Detroit community," especially those myths that served the interests of the auto-motive industry. He also recalled numerous attempts to silence those ministers "who defied the ruling group."[14]

But these conflicting tensions were probably strongest in the city's African American community. Thousands of Black workers eventually found employment at the Ford Motor Company, the leading industrial employer of Blacks before World War II. When one factors in spouses and families, the welfare of thirty to forty thousand individuals—roughly one-fourth of the city's Black population—depended on Ford wages. As one contemporary observer noted, "There is hardly a Negro church, fra-ternal body or other organization in which Ford workers are not repre-sented. Scarcely a Negro professional or businessman is completely inde-pendent of income derived from Negro employees."[15] Black workers, many of whom were drawn from the South by Ford's promise of five dol-lars a day, were understandably grateful for the opportunities offered by the company, as were the ministers, with whom the company formed a "cooperative relationship." This relationship, or alliance, between the company and select Black ministers was inaugurated shortly after World War I and lasted until Ford was successfully unionized in 1941. Through-out this period, Black ministers and churches functioned as agents of the Ford employment office.

To secure employment at a Ford plant, an aspiring Black worker gen-erally had to obtain a letter of recommendation from his minister. For the handful of Black ministers who refused to participate in this arrange-ment, such requests could be agonizing. "I guess the good Lord, the Holy Spirit was guiding me," recalled Fr. Malcolm C. Dade, "but I never got caught in that trap, though it was pitiful to see how many men would come to you and beg you just to give them a letter."[16]

The situation in Detroit was not unlike that described in Liston Pope's seminal 1942 study of southern textile company towns, *Millhands and Preachers*. Pope found that in "normal times" Christianity legitima-tized "capitalist" virtues, such as hard work, sobriety, and responsibility to one's employers, and in times of crisis (such as the infamous Gastonia strike that Pope chronicles) ministers were called upon to directly sanc-tion and preserve the traditional order.[17] While there were certainly differences between a mill town, where industrialists supplied the church's physical structure and paid the minister's salary, on the one hand and Henry Ford's Detroit on the other, the analogy holds. "Company ministers" and parish priests, indebted either directly or indirectly to the industry, were often unable or unwilling to discuss the merits of unionization. Those who bucked this status quo risked various forms of social and economic reprisal.

For ministers such as Father Dade, Reverend White, and Reverend Hill, resistance to the company's allure allowed them to ensure their own personal and political independence. According to Reverend Hill, who went on to become one of the most radical clergymen in the city, he was forced to refuse the overtures of the company time and time again. It was a gamble. Throughout the late 1930s, the Ford Motor Company (the last of the large automotive concerns to unionize) carried on a campaign of political intimidation and economic terrorism intended to prevent Black ministers and their congregations from taking any kind of active interest in the UAW's efforts. Hill, however, allowed union organizers to use his church for clandestine union meetings disguised as prayer services. "If they met in a union hall," Hill explained, "then some of the spies from Ford would take their automobile license numbers and they lost their jobs. By holding it in a church, it would be difficult for them to prove we were just discussing union matters."[18]

All social movements need what historian Sara Evans and sociologist Harry Boyte characterize as "free spaces": communally grounded and autonomous associations that permit people to work out alternative visions of society and to organize collectively.[19] The central role of Hill's church in organizing one of the largest UAW locals (Local 600) testifies to the Black church's institutional significance in protest struggles. At the same time, Hill also understood the *discursive* power of religion. He consistently attempted to bridge the secular and the sacred, to make faith serve the needs of progressive activism. Hill "was really one of the few preachers I could ever sit and listen to," recalled Eleanor Maki, a local schoolteacher and member of the Detroit Civil Rights Federation (CRF) in the early 1930s. She continued, "He was, I think, sincerely, devotedly, really religious. And he made sense, and he was never afraid to go anywhere or do anything."[20]

Although much of the city's civil rights activity took place within seemingly secular contexts, religion, often translated into a diffuse yet powerful moral imperative, provided a readily identifiable subtext— even for those who questioned the efficacy of organized religion. "I turned away from my church and what I felt was a mockery of religion," writes Margaret Collingwood Nowak in her combined autobiography and biography of her husband, Stanley Nowak. The Nowaks worked for years in Detroit's radical Left community "and became involved in the activities of unemployed groups and the Proletarian Party." "Here," said Margaret, "I felt was religion in action; here I belonged. . . . Working for a better world here and now was far more satisfying than the idea of a distant and problematical Heaven."[21] But Nowak never turned her back on the idea that organized religion could be a useful political tool. Both she and her husband befriended and supported Reverend Hill and were often in attendance at Hartford.

Stanley Nowak, who was part of the UAW's Polish Organizing Committee, met Hill during the 1941 Ford strike, and the two went on to work together during the 1942 Sojourner Truth Housing Project incident, in which Blacks and Poles—the two largest cultural minority groups in the city—clashed violently over who would live in the newly constructed federal project. This World War II housing controversy, along with the race riot the following year, would, as historian Thomas Sugrue argues, set precedents for Detroit's public housing policy for another decade. Through all their efforts to prevent the conflicts that Sugrue documents in such ample and depressing detail, Hill and Nowak developed what Margaret Nowak describes as "a wonderful friendship that would take them through two joint campaigns for election to Detroit's Common Council."[22]

The Nowaks, along with Hill, also befriended and supported religious radical Claude C. Williams, a southern white minister who preached a leftist version of the social gospel inspired as much by Marx and Lenin as Christ. Williams's political theology resembled that of religious thinkers and activists Harry Ward and Harry Emerson Fosdick, both of whom believed, as Ward once wrote, that there existed in capitalism "an irreconcilable antagonism to the ethic of Jesus."[23] Williams arrived in Detroit in 1942 to take up a position as "minister of labor" for the Detroit Presbytery. He was attracted by the chance to work with newly transplanted southern workers who had been lured to Detroit by employment opportunities in the "Arsenal of Democracy."

Williams was also energized by the challenge of confronting and working against the reactionary men of God whom he believed held sway over large segments of the white working class, men such as Fr. Charles Coughlin, the famous "Radio priest" of the 1930s, who became enamored of fascism and had to be silenced by the Catholic Church and the U.S. government in the early 1940s, and the Rev. Gerald L. K. Smith, a former devotee of Huey Long's "Share the Wealth" ideology who became a rabid anti-Semite and a trenchant opponent of any form of racial mixing.[24] For activists within the city's civil rights community, the presence of "hate-mongering religious demagogues" was an important civil rights issue in and of itself. And, while many noted the possible connections between fundamentalism and racial violence, none came close to the feverish pitch of Claude Williams's "exposé," which characterized Detroit as a "modern Babel" of religious reactionaries driving the city toward a race war.[25] When a major riot broke out in 1943, leaving 34 dead, 675 seriously injured, and 1,893 jailed, few were completely surprised given the escalating racial violence on the city's streets and in the plants.[26]

In the tense atmosphere of wartime Detroit, Williams was welcomed and appreciated by Detroit's Left community. Admitting that for years "there has been a growing feeling among labor that the church is not interested in the day-to-day problems of the people," Stanley Nowak asserted that "Claude Williams has done more than any other person we know of to counteract this feeling and tendency among labor people."[27] Reverend Hill, for his part, regarded Williams as a man who "in a very practical way" was "making Christianity real," and he literally thanked God for Williams's work in Detroit.[28] Hill's assistant pastor, the Rev. John Miles, became a devotee of Williams and worked closely with his People's Institute of Applied Religion (PIAR). While members of the city's Left were extremely worried about the presence of southern fundamentalists in Detroit (and there were thousands of small storefront churches and congregations catering to the waves of the white southern workers who were flooding the city during the war), Williams actively reached out to them.[29]

Some of Williams's beliefs were extreme. For instance, in his theological universe Jesus, the "Son of Man," had emerged as a "class-conscious leader" of a people's revolutionary movement aimed at destroying "fascist" Rome. His brand of Christianity was stripped of its supernaturalism, which he saw as "an unscriptural invention of theology" or, more specifically, a corruption of Jesus' revolutionary zeal by the "Christ-centered" theology of Paul. God was not so much a Supreme Being as a "Symbol of Struggle for Freedom, Security, Brotherhood." Sin became any manifestation of "ultra-individualism," while salvation was transformed into "a collective effort of the workers and other victims of this world system to save themselves from the oppressors."[30]

This was controversial material, but the idea of a *social gospel* of faith in action, of a liberating theology, inspired religious and secular activists alike. Many of the most politically engaged ministers in Detroit took up the challenge of navigating the sacred/secular divide. One, the Rev. Albert B. Cleage Jr., a founder of Black theology and the Black Christian nationalism movement, was especially eloquent in this regard. In the early 1970s, Cleage changed his name to Jaramogi Abebe Ageyman, which means "liberator, holy man, savior of the nation" in Swahili. His BCN movement was subsequently reformulated as the Pan African Orthodox Christian Church (PAOCC). Since the events narrated in this book deal primarily with the period before Cleage's name change, I have decided, for the sake of clarity and consistency, to use his familial name, along with the original name of the church of which he was founder and eventually holy patriarch. No disrespect is intended to the current members of the individual Shrines of the Black Madonna in Detroit, Houston, and Atlanta or the PAOCC overall.

Much like Claude Williams, Albert Cleage believed that Christianity had become too cluttered and muddled by supernatural ideas and that the "Negro" church—like other forms of ossified organized religion—was failing to address the needs of the poor and marginal. Distressed, too, at the number of young radicals who were leaving the Black church in the 1960s, Cleage struggled to make the church not only relevant but central to the goal of self-determination and freedom. He knew that many young activists agreed with Charleen Johnson, a community organizer and welfare activist, who left the church when she was eighteen because she believed that it contributed to a sense of "powerlessness" in its members' lives and because she was seeking "to overthrow the system."[31] Cleage also knew that the sentiment expressed by Luke Tripp, another young radical in Detroit who would go on to become a key figure in the League of Revolutionary Black Workers (LRBW), was widespread. "Man, I don't operate out of a religious bag," Tripp told a local reporter. "I was baptized a Catholic but now you can say I am a free thinker."[32]

Early on, some older activists and community leaders had hoped that Cleage would provide guidance to the younger radicals and "give them a little discipline."[33] Instead, what Cleage offered to younger activists such as Tripp, General Baker, Ken Cockrel, John Watson, and others affiliated with UHURU, an early Black nationalist group, was encouragement. In a sense UHURU—the name means "freedom" in Swahili—was among the earliest organizational expressions of the diverse intellectual and political trends that converged within Detroit's radical circles as a rejection of nonviolence and the embrace of Black nationalism and third world revolution. Many of the young people involved in UHURU, and later with the independent paper *Inner City Voice*, had been regular attendees of the Socialist Workers Party's (SWP) weekly Militant Labor Forums. Some had been involved in the southern struggle, traveling south to work with the Student Nonviolent Coordinating Committee (SNCC).

The writings and example of Cuban and African revolutionaries were profoundly influential within this circle, as were, closer to home, the works of Robert F. Williams, whose 1962 volume *Negroes with Guns* was "popular early reading," along with texts by Malcolm X and Albert Cleage. Dan Georgakas, who with Marvin Surkin would go on to chronicle the experiences of their generation in *Detroit: I Do Mind Dying* (1974), remembers attending a talk by Cleage on the Cuban missile crisis and "going home thinking we might be dead by morning."[34] Despite a substantial difference in age (Cleage was born in 1911), Cleage shared many of the younger generation's views and positions. At one point, he even put forth the idea of ordaining young civil rights workers in the North and South as a way of protecting them against "the conspiracy to either kill them in Vietnam or take them out of active work by putting them in a penitentiary."[35] And while the *Black Manifesto,* a document written in Detroit and dramatically presented in May 1969 by James Foreman at Riverside Church in New York, expressed an ambiguous relationship with religion—it demanded $500 million from white churches and synagogues—Cleage, the members of the Interreligious Foundation for Community Organization (IFCO), and other budding Black theologians supported the manifesto's goals.[36]

Given the religious dimensions of the political struggles that animated Detroiters in the latter half of the 1960s, we must question the conventional view that the Black power movement was "de-Christianized" and totally secular. Indeed, Reverend Cleage was so central in the creation of what might be called the latter or second civil rights movement in Detroit—as opposed to the "early" movement of the 1930s and 1940s—that I chose to highlight his experiences and political theology in the second half of this book.

Despite the richness of these sorts of connections between political radicalism and progressive religion in both the 1930s and the 1960s, historians and theorists of social movements in Detroit and elsewhere have too frequently addressed religion as a tangential, rather than central, factor in political struggle. My argument is not that religion does or should take precedence over other modes of individual or collective identification but that religion has been a crucial factor in the cultures of opposition that make collective action possible. Gospel hymns and other forms of sacred music, as well as biblical stories—David's defeat of

Goliath, the story of Exodus, and the life of Christ—can be given a political spin and incorporated into an oppositional consciousness. Further, even in its most "otherworldly" manifestations, emphasizing the eschatological transcendence of the material world, religion provides the raw materials for an ethical and prophetic critique. Religion, that is to say, can provide a picture of an ideal world that is continuously—and critically—juxtaposed against an actual social order. "At its worst," argues Black theologian Cornel West, religion "serves as an ideological means of preserving and perpetuating" the status quo, but "at its best" religion has the potential to yield "moralistic condemnations of and utopian visions beyond present social and historical realities."[37]

Thus, if America has historically denied freedom to African Americans and members of other oppressed and marginalized social groups, then religion—from Judaism to the Nation of Islam (NOI, founded in Detroit in the early 1930s) to variants of Christianity ranging from evangelical Protestantism to Catholicism and beyond—has often appealed to a higher standard, a greater authority and source of justice. The content of religious belief and practice need not be "liberal" or "progressive" in order for it to serve this function. The type of Christianity that sustained most Black southern communities in their civil rights activism, for instance, was illiberal, highly emotional, and structured by an "irrational" belief in miracles, faith healing, and other direct manifestations of the Divine.

Historian Christopher Lasch presaged this notion in an almost lyrical way when he wrote:

> Religious contributions to social movements might be characterized as inspirational and inflammatory, disciplinary and morally self-corrective, politically sobering and cautionary, emotionally healing and hopegiving. Only the notion of some higher set of standards prevailed and that these, at least, were not flouted with impunity could give hope to the hopeless or enable them to see themselves as moral agents not merely as victims.[38]

This passage also describes the political faith that guided the words and deeds of some of Detroit's most prominent and politically engaged ministers—a core of belief that sustained the movement culture over more than three decades of militant civil rights activism.

That activism can be divided into two distinctive periods: the first from the early 1930s to the early 1950s; and the second from roughly the late 1950s to the late 1960s. I have framed my investigation within a study of two ministers who are especially representative of religiously inflected activism in their respective periods: the Rev. Charles A. Hill and the Rev. Albert B. Cleage Jr. My two narratives—the history of various civil rights mobilizations from the 1930s to the 1960s and the political biographies of Hill and Cleage—offer a running dialogue between history and biography, with each influencing and hopefully enriching the other.

The great promise of the biographical approach, even in the attenuated version that I employ here, lies in its ability to at least partially personify a moment or in this case a succession of moments. By drawing our attention to the complex processes of identity formation, biography gives us a perspective on an equally complex set of historical trends and social forces—forces that structure our society and its politics. Because all of our lives play out in social and cultural contexts, a biographical narrative should transcend its individual subject and steadily draw us into the webs of friendships, rivalries, aspirations, fears, and circumstances that give his or her life meaning. As pastors of large and politically significant Black congregations who pursued distinct social, political, and religious strategies, Hill and Cleage shaped and were shaped by two distinct yet overlapping communities of protest and struggle. The Left, with which this book is chiefly concerned, looked very different in the 1930s and 1940s than it did in the 1960s. The personal and political and religious lives of Reverends Hill and Cleage do evidence moments of symmetry, but between them lies the redefinition of the social gospel, the transformation of the militant Left, and perhaps the very meaning of civil rights and social justice itself.

THE DIALOGUE BETWEEN HISTORY AND BIOGRAPHY

The first half of *Faith in the City* is organized around the Rev. Charles A. Hill. Born in Detroit in 1893, Hill's activism and implicit political theology—he was not a theologian in the traditional sense—was rooted in the prophetic tradition of African American Christianity and the idealism of early-twentieth-century versions of the social gospel. As it was developed by thinkers such as Walter Rauschenbusch, the social gospel linked ideas about social transformation with an understanding of God's immanence, of his Kingdom as something that was at least partially realizable in this world. As Rauschenbusch himself explained in his *A Theology for the Social Gospel* (1917):

This doctrine [of the Kingdom] is itself the social gospel. Without it, the idea of redeeming the social order will be but an annex to the orthodox conception of the schema of salvation. It will live like the negro servant family in a detached cabin back of the white man's house in the South. If this doctrine gets the proper place which has always been its legitimate right, the practical proclamation and application of social morality will have a firm footing.[39]

In Rauschenbusch's recasting of orthodox Christianity, *sin* is defined as a social or collective expression of selfishness transmitted from generation to generation not through blood forever tainted by Adam's—and therefore mankind's—Fall, but through exploitative social and economic structures. In turn, salvation is reconceived as collective and corporate: "This involves redemption of the social life from the cramping influence of religious bigotry, from the repression of self-assertion in the relation of upper and lower classes, and from all forms of slavery in which human beings are treated as mere means to serve the ends of others."[40] Rauschenbusch arrived at these theological conclusions after spending years toiling in a parish in the Hell's Kitchen neighborhood of New York, working primarily with the area's immigrant and impoverished residents.

As a movement within American social Christianity and Protestant or "evangelical" liberalism, the social gospel is generally said to have begun during the Gilded Age and to have reached its peak in the 1920s, after which it suffered a decline (its insistence on combining theology with practice may explain why the movement never became particularly large or widespread). But the social gospel was also, arguably, a precursor to liberation theology and similar in some respects to a broader compass of ideas, popular in the 1930s, that linked Christianity with Marxism. The stress on justice for workers, immigrants, and (though seldom articulated in older versions of the social gospel) African Americans is echoed, for instance, in the writings and political activism of Harry Emerson Fosdick, Harry Ward, and Claude C. Williams, as well as those of Catholic social thinkers such as Msgr. John A. Ryan, who used his position at Catholic University to advocate the "just wage" theory.[41] While the more radical and anticapitalist applications of these ideas can be seen as a response to urban-industrial problems in the late nineteenth and early twentieth centuries, the social gospel might also be conceptualized as part of a larger tradition of American social Christianity rooted in antebellum voluntary societies, home missions, and reform movements, including abolitionism.

At the same time, the social gospel has been justly criticized for its aversion to the nascent feminist movement, its adoption of paternalistic attitudes toward Blacks and immigrants, its vagueness on practical programmatic matters, and its perhaps excessive optimism about political change. Seen from this perspective, the social gospel's origins lay less in a radical critique of capitalism and more in a "growing conservative awareness that industrial capitalism has been the radical force in American society, generating social change of unforeseen consequences, heedlessly disruptive of human community."[42] Although American social Christianity developed an increasingly radical dimension in the 1930s and 1940s, it did not completely shed its prior affinity with an organic conservatism. This blend of, or perhaps creative tension between, the radical and the conservative is reflected in the complexity of Charles Hill's own political theology.

The commonalities between the social gospel and the prophetic strain in Black religious thought often went unnoticed, but the imperative to reform society—to bring it in line with Christian ethics—has always been central to African American Christian thought. The example of Martin Luther King Jr. is obvious in this context; but, as with many of the topics covered in this book, an argument can also be made here about the ways in which the 1930s laid the foundations for the 1960s. Indeed, a number of even earlier figures, such as Reverdy C. Ransom and Nannie Burroughs, who were active in the late nineteenth and early twentieth centuries, harbored a special affinity for the social gospel tradition and particularly its emphasis on making religious institutions more responsive and relevant to contemporary social conditions.[43]

Hill's rendering of the social gospel was never as radical as that of his good friend Claude Williams, who believed that it was necessary to overthrow capitalism in order to lead men and women from the sins of exploitation to the salvation of justice and human liberation. Yet Hill believed deeply in the tenets of evangelical liberalism. He also believed that the future of African Americans was tied to labor and that the early years of the industrial unionization movement held out the possibility of reconstructing the social order and fulfilling the promise of economic, and by extension racial, democracy.

The pastor of Detroit's Hartford Avenue Baptist Church for over forty years, Hill was dedicated to integrationist civil rights struggles predicated on the viability of interracial, interethnic coalition building in which the left wing of the labor movement, as well as the Communist Party (CP) and its various "front groups," were central. Hill was not a member of the CP, but at a time when individual communists and local fellow travelers made up a sizable portion of the city's Left, he evidenced few qualms about positioning himself within that political and cultural milieu. This openness was not peculiar to Hill or Black activists in Detroit. As Horace Cayton and St. Clair Drake note in their study of Chicago in the 1930s and 1940s, Blacks

> take their friends and allies where they can find them. Most of them were attracted to the Communists primarily because the "Reds" fought for Negroes as Negroes. . . . Every time a black Communist appeared on the platform, or his picture appeared in the newspaper, Negroes were proud; and no stories of "atheistic Reds," or "alien Communists" could nullify the fact that here were people who accepted Negroes as complete equals and asked other white men to do so.[44]

Or, as Detroit's Coleman A. Young put it, "Hell, I would have teamed up with Satan if he could have assured me that I'd have all the working privileges of a white man."[45]

More important, the feeling appears to have been mutual. Few radical organizations in Detroit failed to incorporate some sort of religious presence or dimension. The Civil Rights Federation, for example, which united many of the strains of leftist political activism in Detroit during the late 1930s, including those within the orbit of the Communist Party, always had a religious flavor. The purpose of the organization (which began its existence in 1935 as the Conference for the Protection of Civil Rights, and merged with the national Civil Rights Congress in the late 1940s) was to create "a real united front" and provide a Left alternative to such liberal organizations as the American Civil Liberties Union (ACLU), the Jewish Community Council, and the NAACP. Until the 1940s, when local Jewish radical Jack Raskin assumed the helm, the group was headed by clergymen, including the Rev. John H. Bollens, a white pastor of the Messiah Evangelical Church and a former director of the local ACLU, and the Rev. Owen Knox, a white Methodist minister and proponent of Methodist social action, a movement inspired by Harry Ward. In the late 1930s, Hill served as head of the federation's Negro Department. He was also among the leaders of the Detroit branch of the National Negro Congress (NNC), which was equally committed to religious and ministerial representation. The Federal Bureau of Investigation (FBI) files on the NNC list the Reverends Hill, White, and John Miles (Hill's assistant pastor at Hartford, whose ties to the CP appear to have been much stronger than Hill's), as well as unionists Christopher

Alston, Hodges Mason, John Conyers Sr., Snow Grigsby, and Sen. Charles Diggs Sr., as among those sponsoring the Michigan chapter.[46]

Perhaps because they had to contend with a host of reactionary fundamentalist preachers who took up residence in the city and advocated against racial justice and progressive unionism, local activists from both the religious and secular traditions seemed very much aware of religion's potential. This was true even for those on the Far Left. The assumption that communists, Marxists, and associated radicals are by definition "godless" is simplistic at best: Marx's famous characterization of religion as an opiate, in its entirety, reads: "Religious distress is at the same time the expression of real distress *and the protest against real distress.* Religion is the sigh of the oppressed creature, the heart of a heartless world, just as it is the spirit of an unspiritual situation. It is the opiate of the people."[47] Radical organizations such as the Communist Party or the Socialist Workers Party may not have been in touch with the sigh, the heart and the spirit of religion, but they found numerous opportunities to use the trappings of religion, especially Christianity, to make a political point.

One of my favorite examples of this functional use of religion as political critique is a cartoon by Art Young, which was reprinted in a 1954 issue of the CP's *Daily Worker.* The drawing depicts a wanted poster for Jesus Christ, who is charged with "Sedition, Criminal Anarchy, Vagrancy, and Conspiring to Overthrow the Established Government." The caption underneath the dispirited and disheveled-looking Christ reads: "Dresses poorly, *said* to be a carpenter by trade, ill-nourished, has visionary ideas, associates with common working people, the unemployed, and bums. Alien—Believed to be a Jew . . . *Professional agitator . . .* Marks on hands and feet the result of injuries inflicted by an angry mob led by respectable citizens and legal authorities."[48] Nor was it unusual, in Detroit as elsewhere, to find union organizers drawing connections between unionization and Christianity—Christ as worker—or to see union publications differentiating between "true" and "false" religion. As one CIO publication ventured, true religion "puts its faith in the people, believing in power with, not over them."[49]

For someone like Hill, a belief in the "Brotherhood of Man" and the "Fatherhood of God"—that God is ultimately no respecter of persons—coalesced nicely with the union's and the Left's support of social and racial equality. The plight of African Americans was central to Hill's political activism, but he was involved in a cause and a community that united people from various faiths and doctrines—especially Jews, Poles, the foreign born, and political minorities—in a common struggle for

"Wanted Poster of Christ" by cartoonist Art Young. (From the *Daily Worker*, September 19, 1954.)

social justice. In many ways, that common struggle can be best conceptualized as an "early" civil rights movement conducted by an "early" civil rights community that began to take shape in the 1930s around organizations such as the Civil Rights Federation, the National Negro Congress, and the militant wing of the labor movement; that was active in the 1940s in Detroit's version of the Double Victory campaign (victory against fascism abroad and victory against discrimination at home); and whose existence was severely challenged in the harsh anticommunist climate of mid- to late 1950s. This argument was made most convincingly by historians Nelson Lichtenstein and Robert Korstad in a 1988 article in the *Journal of American History* entitled "Opportunities Found and Lost: Labor, Radicals, and the Early Civil Rights Movement," and it guides the development of the first half of this book.

Building on British historian E. P. Thompson's observation about the "window of opportunity" that seems to define the life cycle of a movement, Lichtenstein and Korstad argue that the narrowing of public discourse in the cold war era contributed to the "defeat and diffusion" of the early civil rights community, that the rise of anticommunism shattered the Popular Front coalition on civil rights, and that the "retreat and containment of the union movement deprived black activists of the political and social space necessary to carry on an independent struggle."[50] It was under these circumstances, they claim, that the civil rights struggles of the late 1950s and early 1960s took on their unique social character and political strategy. While some of this is certainly true, Lictenstein and Korstad overlook the myriad ways in which the movements of the 1930s and the 1960s exist on a single continuum. A closer study of intergenerational transmission, of reflection and continuity, offers a much more accurate model for understanding the movement cultures created in places such as Detroit and the role that key figures such as Reverend Hill, whose activism spans the 1930s–1960s divide, played in making these cultures into rich and vibrant and spiritual and active spaces.

The second half of this study therefore focuses on this question of change and continuity within and among activist communities in Detroit. The main focus is on the Rev. Albert B. Cleage Jr. and what might be called the *reconstitution* of the city's Left from the late 1950s onward. Cleage embarked on his ministerial and political career in Detroit in the mid-1950s as Hill's viability as a spokesperson and community organizer was beginning to wane under the pressures of a repressive political climate. Some of the issues that animated Hill and his allies—the lack of adequate political representation for Blacks, housing and job shortages, police brutality—were also cornerstones of Cleage's activism. Cleage, however, adopted a new approach to the amelioration of these social ills. Preaching a type of gospel very different from the Reverend Hill's—one based on the "realism" of neo-orthodox theology as opposed to the traditional "idealism" of the social gospel—Cleage eventually repudiated the older Left-labor coalitions and their integrationist tendencies. Instead he turned to Black theology and Black Christian nationalism.

In this sense, Cleage was part of a growing national trend in Black religious and political thought, a trend that developed and codified Black theology and linked it with other liberation theologies in Latin America, Africa, and North America. On Easter Sunday, 1967, he unveiled an eighteen-foot painting of the Black Madonna at his Central Congregational Church and began to lay the foundations for his Black Christian nationalism movement. Deploying a political theology based on a Black Christ as a Black revolutionary, Cleage worked to transform the Black church into the foundation of a new, or rather redeemed, Black nation. Calling for community control of institutions in the inner city as well as self-determination in economics, culture, and religion, Cleage offered what he viewed as the only viable alternative to the social and political vision of the mainstream civil rights movement. "You can't fight an enemy that you believe is your friend," he wrote, "dedicated to your welfare and your best interest." For Cleage, as for many other radicals in the mid- to late 1960s, American society—white society—was far too sick to merit the extreme effort of integration: "Every time the cattle prod was used, every time the fire hose was used, every time a black person was beaten, we saw the bestiality to which the white man has degenerated in a racist society."[51]

For Cleage, who was very taken with Reinhold Niebuhr's theology as a young divinity student, the construction of "Heaven on Earth," to use a well-worn phrase associated with the social gospel, was an impossible dream. Racism, as a manifestation of unequal divisions of power and resources, was a deeply entrenched social phenomenon, one that could not be overcome by moral suasion and enlightenment. Led to these conclusions by disillusionment with the ideology and tactics of the southern-based civil rights movement, as well as the liberal and labor-based traditions of its northern counterparts, Cleage represented an important transition for Black political and religious radicalism in Detroit. The "rights of labor," especially equal employment opportunities and increased Black representation within unions, were still a goal of Cleage's activism, but the context within which the struggle was waged had shifted dramatically. As one contemporary commentator noted, the UAW had become a "right-of-center union with a left-of-center reputation" and could no longer be reasonably counted on as a source of support. Yet, the overwhelmingly working class character of the movements remained a constant. It was this character, Dan Georgakas and Marvin Surkin argue, that "clearly differentiated the Detroit experience from other major social movements of the 1960s and early 1970s."[52]

With Cleage and his constituency, which included an array of Black nationalists and separatists, as well as Black and white Marxists, the city's civil rights movement may be said to have entered a new phase—one marked by a new, or at least reconstituted, community of protest, which was located around organizations such as the Group on Advanced Leadership (GOAL, headed by Cleage along with Milton and Richard Henry, who later changed their names to Brother Gaidi Obadele and Brother Imari Obadele), UHURU, the Freedom Now Party (FNP), the Socialist Workers Party, the Inner-City Organizing Committee, the Interreligious Foundation for Community Organization, and of course Cleage's church. Interestingly, Reverend Cleage viewed the years 1963–64, not 1967, the year of the massive uprising in Detroit, as a decisive turning point in the history of the movement. "In the North, the 'Black Revolt of 1963' departed radically from the pattern established in the South," Cleage wrote in his independent paper, *Illustrated News.*

> In northern centers a new kind of "Black Nationalism" began to emerge. The Negro, disillusioned with "integration," began to look for another way—an independent course he could chart and travel alone. Black men began to talk of Black History, Black Art, Black Economics, Black Political Action and Black Leadership. Black Nationalists didn't merely talk black, they began to act black.[53]

For all of his insistence to the contrary, Cleage's "break" with the past was neither sudden nor clean, however. Nineteen sixty-three was hardly the first time that Black men and women in Detroit and elsewhere began to talk and act like Black nationalists. The city was, after all, the birthplace of the Nation of Islam and the home of Temple #1, and Detroit also had a thriving Garveyite movement in the 1920s. Further, a number of the older activists, many of whom were involved in the union movement and the CP, made the transition from the Popular Front ideology of "Black and White Unite and Fight" to the social and political reality of militant Black nationalism, thereby bridging the city's two eras of civil rights struggles. Moreover, the Black power stance that Cleage eventually adopted had a long gestation period, and he was influenced by an array of notable forerunners. One of them was the Rev. Charles A. Hill. Although Hill resisted the turn toward Black nationalism, he sought to enlist the institutional power of the church and the discursive power of religion with a vigor that rivaled Cleage's.

Hill's example was not lost on Cleage. The course of events would increasingly place the two men at political odds, with Hill openly denouncing Black power politics and Black separatism as shortsighted extremism and Cleage retaliating with charges of "Uncle Tomism." But Hill had served as a role model for a number of younger activists, including Cleage. Scorning what he saw as an emphasis on "spirituality" in Hill's social activism, Cleage nonetheless admired the elder man's "radicalism."[54]

As a young man, Cleage attended services and political meetings at Hill's church, even though the prosperous Cleage family belonged to Plymouth Congregational, which was pastored by Horace A. White, another of Cleage's role models. Further, Cleage visited Hartford well into the late 1950s, when Hill defied anticommunist slurs by offering a platform to such unpopular individuals (at the time) as Paul Robeson, W. E. B. DuBois, and Ben Davis and by providing a meeting space for equally unpopular organizations such as the National Negro Labor Council (NNLC) and the American Committee for Protection of Foreign Born. Cleage, for his part, continued this open-door policy at his own church. In fact, such political, ideological, and communal openness was a point of pride and principle for both ministers. "This morning's paper has an article listing all of the Black Nationalist groups in the city," Cleage enthusiastically reported at the beginning of a Sunday sermon, "saying that for all or most of them the Shrine of the Black Madonna is their spiritual home."[55] As this statement suggests, the civil rights movement in which Cleage participated was as porous as the one to which Hill gave much of his life. For all their other differences, the two men shared a pragmatic and moral quest for unity amid diversity. Although actively engaged in seemingly secular movements, they were wholly dedicated to the creation of an open "spiritual home" for political radicals.

The movements and protest communities of both eras also had to negotiate an appropriate space for the labor movement, on the one hand, and a militant, predominantly white Left on the other. For the community of activists in the 1930s, this negotiation took place during the early years of what was then an unpopular UAW-CIO and an active period for the Communist Party and its front groups. In the late 1950s and 1960s, the negotiation was between a UAW dominated by Walter Reuther and liberal anticommunism and the Socialist Workers Party, which was particularly active in Detroit after the CP was weakened by McCarthyism. Throughout the late 1950s and 1960s, the SWP became increasingly supportive of the politics and ideology of revolutionary Black nationalism, and its members were among the earliest white supporters of Malcolm X. In fact, generations of students have been introduced to the words and philosophy of Malcolm X via the collection *Malcolm X Speaks,* which was edited by the SWP's George Breitman and published by Pathfinder, the party's press. The SWP also sponsored a Friday Labor Forum that attracted dozens of young radicals, many of whom would go on to work with Reverend Cleage and found some of the most important organizations of the late 1960s, including the League of Black Revolutionary Workers and the Revolutionary Union Movement (RUM), the West Central Organization (WCO), and the Black Economic Development Conference.

Local radicals such as James and Grace Lee Boggs had ties to the SWP, as did national figures such as Conrad Lynn and William Worthy. Cleage and others worked with all of them in groups such as the Freedom Now Party, and many from within the SWP's orbit worked on Cleage's campaign when he ran for governor of Michigan in 1964. By noting these sorts of connections, I hope at least to begin to explore the often contentious yet relatively cooperative relationship between the SWP and the rise of Black (Christian) nationalism in Detroit during the late 1950s and 1960s.[56]

One way to chart the development of political radicalism and civil rights militancy in Detroit, then, is along a line from Hill to Cleage. This is a line that highlights the significance of religion. The point is not to pit Hill against Cleage and thereby create a false dichotomy between integration and Black nationalism or civil rights and Black power. Like Hill and Cleage themselves, these strategies coexisted on a single ideological continuum as different inflections of the struggle for social justice that informs various protest movements throughout African American and American political culture. Nor is it my intention to elevate the Reverends Hill and Cleage to the status of prophets preaching in the wilderness. As historian Evelyn Brooks Higginbotham rightly cautions, "In portraying the church's role, historians tend to rely too heavily on the speeches and actions of outstanding ministers. Too often, 'minister' functions as a metonym for church and the embodiment of the church's public identity." A church may serve as the power base for the activism of a highly political minister, but in the end ministers remain accountable to their congregants, who may have divergent social and political and economic interests.[57]

Hill and Cleage are important historical figures because through the courage of conviction and faith they worked on the local, grassroots level to bring about social change. It is difficult to avoid the pitfalls identified by Brooks Higginbotham, especially in a book that relies so heavily on biography and intellectual history; yet it is obvious that neither man worked alone and that neither, studied in isolation, fully reflects the rich and varied nature of Detroit's multilayered civil rights communities. This book, therefore, is crowded with the presence and voices of dozens of individuals, as well as organizations, networks, and social forces, struggling with—and against—the Reverends Hill and Cleage.

ONE

EVOLVING FAITH

Rev. Charles A. Hill and the
Making of a Black Religious Radical

In the short story "Fire and Cloud," published in the 1940 collection *Uncle Tom's Children*, African American writer Richard Wright explores the conflicts among religion, politics, race, and class by focusing on the inner turmoil and external pressures besetting Reverend Taylor, the story's protagonist. The tale commences with Reverend Taylor, a Black minister in a small southern town, returning from a discouraging meeting with the town's white relief officer. Taylor had gone, hat in hand, to plead the case of the town's nearly destitute and increasingly desperate Black population. He was rebuffed, told only that "Everybody's hungry, and after all, it's no harder on your people than it is on ours."[1] The officer's only suggestion is that Taylor tell his congregation "they'll just have to wait." Mulling over how best to convey the bad news, Taylor begins to think, "Lawd, mabe them Reds is right," which is to say maybe the community should band together, stage a massive interracial march downtown, and "scare 'em inter doin' something!"[2] At the same time, Taylor is worried that such a militant course of action would offend the mayor and the town's white elite, endangering his flock and the entire Black community by stirring up the antagonism of local whites. It would also, he fears, place his own position as minister of his church in jeopardy, especially since Deacon Smith—"A black snake in the grass! A black Judas!"—is looking for any excuse to engineer Taylor's ouster.

By the time Taylor arrives at his home, all of these pressures and worries and competing constituencies have been gathered under one roof, literally. The Reds, Hadley and Green, are in the Bible room; the chief of police, who has been sent by the mayor, is in the parlor; Deacon Smith, who has been using the rumor of a demonstration in his campaign to discredit Taylor and curry favor with the local white political bosses, is in the basement with the other deacons; and a distressed and agitated delegation from his congregation is crowded into the front hallway. The physical structure of the house, then, operates as a symbolic representation of Reverend Taylor's internal conflicts—conflicts that are resolved when Taylor is abducted and savagely beaten by a gang of white men, after which he agrees to support the interracial march. In preparation for that march Wright has Taylor preach an uncompromising sermon, urging his audience to take collective action on its own behalf.

> Sistahs n Brothers, Ah *know* now! Ah done seen the *sign!* Wes gotta git together. Ah know whut yo life is! Ah done felt it! Its *fire!* Its like the fire that burned me last night! Its sufferin! Its hell! Ah can't bear this fire erlone! Ah know now wut t do! Wes gotta git close t one ernother! Gawds done spoke! Gawds done sent His sign. Now its time fer us t ack.[3]

Characteristically, Wright leaves the question of the march's success unanswered. We are not told whether the Black and white marchers, united at least for the moment around shared class interests, are able to force the hand of the town's elite. While he suggests that *all* of the participants, especially the African American ones, have been transformed by the experience of interracial collective struggle, Wright ends with Taylor's newfound conviction that "This is the way!" "Gawd ain no lie!" he tells himself, and the story concludes as he "mumbled out loud, exultingly: *'Freedom belongs t the strong!'* "[4]

This story of one religious man's, one minister's, conversion to the necessity of collective action is instructive for a number of reasons, not the least of which is Wright's ability to capture the complex relationship of faith to action. At the beginning of the tale the sympathetic Taylor is a man of God, whose authority as a minister anoints him a mediator between the Black community and the white power structure. Sustained by his faith, he accommodates himself to the racial and class status quo, viewing his passivity as the only viable option in a town (and a world) where "the white folks jus erbout owns" everything. At the story's end, Taylor's faith continues to shape his identity and his actions, but now those actions are geared toward a nonaccommodationist and potentially progressive politics. What has changed is Taylor's interpretation of what God demands and his vision of how best to serve his congregation.

Reverend Taylor had many real life counterparts in the Depression era, ministers who, like Taylor, were driven by faith and circumstance to participate in mass demonstrations, strikes, and other political actions. Progressive activists and unionists in Detroit in the 1930s and early 1940s were blessed with the presence of three such men: the Rev. Horace A. White, Fr. Malcolm C. Dade, and the Rev. Charles A. Hill. All three played a key role in the city's early civil rights movement, and all three are intriguing in their own right. It was the Reverend Hill, however, who developed the most extensive and militant set of positions and alliances with the Left and whose story therefore seems the most compelling. His biography embodies the dynamic confluence of religion and politics during the formative years of Detroit's early civil rights community.

Charles Hill did not start as a radical in either a political or a theological sense. In fact, he was once described as "an old-fashion Bible thumping preacher whose only political concern was making things right in the sight of the Lord."[5] This wonderfully descriptive statement from Hill's close friend and ally, Coleman A. Young (the labor radical who became Detroit's first Black mayor, in 1973), captures the intriguing admixture of conservative and progressive uses of religion that formed the beating heart of Hill's political theology and activism. Like the fictional Reverend Taylor, there was nothing particularly radical about Hill's understanding of evangelical Christianity. Unlike the radical theologians active in the 1930s—figures such as Claude Williams and Harry Ward, one of the founding members of the Methodist Federation for Social Action—Hill never articulated a direct connection between Christianity and Marxism; nor did he ever directly urge the overthrow of capitalism. And yet this Bible-thumping minister became one of the most militant religious leaders in the city.

Reverend Hill was not a practicing theologian, and unfortunately few of his writings and sermons survived his death in 1970. Yet Hill's early life and young adulthood offer a number of clues to the sources of his later political activism. Born in Detroit on April 28, 1893, Hill was the surviving twin born to Edward Hill, an African American dentist, and Mary Lantz Hill, a second-generation German American. There are two family stories, or legends, about this union. The first, told by Hill's eldest son, Charles A. Hill Jr., maintains that the union was little more than a one-night stand. Edward Hill had come to town "for a convention, you know," and Mary Lantz was "a waitress, I think, at a local place. They met and, well, one thing led to another." The other version, told by Hill's daughter, Bermecia Morrow McCoy, insists that Mary Lantz and Edward Hill were formally married, even though there is no trace of a marriage license or official record. She also points out that Mary Lantz went by the name Mrs. Hill until her death.[6]

In both heavily gendered versions, Edward and Mary defied the racial and sexual norms that structured social interactions in what was then still a small city teetering on the brink of industrial greatness. Although an 1838 statute prohibiting marriage between Blacks and whites had been repealed by the Michigan legislature in 1882, the social stigma attached to such a union at the time of Hill's birth would have been substantial. And, while Blacks were scattered across the German east side, virtually no intermarriages were officially recorded before the early 1900s.[7] The union between Mary and Edward may not have been prohibited by the state, but it was certainly not sanctioned by members of the Lantz family, who, like many other older German immigrants, had become relatively prosperous as skilled workers. As a result of the unpopular marriage/ elicit rendezvous, Mary was forced to sever her familial ties.

Whatever the truth about the nature of their relationship, it ended, but not before a child was conceived. There is no evidence as to whether Edward Hill ever saw his son or provided any type of emotional or financial support for his estranged wife and child. In fact, Hill's birth certificate lists his father as "Unknown."[8] Apparently, Edward Hill returned to Chicago. According to both Hill children, Charles Hill rarely mentioned his father; both children also agree that the two men never met. For his mother, however, Charles Hill seemed to harbor only love and affection. Mary Hill's life was not an easy one. She was left alone with a redheaded infant who in his third month began to "darken"—much to the consternation of her friends and neighbors in the German community near Jay Street and Gratiot on Detroit's east side. His birth certificate lists him as "White," but this did not stop gossip about Mary's "colored baby" from spreading through the community and compounding the hardships faced by the young, ostensibly single mother. Eking out a living for herself and her child without a strong support network in turn of the century Detroit soon proved overwhelming. Shortly after Charles was baptized into the Catholic faith, Mary Hill took the drastic step of placing her son in the care of an orphanage, the German Protestant Home, where he would remain for the next eleven to twelve years.

That she was able to place her "colored" baby in the home was fairly remarkable in itself since nearly all of the city's orphanages practiced a policy of racial exclusivity.[9] In fact, in a June 1916 exchange of letters between the Rev. John Webster, superintendent of the German Protestant Home, and Forrester B. Washington, the first director of the Detroit Urban League (DUL), Webster reported that "we have never had any colored children in our Home" and had none presently.[10] Throughout her son's tenure as a ward, Mary continued to work odd jobs—taking in laundry and hiring herself out as a maid—and visited Charles sporadically. Aware of his ambiguous status as both "son" and "orphan," not to mention as both legally White and socially colored, his years at the German Protestant Home passed slowly.

As an adult, Hill rarely mentioned these years. The one story that his eldest son was able to clearly recall had to do with Hill sneaking into the cellar of the orphanage to lick the sides of the maple syrup barrels. While humorous, Charles Hill Jr. remembers this as a story of deprivation. Although Charles Sr.'s love for, and loyalty to, Mary Hill was never questioned by friends or family, there is little doubt that he was deeply affected by his experience in both negative and positive ways. "I think that's why Daddy was such a good father," Bermecia recalled. "I mean not having a father, and the orphanage, made him value fatherhood that much more."[11] But the implications of his years in the orphanage extend even further. On the one hand, his early and prolonged exposure to white children and administrators may have accounted in part for his later ease in interracial and majority-white settings. Perhaps it even formed the basis for his abiding faith in the possibility of integration and racial reconciliation. If a much later remark by his grandson, David Morrow, is accurate, then Hill found a certain amount of acceptance and support at the home. "During his early years," Morrow said in a speech entitled "Charles Andrew Hill—the Family Man" delivered at his grandfather's retirement celebration in 1968, "his teachers in the home recognized his strong character and depended on him to escort them to and from evening prayer service."[12]

On the other hand, it is surely the case that his early experiences complicated Hill's efforts to work out his own racial, or interracial, identity. By his eleventh or twelfth year, Hill had had enough. He returned to his mother's house on Jay Street determined to assist her and continue his education. The character of the Jay Street neighborhood, like the city as a whole, had begun to change. Jay Street was still part of the area near Gratiot Avenue populated by less affluent Germans, but by 1905 the area also included "the better class of the colored people," as well as Jewish families. Naturally, he would have explored his new surroundings as he traveled from home to school to whatever after-school jobs he could secure to augment the relatively meager family income. West of Gratiot, near the heart of what had been known as "Little Berlin," was Woodward Avenue, the broad main boulevard that bisected the city, stretching from the river outward past Detroit's ever-expanding northern boundaries. To the far east lay DeQuindre Avenue, with an ethnic and racial patchwork in between.[13]

Detroit's near east side, the center of Hill's geographical existence, was the traditional point of entry for immigrant Detroit, first for the French, then for (relatively fewer) Irish, and later for innumerable Germans. In the 1880s and 1890s, it became the portal for immigrant Italians, who established a colony near the river called Paradise Valley, and for Greeks, Jews, and waves of Poles, who would quickly become the largest cultural minority group in the city. By the turn of the century, the deep east side was identified with Irish, Gratiot with Germans, Hastings Street with Poles and Russian Jews, and Paradise Valley with Italians. The narrow sector to the south of Jefferson, the major avenue following the contours of the Detroit River, was filled with dilapidated old warehouses, decaying housing stock, vice, crime, and the poor from all racial and ethnic groups. In a pattern that was replicated generation after generation, each group would establish a beachhead within the east side and gradually move out—and up, socioeconomically speaking—generally toward the city's northern reaches. This is what the better-off, native-born white population managed to do as Detroit experienced its first major population boom, from 132,956 residents in 1884 to 205,876 in 1890. The last group to manage this transition in class and social space would be African Americans, who occupied more and more of the east side as others moved on.[14]

In the early 1900s, when Hill first encountered it, this African American enclave was still relatively small. Before the Civil War, the tiny Black population of roughly 580 souls had been clustered in the area between Randolph Street on the west, Hastings on the east, Gratiot on the north and the river to the south. By the 1870s, Blacks, who made up less than 3 percent of the population, began to settle in the old Kentucky district, twenty blocks north of Gratiot and St. Antoine, and throughout the east side. As the Black population increased (from 4,111 in 1900 to 5,741 in 1910), so did its concentration, creating the early outlines of what would soon become a city within a city, with a variety and breadth of institutions that could match those of Detroit itself.[15]

Mary Hill gradually withdrew from friends and neighbors in the years following her son's return, but she never stood in the way of Charles's desire for increased interaction with African Americans. Indeed, she would periodically accompany him to the various Black churches that he attended—faithfully—every Sunday. Her own ties to Catholicism and the local parish had weakened over the years, and she did not prevent her son from exploring other religious options. Hence, Hill was free throughout his high school years to frequent no less than three churches: Ebenezer African Methodist Episcopal (AME); Bethel AME at the corner of Napoleon and Hastings; and Second Baptist, the oldest of the city's Black churches, with a stately brick edifice on Monroe (originally called Croghan) Street. It was largely through these religious institutions that Hill came to identify with the struggles, hopes, successes, and indignities that were part of the day-to-day existence of Detroit's Black population. Indeed, it is difficult to underestimate the importance of Black churches in urban centers during this period. They were often the first institutions to provide social services, and they offered spaces for meetings and gatherings, both spiritual and secular. Moreover, they endowed their congregants with a sense of belonging, a source of stability in a chaotic world.[16]

These institutions also, arguably, augmented Hill's understanding of class stratification. In Detroit, as elsewhere, church membership was an excellent measure of class and social status within the Black community. Hence it is significant that Hill did not seem to have much contact with churches such as St. Matthew's Episcopal (at the intersection of St. Antoine and Elizabeth), which catered to the Black elite, particularly the city's small group of established Black families. The St. Matthew's congregation included doctors and lawyers and was always led by well-educated clergymen. There was widespread acknowledgment that the church's ornate chapel was the most popular site of worship for members of the "blue book of colored society in Detroit," and the parish actively cultivated its reputation among "those who fancy themselves to the intelligentsia and the better paid workmen and businessmen."[17]

This tendency shaped much of the church's history. In an internal document, "A Brief History of St. Matthew's Church," probably drafted in the early 1920s, the anonymous author makes repeated reference to the "upstanding, courageous, intelligent, high type class of men who played a role in the establishment and maintenance of the church in its early years." Among this group were men "who had been free since birth and whose ancestors before them had been free." These men are mentioned not only because of their accomplishments, the author relates, but also because "we believe it to be a just and Christian act to dissipate the impression of illiteracy of the men of that time."[18]

Along with the "high type" of the congregation and the impressive education of the clergy, the typewritten history also notes, "Our splendid contacts with the best and most influential citizenry of the white race has always worked for the best interests of our group, as in the past this fact is still apparent." This fact was also apparent throughout the first half of the twentieth century, especially as the church continued to enjoy contacts with Henry Ford and others. Thus, under the direction of Robert W. Bagnall from 1911 to 1921, when Bagnall left to become the NAACP's director of branches in New York, and Fr. Everard Daniel until 1939, St. Matthew's membership strove to be "a group conscious of their role as community leaders and separate from the 'masses of the laboring classes.'"[19] It was to those "laboring classes" that Hill, the son of a working-class mother, was drawn.

Eschewing the cachet of St. Matthew's, Hill favored churches, such as Bethel AME, whose congregants were from the "middling classes"—factory workers, carpenters, tailors, janitors, laundresses, and cooks—and Second Baptist, which also had a predominantly working-class congregation. Bethel was a driving force behind Detroit's Black institutional development in the late nineteenth century. It was particularly active in the field of education and was the first church to do extensive social work among the Black population.[20] It was in such institutions, moreover, that Hill found an edifying religious emotionalism to match the evangelical style that he would come to adopt in his own preaching decades later. But that is not all that he found. Members of all three congregations became his friends; their respective pastors became mentors and role models, perhaps becoming the extended family (and father figures) he had never had. Hill was particularly drawn to the children of these congregations. By the time he entered his final year of high school he had managed to have himself appointed superintendent of the Sunday schools at Bethel and Second Baptist while serving on the usher board at Ebenezer.

It was during these years of immersion in Black religious life that Hill began to struggle with the question of whether he truly felt "the call" of the ministry, that urge to preach, as a vocation, that is so central to African American (and Christian) religious expression. In narratives of the call experience, conflict, resistance, and uncertainty are tropes of the struggle to understand and answer. Those who are called to the ministry often have to come to terms with feelings of inadequacy, loneliness, and doubt about their competence to fulfill a religious vocation.[21] Hill's experiences fit this arc. His devotion was strong, yet he remained uncertain. The idea of becoming a minister competed with dreams of pursuing a career in law or business. With high school graduation swiftly approaching, Hill chose business. He was wary of leaving home, and the family finances were as precarious as ever, but, with his mother's blessing, he headed to Ypsilanti, Michigan, to attend Cleary Business College, where he earned a degree in business administration.

Cleary was a relatively good vocational school. It was predominantly white but not racially exclusive. Moreover, and perhaps more important, it was close enough to Detroit (about thirty miles) that Charles could return home nearly every weekend to continue his Sunday school and other church duties. The short bus ride home every Friday or Saturday also gave him the opportunity to visit with his mother. She never failed to prepare his favorite foods or to hand wash and press a stack of white shirts so that he would look "presentable" throughout the week.[22] He did well in his courses. His transcripts reveal a very basic selection of classes top-heavy with arithmetic, bookkeeping, and office practices.[23]

As Hill struggled to blend the secular world of weekday business studies with the spiritual world of the church, he also continued to wrestle with the question of whether he felt truly called to preach and minister. His chosen path reflects this doubt and struggle. Hill finished Cleary in 1912 and accepted an apprenticeship in the downtown offices of Black attorney William Patrick Sr. with the intent of pursuing a legal career. At the same time, he enrolled in a correspondence course offered by Moody Bible College in Chicago. This dichotomy is significant for at least two reasons. First, Hill's actions reveal the extent to which he was conflicted over the call and his future. Second, his choice of Moody tells us something about how Hill conceptualized the role of a minister.

Named in honor of Dwight L. Moody, a nineteenth-century evangelist who operated schools for "Bible work" in the slums of Chicago for sixteen years, Moody Bible College was not a traditional seminary. Rather, the institution was in many ways the perpetuation of Dwight Moody's desire to outfit laymen for the "practical work" of reaching the masses.[24] This appreciation for the practical side of the ministry would mark Hill's long career. He also adopted much of Moody's theological framework, which was conservative and evangelical. Hill was comfortable with fairly literal scriptural readings and interpretations—he was not a theologian in the scholarly sense—and, not surprisingly, he chose to take the "Bible Doctrine Course," ultimately receiving a degree in "The Doctrine of God, the Doctrine of Jesus Christ, the Doctrine of the Holy Spirit, the Doctrine of Man, and the Doctrine of Angels and Satan." As a field of theological inquiry it seems to have emphasized the place of mankind after the Trinity and to have regarded Satan as a real presence in the world. This type of theological conservatism is not inconsistent with a radical politics, and it had the potential, realized in Hill's later work, to fuel a forthright critique of capitalism, racism, and exploitation.

Hill's degree from Moody also gave him credentials sufficient to enroll in the seminary at Lincoln University in rural Chester, Pennsylvania. On the eve of World War I, he matriculated as a probationary student. Lincoln was an all-Black and all-male college funded by the Presbyterian Church and endowed with a reputation for producing outstanding graduates. "The Black Princeton," as it was known, was an ideal site for ambitious and upwardly mobile young Black men, many of whom would go on to become doctors, lawyers, businessmen, and, of course, ministers.

Religion played a major role in the founding and running of the school. When Lincoln was founded in 1854, its primary mission was to oversee the Christian education of Black men and prepare them to evangelize in both the United States and Africa. By the time of Hill's arrival in 1914, this mission had become broader and much more secular overall. Simply put, the impetus to evangelize became wedded to and perhaps submerged within the drive to "uplift" socially, economically, and politically. Moreover, as one of the first institutions dedicated to higher learning for African Americans, Lincoln's administrators eschewed the Tuskegee-inspired trend toward industrial education. Instead, they chose a path that would make their university "a leading example of an institution devoted to the creation of W. E. B. DuBois's 'talented tenth.'"[25]

The talented-tenth ideal is often derided (in some cases rightfully so) as mere elitism. As historian Kevin Gaines points out, "this emphasis on class differentiation as race progress," could produce distressing results. "Amid the legal and extralegal repression," he argues, "many black elites sought status, moral authority, and recognition of their humanity by distinguishing themselves, as bourgeois agents of civilization, from the presumably undeveloped black majority; hence the phrase, so purposeful and earnest, yet so often of ambiguous significance, 'uplifting the race.'"[26] This is not to suggest that racial uplift was completely devoid of positive features. Indeed, uplift was also rooted in a tradition of service and social responsibility—an "each one, teach one" understanding of collective struggle and social emancipation. When underpinned by religious faith, particularly the desire to see to it that others were right with God, uplift focused on both this world and the next. Such a call to service shaped Hill's life and career. It had been inculcated years ago in the churches he joined as an adolescent, cultivated during his years at Lincoln, and fully expressed in his ministry at Hartford, whose motto was "We gather to Worship, We depart to Serve."

The Lincoln experience seemed to shape Hill in other ways as well. Its diverse student body afforded him the opportunity to interact with young men from different geographical regions; because of Lincoln's continuing commitment to training African students, he also met students from different countries. The entering class of 1917, for example, was almost evenly divided between men from southern states, especially Georgia, and northern ones, especially Pennsylvania. The student body was also socioeconomically diverse. The administration kept tuition low and often allowed students to graduate with debt. While this policy would eventually prove disastrous from an administrative and financial standpoint, it gave financially insecure students such as Hill the chance to receive a first-rate, liberal-arts-based education.

Lincoln had an all-Black student body, but until 1930 its faculty was exclusively white. It was also a nonreformist institution that sought to "minimize militant attitudes and maintain a low profile in the region."[27] Relatively conservative in outlook, the administration struggled to articulate the potentially nonconservative goal of educating a Black elite in neutral terms. Thus, the students relied on one another to collectively negotiate the ambiguities at the heart of the institution. The faculty, while charged with the responsibility of cultivating a group of exceptional Black men capable of "redeeming" their race, tended to remain aloof from students both socially and ideologically. By all accounts, racial equality and racial justice—national and international—were rarely discussed in the classrooms, where strict decorum was maintained at all times. This neglect of pressing racial issues, coupled with the social distance between students and faculty, surely helped to encourage the creation of an extracurricular culture of evening "bull sessions" and informal debates on such topics as national and international politics, the Black rights agenda, the war, and colonialism. Copies of Black publications such as the NAACP's *Crisis* magazine were circulated and discussed among students, and the need for heightened militancy in the struggle for equality was always a topic of conversation.[28]

A religious sensibility was also pervasive at Lincoln, both inside and outside the seminary, where Hill was enrolled. In keeping with the school's heritage, all students were required to take two academic semesters of religious studies, and attendance at weekly chapel services was mandatory. In this regard Lincoln was part of the mainstream of Black education, in which all education was to some degree religious. According to Horace Mann Bond, a Lincoln graduate who became the college's first Black president in 1945, the university was constructed on a set of well-defined religious principles. "Lincoln University," he wrote, "is a spiritual, intellectual and social institution."

> Its basic theme derives from the idea that there is but one God. A monotheistic religion, principally the handiwork of the Jews, has the necessary corollary that God is the Father of all mankind: the children of God are Brothers.[29]

The "Fatherhood of God" and the "Brotherhood of all Mankind" are concepts whose deeper meaning and significance exceed their prima facie simplicity. If, as the Bible insists, "God is no respecter of persons" and all men and women are equal in His eyes, then racial prejudice and social intolerance are necessarily sinful and immoral.

All the available evidence about Hill's style of preaching and ministering to his flock, not to mention his broader political theology, shows that this ethos infused his life and work. "He preached the Bible," as his son put it. He was also "holistic in his theological view," recalled the Rev. Charles G. Adams, who grew up in Hartford, was mentored by Hill, and assumed the pastorate of the church when Hill retired. "He was very cosmopolitan and universalistic."[30] This universalism, or religious ecumenicalism, is hardly surprising given that Hill was baptized Catholic, raised at a German Protestant orphanage, prayed at both AME and Baptist churches, and graduated from a Presbyterian seminary. This same ecumenical spirit extended to his later political associations.

Hill's seminary training was strict and traditional; basic requirements would have included course work in biblical archaeology, homiletics, systematic theology, apologetics, Old Testament exegesis, pastoral theology, and expression.[31] Like many of his classmates, he no doubt came to Lincoln with his own ideas—many of which had been formed through his experiences, especially in Black churches, and in his correspondence course at Moody—about the Bible, Christianity, and their place in the world. In Hill's case these ideas translated into "a brand of Christianity [that] demanded activism in society on behalf of the oppressed, the underdog,"[32] which is a classic expression of both the social gospel and the prophetic strain within African American Christianity. This is not to suggest that either the social gospel or prophetic Christianity was part of the Lincoln curriculum, but certainly students were free to work out their own understandings of the relationship between these traditions and the theology they studied in the classroom.

At the time of Hill's tenure at Lincoln most of the faculty were either Presbyterian clergymen or laymen, many of whom had trained at Princeton. The seminary's orientation was therefore toward a blend of Calvinism and religious humanism. If the humanist idea that all men and women are equal in the eyes of the Lord formed one pillar of religious education at Lincoln, then the Calvinist doctrine of election—the idea that God has chosen a particular group of people for a particular destiny and that salvation comes through grace not works—formed the other. This doctrine of election and salvation not only conformed to the university's missionary outlook; it also offered a religious justification for the notion of a talented tenth that would go forth and uplift the race.

Hill imbibed this spirit as he worked out his own political theology. At its heart, this theology can best be thought of in terms of the "evangelical liberalism" constructed by "serious Christians" searching for a theology that could be believed and embraced by "intelligent moderns." This evangelical liberalism was both Christ-centric and biblically based. It was Christ-centric to the degree that it expressed the essential features of Christianity—the person and work of Jesus Christ as savior—in terms suitable to a modern world plagued with the social sins of racism and exploitation. And it was biblically based insofar as the scriptural teachings were accepted because of their intrinsic worth and epistemological value.[33] Even during these years (roughly 1914 to 1918), glimmers of Hill's affinity for evangelical liberalism can be seen, whether in his volunteer service as secretary of the Young Men's Christian Association's (YMCA's) National War Work Council or in his pursuit of an advanced teaching certificate through the Pennsylvania Sunday School Association. The Sunday school movement has, after all, always been part of a broader evangelical mission.[34]

After four years of wrestling with theological concepts inside the classroom and debating racial politics with his fellow students after hours, Hill was prepared to begin his career as a licensed minister. His mixture of Bible-thumping evangelism and social activism was already in evidence. Selected to give one of the commencement addresses for the graduation of the class of 1918, Hill chose the provocative title "Religion, a Man's Job" (sadly, the text of the speech has not survived). He and many of his classmates listening that afternoon had forgone military service—a major expression of Black manhood at the time. But perhaps they saw themselves as soldiers of a different kind, as young men able and willing to do the "man's job" of ministering to the faithful and pressing the cause of Black rights. Like their counterparts returning from the war, Hill and his classmates were no doubt inspired by what many took to be a new and growing African American militancy. During the war, W. E. B. DuBois had echoed the sentiments of many when he advised Blacks to "close ranks" around the country and engage in patriotic, albeit segregated, service. Now, at war's end and with segregation unabated, he proclaimed: "We return. We return from fighting. We return fighting. Make way for Democracy! We saved it in France, and by the Great Jehovah, we will save it in the United States of America, or know the reason why."[35]

Hill would have surely seen himself as one of DuBois's "soldiers of democracy." He would have also seen himself as one of the "new" Negroes. The same generation that would discover "newness" all round itself—New Humanism, New Thought, New Woman, New Criticism—would also discover a New Negro. As Asa Philip Randolph, then editor of the *Messenger* (billed as the only "radical black socialist magazine in America") put it at the time, "The New Negro arrived on the scene at the same time of all the other forward, progressive movements."[36] A product of both war and migration, this New Negro was, or so many claimed, no longer willing to turn the other cheek while his political rights were ignored and trampled, his labor exploited, and his demands for social equality and social justice mocked. Black Americans, declared Alain Locke some years later, were no longer willing to be "something to be argued about, condemned or defended, to be kept down or in his place or helped up, to be worried with or worried over, harassed or patronized, a social bogey or a social burden." Although this New Negro was partially the product of artists, intellectuals, and middle-class activists, it was not without a material basis in the changing everyday lives of large segments of the African American population.[37]

The beginning of the "Great Migration"—from rural to urban and South to North and West—was an important expression of agency and self-determination, as millions of African Americans struck out in search of better lives for themselves and their children. The scattered outbreaks of anti-Black violence that greeted the appearance of this New Negro—especially during the Red Summer of 1919—are one indication that white communities across the country felt the need to keep Blacks, new or not, in their (subordinate) places.[38] "When some of the soldiers came from World War I," Hill recalled, "they had gotten used to larger privileges and so they were making a demand and being pushy."[39] And Hill, who pledged to take up the man's job of religion during this sickening wave of anti-Black violence, was in favor of pushiness.

In the midst of the celebration of the New Negro and the concomitant racial violence, Hill returned home to Detroit and was ordained in the Baptist faith. Although Detroit escaped the outbreak of a full-fledged race riot, there were a number of clashes between Blacks and whites, especially during the spring of 1919, as the postwar recession led to a more competitive job market. Periodic violence at the factory gates, particularly when Black workers were used as strikebreakers and scabs, also helped to keep racial tension high. Moreover, the bombing of homes as a means of forcing Blacks out of previously integrated neighborhoods and preventing new arrivals, which had begun as early as 1917, became frequent by 1920.[40] But Hill returned not only to a city of increasing racial tensions and violence. He also returned to his mother's Jay Street house and one of the churches, Second Baptist, that had provided him with a spiritual home. Accepting a position as assistant pastor, Hill benefited from a familiarity with the congregation's older members that came from his being a former member and Sunday school superintendent. Less familiar were the church's newcomers—the steady flow of Black southern migrants who had been arriving in the city since the beginning of World War I.

Detroit had become one of the leading destinations for Black workers migrating out of the South in search of work. Between twenty-five and thirty-five thousand African American migrants took up residence there in 1916 and 1917 alone, meaning, remarkably, that the majority of the city's Black population—which numbered over forty thousand in 1920—had arrived in that one year. A second wave of migration in 1924 and 1925 brought an additional forty thousand men, women, and children. By 1926, 85 percent of Detroit's Black population had arrived in just one decade. At the same time, the city's total population also doubled, making it the fourth-largest city in America by 1920.[41]

While astonishing in their own right, these numbers fail to reveal the energy and hope, as well as the misery and despair, that gripped the city's residents in the immediate post–World War I period. For some, there was a sense that the city was on the move. New industries, especially the automotive industry, were in a period of intense growth. But for others—especially the majority of the city's southern migrants, both Black and white—the "promised land" turned out to be a hell of poverty and social dislocation. Many Black migrants watched their dreams slowly die in the thirty-four crowded city blocks that comprised Paradise Valley, the old Italian east-side enclave where the vast majority of the Black population was confined from the 1920s to the 1940s.

Under the pastorate of Rev. Robert Bradby, Second Baptist had welcomed these troubled newcomers from the start. From 1915 to 1920 alone, over nine hundred new members were added to the church's rolls. Hill owed his position as assistant pastor in charge of charity and educational programs to the influx. Given that so many Black southern migrants were Baptist, the church automatically benefited from the increase. But Bradby was also dedicated to outreach. In 1917 he set up a system of committees to meet the trains arriving at Michigan Central Station with offers of housing and employment assistance. As an assistant pastor, Hill was thrown into the thick of the Black community's social crisis, where housing and jobs were the most pressing concerns.

The district on the city's lower east side that young Charles had explored as a teenager was now bursting at the seams. In 1918, twelve to fifteen thousand African American residents were crowded into three square miles that had previously housed half that number. Although a number of other, smaller districts had been developed, the high-rent, poverty-ridden east side would remain the city's chief point of entry for migrants for decades. Excessive rents (as much as 50 to 60 percent higher than what whites and white ethnics were paying in other parts of the city), coupled with lower-paying, unskilled jobs, posed enormous difficulties for southern migrants.

One of Hill's duties was to assist new migrants in finding adequate housing and decent jobs. While the assistant pastor no doubt considered this part of the man's job of religion in action, it was actually a job in which women, most notably the church's Big Sister auxiliary, played the dominant role. In less than four years, this group of one hundred women had recruited hundreds of volunteers, raised over five thousand dollars, and founded a home for young women that was to stand "as a beacon-light for the protection of our girls."[42] The women of Second Baptist, along with other churchwomen and club women in the city, expended thousands of hours in charity work, organizing groups and societies to tend to the needs of Black southern migrants.

Second Baptist was thus a prominent place for a young, newly ordained minister to begin his career. Founded in 1836 after the First Baptist congregation split over allowing its Black congregants to vote in church matters, Second Baptist is the oldest Black church not only in Detroit but in the entire state. Second Baptist has a long and proud history of going beyond the spiritual needs of the congregation and extending itself into politics and social life. The church was a stop on the Underground Railroad (one can still see the basement rooms used to hide fugitive slaves) and hosted Frederick Douglass and John Brown.

Reverend Bradby was a distinguished leader of this important institution. Born into poverty in a rural area outside Chatham, Ontario (a background that might explain his tremendous sympathy for southern migrants), Bradby was schooled at McMaster University, a Baptist Col-

lege and Seminary in Toronto. Before accepting the pastorate at Second
Baptist in 1910, he had served congregations in Amherstburg and Wind-
sor, Ontario, and Toledo, Ohio.[43] A self-made man and prominent religious leader, Bradby was a good role model for the young minister Hill.

Hill did not remain in the position for long, however. In 1920 he
married Georgia Roberta Underwood, the daughter of a Seventh Day
Adventist minister. Born in Longsport, Indiana, Georgia had lost both
parents by the age of ten and was sent to live with an aunt in Ann Arbor,
Michigan, where she met Hill at a convention of Sunday school teachers
and administrators. Georgia Underwood Hill was a deeply religious con-
vert to the Baptist faith. As a young woman she had once vowed that she
would never be a minister's wife and would never live in Detroit. Nevertheless, she married Hill and moved into his mother's Jay Street house
during the early years of their marriage. She recalled these years as hard
but happy. As a profile in the *Michigan Chronicle* reports, "There was a
time when she baked cookies and cakes to supplement her husband's
salary. They made it a family project, and everyone was happy doing it."
The family—Georgia, Reverend Hill, and his mother—were also among
the first to take an active interest in selling Black newspapers, especially
the *Detroit Courier*. Mother Hill would continue to sell the paper well into
old age.[44]

Such measures were necessary because in 1920 Hill had also taken
on the pastorate of his own congregation with a modest salary. His new
church, Hartford Avenue Baptist (at the corner of Hartford and Milford
Streets), was, in 1920, little more than a wooden shack. Organized in
1917 by Second Baptist, the church was an urban outpost located across
Woodward Avenue—a neighborhood into which Blacks were slowly
beginning to flow. These "west siders," who no longer wished to travel
east of Woodward (the broad avenue that once served as the city's racial
divider), solicited the aid of Reverend Bradby and Second Baptist—"the
Mother of Hartford"—for help in establishing their own congregation.
Originally known as the Institutional Baptist Church, Hartford's early
membership was "made up of people of all faiths for this was the first
church in the area" and was first pastored by Rev. E. W. Edwards, whose
salary was paid in part by the Detroit Baptist Union and Second Baptist.[45]
In many ways, Hartford was part of Bradby and Second Baptist's uplift
effort, but it was Hill who made Hartford his own. He aspired, he once
said, to make Hartford "a haven of spiritual resources for all the contin-
gencies of life."[46]

Sadly, less than a year after the Hills were married their first child,
Lucia, died within a week of her birth. Some eleven months later, how-

ever, Charles Jr. was born, followed fifteen months later by Georgia Roberta. Within the next several years, Wesley, Lovica, Bermecia, Sylvia, Brent, and Lantz Hill were added to the clan. And as Hill's family continued to grow, so, too, did his church. From a membership of thirty-five in 1920, Hartford grew by 1926 to one of the ten largest Black churches in the city, with a membership of over twelve hundred. In part, this impressive growth can be linked to the influx of southern migrants into the neighborhood, as well as to relationship between Hartford and Second Baptist, but part of the explanation also lies in Hill's quiet charisma and his dedication to outreach and service.

Hill initiated an ambitious building project while Georgia came to relish her role as "first lady" of Hartford. She was a founding member of the Ladies Aid Society, served on the Women's Day Committee, and was a steady and dignified presence at most social functions. Once their children were a bit older, she extended her sphere of social involvement, serving on the board of the Lucy Thurman branch of the Young Women's Christian Association (YWCA). She also became an avid "club woman." Indeed, her extensive range of memberships led her children to joke that if she did not have a club to join for a particular purpose then she would surely invent one. And she did help to invent them. Over the years of her marriage, Georgia Hill assisted in organizing the Abatenjwa Club (for Detroit ministers' wives), the Interdenominational Wives Organization, and the Baptist Ministers' Wives Association.[47] Throughout the 1920s, both husband and wife poured their energies into church and family. While forced to live with Hill's mother to make ends meet, the family was still better off than the majority of the church's members.

When the Ford Motor Company shut down its plants in 1927 because of a model change, thousands of African American men were suddenly cast out of work, increasing the hardships suffered by workers and their families—many of whom were still reeling from the economic recession of 1920–21. Hartford's resources for coping with this disaster were minuscule compared to Second Baptist's, but Hill strove to find ways to lessen the hardships faced by his congregants, not only through the word of God and weekly spiritual communion but also through various forms of cooperative economics. He urged his congregants not to stay away from the church just because they didn't have money. Operating under the belief that God helps those who help themselves, the church held coal drives and arranged for the distribution of day-old bread from Detroit's Awrey Bakery. Although Hill stolidly refused "favors" from powerful "outside sources," Hartford also had some success in running its own small employment agency.[48]

But life was not all work and struggle. Reverend Hill saw to it that the church held dances and social forums, especially for young people, and he often organized the church's athletic programs himself. He had been an avid volleyball player while at Lincoln and even did some traveling on the Black volleyball circuit; he was always willing to get a game up. During these years and throughout the Depression, Hill would also make pancakes every Saturday for his children and their many friends. His eldest son remembers that the operation required at least two massive bags of flour and a good deal of coordination. Reverend Hill also made his own syrup—which calls to mind his late-night forays into the orphanage cellar.[49]

Hill and family also valued more restful types of recreation. Every summer they spent at least two weeks at various lakefront spots, where they would slow down, commune with nature, and take stock of their lives. Initially these family vacations were based in Mackinac City, at the very northern tip of Michigan's Lower Peninsula, where other Black families were few and far between. While the Hill family escaped the hustle and bustle of city life during these outings, they did not escape racial prejudice and de facto segregation. Indeed, Hill's children still recount stories of their summer experiences with racism—not being allowed in certain hotels, restaurants, and, significantly, certain white churches. Still, church services were mandatory. When they could find nowhere else, the family held its own private services presided over by Reverend Hill.

The family eventually saved enough money to secure the purchase of a piece of land in Harbor Beach, Michigan, in 1951, which they christened Cha-Hill-Gia, an odd amalgamation of their names. The actual purchase was accompanied by racial indignities—a white friend had to close the deal on Hill's behalf—but the lakefront site became a personal retreat for Hill, his family, and, on numerous occasions, friends and members of his congregation.

Harbor Beach was also the birthplace and hometown of Frank Murphy, whose famed career intersected with Hill's and many of those within the city's Left at numerous points. Murphy was rising during this period from a liberal Recorder's Court judge in Detroit to the city's mayor throughout the Depression, and then later to governor and Supreme Court justice.[50] The town of Harbor Beach, however, was not always as liberal and fair-minded as its favorite son. Georgia Hill recalled that when the family first arrived "we noticed that they seemed to resent us. Even when I would go to the drugstore, they always gave us what we wanted, but it seemed as if they didn't want to touch our hands."

Undaunted, the Hills continued to make friendly overtures, and the tensions gradually subsided or were at least pushed below the surface. Revealing her own class predispositions (attitudes that she shared with her husband), Georgia Hill continued: "We'd get a little odd feeling, but afterward they found out that we dressed as well as they dressed and we ate the same food, and our place looked as nice as theirs and better."[51]

Owning their own home in Detroit and a lakefront summer cottage far outside the confines of the city were still years away for the Hill family. By the late 1920s, however, Hill's life was good. He had his own church, a growing family, and a solid reputation within the Black community. Approaching his late twenties, he was in good health and well on his way to achieving middle-class standing. To all of these blessings he would add the harsh realities of political struggle.

WHAT KIND OF ACTIVISM?

The details of Charles Hill's political development are a bit fuzzy, but some basic observations can be made from the evidence. It is clear, for example, that throughout the 1920s, as Hill worked to build his church and enlarge his congregation, he was still negotiating his class identity. On the one hand, his educational pursuits suggest aspirations to become a solid citizen and a member of the Black middle class like his absent father, Edward Hill. On the other, he must have retained some loyalties to the working-class life of his mother, Mary, who continued to work at the various odd jobs that had financed her son's education until, in the early 1940s, a leg injury failed to heal properly.

Happily, the church provided a perfect opportunity for Hill to reconcile these two aspects of his identity. Hartford's decidedly working-class character allowed the young pastor to satisfy his aspirations for middle-class respectability without betraying his loyalty and sense of belonging to the class of his birth and childhood. To this end, Hill infused every aspect of Hartford with an ethos of service. Moreover, the church provided him, as it had so many others, with a fast track into politics. As one close observer put it, "For answers—for salvation—people turned to the church and politics. In many cases, the two were symbiotic. Every pastor had a political position, and every address had multiple purposes."[52]

At this point in his career, Hill's political outlook did not place him too far outside the mainstream of the Black middle class and the city's Black clergy, most of whom seemed to accept the prevailing ideology of racial uplift. The idea of an educated elite responsible for "lifting as they climbed" and providing services to their less fortunate brothers and sisters was, after all, entirely consistent with the tenor of his education at Lincoln and his prior experiences within Black religious communities such as Bethel and Second Baptist. Hill, who maintained the habit of wearing crisp white shirts, would most likely have approved of such initiatives as the "Dress Well Club," which stressed the necessity of proper attire and deportment in public. Outside the church, but within this ideological framework, Hill worked with the local YMCA and maintained a membership in Detroit's NAACP chapter. The former seemed to satisfy his continuing interests in Christian education, while the latter probably spoke to his interests in the law, social justice, and integration.

Hill was a mighty proponent of integration—so much so that he made a habit of welcoming whites into his church. This upset some of the Black congregants. There is an old joke that eleven o'clock Sunday morning is the most segregated hour in America. Some wanted to keep it that way. "I remember when I first took the church," Hill remarked, "at any time when a white citizen came in, they'd [his congregants] ask what business they had here. Why didn't they go to their own churches?" His characteristic response was to chastise his congregants for their "black chauvinism," which was, according to Hill, was "as bad as its white counterpart."[53] Given his long-standing commitment to integration on all levels of society, he began working with the local NAACP while he was still an apprentice to attorney William Patrick.

Working with Patrick, Hill had aided in the preparation of the fourteen lawsuits that the Detroit branch had brought against local movie houses and theaters, which confined Blacks to specific sections or barred them altogether. He also had the opportunity to participate in a vigorous NAACP campaign against a state bill outlawing interracial marriage.[54] The local NAACP attracted further national attention in the wake of its successful handling of the 1926 Ossian Sweet case. Sweet was an African American dentist indicted for murdering a member of a white mob that had threatened his family while it was moving into a previously all-white neighborhood. Clarence Darrow's defense work on behalf of the NAACP and the Sweet family made this an especially high-profile trial.[55] For Hill, who had begun to contemplate moving his own family into a predominantly white neighborhood on the city's west side in order to be closer to his church, the Sweet case must have touched not only a political nerve but personal one as well. His attention to the case is evident in the many updates and pleas for financial assistance that he inserted into his Sunday sermons. In 1945 he did purchase a home on the west side on West Grand Boulevard. As with the purchase of the lakefront property, a white friend closed the deal on his behalf.[56]

Throughout the 1920s, Hill hovered on the periphery of both the NAACP and the YMCA leadership. Whether by choice or circumstance, he was not admitted into the upper echelon of common leadership that linked the NAACP and the Detroit Urban League with influential Black churches, newspapers, and other high-profile community organizations such as Dunbar Hospital. Reverend Bradby of Second Baptist and Rev. John Bagnall of St. Matthew's Episcopal, for instance, worked closely with the DUL, and were contributing editors of the Black-run *Detroit Tribune;* over the years both served as president of the Detroit NAACP, with Bagnall moving on to the national office as director of branches. Another former president of the Detroit NAACP, William Osby, was a member of the DUL Board, a trustee at Dunbar Hospital, and a trustee at Second Baptist. John Dancy, head of the Detroit Urban League, had ties to at least six different race-improvement agencies and organizations, including the state Negro Welfare Bureau, Alpha Phi Alpha fraternity, the YMCA, and the Detroit Federation of Settlements. Along with Reverend Bradby, he also maintained a close connection with the Detroit Council of Churches (DCC). While Hill associated with these men—some of whom were, like Hill himself, members of the Masons—he was not yet their social or political equal.[57]

Nor is there much evidence to suggest that Hill was willing, at least in the 1920s, to join those who challenged the power of these men and their organizations. J. H. Porter's Good Citizenship League (GCL), for example, which was incorporated in 1918, complained that the political elites associated with the DUL were "political bums" willing to sell their souls to the devil in their negotiations with the white establishment.[58] Moreover, they charged that the Urban League unduly limited the sphere of Black representation. "We are tired of picked leaders," the GCL stated in a 1921 pamphlet.

We haven't a man in Detroit that the masses of colored people can point to and really trust as a leader. Negro ministers and other worthy citizens can't reach the Civic Boards now on account of the Urban League, being the accepted channel through which all matters pertaining to Negro welfare must pass. As far as we have been able to learn, every application for aid of any kind, worthy or unworthy, that has been presented to the Board of Charity, during the last year or more, has died in the office of the Urban League, the application seldom receiving a reply.[59]

For all of its outspokenness, the Good Citizenship League never achieved a mass base. Foreshadowing the anticommunist tirades that hampered the effectiveness of Black militant groups in the 1940s and 1950s, the DUL dismissed the GCL as a tiny group of "crabby, muddle-headed near reds." The group was virtually destroyed when police raided a league member's home office and arrested Porter and the group's secretary, Mary E. Jones, for distributing "inflammatory materials" in 1927.[60]

A much stronger challenge to the DUL-aligned Black elite came from Jamaican-born Marcus Garvey, who urged the thousands of Detroit members of his Universal Negro Improvement Association (UNIA) to cease their subservience to the "modern Uncle Toms seeking the shelter, leadership, protection and patronage of the 'master' in their organization and their so-called advancement work."[61] The Detroit Division of the UNIA was founded in 1920 by a minister, A. D. Williams, who attended a UNIA convention in New York and returned home "with a red, black, and green flag" and a passion for the principles and practices of the organization. With the guidance of F. Levi Lord, a native of Barbados, who accepted the assignment of creating the Detroit branch, the division grew rapidly. It purchased a building, Liberty Hall, at 1516 Russell Street, bought stock in the Black Star Line, established drugstores, shoeshine parlors, restaurants, theaters, and a gas station, while also developing a range of internal participatory groups—the Black Cross Nurses, the Motor Corps, and so forth—that were typical of the UNIA overall.[62]

The interracially minded Reverend Hill would have found Garvey's brand of "racial chauvinism" unappealing. Yet the local chapter of the UNIA gained a large following in the city, especially among women. Their meetings and marches attracted upward of fifteen thousand men and women during the early 1920s. Ruth Smith, who migrated with her parents from Gadsen, Alabama, has fond memories of growing up within the organization. "My mother carried all of the girls into the UNIA so I was a member at a very young age," she recalls. "Instead of going to church on Sunday, we would get up early and go to the Detroit division of the UNIA, diligently every Sunday." A member of the Women's Motor Corps, she reminisced in a 1975 interview about large parades through the streets of the city and the extent to which "my life, my ideals" revolved around the local UNIA. She even met and married her husband through the organization.[63]

Smith's experiences are not unique. At its height the Detroit Division had at least four thousand members, the majority of whom were employed in the plants, and a paid staff that included a president, two secretaries, and a janitor.[64] The division also attracted a number of Black middle-class businessmen and professionals, including attorney Alonzo Pettiford, who served as president in the early 1920s; J. Milton Van Lowe, legal counsel for the division and also a member of Bethel AME; and Charles Diggs, who served as the director of the board of trustees.[65] Years later, Diggs, an undertaker by profession, would go on to play a leading role in the city's civil rights community as a Democratic state senator. Along with fellow UNIA member Joseph A. Craigen, an immigrant from British Guiana who was appointed in 1937 to the Michigan Workmen's Compensation Commission by Governor Frank Murphy, Diggs helped to establish Democrat Clubs as an alternative to the power of the Republican Party in Black Detroit.

Like the members of the Good Citizenship League, local Garveyites, and in some cases Garvey himself, directly attacked the common leadership provided by the Black elite but not because it blocked access to white philanthropy. For Garvey, the problem with groups such as the NAACP and the Urban League—whether in New York or Detroit—was not only that they were dominated by integrationists and light-skinned Blacks but also that they were not sufficiently self-reliant and dedicated to the promotion of economic nationalism. He claimed, for instance, that Reverend Bagnall, the pastor of St. Matthew's, refused to allow dark-skinned Blacks to join his church. In an exchange of insults typical of Garvey's interactions with the Black elite in the United States, Bagnall, who was still new to his position in the national office of the NAACP, denounced Garvey as a "Jamaican Negro of unmixed stock, squat, stocky . . . with protruding jaws . . and rather bull-dog-like face. . . . Boastful, egotistical, tyrannical, intolerant, cunning, shifty, smooth and suave . . . gifted at self-advertisement, without shame in self-laudation . . . a lover of pomp and tawdry finery and garish display, a bully with his own folk but servile in the presence of the Klan, a sheer opportunist and a demagogic charlatan."[66]

Even though the local UNIA lost much of its momentum after Garvey's deportation in the late 1920s, the organization's influence continued to shape later developments in the city, from the establishment of the Nation of Islam during the Depression (Elijah Mohammad, né Elijah Poole, was a member of the Detroit UNIA) to, arguably, the Rev. Albert B. Cleage's Shrine of the Black Madonna and the Black Christian nationalism movement.[67] Some, such as John Charles Zampty, a loyal member of the Detroit Division from the 1920s through the 1970s, became living links between these two eras of Black religious nationalism. In fact, the similarities between Garveyism with its African Orthodox Church (AOC) and Cleage's Black Christian nationalism are striking, especially their common belief in a Black God. Why, Garvey asked in a 1924 UNIA convention speech, is God white? "If God be our Father, and we bear His image and likeness, why should we not teach our children that their Father in Heaven resembles them even as they do Him?" Linking the question to racism and power, he continued: "Why should we permit the Caucasians to constantly and indelibly impress upon their youthful minds that God is white?" "No longer," he concluded, "must we permit white religious 'pastors and asters' to hold us in spiritual serfdom and tutelage."[68]

While Garvey himself was often critical of ministers who regarded themselves as "so-called leaders of the race" and reserved special scorn for those who preached a delayed and otherworldly belief in divine justice, he nonetheless understood and built on the indigenous faith of Black folk. His own expression of faith tended toward the ethical and the pragmatic. "I would rather stand alone," Garvey once wrote, "and be framed for the prison a thousand times than deny the [Black] religion of my mother—mark you, not the [white] religion—the religion that taught me to be honest and fair to all my fellowmen."[69] Under the banner of "One God, One Aim, One Destiny," Garveyism encouraged its followers to see the One God, in whose image we are created, as Black. Further, members of the African Orthodox Church, the movement's official religious institution, were urged to "erase the white gods from your hearts . . . [and] go back to the native church, to our own true God." At a session of the fourth international convention, AOC bishop George A. McGuire also advised the audience to "name the day when all members of the race would tear down and burn all the pictures of the white Madonna and Child, and replace them with a black Madonna and Child." Thus, although careful not to offend Muslims and non-Christians, Garveyites effectively placed Christianity within a Black nationalist framework that advocated separatism from the United States and the redemption of Africa—as "Ethiopia shall arise and stretch forth her hands onto God"—from European colonial domination.[70]

None of this would have resonated with Reverend Hill, especially the idea that God could be Black or any other color. Hill's scattered statements on Black nationalism, made in the 1960s, were always derogatory, and his staunch commitment to interracialism suggests that he would have been uncomfortable with aspects of the nationalists' Afrocentric theology. Or perhaps he would have agreed with the assessment of Ruth

Smith, who observed that "years ago you had to join the UNIA or the NAACP."[71] At this point in his political career, Hill chose the latter.

Hill's own challenge to the Black political elite would come later, as his activism began to focus on the working class. His movement from a mainstream thinker on the margins of the elite to a militant religious activist aligned with workers had as much to do with his identity as a minister and the Black son of a white working-class mother as it did with Depression era changes in Detroit's political geography. The power of the Black elite, that is to say, was weakened not by the admonishments of Garveyites and groups such as the Good Citizenship League; instead, it was weakened by social forces arising out of the Depression, which opened up new opportunities for members of the working classes and middle-class supporters such as Hill.

THE DEPRESSION YEARS

The Great Depression plunged Detroit and its Black community into a pit of despair; but it also, ironically, allowed the emergence of a working-class politics. The city as a whole suffered the highest jobless rate in the country, and many of the businesses that did not fold were forced to implement massive layoffs. The Ford Motor Company, which had employed 128,000 people in March 1929, had only 37,000 left on its payroll in August 1931. By then 210,000 people were on city relief. And they were the "lucky" ones, the "deserving poor," able to take advantage of the city's limited relief programs. With 46 percent of the workforce in Michigan unemployed by 1933, conditions were becoming increasingly desperate, particularly in African American communities, where unemployment reached as high as 80 percent.[72] One result was that established race improvement organizations such as the NAACP and DUL and churches such as Second Baptist were severely constrained by financial difficulties precisely when their help was most needed.

Back in 1918 the Detroit Urban League had placed over ten thousand Blacks in jobs. By June of 1931, when the Employers' Association of Detroit, the league's primary source of funding, withdrew its support, John Dancy noted that the group's effectiveness had been severely curtailed. By 1933 the DUL only maintained two full-time employees. The NAACP suffered a similar fate. Between 1930 and 1934 the national office's operating budget dropped from sixty to thirty-eight thousand dollars. Many Black Detroiters were simply unable to pay dues and support NAACP activities; as early as 1930 the Detroit branch had ceased all regular meetings. Finally, as one author notes, "the black churches, in the main, were either financially unable, or philosophically unwilling to assert any meaningful leadership in the black community to deal with mass unemployment."[73] In fact, as a poll conducted by the Baltimore *Afro-American* bears out, most Black ministers refused to call on their churches to confront pressing economic struggles. Seventy-five percent of their sermons dealt with "the other world and the rewards of heaven" while only twenty-five percent focused on "how Christianity could be applied to the economic problems of everyday life."[74]

New groups began to fill the gap left by these churches and traditional race improvement organizations, all of which had depended to some degree on white philanthropy. In Black Detroit the new organizations spanned the ideological spectrum. Hill worked with three in particular: the Booker T. Washington Trade Association (BTWTA) and the affiliated Housewives' League, the Civic Rights Committee, and the loose collective of groups and councils associated with the Communist Party. They are therefore useful for tracing the evolution of his interest in social, political, and economic issues during the 1930s. More important, they are also representative of the different ways in which various segments of the city's African American community attempted to make a better life.

The Booker T. Washington Trade Association was organized in 1930 by the Rev. William Peck. A graduate of the Oberlin College seminary, Peck came to Detroit in 1930 to take over the pastorate of Bethel AME, one of the churches that Hill had frequented in his youth. Soon after his arrival, Reverend Peck called together a group of Black businessmen and professionals, including Hill, in order to discuss the situation in Detroit and to seek ways of addressing the community's hardships. As a result of these initial meetings, the BTWTA was formed to encourage the patronage of existing Black businesses and support the development of new ones. This was also the mission of the Housewives' League, which was founded as a sister organization by Reverend Peck's wife, Fannie.[75]

In keeping with the social philosophy of its namesake (not to mention—and few did—the mission of Marcus Garvey and the UNIA as well), the BTWTA and the Housewives' League were rooted in the premise that "only through the development of black business and industry will the race gain its economic freedom." Although ministers and their wives played a role in the groups' founding, the BTWTA and the Housewives' League were not religiously oriented, nor were they particularly involved in organized political activism. Indeed, the BTWTA was quick to point out that it was "not an organization which seeks to right the many injustices we have forced upon us or as a result of discrimination within the field of civil and property rights."[76] But within their self-proscribed sphere both groups were relatively successful. The BTWTA organized two Black merchant clubs that met twice weekly to discuss the state of Black business in the city and offer mutual support. It also organized several well-attended trade exhibits and established a trade school. By the end of the Depression, the Housewives' League, which canvassed Black neighborhoods on behalf of Black establishments, was widely credited with aiding Black merchants.

Other groups took a more confrontational approach to the problems confronting the city's African American community in the early 1930s. The Civic Rights Committee, founded in 1933 by Snow Grigsby, was more vocal and militant in its efforts to secure economic justice. Instead of focusing on the development of Black business, the committee attacked discriminatory hiring practices in the public sector. Grigsby, a Black postal worker who moved to Detroit from Chatsville, South Carolina, in 1920, considered the local NAACP leaders "dilatory in their activity," and set out to form a political association that was able and willing to adopt a more forceful position on employment discrimination.[77] Like the BTWTA and the Housewives' League, the Civic Rights Committee was not a religious organization, but it was intimately tied to the Black church. A number of ministers supported Grigsby's work and allowed him to use their facilities for meetings, and Grigsby himself was a deeply spiritual man who wrote and lectured on religious themes, insisting that churches become a more responsible and forthright agent for social change. As historian Victoria Walcott notes, however, Grigsby adopted a condescending attitude toward the hundreds of small storefront churches dotting the streets of the city's Black neighborhoods, whose preachers Grigsby, like many within the Black elite, regarded as "parasites" and practitioners of a "bootleggers religion."[78]

The reasons for Grigsby's dismissive attitude toward these small, often charismatic and Pentecostal churches stemmed as much from his activist vision of Christianity as from his unwillingness to see the spiritual beauty or social security and solace provided in the storefronts. In "Christianity and Race Relations," a speech originally delivered at the People's Church in East Lansing, Michigan, and reprinted in Grigsby's 1937 volume *White Hypocrisy and Black Lethargy*, he surveyed a range of people on how they defined Christianity. Most respondents he found wanting. "I believe that Christianity should be defined as an inward inclination which compels one, of his own initiative, to give equal opportunity to all men," he wrote, noting that the way the religion was practiced at the time was often "a joke and hypocritical in the superlative degree."

Grigsby, who was a member and later an elder and trustee of St. John's United Presbyterian, focused almost exclusively on the ethical dimensions of faith and creed. Chiding Christianity as "the only religion that draws the color line" and arguing that Blacks had become increasingly disillusioned by the "differences between our creeds and our deeds," he urged that a more authentic practice be brought to Detroit.[79]

"Our articles of religion speak of the original sin of Adam," Grigsby continues, in a language reminiscent of Walter Rauschenbusch's, "but very little is said of the modern sins of Adam's white offspring.

> They say nothing of the high rentals built up by white Christian land-lords, dilapidated houses; nothing of the unsanitary conditions of our city where the black brother is forced to live. . . . It is a sin to deprive men of an opportunity for their own growth and development, a sin to hold them down by force, a sin to impede their advancement, as well as to hinder them in educating their children and securing work to care for their dependents. All racial discrimination is sinful as well as wicked.[80]

By focusing on the sins of economic injustice, the committee functioned as a counterpart to the urban boycott campaigns—the "Don't Buy Where You Can't Work" movement—that emerged around the same time in Black communities throughout the nation.

While the BTWTA and the Housewives' League occasionally stepped beyond their limited role as booster organizations to picket stores in Black neighborhoods that did not hire African Americans, the committee went on the offensive more often. Emphasizing the importance of researching his targets, Grigsby spearheaded attacks on the racist hiring practices of the Detroit Board of Education, the Postal Service, the Fire Department, and, most impressively, the electric company, Detroit Edison.[81] When he and the committee discovered that Detroit Edison employed only forty African Americans out of a workforce of eight thousand, the group paid high school students to go door-to-door collecting light bills. The committee, joined by groups that included the BTWTA and NAACP, confronted Detroit Edison with evidence of the level of Black energy consumption. After a series of negotiations they were successful in convincing the company to hire more African Americans.

The group used such tactics repeatedly, adopting a two-pronged approach. First, it generally focused on public employment: hence, the use of *Civic* as opposed to *Civil* in the organization's name. Second, it targeted the silence of three broad groups within the community, each of which was represented by one of the three monkeys who see, hear, and speak no evil, as depicted on the cover of the committee's 1933 booklet *An X-Ray Picture of Detroit*. The monkeys are labeled "Negro Politician, Urban League, Medical Society"; "Local branch NAACP"; and "Civic and Christian Leadership."[82]

The Reverend Hill participated in the activities of the Civic Rights Committee almost from the beginning, although he does not seem to have been among its founding members. When the newly instituted Hatch Act, which prohibited federal employees (including postal workers) from engaging in "pernicious political activity," forced Grigsby to leave his position as the group's chairman, Hill became the new chair.[83] Overall, Hill participated more actively in the committee, which tended to stage public, community-based forms of protest, than in the BTWTA. His membership in both groups, which was hardly uncommon, suggests a holistic approach toward Black social advancement—one that incorporated the concerns of both the emerging middle classes and at least some segments of the working classes.

Hill's activism on behalf of African American industrial workers, who were well represented in his congregation, took more time to manifest itself in a public way. This was partly a consequence of timing, since there had been very little organizing among industrial workers before 1935 and even less that embraced Black workers. Still, at the same time that Reverend Peck was organizing the BTWTA and Snow Grigsby was forming the Civic Rights Committee, Black industrial workers were beginning to organize their own associations. That many of these groups were founded by African American members of the Communist Party is important not only for the political biography of Reverend Hill and the development of Black radicalism in Detroit but also for the emergence of the city's early civil rights community in general.

A LABOR–CIVIL RIGHTS COMMUNITY TAKES SHAPE

The long, hard years of the Depression gave the Communist Party an opportunity to expand its sphere of influence, and it was during the early 1930s that Hill and hundreds of other Black Detroiters would have first become aware of the party and its activities. There is little evidence regarding the precise nature of Hill's involvement with CP-inspired groups during this period. But it is fair to say that he was aware of the events and organizations that gradually drew segments of the Black community and the CP closer together in the early 1930s. These years were, in effect, foundational ones for the groups and individuals who would

An X-Ray Picture of Detroit

December. 1933

Bulletin No. 1   Single Copy 10 Cents

Special Price on quantities over 10 copies.

"IS THIS SILENCE PERPETUAL?"

By

SNOW F. GRIGSBY

3762 Seyburn Avenue

Detroit, Mich.

Cover from Snow F. Grigsby's *An X-Ray Picture of Detroit*, 1933. (Michigan Historical Collections. Courtesy of the Bentley Historical Library, University of Michigan.)

come to align themselves with the city's civil rights community after 1935. A few such groups—the Auto Workers Union (AWU), the League of Struggle for Negro Rights, the Unemployed Councils, and the International Labor Defense (ILD)—were particularly important.

In spite of its small numbers, the CP, having wrested control of the Auto Workers Union from the Socialist Party, did make significant attempts between 1924 and 1930 to spread the gospel of interracial unionism. Along with appeals to the foreign born, women, and young workers, the AWU also made a special appeal to Black workers, advocating "equal pay for equal work" regardless of race and insisting that "All workers must get together—men, women, young workers, all nationalities, all races, for their own protection."[84] Throughout the 1920s the CP and the AWU achieved their greatest success in recruiting white ethnics, especially Slavs. A few African Americans joined as well, most notably Joseph Billups, the son of a Mississippi preacher, and Walter Hardin—both of whom had earlier been members of the defunct (but not forgotten) Industrial Workers of the World or Wobblies—as well as Alabama-born Paul Kirk, another minister's son, and William Nowell, who ran for Congress in 1930 on the Communist Party ticket. The activities of these men within and for the CP were shaped, to some extent, by a change in policy on the "Negro question" in 1928. Instead of working (or "boring") within preexisting organizations such as the NAACP, the new policy called for the creation of parallel revolutionary groups. The party, like Garvey's UNIA, now viewed Blacks as an oppressed nation and adopted a program of "Self-Determination for Negroes in the Black Belt."[85]

This so-called Third-Period (1928–34) policy coincided with a change in the local CP leadership following the election of Phil Raymond as general secretary of the Detroit branch and, by extension, as head of the AWU. Under Raymond's direction the AWU evolved from "an independent and apolitical union into the nucleus of a self-proclaimed 'revolutionary union'" affiliated with the Communist Trade Union Unity League.[86] In the early 1930s, the member organizations in this union participated in strikes in area plants, including the Fisher Body plant in Flint and the Detroit strike wave of 1933. Following the CP line, and in an attempt to unite organizing on the shop floor with organizing in the community, Black Communists in Detroit worked within both the AWU and the League of Struggle for Negro Rights (LSNR), the organization that succeeded the American Negro Labor Congress in 1930. The LSNR was charged with bringing revolutionary and proto-nationalist ideas to urban centers of Black discontent such as Detroit.

When the CP adopted its Popular Front policy in 1935 and replaced its dual revolutionary strategy with one that called for working in broad coalitions with liberals, the league disbanded and most of its members joined the National Negro Congress.[87]

Despite these changes in policy and approach, the CP's visibility increased exponentially in the early 1930s in large part because of the opportunities afforded by worsening economic conditions. Indeed, Detroit was an important center of CP activity during these years, and there is ample evidence that the party was stronger there than in most other U.S. cities.[88] African Americans and others became aware of the party not so much through its organizing efforts within the plants but as a result of its community organizing efforts among unemployed workers and, most especially, because of its practice of "unevicting" families. "When people were evicted," recalled Joseph Billups, "we would place them back in their houses, and I've seen times when we would have four or five evictions in one block."[89] This practice was evidently widespread; since landlords would have to return to court for a new eviction order each time it happened, evictions quickly ceased to be cost effective.

To structure these and other activities, Detroit area Communists created at least fifteen Unemployed Councils. The councils' main goal was "to convince the jobless they had to overcome ethnic and racial divisions and unite, and [to] convince people that it was the government's responsibility to provide relief."[90] To this end, the CP organized a number of councils along neighborhood lines: one for the Hastings–Ferry Street area; one along Woodward Avenue north of Grand Circus Park; and a large one for the east side, where Italian, Jewish, and Eastern European families still lived and the African American enclaves were located. At their peak, Detroit's Unemployed Councils—which were among the first in the nation—were estimated to possess a combined membership of almost thirty thousand. The CP may not have been very successful in encouraging people to overcome their racial and ethnic divisions, but it did manage, on a number of occasions, to bring diverse groups of people together for mass rallies and demonstrations. Grand Circus Park, in the middle of the downtown business district, became the prime site for protests, and Left organizations used it to keep up a running dialogue on the faults and failures of capitalism. Joseph Billups recalled:

> Well, the Unemployed Councils we had used to hold meetings down there, day and night, in Grand Circus Park. And that's where the idea of unemployment insurance was raised, in Grand Circus Park. "Work or bread" was the slogan. . . . Grand Circus Park was full, day and

night, and always there was someone up speaking and it didn't make any difference at the time, for those fellows, because they didn't have any place to stay, and they were sleeping in the park.[91]

Not everyone who joined the Unemployed Councils or participated in the CP-sponsored rallies was entirely sympathetic to the party's ideology, but a large number of residents were willing to give the CP a fair hearing on the basis of its practical work. When a Ford "goon squad" and Dearborn police attacked a 1932 hunger march at Ford's Dearborn, Michigan, plant, killing three marchers (a fourth died later from injuries sustained during the assault), an estimated sixty thousand Detroiters joined the funeral march to protest what the radical press labeled the "Ford Massacre." Josephine Gomon, the mayor's secretary, remembered it as "a very dramatic scene. . . . The paraders marched down Woodward Avenue behind the four flag-draped caskets; and as they came, they sang the *Internationale*. It was said that 60,000 people marched and the volume of singing could be heard all over the city. It reverberated."[92] The event itself reverberated throughout the city and the nation.[93]

Roger Baldwin, head of the American Civil Liberties Union, denounced Ford and the Dearborn police. The situation, according to the ACLU, was not so much about communism—"or any other 'ism'"— but about the rights to freedom of expression, assembly, peaceful demonstration and political thought.[94] Baldwin and the ACLU did not agree with local Communists, however, in assigning some of the blame to Frank Murphy, Detroit's liberal mayor. For the party it was crucial, under the logic of the Third Period strategy, that workers and the unemployed see Murphy, the liberal, as a threat as great as Ford, the capitalist. Hence the banners unfurled along the parade route read "Smash the Ford-Murphy Police Terror."[95]

For some, such as David Moore, a Black auto worker who was just a teenager at the time of what came to be called the Ford Hunger March and its aftermath, the protest was "a turning point in my life. . . . The more I'd gotten involved in the Councils, the more I learned about the system . . . [and] when I saw the blood flowing there on Miller Road [near the plant], that was the point I became a radical. From that day on."[96] Young Christopher Alston, whose family had moved from Florida to Detroit in 1916, was similarly affected—even more so since the eighteen year old had attended the march with a high school friend, Joe Bussell, one of the men killed later that day. Alston joined the party soon after. From 1933 to 1935 he worked in Harlem, organizing the Young People's Progressive League, and in 1936 he went south to organize the

All Southern Negro Youth Congress. In 1938, after helping to found what became the Tobacco Stemmers' and Laborers' Industrial Union in Richmond, Alston traveled through Virginia, North Carolina, and Tennessee, organizing Black workers for the CIO. He returned to Detroit just in time to get a job at Ford's River Rouge complex and to begin the long, hard campaign to organize workers in that massive facility.[97]

The funeral/mass march was not the end of the hunger march tragedy. Four days after the massacre, a fourth marcher, Curtis William, a thirty-seven-year-old Black worker, died from injuries sustained during the melee. A group of Black organizers led by Joseph Billups requested that Williams's body be interred alongside those of the other three casualties in the (segregated) Woodlawn Cemetery overlooking Ford's River Rouge plant. When that request was denied because of the cemetery's all-white policy, Billups threatened to bury the body in Grand Circus Park. A group of disgruntled mourners actually gathered with picks and shovels to dig up the pavement in the middle of the city's business district, only to be turned away by city officials—all of whom, including Mayor Murphy and other noncommunists, were denounced as "social fascists." In the end, Billups opted for the equally dramatic solution of having the body cremated, renting an airplane, and scattering the ashes over the River Rouge plant.[98]

As the Depression wore on and the incidents of racial injustice mounted, a number of African American activists, like Alston and Moore, were pulled into the orbit of the city's Left and the Communist Party. Shelton Tappes, a Black worker and future union official, recalled that all the Communist organizers had to do was "run off handbills and go up and down the main streets in the Negro community, and whatever the site of the demonstration was to be, at the time it was to take place, there was usually a considerable crowd there." To increase its presence in the Black community, the party encouraged its African American members to organize their own councils, known as Nat Turner Clubs. These groups often held rallies "right in the Negro community," on and around Hastings Street.[99]

The opinions of Black Detroiters tended to reflect national trends. When the NAACP conducted a poll of the major Black newspapers in 1933, it found that most editors agreed with the idea that, while the CP was far from perfect, the party's stance on racial equality put it far in advance of other predominantly white organizations. As a result, the CP was making headway among African Americans. "How, under such circumstances, can we go to war with the Communist Party?" asked the *Chicago Defender,* a Black weekly avidly read in Detroit.

Is there any other political, religious, or civic organization in the country that would go to such lengths to prove itself not unfriendly to us? We may not agree with the entire program of the Communist Party, but there is one item with which we do agree wholeheartedly and that is the zealousness with which it guards the rights of the Race.

This was quite an endorsement. Even the NAACP had to admit a grudging respect for the party's race work.[100]

The CP's reputation among African Americans was also greatly enhanced by the work of International Labor Defense, the legal arm of the party, and its involvement in the Scottsboro case. "It aroused the interest of all Negroes," remembered Rose Billups. "There wasn't any question of left, right, or middle. It was a question of save the boys."[101] On March 25, 1931, nine young Black men and two white women who had been traveling on a southbound freight train were arrested. The men were subsequently charged with rape. With indecent speed, they were indicted by an all-white jury, assigned an all-white defense team by a white judge, and convicted and sentenced to death by another all-white jury. In Alabama, the Scottsboro case was nothing more than another legal lynching; but it was rescued from obscurity by the activism of Communists and the ILD. Thanks to their efforts, the U.S. Supreme Court remanded the case to the state on due process grounds. In 1934, as the ILD was preparing for a new trial, the CP called for "a solid front in the fight for the unconditional freedom of the Scottsboro Boys," and by 1935 other organizations, including the NAACP, church groups, and civic associations had gotten involved.[102]

As the case dragged on throughout the decade, moving from the state courts to higher courts and back again, it came to symbolize the faults of the American legal system and the collective struggle of African Americans. Clubs were organized in Detroit, as elsewhere, to support the boys and their defense. The families of the nine young men, along with Communists such as William Patterson, the Black Central Committee member in charge of the Scottsboro Defense Fund, came to the city to speak at large rallies and church forums. Reverend Hill, along with Fr. Malcolm Dade of St. Cyprian's, were among those who formed the committee that coordinated the defense fund's activities in Detroit. The protest around the case is the first direct mention of Hill's interaction with the CP that I have been able to locate. It may also have been one of his first public steps toward a radical politics, introducing him to the expanding ranks of the city's Left.[103]

The ILD retained the services of Maurice Sugar, a radical lawyer who had defended most of those indicted for their supposed role in the Ford Hunger March. Born in 1891 in the Upper Peninsula lumber town of Brimley, Michigan, where his Lithuanian Jewish parents ran the general store, Sugar was a Marxist who believed in struggle "within the existing law and culture of capitalism while working for socialist change." He also believed in relating legal work to the overall class struggle and was a prominent supporter of Black rights.[104] Through Sugar, the ILD became involved in a number of local cases in which African Americans were wrongfully charged. As a result, Sugar and the ILD were widely recognized as leading defenders of persecuted Blacks in the city. In fact, when Sugar ran for a position on the Detroit Recorder's Court in 1935 he was warmly received in Black churches and at civic functions. He even won the unanimous endorsement of the fifty-nine-member Detroit Metro Baptist Alliance and the conservative *Tribune Independent.* Reverend Hill was a firm supporter of Sugar—a fact much noted in Sugar's Black-directed campaign literature—and over the years the two men and their families developed a close friendship. Reverend and Mrs. Hill, for instance, were annual attendees at Sugar's Buck Dinner, a fund-raising event for radical causes begun in 1929 for which Sugar supplied the main course from his hunting trips.[105]

In the years to come, Sugar would become a central figure in Detroit's Left community, which was always seeking to increase its ranks. "Overall," as one student of political radicalism in Detroit has noted, "it can be argued that Sugar's Recorder's Court campaign served as the catalyst in the emergence of the black community's acceptance of unions and in opening a window to the left."[106] There was indeed a window created in the early 1930s and not only by Sugar's campaign. The organization of the League of Struggle for Negro Rights, the work of the Unemployed Councils, the hunger marches and protest rallies, and the fight to free the Scottsboro boys, as well as the work of groups such as the Civic Rights Committee, the Booker T. Washington Trade Association, and the Housewives' League, all contributed to the civil rights struggles of Depression era Detroit. By weakening traditional race improvement associations that depended on white philanthropy, the social and economic hardships of the Depression had opened up new spaces for working-class activism. Reverend Hill and others like him began to appreciate the working classes, the Communist Party, and the need for militant (and interracial and interethnic) collective action as central to their struggle for social justice. For (barely) middle-class activists such as Hill, the ideology of racial uplift and service did not entirely dissipate. Instead, *service* was redefined—away from "service to" the working classes and toward a position of "struggle with" them.

Hill's transformation into a religious radical was occasioned by nothing as dramatic as the savage beating at the hands of angry whites endured by Reverend Taylor in Richard Wright's "Fire and Cloud," but the spirit of the transformation was similar. Neither Hill nor the fictional Taylor faltered in his faith. Neither developed, that is to say, a particularly radical political theology. Both did, however, develop new ideas about what it means to do the Lord's work. Thus, by the mid-1930s, when the city's civil rights community was taking on a definite shape, the Reverend Hill found even greater opportunities to do the "man's job" of working for faith and social change.

TWO

TRUE VERSUS
FALSE RELIGION

The Labor–Civil Rights Community
and the Struggle to Define
a Progressive Faith, 1935–41

> True religion puts its faith in the people, believing in power with
> them, not over them. True religion adopts the ethical standard of
> Christ: "The Spirit of the Lord is upon them, because He has
> anointed me to preach the gospel to the poor; He has sent me to heal
> the brokenhearted, to preach deliverance to the captives and to set at
> liberty they who are oppressed."
>
> —CIO, *Labor and Religion* (1944)

Religion, or more specifically the role of churches and clergy, was the subject of increasing dispute throughout the 1930s as Detroit's labor–civil rights community continued to develop. In the debate over "true" versus "false" visions of Christianity, progressives implicitly followed the lead of theologian Harry F. Ward and his Methodist Federation for Social Action, who expressed an unflagging belief in "the revolutionary tradition of Christianity."[1] At the same time, the question of the proper relationship between religion and labor was broached by antiunion clergymen of various denominations and most dramatically by Fr. Charles Coughlin, whose increasingly vitriolic sermons warned of the dangers of a communist-dominated CIO.

At the same time, the question "Who owns the Negro church?" continued to occupy progressive activists, including those Black ministers and priests—Charles Hill, Horace A. White, and Malcolm C. Dade—who openly opposed the powerful alliance between the Ford Motor Company and select members of the established African American clergy.

THE PRIESTLY AND THE PROPHETIC
Hill, Bradby, and the Church-Company Alliance

When Charles Hill left his position at Second Baptist for the pastorate of Hartford in 1920, he also left behind a system of white patronage that was divisive within the Black community and generally troublesome for the labor–civil rights community as a whole. The system was rooted in a cooperative relationship that developed over the years between the Ford Motor Company and well-established Black ministers such as Second Baptist's Rev. Robert Bradby and illuminates the complex interactions among race, religion, economics, and politics in interwar Detroit. The special relationship between church and company was initiated in 1918 or 1919 when Charles Sorenson, Ford's production chief, invited Reverend Bradby to lunch with him, Henry Ford, and other company executives with the intention of discussing recent problems with and among Black workers. Over lunch, Ford "personally outlined to Bradby his desire to recruit carefully selected Negro workmen"; Bradby duly promised to recommend "very high type fellows."[2]

Operating as a thinly veiled extension of the company's employment department, Detroit's leading Black ministers were called upon to supply the "right" type of applicant—reliable, compliant, and decidedly not pro-union—with a letter of recommendation. In a typical letter, dated October 18, 1926, Reverend Bradby asks the employment department to "investigate [a case] and do whatever you can for him."[3]

Ministers were also occasionally called upon to mediate disputes between workers in the plant itself. In another letter, this one to the general superintendent of Michigan Copper and Brass—which, like other local companies, used an informal version of this same referral system—Bradby intervened on behalf of "one John Biggs," a deacon at Second Baptist and "one of the most conscientious men whom I have known." Biggs was charged with fighting and had been dismissed by the foreman.[4] In some ways, the alliance between church and company was a practical solution to a pressing problem rather than opportunism on the part of the ministers or antagonism toward Black workers' interests. Hundreds of Black men were able to obtain gainful employment through this system, and ministers were able to provide valuable assistance.

Ministers routinely performed this sort of service for their congregants. Interspersed in Reverend Bradby's papers with letters to representatives of the Ford Motor Company are other letters vouching for church members who were seeking employment elsewhere (at the city's Welfare Department, for example) and members who had lodged complaints such as a missive protesting the "segregation and mistreatment" of students in a class at Northwestern High School.[5] Such acts were a normal part of the priestly function. Care for the church as an institution and for congregants as individuals is, arguably, the highest duty of a minister. Further, as one student of the "community-building process" has argued in defense of what he calls the "Ford–Black Minister Entente": "At a time when blacks in Detroit, as elsewhere, had few friends and more than enough enemies, black leaders could not afford the luxury of being too choosy."[6]

It was also a service that congregants expected and appreciated. For example, Fr. Everard W. Daniel of St. Matthew's Episcopal joined the entente in 1923, and by 1925 he had received so many requests for letters of recommendation that he found it necessary to solicit funds from the vestry for a new employment office with a paid investigator and secretary. "Dear Father Daniel," began one letter from October 1929.

> My husband got reinstated with the Ford Motor Company on Thursday. . . . We called on the phone to let you know, and though did not get you personally, we felt sure the message was delivered. Words fail to express our deep gratitude and appreciation for your kind help in the matter. But we know you will understand our feelings though we express them so poorly.[7]

Although they were not nearly as successful in placing Black workers as was the employment department of the Detroit Urban League, which, backed by the Detroit Employers Association, found work for thousands of Black men and women, a significant number of workers were hired into the auto industry via these church connections. Many of these workers, the majority of whom were recent migrants drawn from the South by Ford's promise of five dollars a day, were, like the authors of the letter to Father Daniel, grateful for the opportunity. As Reverend Hill put it, "[S]ome of them [the workers] looked upon Ford as almost being a god."[8] Indeed, men proudly displaying company badges on the breast pockets of their best suits were a common sight at Black churches on Sunday mornings. The phrase "I work for Henry Ford" became an immense source of pride, even though the company relegated all but a fortunate few Black workers to the dirtiest, most hazardous jobs. In his 1940 booklet *Henry Ford and the Negro People*, Christopher Alston, a Black auto worker and Communist union organizer who had been radicalized by the 1932 Ford Hunger March, pointed to the fact that 6,457 of the 9,852 Blacks who were employed by Ford in 1937 "worked in the worst and hardest jobs in the company—namely: the foundry, rolling mill and open hearth." "The remaining 3,386," he continued, "were to be found in the motor building, the foundry machine shop, the 'B' building, the spring and upset building, the pressed steel building, in tool rooms, construction departments, as sweepers and on miscellaneous jobs." Although the larger of these departments, especially the foundry, would become prime sites of Black influence once the company was unionized, before 1941 thousands of Black men risked their health and their lives in these so-called nigger jobs.[9] Many—too many—accepted the dangers as a fact of life.

Almost everyone profited from the alliance, however. Workers got an avenue to employment, which benefited them and their families. The city's emerging Black middle class—the owners of saloons, hotels, funeral homes, drugstores, coal yards, and financial and realty agencies—profited from the wages of the growing workforce. Black ministers benefited, too, for some of the same reasons. In return for their services, clergymen gained not only congregants able to tithe the customary 10 percent of their income but also donations to church funds and building committees and nonmonetary gifts such as concert tickets, coal, and building materials. The alliance also increased the ministers' social status and capital. Father Daniel was a particular favorite. A native of the Virgin Islands, tall and handsome, and a graduate of both New York University and the Union Theological Seminary, the Episcopal Daniel was deemed a suitable companion for the top Ford executives with whom he lunched on a fairly regular basis. Moreover, his church was favored by a yearly Sunday visit from Henry Ford himself, who was also Episcopalian.[10]

Not everyone, however, viewed the situation as ideal. Although he presumably could have joined the alliance through his connection to Bradby, Reverend Hill doggedly resisted. From his first years at Hartford, Hill struggled to maintain his and his church's independence, refusing offers of "assistance" at every turn. The propriety of the church-company alliance was something on which Hill and Reverend Bradby, his mentor, could not agree. "Reverend Hill had grown up under Reverend Bradby even as I grew up under Reverend Hill," recalled Charles G. Adams, the current pastor of Hartford. "Reverend Hill agreed with Bradby that the church should be relevant to the social position and social struggles of the people. But whereas Reverend Bradby wanted to accommodate them to certain strictures upon which they were dependent, such as the Ford Motor Company, Reverend Hill came in on the side of the labor movement."[11] Although it became clear only in hindsight, there was also a downside to the alliance, which Hill perhaps sensed.

In return for reliable workers, the company secured a fair amount of social control over not only workers but also prominent ministers. This control was asserted most dramatically through men such as Donald J. Marshall and Harry Bennett. Marshall, a Black policeman who was a member of St. Matthew's, was hired by the Ford Service Department in 1923; within a few months he had achieved supervisory and hiring authority over Black personnel, reporting directly to Charles Sorenson (the architect of the church-company alliance) and Bennett, the head of Ford's notorious Service Department. Marshall, whose official title was special investigator, became increasingly cynical and arbitrary as his power grew. He may well have been influenced in this respect by his boss, Bennett, who oversaw a department, in reality a private army, of ex-convicts, ex-boxers (like Bennett himself, who boxed in the navy), gangsters, and assorted sociopaths.[12]

Bennett's department was well organized and heavily armed. While such control organs also existed in other industries, Ford's was the largest in the nation, employing over three thousand men. Initiated at the express direction of Henry Ford, its primary purpose was to suppress unionization and other sources of "trouble" through espionage, intimidation, and force. Branches of the main department, located in Ford's Dearborn headquarters, were a fixture in every Ford plant across the country. Bennett's Service Department was also responsible for the policing of Black workers, a task generally delegated to Marshall and Willis Ward, a former University of Michigan football star hired as part of Marshall's personal staff in 1935. Both Marshall and Ward attacked their overseeing duties enthusiastically; by the mid-1930s it was exceedingly difficult to obtain a position at the Rouge plant without a letter from a minister or other prominent members of the Black elite.

Hill was hardly alone in sensing the potential dangers of the church-company alliance. His actions are probably best seen in light of a growing restlessness among more militant activists, a trend that would encompass the critiques of the Black elite launched in the 1920s by groups such as the Good Citizenship League, the local UNIA, and Snow Grigsby's Civic Rights Committee. Given the social and political prominence of the clergy, it was almost inevitable that a new generation of ministers and activists would eventually come to question and even challenge the alliance with Ford. Hill was part of this "new crowd," which rejected the "somber, reformist stance" of older, more established ministers and leaders of race improvement agencies such as the Urban League. As Beth Tompkins Bates has argued, a new crowd of activists, much more closely aligned with grassroots and working-class politics, emerged from the economic turmoil of the Depression and the social dynamics of the migration. Whereas the "old guard" tended to rely on white philanthropy and patronage, the new crowd turned to direct action, mass pressure, collective organizing, and a much more confrontational style.[13] Hill's stance may also have been shaped by the ever-present tension between the priestly and the prophetic functions of African American clergymen. The priestly represented care for congregation and community, even at the price of accommodation, and the prophetic represented a forthright resistance to racism and other modes of exploitation and oppression. These two aspects have always existed in a dialectical relationship whose balance is dependent as much on individual propensity as on objective circumstances.[14] As the decade wore on these two strains of Black religious thought and practice were brought increasingly into conflict.

THE NEW CROWD AND THE RISE OF A LABOR–CIVIL RIGHTS COMMUNITY

By the mid-1930s, a new crowd was emerging in Detroit made up of ministers, such as Hill, White, and Dade, who rejected the alliance with Ford. Father Dade was a graduate of Lincoln University and the Episcopal Theological Seminary in Cambridge, Massachusetts. He arrived in Detroit in 1936 to serve first as vicar of St. Cyprian's and later, when it officially joined the Michigan Diocese as a parish in 1944, as the church's first rector. He remained at St. Cyprian's until his retirement in 1972. Detroit must have been quite a change of pace for the energetic New Englander (he was born in the Massachusetts whaling town of New Bedford in 1903), and he was certainly struck by the implications of the church-company alliance. When Dade asked one of his parishioners why he belonged to both the St. Cyprian's and St. Matthew's men's clubs, the man replied: "I belong to St. Matthew's Men's Club because of Mr. Marshall. All the men who belong to St. Matthew's Men's Club have some sort of tie-in with Mr. Marshall and Father Daniel, and through them you have to buy a car and also you're assured of work and continuing to work at the Ford Motor Company."[15]

Dade once remarked that he felt the "good Lord" guided him in avoiding the "trap" of the church-company alliance, but courage must also be an important element in the explanation. Father Dade had not felt particularly friendly toward labor before coming to Detroit, which is unsurprising given the racial exclusion policies adopted by most unions prior to the founding of the CIO. Rather, his union sympathies grew out of his belief that "the church had to be relevant to whatever was good for people in all phases of their life, whether it was economic, political, or social." "And here I came into a community," Dade reminisced, "and here was a situation having to do with the working life of people that was just flagrantly bad, wrong, certainly not good." By 1936 some of the more negative attributes of the patronage system were becoming evident, but acknowledgment of these drawbacks was a risk for a young minister of a church that had yet to achieve parish status. Not only was St. Cyprian's under the direct control of the diocese, but it was also a west-side outpost of St. Matthew's. There is a clear parallel between Hill and Hartford's relationship to Reverend Bradby and Second Baptist, and Dade and St. Cyprian's connection to Father Daniel and St. Matthew's.

The contrast in power and privilege was even evident in the churches' architecture. Second Baptist and St. Matthew's were both stately brick structures with wide aisles, comfortable pews, and decorative altars. Early photographs of Hartford, by contrast, reveal a little wooden structure poised precariously on short stilts and sitting in the midst of a dusty lot. Similarly, Father Dade recalls being "surprised" that the physical structure of St. Cyprian's offered him "practically nothing to work with." "The church hadn't been developed" and was closer in appearance to a storefront. Hill and Dade, the less-established ministers of less-established but growing institutions, sided with the UAW and opened their respective churches to union meetings. In so doing, both implicitly rejected the cautious path charted by their elder pastors.

As a result, both ministers were occasionally targeted for retribution. Dade was shocked to find that Father Daniel had complained to the local bishop that he (Dade) had hosted a "radical" political meeting at his church. "If the union had not succeeded," said Dade, "I would have had to resign." Looking back on the situation nearly three decades later, Dade adopted a generous view of his former senior cleric and the relationship Father Daniel had helped to build with the Ford Motor Company. "Father Daniel was a person of such intellectual standing that I could see why Mr. Ford and he would be friends," he noted.

But, I think he was off base when he couldn't see the union or anything to do with the union. I mean, he let his friendship with Mr.

Ford blind him to the real need and so forth of the black working man. Now, whether he knew what Mr. Marshall was doing, I don't know.[16]

Whether the elder clergyman knew it or not, Marshall was certainly Ford's main enforcer within the Black community. Dade and Hill both weathered his threats. Marshall once swore to "fire every Negro in the neighborhood" if Hill went through with plans to hold a UAW-sponsored meeting at his church.[17]

The third member of this triad, the Rev. Horace A. White, took similar risks and by all accounts did so gladly. A graduate of Oberlin College's Divinity School, White had come to Detroit in 1936 to pastor Plymouth Congregational. An advocate of the social gospel, Reverend White was as well spoken as he was outspoken, and he was often asked to address mass meetings of workers and unionists. He firmly believed in the rights of labor and insisted that "The Negro should not stand on the outside and look in; but should step in and join" the union.[18] At the height of the 1939 Chrysler sit-down strike, he even did verbal battle with Don Marshall during a debate on the merits of the UAW. He would also come to play a leading role in community support for the UAW during the 1941 Ford strike. In later years he emerged as a prominent liberal political figure, heading the local NAACP's Legal Redress Committee; serving, by appointment, on the Detroit Housing Commission; and winning a seat in the state House of Representatives on a Democratic ticket.[19]

White, Hill, and Dade formed the core of a pro-union Black religious movement, but they were also part of a much larger network of progressive activists. The same year that White arrived in Detroit, Louis Martin, a recent graduate of the University of Michigan, became the editor of the *Michigan Chronicle*, a local subsidiary of the *Chicago Defender*. In the years to come Martin, an ardent supporter of the CIO, the New Deal, and the Democratic Party, managed to transform the *Chronicle* into an unabashedly pro-union alternative to the other major Detroit-based Black weekly, the *Detroit Tribune*, which was staunchly Republican and generally antiunion. Like White, Louis Martin eventually entered the political arena, joining the staff of the Democratic National Committee in 1944.

White and Martin, both of whom were in their early twenties when they arrived in Detroit, swiftly gravitated toward Charles C. Diggs, "a symbol and a model of progressive black political leadership unprecedented in Detroit's black political history."[20]Diggs was born in Tallula, Mississippi, in 1894 and came to Detroit in 1913. A member of the Garvey movement in the 1920s, he was also the proprietor of a highly successful funeral home located on the lower east side. While he began his political career as a Republican, in 1932 Diggs changed his party affiliation and became active in Democratic ward politics. Diggs, along with attorney Harold Bledsoe and fellow ex-Garveyite J. A. Craigen, organized the first Black Democratic club in Detroit and by 1936 was confident enough to run for the state Senate, representing a district composed mainly of Blacks and Poles. Like their white ethnic counterparts, Black voters were increasingly turning toward the Democratic Party, and away from their traditional affiliation with the Party of Lincoln. The 1936 election that brought Diggs to the Michigan legislature as the first Black Democratic senator in the state's history also marked the first time that major Black districts in Detroit voted solidly for the Democrats in statewide and national races.[21] Neither unions nor Democrats had previously earned the trust of African Americans; hence, the decision to vote Democratic was still controversial.

Diggs proved to be a powerful ally for the city's emerging labor–civil rights community. During his tenure in the legislature, he introduced a series of bills designed to strengthen Michigan's civil rights laws. Public Act 117 (the "Diggs Law"), for example, made discriminatory service on the basis of race, color, or creed a misdemeanor.[22] He was also one of the two most-recognized "friends of labor" in the legislature, the other being Stanley Nowak, another key addition to the city's Left community in the 1930s. Nowak was a Polish immigrant who came to the United States with his family in 1913 and was raised in the slums of Chicago. After a parochial school education and several years spent as an altar boy, he began his political career as a newspaper reporter and a tireless organizer for the Unemployed Councils, as well as for the Amalgamated Clothing Workers, in Chicago. Having traveled throughout the country in the early 1930s he finally settled in Detroit, where he met his future wife, Margaret Collingwood, at a social gathering sponsored by the Proletarian Party—a forum for the discussion of radical ideas.[23] The party, which focused on "educational communism" and ran the Proletarian University of Detroit, was the perfect intellectual home for a young woman like Margaret, who was searching for ways to translate her early religious beliefs into progressive social action. The two were a perfect match. Stanley, who had long ago lost his faith in the Catholic Church, dedicated his life to labor organizing and working-class politics, and Margaret, who had been a member of the Brethren church, quickly joined him. The Nowaks made their home in a Polish neighborhood on the city's east side, just blocks away from the home of another local activist, Mary Zuk, who was to become a friend and political ally.

Because of his bilingualism and his connections with the Polish community, Nowak was appointed creator and head of the UAW Polish Trade Union Committee in 1936, a position that involved him in many UAW strikes from 1936 to 1941.[24] By 1938 Stanley had decided to run for elected office, which would enable him to use his community-based campaign as an organizing and publicity tool for industrial unionism. Much to his surprise, he won a seat in the Michigan Senate representing the Twenty-first District, which included the municipalities of Ecorse, predominantly Black Inkster, Allen Park, Dearborn, and River Rouge; he was returned to office four times, three times after running joint campaigns with Charles Diggs. In Diggs, "Stanley found a staunch ally on civil liberties, the rights of minorities, and organized labor," wrote Margaret Collingwood Nowak. "A friendship developed, and Diggs often rode with us to Detroit on Friday afternoons, sometimes having dinner when we took him home." Their friendship with the Diggs family also gave the Nowaks an intimate glimpse into the workings of racism. The Nowaks, for instance, were distressed to learn that Diggs could not find accommodations near the state capital, and was forced to reside in one of Lansing's segregated neighborhoods during the week. Together the two men initiated investigations into the misuse of welfare funds, fought "antisubversive" legislation, and introduced bills on academic freedom. When Nowak was repeatedly threatened with deportation for his ties to radical organizations, Diggs, along with Reverend Hill, Mary Zuk, Louis Martin, and others, rallied to his defense.

Friendships were an important medium for the growth of the city's interracial and interethnic Left—a simple point that is too often overlooked in histories of social movements and the communities of activists that support them. And friendship may in fact be even more important to social formations that involve more than one racial, ethnic, or cultural group. "The first time I came to Detroit," recalled Black attorney George Crockett, who would become yet another leading figure in local labor and civil rights activism, "the best way you could describe me was apolitical. . . . I suppose the way I got interested in politics in the broad sense of the term was my contact with Maurice Sugar, who was general counsel of the UAW and one of the leading labor lawyers in the city."[25]

Crockett worked with the radical lawyer Sugar to desegregate city bowling alleys so that the union's "mixed teams" could play. It was a small but significant beginning. Crockett also got to know Reverend Hill and eventually became a member and later a trustee of Hartford Avenue

Baptist Church. Ernest Goodman, another prominent labor lawyer, tells a similar tale. Goodman grew up in one of the city's Jewish ghettoes—"a completely Jewish environment"—and although it was not far from a Black neighborhood, he recalls the social distance as immense. After graduating from law school, Goodman joined the ACLU in 1935 and began to take a more active interest in union politics after he, like Crockett, met Maurice Sugar.

Goodman joined the left-leaning National Lawyers' Guild a few years later. "Through the Guild," he explains, "I became acquainted with lawyers across the country who held social and political views to suit my own. They formed a network of lawyers who were involved in the development of labor law, civil rights and liberties, and other people's struggles."[26] Such identifications and sensibilities were central to the creation of Detroit's early civil rights movement—which is not to suggest that friendships and political affinities alone were able to erase social tensions or interpersonal (and at times cultural) conflicts. Goodman, for example, tells a story about his lack of cultural knowledge of the Black community. Asked to speak at a Black church, he showed up without a coat or a tie, thus violating Black norms regarding appropriate church attire. For this he was politely and firmly chastised by the presiding minister. "I wouldn't have gone into a white church the way I was dressed," Goodman admits. "It was lessons of this kind, over a period of years, that helped me to feel more comfortable with Black people."[27]

There were growing pains of all sorts as the labor–civil rights community took shape, and its leadership was shaped, in turn, by the local and national trends that began to converge in 1935–36. By 1935, having made few structural gains, most of the city's Unemployed Councils had ceased to exist. Yet community- and neighborhood-based militancy, in which women were often central, continued even as the economic situation began to show signs of improvement. Black women associated with the Housewives' League, the sister organization of the Booker T. Washington Trade Association, continued the effort to support Black businesses and target white-owned businesses in their neighborhoods that engaged in price gouging or refused to hire Blacks.

This sort of activity was hardly confined to the Black community. Struggling to make ends meet in the summer of 1935, Mary Zuk, the wife of an unemployed auto worker, and several of her friends decided that they had had enough. Demonstrations by women responsible for household economics broke out in Hamtramck, the east-side Polish neighborhood where Zuk and her allies resided, and these sporadic protests swiftly turned into a full-fledged meat boycott. The boycott spread to other immigrant neighborhoods and adjacent Black areas in a matter of days and weeks.

These protests generated a harsh and sometimes violent response, especially in the Polish neighborhoods at the epicenter of the protest. Police arrested a growing number of housewives, but the women would not be deterred. An organizational structure, mostly Polish but also including native-born white women, Jews, and at least one African American woman, Irene Thompson, was soon devised. Its representatives, including Mary Zuk and Irene Thompson, were sent to Washington to testify before a congressional committee on food prices. Having won much publicity but few substantial gains, the movement faded by the fall of that year. But it launched the political career of Mary Zuk, who, despite charges of communist leanings and the endorsement of the CP, won a seat on the Hamtramck city council in 1936. Further, the meat boycotts led to the formation of the Peoples' League of Hamtramck, which was later instrumental in mustering public support for CIO organizing drives and sit-down strikes. Moreover, Mary Zuk and the women of the Housewives' League against the High Cost of Living gave working-class immigrant women a greater sense of their own political power and a greater appreciation for the importance of direct action and mass organization.[28]

While such moments of grassroots protest developed on the local level, important developments were also under way on the national stage. The post-1935 shift in Roosevelt's New Deal administration—away from short-range palliatives and toward long-term modifications in the nation's economic and social structure—ushered in a new era of social reform. The New Deal itself was one of the forces that transformed civil rights into a national political issue, as its liberal advocates became part of a developing coalition of Black civil rights organizations, leftist activists, labor unionists, and intellectuals. Although Roosevelt was unwilling to antagonize powerful southern Democrats in Congress, and his administration's policies often sanctioned racial discrimination, the New Deal recognized the aspirations of Black Americans and other marginalized groups to a greater extent than any previous administration in the twentieth century.[29]

Roosevelt's staff was even more acutely cognizant of the rising tide of labor activism. The second phase of the New Deal, 1935–40, witnessed the passages of the National Labor Relations Act, also known as the Wagner Act, in honor of Sen. Robert F. Wagner. Signed by Roosevelt in 1935, it gave workers the right to organize and vote for the union of their choice, outlawed unfair labor practices, and established the

National Labor Relations Board, which was imbued with mediation and enforcement powers. The act replaced section 7(A) of the National Recovery Act of 1933, which had generated a wave of grassroots organizing efforts and wildcat strikes but the Supreme Court had deemed unconstitutional.[30] Thus, the Wagner Act not only revived the rights of workers to unionize but also helped shape the public discourse on rights in general. Castigated by its detractors as an unconstitutional violation of individual rights to contract between employers and employees and heralded as "labor's bill of rights" by its supporters, the Wagner Act advanced the idea of state-protected corporate rights adhering not to individuals but to groups (e.g., workers). In 1937, when a slightly more liberal Supreme Court upheld the constitutionality of the act, Chief Justice Evan Hughes noted that the right of workers to unionize and seek the collective representation of their choice was a "fundamental" one.[31]

By instituting a new class of rights that were protected under the First Amendment and by federal action, Wagner encouraged the activities of the newly formed Congress of Industrial Organizations. Unlike the American Federation of Labor (AFL), which organized workers according to trades and skills and thereby excluded nonskilled industrial workers, the CIO was committed to organizing all workers into industrial unions across technical specialties and, more important, across lines of race, nationality, religious affiliation, and (albeit with less conviction at first) gender. With its desire to unionize heavy industries such as steel and automotive production now sanctioned by the state, in 1936 the CIO began the most massive organizing campaign in American history. From the start, the CIO received the support of the Communist Party, which had been pursuing a similar strategy in its own unions, including the Auto Workers Union, though with limited success. With the 1935 decision of the Seventh Congress of the Communist International to dismantle these "dual unions" in favor of constructing a "popular front" with other progressive forces and even liberals (as long as those groups did not express overt hostility toward the Soviet Union), the CP sent hundreds of seasoned organizers into the ranks of the CIO-affiliated unions, including the UAW. Indeed, labor organizing, especially industrial unionism, was, along with the fight against fascism, a key focal point of the Popular Front strategy lasting, in its first official phase, from 1935 to 1939.[32]

The timing of the Popular Front was crucial. At the same time that labor organizing assumed a new legitimacy and militancy, *communism* was redefined, in the words of Earl Browder, the CP's 1936 presidential candidate, as "twentieth-century Americanism," with the party trans-

formed into "the standard bearers and pioneers of that revolutionary tradition out of which the United States was born." For the CP, then, the
primary political choice was not so much between socialism and capitalism as between democracy and fascism—at least until the 1939 Hitler-
Stalin pact undermined the CP's official Popular Front ideology and
severely hampered the effectiveness of Communist organizers within
unions, including the UAW.[33] As historian James Pickett notes, during
the initial phase of the Popular Front, Communists inside the UAW
embraced a "self-effacing affability" and a deferential posture in order to
avoid clashes with other "progressive forces." This deference came to an
abrupt end eighteen months later when the pact was announced and
Communists "stopped deferring to the Roosevelt administration and the
liberal CIO leadership." At least two strikes—at Allis-Chambers in Wisconsin and North American Aviation in California, along with, less dramatically, the Ford strike in Michigan—were affected by these changes
and ongoing factionalism within the CIO itself. Of course, after the
United States entered the war in 1941 the CP enthusiastically endorsed
the CIO's "no strike" pledge.[34]

Another difficulty internal to the party had to do with criticisms of
the Popular Front by African American members such as Harry Haywood. Historian Mark Naison is surely correct on one level when he
notes that initially the Popular Front policy "engendered a spirit of cooperation between liberals and radicals that facilitated the empowerment
of North America's least privileged citizens and placed ethnocentrism
on the defensive in U.S. intellectual and political life."[35] Yet for many
Black Communists, including Haywood, the new policy sacrificed revolutionary antiracism and the long-standing dedication to Self-Determination in the Black Belt. Indeed, Haywood dated the beginning of the
party's backsliding on Black liberation to 1936, when in a fit of popular
frontism the Communist leadership of the Alabama Sharecroppers
Union pushed for the union's incorporation into the Agricultural Workers Union and the Farmers Union of Alabama, which were, Haywood
argued, "strongly influenced by the racist and right-wing Coughlinite
forces." Haywood was also highly critical of the party for backing away
from A. Philip Randolph's March on Washington movement in the
name of "'unity' in the face of the fascist enemy" as well as of its general
hostility toward the African American "Double-V campaign" during the
war.[36]

West Indian Marxist C. L. R. James, then a member of the newly
founded Socialist Workers Party, similarly viewed the Popular Front as

the "chief reason" why the CP "cannot gain the allies it wants if it fights the difficult fight for Negro rights." "The C.P. is now an American Party," James continued, "and the petty bourgeois supporters of democracy who are coming into it have nothing in common with the Negro, who, finding himself an outsider, has simply left the party."[37]

All of these national, and indeed international, developments were followed closely in the ranks of Detroit's labor–civil rights community and the newly formed UAW. Communist Party members had laid the foundations for industrial unionism in several of the city's plants. The Michigan CP, then under the direction of William Weinstone and Phil Raymond (both secular Jews), had established associations of the Popular Front sort even before this became official policy. In backing the 1935 campaign of Maurice Sugar for a position on the Recorder's Court, for instance, Communists joined hands with Frank X. Martel, the local head of the AFL; with Black ministers, including Reverends Hill and Peck; and with the full array of the city's Left community—with the notable exception of the Socialist Party, which maintained its traditional aversion to the CP. Although Sugar lost the election, before it was over "the cause of organized labor was preached in virtually every fraternal hall and political club in the city, and more impressively, in black churches where the very word 'union' had been traditionally uttered in low whispers, if at all."[38]

Sugar was extremely popular among Black Detroiters, who regarded him as a "champion of the underdog," largely due to his spirited defense a year earlier of James Victory, an African American World War I veteran accused of slashing the face of a white woman in an alley and stealing her purse. Victory's alibi was solid, he had no prior criminal record, and the method used by the police for witness identification was faulty. Armed with these facts, Sugar successfully argued the case before an all-white jury and, luckily, a sympathetic judge by the name of Edward L. Jeffries. Black Communist Harry Haywood, who was then head of the CP's Negro Department, came to Detroit to organize around what he called "Detroit's Scottsboro." In his memoir *Black Bolshevik*, Haywood vividly recalls Victory's case and the work of the Detroit branch of the League of Struggle for Negro Rights, headed by Joe Billups, as well as the efforts of the ILD and Maurice Sugar. Victory's arrest and trial came, Haywood notes, "in the midst of one of the most vicious campaigns of racist incitement in Detroit's history," orchestrated by Police Commissioner Heinrich Pickert, who boasted that an average of fifty arrests were being made each day. The local papers, especially the *Detroit Times*, carried on an equally vicious campaign of "slanderous race-baiting in which Blacks were depicted as natural rapists, voodooists, murderers and all-round thugs who were conspiring to assault white women."[39]

Various segments of the Left sprang to Victory's defense. Haywood remembers addressing a large mass rally held at the Israel Baptist Church along with the Rev. John Bollens, Joe Billups, Black attorney C. LeBron Simmons, William Weinstone of the Detroit CP, and Nat Ganley, the trade union director for the CP. The decision of this quickly organized committee to retain Sugar as defense counsel proved decisive. While Sugar could not match the oratorical power of Clarence Darrow, his sharp defense of Victory recalls Darrow's strategy some ten years earlier in the Ossian Sweet trial. In both cases, white lawyers argued in front of white juries that the existence and pervasiveness of white supremacy was an issue in the indictments. Sugar began his long closing statement by pointing out the obvious: "Every one of you is a white person—every one. The defendant is black. Many of his witnesses . . . are black." He continued:

> Well, I asked you if you had any prejudice against a man because of his color and you said "No." I believe that you believe it. But is it really possible for a white person not to be prejudiced? . . . The man who participates in the lynching of an innocent Negro in the South doesn't think he is prejudiced; he thinks he has a proper view of things. "That's the way to handle these niggers,"—that is his view. That does not apply to the same degree in the North, but unfortunately it seems to be growing in the ideas of a good many people. . . . Be careful, oh, be careful, because if there is a verdict of guilty in this case, then I am telling you that it can be only because white people are unable to overcome prejudice when it is about them. That must not happen here!

At the close of his statement, Sugar made an impassioned plea for the jury to see past the barrier of color and understand that Blacks have "the same hearts, they have the same pleasures, they have the same joys, they have the same pains, they have the same agonies as other people." At the same time, he called on the jurors to acknowledge the differences that racism had produced, namely, that the "Negro is doubly exploited. He is exploited as a worker and he is further exploited as a colored worker." It was a risky strategy, to be sure, but it paid off, and James Victory was set free.[40]

Sugar encouraged the comparison between himself and Darrow by featuring Darrow's endorsement on Black-oriented campaign literature during his 1935 run for a seat on the city's Common Council as part of a labor ticket. The pamphlet "United Labor Candidates for Council: William McKie, Maurice Sugar, Fay O'Camb on Equal Rights for Negroes" carries Darrow's endorsement on the back cover and includes an open letter from Snow Grigsby and the Civic Rights Committee to all councilmen and candidates about the patterns of racial discrimination in Detroit's public and municipal employment. Sugar, O'Camb, and McKie were the only candidates to respond to the letter. They assured their readers that they were "fully aware of the gross discrimination practiced against Negroes in the City of Detroit" and pledged to fight it "with all our power."[41] The campaign also distributed copies of Sugar's closing argument in the Victory case under the title *A Negro on Trial for His Life: The Frame-Up of James Victory Exposed!*

Sugar's campaign, and the public circulation of materials like those just mentioned, drew the city's progressives closer together in 1935–36. Other factors contributed to this process as well. Black Communists such as Joseph Billups, Paul Kirk, Veal Clough, and William Nowell—all of whom had been active in the old AWU and the Unemployed Councils—were willing to make common cause with activists such as Maurice Sugar and Charles Hill, with others who had worked in the councils or on the Scottsboro defense, with Snow Grigsby, and with those who, like Coleman A. Young, had forged their radicalism through endless discussions in such places as Maben's barbershop on the city's east side.[42]

During these years the labor–civil rights community also began to develop a more stable organizational infrastructure. Its major components included the UAW and its various organizing committees (e.g., the Polish Organizing Committee and the Negro Organizing Committee), the CP and its various "front groups," and the two significant labor–civil rights organizations founded in 1935–36: the local branch of the National Negro Congress and the Conference for the Protection of Civil Rights (CFPCR, later known as the Civil Rights Federation and still later as the Michigan division of the Civil Rights Congress [CRC]), both of which proclaimed the rights of labor to be indivisible from the rights of Blacks and other minorities and both of which were infused with the spirit of religious radicalism. The NNC and the conference went beyond the effort to protect civil rights in this period by seeking to both broaden and extend them.

The leftists' perspective on rights in general was very much informed by their understanding of the rights of labor in particular. When thousands of workers "sat down to stand up for their rights"—as they did so

A NEGRO ON TRIAL
FOR HIS LIFE

The Frame-up of James Victory Exposed!

SPEECH TO JURY BY
COUNSEL FOR DEFENSE

MAURICE SUGAR

CANDIDATE FOR JUDGE
OF RECORDER'S COURT

NON-PARTISAN
Election, April 1, 1935

Price **5c** per copy

Cover from *A Negro on Trial for His Life: The Frame-Up of James Victory Exposed!* (Maurice Sugar Collection. Courtesy of Walter P. Reuther Library, Wayne State University.)

dramatically during the 1936–37 Flint strike against General Motors (GM)—both the conference and the NNC argued that even if the sit-down strikes were illegal workers had a moral right to engage in such activities. "There's no doubt that the sitdown is illegal," stated Michigan's newly elected pro-labor governor, Frank Murphy, "But laboring people justify the sitdown on the grounds that it is effective. They claim that it is moral."[43] As with the sit-ins in the 1960s, activists used moral reasoning to justify acts of civil disobedience.

"We start by asserting that every worker in America has the right to live in decency and as a free man," argued Maurice Sugar in his defense of the sit-down tactic. "Now, when the workers engage in a sit-down strike. . . . [i]s this an encroachment upon the property rights of the employer? Of course it is. But encroachment upon property rights is not *ipso facto* illegal." In contradistinction to the supposed illegality of this form of protest, Sugar, who eventually joined the UAW's Legal Department, insisted that because the sit-down strike is "legal to millions of workers" and no one would "dare say that millions of American workers have suddenly become criminals" labor had, in essence, already caused the law to be changed: "Now we await only the acceptance by the courts of the change which has already been made."[44]

Although the virtual occupation of private corporate property by hundreds—at times, thousands—of workers was never ruled legal by any court, this powerful tactic proved wildly popular among protesters for a time and helped structure arguments for the extension of rights and freedoms. As Detroit's Conference for the Protection of Civil Rights defined the issue in its statement of purpose, civil rights included "the rights of free speech, press, assembly and worship as granted in the Bill of Rights . . . the rights of labor to organize and carry out the functions essential to collective bargaining as guaranteed in the Wagner Act," and "equal rights with all others in the community of religious, racial and political minorities."[45]

The statement's mixture of civil libertarian fears and pro-labor idealism neatly encapsulates the CFPCR's understanding of rights. First, by invoking the Bill of Rights, the conference demonstrated an affinity with the traditional sphere of constitutional liberties and the underlying philosophy that all individuals possess a class of fundamental or "natural" rights, which the state cannot unduly interfere with or violate. Second, by citing the rights of labor and minorities the statement identifies the conference with an understanding of group or corporate rights, which the state must act not only to protect but also codify and extend. Finally, the conference's statement reflects the growing importance of economic and social rights (along with civil and political ones) within segments of the Left, where the call for economic justice and industrial democracy was becoming commonplace.

In a 1938 article in the CFPCR's *Civil Rights News,* the Rev. John H. Bollens, pastor of the Messiah Evangelical Church and executive director of the conference, reflected on the circumstances that led to formation of the conference and the concomitant shift in thinking about civil rights. Before the conference, Bollens writes, "civil rights work in this community was handled by the Detroit branch of the ACLU, of which I was chairman." He continues:

> The cases were practically all infringements upon an individual's civil rights. . . . When the depression came, we noted not only a change in the attitudes of the workers but also a definite change in the trends of civil rights cases. As the men in the factories came to realize that they were being victimized not as individuals, but as a group, they spontaneously began to bond themselves together. . . . This spontaneous movement, being driven by necessity, brought with it opposition from the side of reaction. . . . The reactionary forces sought legislation which would not only curtail, but make this movement impossible.[46]

The piece of "reactionary" legislation to which Reverend Bollens referred was the Dunckel-Baldwin bill, which was introduced in the state legislature in 1935 and was supported by the conservative Liberty League.[47] The bill, which Bollens denounced as "the most vicious anti-civil liberties piece of legislation that had ever been introduced into any legislature in the United States," would have outlawed most forms of strike activity and made possible the "abolition of any kind of labor or liberal activity in the state" under the guise of stopping "subversive activities." Instead of adopting the usual policy of the ACLU and waiting to see if the state Supreme Court would render the bill unconstitutional in a test case, Bollens and other concerned citizens launched a frontal attack while the bill was still under consideration. "Since the proposed bill endangered the existence of even a civil rights organization," he explained, "we decided that it would be necessary to change our policy and organize anew so that we might get to the people, arouse public opinion to the extent that this bill could not become law."[48]

The idea was to create a "real united front" of labor and farm groups, as well as fraternal, language, race, civic, professional, women's, and youth organizations. They realized that such groups differed widely in their primary aims and interests but believed that the ideological glue holding them all together was "a desire to preserve democracy" by protecting the rights of all. "The effort now being made by organized labor to unionize the workers in all industries and occupations," conference spokespersons insisted, "is of vital concern to every American who cherishes our democratic institutions." Unionization, according to the conference, transcended "the ordinary objectives of a labor controversy" and became, in essence, "a crusade for the political and economic emancipation of a great multitude of our fellow citizens who are employed in industries which deny them the elementary rights of free speech, free association and free assembly."[49]

Middle-class professionals, who compromised a major portion of the group's membership, should be engaged in this emancipatory struggle, the conference proclaimed, because what was at stake was not only the rights of workers "but even more the liberties of every American citizen irrespective of his immediate concerns in labor controversies."[50] Working closely with Sugar (who belonged to both the ACLU and the ILD), as well as Frank Martel of the Detroit Federation of Labor (the local branch of the AFL), the conference sent delegates to Lansing and throughout the state to publicly debate the merits of the Dunckel-Baldwin bill. Although they did not succeed in killing the measure completely, the bill that was finally passed by the legislature was a pale reflection of its former self.[51]

Inspired by this success, the conference became a permanent organization, with Reverend Bollens as its chief executive and another white minister—the Rev. Owen Knox, pastor of the Bethlehem Methodist Episcopal Church—as treasurer. Over the years, the group retained its mass-action and legalistic bent. In fact, it attracted some of the best legal minds in the city, including Michigan attorney general Patrick O'Brien and lawyers Ernest Goodman and Ned Smokler, both of whom had ties to the local branch of the National Lawyers Guild, thus ensuring a close connection between the guild and the federation.[52] "We had representatives from most of the language groups in Detroit," recalled Eleanor Maki, who joined the conference after a friend alerted her to the censorship power of Dunckel-Baldwin, "and from some of the union groups, and of the Socialist Party, the Communist Party and the Progressive Party. All sorts of different people, very different, who would come together and they were concerned about the inroads being made on civil rights."[53] A teacher at Detroit's Northwestern High School and a member of the first teacher's union organized in the city's public schools, Maki was also one of dozens of women who became involved in the movement around this time. By October 1935, the conference claimed to be composed of 295 Michigan-based organizations representing over 465,000 individuals. Those numbers are grossly inflated; in terms of active membership the number was closer to 1,200 persons at its height, although this is still impressive for a local radical organization.

Like a few of her fellow white members, Eleanor Maki was also a member of the Detroit chapter of the National Negro Congress. The conference was conceived as an interracial organization but increased its standing in the Black community primarily through its ties with the local NNC, which was formed in 1936. Arthur McPhaul, a Black Communist and auto worker who joined both the conference and the NNC, recalled that the former "was organized mainly as a sort of defense for the struggling trade union organizations at the time" while the latter was primarily "interested in fighting against brutality, for the rights of Negroes." For McPhaul himself, his priorities were "Number one, black people, and number two, left progressives."[54] The NNC attracted Black unionists such as McPhaul, Christopher Alston, Coleman Young, Hodges Mason, and Joseph Billups, as well as Black women such as Rose Billups and Vera Vanderberg. The participation of McPhaul, Alston, the Billupses, and Mason also contributed to the charges, especially common after 1940, that the NNC was a Communist front.

Unlike the Conference for the Protection of Civil Rights, the NNC was national in scope. The idea for its creation grew out of a conference on the economic status of Blacks held at Howard University in May 1935. Sponsored by the university's Social Service Department and the Joint Committee on National Recovery—a short-lived coalition of twenty-two Black organizations formed to lobby the federal government—the Howard conference brought together a number of young militants committed to aggressively bettering the plight of the Black working class. Having agreed that the situation called for coordinated strength, John P. Davis, an economist and head of the joint committee, along with Ralph E. Bunche, then head of Howard's Political Science Department, invited a select group to Bunche's home to discuss plans for the formation of the NNC.

Their discussions consciously harked back to a venerable African American political tradition from the mid–nineteenth century. The Negro Convention Movement, initiated in Philadelphia in 1830, was the "first effort within the race to effect united action on a national scale." Beginning with antislavery agitation before the Civil War and focusing on injustices toward Blacks thereafter, the Negro Convention Movement continued to function until the close of the century.[55] Well aware of this precedent, Bunche, Davis, and more than 250 other men and women signed a call to hold the first national meeting of a new organization in Chicago in February 1936. Local sponsoring committees were set up in cities, including Detroit, Chicago, and New York. In October 1935, the pamphlet "Let Us Build a National Negro Congress," written by Davis with an introduction by A. Philip Randolph, rolled off the press. It was both a manifesto and a call to arms.

> We believe that this Congress will furnish the opportunity for consid-
> ering the problems that face all the Negro people and that a plan of
> action—the collective wisdom of all freedom-loving sections of our
> population—can be intelligently worked out for the solution of these
> problems. By unity of action we can create a nation-wide public opin-
> ion which will force real consideration from public officials, such as
> no single organization can hope to muster. The sincerity of purpose
> of all organizations to whom this call is addressed assures harmo-
> nious cooperation in the common cause for justice.[56]

At the Chicago meeting, which was attended by 817 delegates representing 585 organizations, including labor unions, religious bodies, fra-
ternal organizations, and political parties, Randolph was elected president and Davis agreed to serve as executive secretary. Before the meeting
was officially adjourned, the NNC had established itself as a permanent
body and passed resolutions on issues ranging from the rights of women
and the support of Black business to a lynching and the invasion of
Ethiopia.[57] The invasion of Ethiopia, like the Spanish Civil War before it,
provided common ground between the CP and the Black community,
including in some areas the surviving sections of Garvey's UNIA.[58]

From the beginning, however, the presence of leading Black Communists such as James W. Ford, the CP's 1936 vice presidential candidate, was a source of tension in the congress. Indeed, in an attempt to
procure the endorsement of Walter White, executive secretary of the
NAACP, Randolph gave his assurances that "so far as I have any power,
the Congress shall not be 'sold down the river' to any political group
[e.g., the Communist Party] and I think this is the sentiment of numerous forces in it."[59]

The friction between the NNC and the NAACP did not end there,
nor did the constant accusations of Communist infiltration and control.
The Detroit branch of the NAACP, then headed by the Rev. Robert
Bradby of Second Baptist, was not enthusiastic about the NNC's presence in Detroit. But the Detroit NNC did manage to circumvent one of

the other flash points on which the national organization stumbled, namely, the religious question. During its first convention, the NNC passed a resolution insisting that the churches devote every fifth Sunday to the work of the congress. It also urged ministers to preach a "social and economic gospel as well as [a] spiritual gospel." Yet shortly after the Chicago meeting a group of disgruntled clergymen drafted a letter criticizing the congress for its inattention to religious issues.

"We know that the interest and cooperation of church leaders, clergy and lay, is important to the success of any race movement," the statement read.

> We also know that a neglect or shunting of the Christian Church Leadership causes resentment from the church. We know, too, that the church leadership is rightly jealous of maintaining spiritual notions and injecting Christian ideals in all community, race, or national efforts. The church's program must be labor, industry, education, human rights, human justice, plus a baptism of the truly spiritual and Christian attitude.

Arriving at the crux of the matter, the statement continued:

> Our displeasure with the program, such as in [sic] presented in the National Negro Congress that includes no outstanding church positions of sentiment making—only to pray or pronounce benediction on general programs, was voiced in executive and council meetings and herein expressed.[60]

The churchmen, headed by the (AME) Bishop J. A. Bray, knew that they had history on their side. The first Philadelphia meeting of the nineteenth-century Negro Convention movement had been presided over by Bishop Richard Allen, founder of the African Methodist Church, and prominent religious figures had provided leadership throughout the history of the movement. In dealing with the NNC, it is difficult to determine what caused the group of religious leaders more displeasure: the extension of secular radicalism symbolized by the presence of Communists in the NNC ranks; the inroads being made on their own position; or the NNC's general usurpation of their moral high ground, which placed the clergy in the marginal role of "merely" praying and pronouncing benedictions. Whatever the case may have been, the religious issue became problematic for the congress at the national level.

The Detroit NNC had more success in this area. Snow Grigsby, chairman of the Civic Rights Committee, head of the Michigan Sponsoring Committee for the NNC, and an active member of St. John's United Presbyterian, had established warm relationships with members of the local clergy, including Reverend Hill. Moreover, the religious community was generally supportive of the Civic Rights Committee's efforts to desegregate the post office and other municipal entities, and, due in part to Grigsby's influence, the local NNC was very sensitive to the politics of religion in Detroit. Members of the Detroit NNC were also well aware of the long-standing ties between Black clergymen and the Ford Motor Company, and any minister willing to buck Ford's paternalist system was a welcome addition. The Rev. G. W. Barber, pastor of Detroit's Ebenezer AME, and Reverend Peck, pastor of Bethel AME and founder of the Booker T. Washington Trade Association, were both given highly visible positions in the congress. The Executive Committee was rounded out with young militants such as C. LeBron Simmons, a recent graduate of the University of Michigan Law School; Coleman Young; and Communists Paul Kirk and William Nowell.[61]

The Conference for the Protection of Civil Rights was equally adept at navigating the religious terrain. It was not until 1940 that a secular radical took over as its head: Jack Raskin, a secular Jew who took the CFPCR's helm after the terms of Reverends Bollens and Knox. From the beginning, the conference was stamped with the imprint of progressive religion. Both Bollens and Knox had been shaped by the example of Harry F. Ward, a major figure in the national ACLU until 1940 and one of the country's leading proponents of a radicalized social gospel. Aside from his position on the ACLU's Executive Board (from which he resigned in 1940 in response to the organization's increasingly anticommunist positions), Ward was also one of the five founding members of the left-leaning Methodist Federation for Social Action (MFSA).

Ward wrote and lectured widely on the need for an activist Christianity in which churches and religious institutions would engage in movements opposing oppression and social inequality, especially on behalf of industrial laborers. Once the pastor of a congregation abutting the Chicago stockyards, Ward gradually came to believe that "wage slavery" was the most pressing problem of his time. Under his guidance, the MFSA sought to bring the same moral passion to the alleviation of this social affliction as the abolitionists had brought to their fight against racial slavery. Throughout the 1930s and 1940s Ward's politics and theological writings, which paired Christ and Marx, moved even farther to the left. As an activist and clergyman, Ward lent his time and his name to a number of organizations, including the American League against War and Fascism, the American Friends of Spanish Democracy, and the National Council of American-Soviet Friendship.[62]

Reverends Bollens and Knox, like Ward, believed that the clergy should play a commanding role in the creation of a just social order, and they brought these insights to their political work in Detroit. Ward and Bollens had both held positions with the ACLU, and both became critical of what they saw as the liberal organization's lack of moral perspective. One local activist also recalled that problems developed between the ACLU and the conference over the ACLU's so-called purist concept of civil rights. For the ACLU, all rights had to be protected—the rights of workers and industrialists alike. Such an abstract approach clashed with the perspective that pro-labor religious activists such as Bollens and Knox were attempting to articulate and act on.

For Reverend Knox, the point was to secure the rights of workers now and worry about the industrialists later if at all. Knox had been raised in the West, but his first assignment as a clergyman was in Camden, New Jersey. While there, he witnessed the exploitation of workers and became involved in their strikes. Feeling that his religious calling was to minister to industrial workers, he moved to Detroit in 1936, where he joined the conference almost immediately. An ardent pacifist, Knox resigned from both the conference and the National Federation of Constitutional Liberties after Germany invaded Russia and both organizations threw themselves into the war effort.[63] Still, the organization was fairly successful in recruiting clergymen. Because of the early influence of figures such as Bollens and Knox; Reverends Barber, Peck, Hill, and Horace White; and Snow Grigsby, both the CFPCR and the NNC had strong religious underpinnings from the start. Most of these men would likely have agreed with Hill's statement that "The church can lead the fight for democratic rights, all we have to do is use it. That's what we're doing here in Detroit."[64]

The activists involved in these two local organizations came from varied religious backgrounds, as well as secular humanist traditions. They also came from disparate racial, ethnic, and class backgrounds. And yet there was a common commitment to civil rights and social justice. "But most important," Coleman Young summarized, "for all our social, ethnic, and ideological differences, we shared the same preoccupation with the plight of the working class—particularly the black working class."[65] That activists such as Hill, Father Dade, Young, Simmons, and others would be attracted to such groups as the Conference for the Protection of Civil Rights and the National Negro Congress is understandable. Each of these men was excluded, by choice or circumstance from the leadership of established race improvement organizations such as the NAACP and the Detroit Urban League.

Much has been made of how the struggle between the old and new guards shaped African American politics in northern industrial centers during this period, but similar struggles were going on in the city's other ethnic communities. For instance, it was the need for a more militant approach to the social and economic ills confronting Poles, combined with the conservatism of some segments of the Polish Catholic Church, that gave rise to Mary Zuk's political career and the People's League of Hamtramck. The league combined with the Polish section of the International Workers Order (IWO) and the Slavic factions of the Communist Party to form an important pro-labor cadre. Likewise, the conference offered Jewish radicals such as Jack Raskin an alternative to the more conservative Jewish Community Council (JCC) and American Jewish Congress, both of which tended to keep a low profile.[66]

Such intraracial and intraethnic tensions, particularly among Blacks, Poles, and Jews, fueled the growth of Detroit's early civil rights community. Activists joined the more militant factions of the city's Left community not only in sympathy for what the civil rights community represented but also in opposition to the ideas of their racial and ethnic compatriots. Generating an "enemies list" and defining one's position as more militant than that of groups such as the NAACP and JCC were important organizing actions that produced and sustained an oppositional consciousness. Indeed, identifying the individuals and groups that the civil rights community defined as external adversaries is a helpful step in understanding how this community constructed its own identity and particular commitment to civil rights and social justice.

US VERSUS THEM
Fighting Fascism

The need to distinguish themselves from more moderate groups was important, but the fight against fascism, both international and domestic, lay at the core of the "us versus them" mentality that shaped the formation of Detroit's civil rights community. Members of the community drew parallels between their experiences and events unfolding in the international arena, especially the Spanish Civil War and the invasion of North Africa. Domestic fascism, however, was defined quite broadly, perhaps too broadly. In the mid- to late 1930s, activists identified local "fascistic threats" to civil rights and social peace in the antilabor and anti-Black practices of the Detroit Police Department, and its complicity with splinter groups of the Ku Klux Klan (KKK), in the rhetoric of Fr. Charles Coughlin and other religious demagogues, and in the union-busting policies of the Ford Motor Company. Propaganda and protest campaigns against each of these groups played a major role in the self-definition of the civil rights community.

The NNC's first major action (with the aid of the Conference for the Protection of Civil Rights) was against the Black Legion, a splinter group of the KKK. Founded in Bellaire, Ohio, in late 1924 or early 1925 and dedicated to the extermination of "Anarchists, Communists and the Roman [Catholic] hierarchy," the Black Legion targeted African Americans, trade unionists, and radicals for condemnation and at times violent attack. Drawing on the growing numbers of white southern migrants who arrived in Michigan and Ohio between 1933 and 1936, the Legion's sixty to one hundred thousand members created a climate of fear that hampered the efforts of union organizers. Although the group was similar to the KKK (which it supplanted in Michigan, Ohio, Indiana, and Illinois) in its location in heavily industrial states, and its ability to recruit among southern-born whites thrown into competition with Eastern Europeans and Blacks, the legion was much more antiunion than the Klan. Its propensity for violence and its ties to police departments and industrial espionage units made the legion a significant menace.[67]

The civil rights community encouraged public investigations into the legion's activities. When there was "a danger of the campaign against the Black Legion slowing down," the conference organized people to complain to the Detroit Common Council, the state legislature, and various federal agencies.[68] They also kept extensive files on the legion and other Klan-like groups and even sent their own undercover operatives into meetings to gather firsthand information. At least two activists suffered personal reprisals for these activities. Walter Hardin, a Black unionist with ties to the CP, was kidnapped and flogged by a vigilante mob, while Maurice Sugar, targeted as a "communist nigger lover," received death threats from the legion on a regular basis. As it turned out, the NNC's fears were well placed. From 1936 to 1937, various trials of legionnaires uncovered no less than fifty-seven murders and attempted murders—some of them committed, as legion triggerman Dayton Dean admitted, just for the thrill. Many of the victims were members of religious and ethnic minorities or the nascent movement for industrial unionism. "The night-rider 1936-style, in Ford's Detroit," commented a writer for the *New Republic*, "is likely to be a labor spy as well as a Catholic baiter. The lash that speaks his dark will may as well be hatred of Communists, i.e., union organizers, as well as distrust of Jews."[69]

It also came as no surprise that many of the Black Legion's crimes were committed by workers, factory foremen, and, not inconsequentially, off-duty policemen. Labor spies had long been a problem for unionists. The Detroit Employers Association, a major contributor to the coffers of the Detroit Urban League, had a history of hiring spies, including policemen and foremen, to keep track of any labor organizing being carried out in area plants. As early as 1912 the association compiled a blacklist of nearly eighty thousand people who had had contact with unions or organizers. One legionnaire, who was also a policeman, admitted that he had personally delivered a list of suspected "communists" working in local factories. In some suburban communities the legion network included not only policemen and workers but mayors, police chiefs, and the area's leading officials.

Although arrests, trials, and convictions essentially destroyed the Black Legion, new threats arose from different quarters, including the Detroit Police Department.[70] The department, then under the direction of Commissioner Heinrich Pickert, a Black Legion sympathizer who was appointed in 1934, had been a source of tension for a number of years, especially within the Black community. Under Pickert's tenure the police force became even more militaristic and openly antilabor. As a result, the ongoing fight against police brutality became a central concern of Detroit's civil rights community. Police brutality, like the antilegion campaign, was an issue around which Blacks, labor organizers, workers, and political dissidents could be rallied. Pickert organized the police department's Special Investigations Division, colloquially known as the Red Squad, headed by Sergeant Harry Mikuliak and Sergeant Leo Maciosek—"Mic and Mac"—two self-proclaimed experts on local "Reds." While the regular police divisions were called on to directly intervene in strikes and other actions, the Red Squad worked behind the scenes, infiltrating organizations, compiling files, and engaging in covert surveillance. When the ACLU issued its 1939 report on the state of civil liberties in the major urban centers of the nation, the Red Squad was identified as the cause of "perhaps the most flagrant violations of the civil rights of Detroiters."[71]

Pickert's policies also deepened tensions between the police and the Black community, making a bad situation worse. A 1926 study by the Mayor's Committee on Race Relations had identified the racist practices of the police as the chief cause of poor race relations in Detroit, and this problem only worsened during the 1930s. In 1933, the Detroit branch of the NAACP, along with local representatives of the International Labor Defense, lodged formal complaints against the "promiscuous" shootings of African Americans. These complaints, and others like them, fell on deaf ears; year after year, the "orgy of police brutality" against Blacks increased. A report on the main activities of the Conference for the Protection of Civil Rights from 1938 to 1939 listed the "defense of the rights of the people against an arrogant and nazi-like police administration" as its most important task. In 1938 alone, the conference, which changed its name to the Civil Rights Federation that year, identified three killings and numerous arrests and beatings of Blacks by white officers. Linking the conditions facing Blacks with the conditions facing workers in general, they also charged that in the summer of 1938 large corps of police were used as strikebreakers in five successive labor conflicts, resulting in hundreds of illegal arrests and injuries to at least two hundred persons on the picket lines and in adjoining neighborhoods.[72]

The Civil Rights Federation and the Detroit NNC continually monitored these incidents of police brutality. Indeed, the categories of police brutality and domestic fascism were regarded as complementary elements of big industry's "divide and conquer" strategy. Some activists, such as the UAW's Emil Mazey (a socialist) drew an analogy between anti-Black violence in the United States and anti-Semitism in Europe. "The Negro worker in America today is facing many of the conditions recently imposed upon Jewish people in Germany," Mazey wrote. "The Ku Klux Klan and the Black Legion are avowed enemies of the Negro people. . . . Why have officials ignored the Negro problem? Can it be that industrialists in America are waiting to play the Negro in a similar role as the fascists in Germany are using Jewish people?"[73]

White leftists tended to eschew such ideas, instead placing the blame for racial and ethnic tensions on the existence of secret societies and subversive organizations or on the specter of fascism and the supposed connections between fascism and industrialists bent on dividing the working class. (This tendency became even more pronounced among Communists after the invasion of the Soviet Union encouraged them to "close ranks" with the war effort and subordinate all other struggles.) Black activists, however, tended to see the attacks in narrowly racial terms. Reverend Hill, for one, viewed police brutality as a manifestation of the influence of uneducated southern whites, who "said they know how to handle a Negro."[74] Even though there was disagreement on the primary causes of police brutality, African Americans, unionists, and the Left community returned to the issue again and again. There was general agreement that brutality toward Blacks was part of a larger pattern of violence and intimidation that had to be addressed.

By 1938 it was becoming clear that the civil rights community would have to take matters into its own hands. When a delegation from the Civil Rights Federation managed to secure an audience with Commissioner Pickert, he only confirmed their worst fears. The delegation, composed of Reverends Bollens and Knox, Ernest Goodman, and Milton Kemnitz (the CRF's executive secretary), got a chilly—and chilling—reception. "The police department," Pickert is reported to have said, "will continue to arrest people and search homes without warrants whenever, in the personal opinion of the Commissioner, such actions should be taken. Until Federal, state and local laws are changed, this will continue to be our policy." Not only did Pickert refuse to take any responsibility for the violation of civil (and basic human) rights committed by his officers; he also questioned the integrity of the two "ministers of the Gospel," whom he openly suspected of being communists.[75] At one point the situation in Detroit got so bad that Reverend Bollens solicited the aid of Sen. Robert M. La Follette Jr. of Wisconsin and his Senate Civil Liberties Subcommittee, which was then holding nationwide hearings on civil rights violations in connection with labor organizing.[76]

La Follette's committee was never able (or willing) to hold hearings in Detroit, but another committee, the Dies Committee, took up the challenge. The House Committee on Un-American Activities (known as HUAC), headed by Texas Democrat Martin Dies, was authorized to "investigate (1) the extent, character, and objects of un-American propaganda activities in the United States, (2) the diffusion within the United States of subversive and un-American propaganda that is instigated from foreign countries or of a domestic origin and attacks the principles of the form of government as guaranteed by our Constitution, and (3) all other questions relating thereto that would aid Congress in any necessary remedial legislation."[77] Since the city's civil rights community tended to equate "un-American" activities with domestic fascists, it originally hoped to influence the tenor of the hearings.

Citing the existence of "Nazis, the Black Legion, the Patriotic League and the Silver Shirts as subversive elements in Detroit which should be investigated," Reverend Bollens wrote, "[W]e welcome therefore the investigations of the obviously Un-American . . . elements."[78] This was a "welcome" that Bollens, the CRF, and the entire Left community would soon come to regret, as the Dies Committee quickly shifted its definition of *un-American* from nazis to communists. With this change the committee launched a political assault on the CIO and civil rights organizations, including the CRF. When Dies sent an advance team to Detroit to prepare for the committee's October 1938 hearings held in the city, he found the police department's Red Squad a willing ally.

During the hearings Sergeants Mikuliak and Maciosek were both called to give "expert" testimony on the communistic leanings of local activists. The proceedings of the three-day hearings read like a who's who of the city's Left. Maurice Sugar and his ex-wife Jane Mayer; Mary Zuk; Reverend Bollens; state senator Stanley Nowak; Joe Billups; Patrick O'Brien; Phil Raymond and his wife, public school teacher Vera Katz; William Weinstone, Nat Ganley, and William Allen, all associated with the Michigan Division of the CP; Walter Reuther, then president of the UAW's west-side Local 174; and Rabbi Leon Fram, among others, were identified as part of Michigan's "subversive network."[79] The committee heard days of testimony not only about individuals but about organizations as well, especially the Communist Party.

"The Communist Party," stated Walter S. Reynolds, head of Michigan's American Legion, "is an organization to fit any purpose and every purpose."

> If it happens to be a question of war, the protection of the Soviet Union, they have an organization for that in the name of the Friends of the Soviet Union. If it is a question of legislation, they have the Conference for the Protection of Civil Rights [the Civil Rights Federation]. If it is a question of deportation, they have the International Labor Defense. If it is youth, it is the American Youth Congress, and if it is trade-union work, today it is the CIO and the American Federation of Labor.[80]

At times, the testimony descended to the level of the bizarre, particularly when the issue of race was raised. White women, one witness testified, were being used by the CP as a means of "ensnaring young Negroes," even though the idea of racial equality is "unnatural and repugnant to the American Negro." As proof that white women were being used in this regard, the witness cited a number of interracial marriages within the Left community, including CP member William Nowell's marriage to Pearl Demercy, a Ukrainian woman; Christopher Alston's marriage to Sylvia Hornstein; and William Brown's marriage to a white woman (there was also a seemingly contradictory allusion to his "homosexual tendencies").[81]

There were indeed quite a few interracial marriages among local radicals, and the witnesses were to some extent justified in their description of the existence of a radical network of organizations, institutions, and individuals—though not one necessarily plotting the violent overthrow of the nation. Not only did members of the city's Left community share information, strategies, and fund-raising sources; they were also tied together by friendships, loyalties, and in some cases love. This may or may not account for what the Dies Committee saw as a disturbing number of interracial couples, but it certainly does speak to how communities of protest form and sustain themselves on both the institutional and interpersonal levels. As Coleman Young recalled, members of the Left community "went to the same houses, the same picnics, the same fund-raisers and the same black-and-tans (integrated clubs)."[82] There was, in short, a communal feeling that helped to reinforce their shared political commitments.

One would also expect that these social and emotional ties only intensified in the face of collective attack. Hence the Dies Committee probably served, unintentionally, to further unify the city's growing civil rights community. Confronted with state repression and the willful violation of civil liberties, Detroit's Left forces were driven—and drawn—closer together.

THE RELIGION OF FASCISM

Yet this Left community was hardly content to adopt a defensive posture. In the midst of the accusations and counteraccusations of the Dies hearings, local activists attempted to keep the public's attention on what they identified as the "real" subversive threat: the local reactionaries who were striving for a mass following.

Once again, religion and religious activists were deeply implicated. "To be a Klansman," began one typical recruiting letter, "one must subscribe to the Christian religion."

> There was never a time when our members as well as the whole citizenry of the nation need more firmly to imbibe their thinking in these tenets and shape their course of action thereby. In these days of vague ideas and confused voices it is well for us to pause sometime and renew our indebtedness to the Christian religion. . . . From His teachings there has come the impetus for every really worthwhile social improvement.[83]

This flyer was among many collected by the Civil Rights Federation. Throughout its existence, the federation was particularly interested in the reactionary uses of religion among what it termed "nativist fascists," especially Fr. Charles Coughlin, Gerald L. K. Smith, and the Rev. Frank J. Norris. Like police brutality, "nativism" was an issue that the Left used to unite African Americans, Jews, Catholics, and political radicals in a politics of fear, revulsion, and anger. Coughlin is a particularly instructive example. By the late 1930s, Detroit's famed "radio priest" was growing more and more extreme. Interestingly, he was as dedicated to a politics built on a moral foundation of religion and faith as were Reverends Hill, White, Bollens, and Knox. In this regard, Coughlin is a useful reminder that the connections between religion and oppositional political activity are not inherently leftist or liberal.

Born in Hamilton, Ontario, and educated at St. Basil's Seminary in Toronto, Coughlin arrived in the Detroit area in 1926 with the intention of building up the Shrine of the Little Flower parish in Royal Oak, a near suburb of Detroit. Royal Oak and its environs had long been a stronghold of anti-Catholicism, and the community provided a relatively congenial home for an active branch of the KKK. A cross had been burned on the lawn of Coughlin's church shortly after its construction, and Klan activity had ensured the small size of its congregation and the size of the mortgage payments they could carry. Coughlin originally took to the airwaves in 1926 to pay off parish debts and counteract this rabid anti-Catholicism. Although he initially limited his Sunday radio hour to dissertations on biblical themes, by 1930 he was preaching strong and increasingly popular denunciations of *both* communism and capitalism in the name of compassion and justice for workers. He was soon broadcasting on nearly thirty stations, reaching every major population center in the East and Midwest, and was reportedly receiving more than ten thousand letters and cards each day—most of them, he claimed, from non-Catholics. A Hollywood studio offered him five hundred thousand dollars for the rights to his life story, "The Fighting Priest," with a proposal that Coughlin himself accept the leading role. (He refused both offers.) In the fall of 1930, when the Fish Committee—a precursor to the Dies Committee—invited Coughlin to testify on the threat of communism, his popularity soared. To the chagrin of the committee, he did not speak of subversive activity among dangerous Reds but instead denounced Henry Ford and the Ford Motor Company as "the greatest force in the movement to internationalize [i.e., communize] labor throughout the world."[84] The Hoover administration and a mysterious conglomerate of Wall Street bankers also earned his ire.

As a major figure in Detroit who enjoyed the support of both liberal politicians (including Frank Murphy) and the Catholic hierarchy, Coughlin could scarcely avoid contact with the city's emerging drive for industrial unionism. In a more general sense, he had long been a voice in defense of workers. He advocated better working conditions, higher wages, and shorter hours and spoke of the responsibilities of industry and government for the welfare of laborers. Thus far, none of Coughlin's ideas had placed him at variance with the general principles of Pope Leo XIII's 1891 encyclical *Rerum Novarum* (*On the Condition of the Working Class*).

Although in many ways it is a vague and ambiguous document, *Rerum Novarum* was the Catholic Church's official response to the growing "menace" of socialism in Europe. While reaffirming the Church's traditional teachings on the rights and duties of property ownership, it also harked back to the teachings of Saint Thomas Aquinas, renewing Church and state obligations to have

> special consideration for the weak and the poor. For the nation, as it were, of the rich, is guided by its own defenses and is in less need of governmental protection, whereas the suffering multitude, without the means to protect itself, relies especially on the protection of the State. Wherefore, since wage workers are numbered among the great mass of the needy, the State must include them under its special care and foresight.

The encyclical further affirms the concept of social justice, the idea that "justice demands that the dignity of the human personality be respected," and defines *special care* and *foresight* most prominently in terms of a fair and living wage for workers: "The oppressed workers, above all, ought to be liberated from the savagery of greedy men, who inordinately use human beings as things for gain." In one of the long document's more stirring passages, it reminds all Catholics that the Church must not "so concentrate her energies on caring for souls as to overlook things which pertain to moral and everyday life."[85]

Although impressed with the teachings enshrined in *Rerum Novarum* as a seminary student, it was not until 1935 that Coughlin sought any active involvement in union politics. Sharing (and indeed inciting) many Catholics' fears that the newly formed CIO was dominated by communists, Coughlin sought to influence the Automotive Industrial Workers Association (AIWA), an independent union that had competed with the UAW-CIO until the two unions merged. To the leaders of the AIWA, Coughlin appeared to be a valuable ally. After Richard Frankensteen, then head of the AIWA, solicited Coughlin's aid in June 1935, the energetic young priest appeared to be everywhere within the organization. "Father Coughlin seemed to feel that this was his organization," recalled Frankensteen. "He started to say, 'Your dues are this—we will have this meeting.'" Coughlin's influence had grown to the point where many considered the AIWA Coughlin's union. While Frankensteen remembers being "tickled pink because of the strength of his [Coughlin's] name," the CIO and its supporters within the civil rights community saw Coughlin's popularity among Catholics and non-Catholics alike as a cause of great concern.[86]

This concern continued to grow as Coughlin's religious and political views took a sharp turn to the right in the late 1930s after the failure of his Union for Social Justice (his next major undertaking after the AIWA merged with the hated CIO) and the third-party presidential bid of his associate, William Lemke. (Lemke, who ran on the ticket of the National Union Party, which united the anti–New Deal organizations of Coughlin, Francis Townsend, and Gerald Smith, received 2 percent of the vote nationally; in Michigan, he received 4 percent.) Coughlin's attacks on Roosevelt and the New Deal—both of which he had once praised—now grew more extreme every month. Proclaiming that no true Catholic would join the CIO, Coughlin formed his own "independent" (but actually company backed) union, mainly in the Dodge, Chrysler, and Plymouth plants. At the same time, his radio sermons and articles in his paper, *Social Justice,* were becoming openly anti-Semitic and racist. In 1938, for instance, *Social Justice* serialized the bogus "Protocols of the Elders of Zion" in Coughlin's "From the Tower" column and named Mussolini as its "Man of the Week."[87]

Denunciations of Coughlin's anti-Semitism, racism, and anti-CIO position issued from a number of quarters. Archbishop Edward Mooney did his best to counter Coughlin, telling readers of the *Michigan Catholic* that the Church certainly did not discourage membership in CIO-affiliated unions. Nor did the Association of Catholic Trade Unionists (ACTU). Fr. John Clancy, a pro-union priest, also took to the press to denounce Coughlin. In an article published in the Civil Rights Federation's *Civil Rights News* under the heading "Pope's Words Aren't Safe When Coughlin Quotes Them," Clancy wrote, "Not even by the wildest stretch of the imagination can a careful reader of the encyclical [*Rerum Novarum*] possibly mistake Coughlin's words for anything but what they were intended to be; namely a description of the Fascist system." The CRF itself was equally vigilant. It held a number of rallies and mass meetings—the largest of which attracted fifteen thousand people to Detroit's old Olympia Stadium—aimed at repudiating Coughlin's views.[88]

This local effort was part of a much larger, national anti-Coughlin movement. The publication *Equality,* which was launched by movement activists in 1939, was "dedicated to an uncompromising fight against anti-Semitism and racism" with Coughlin a chief target. *Equality* was financially backed by a variety of Jewish individuals, and many Jews served on its editorial board. Several Catholics also served on the board, and contributors with a variety of religious (and nonreligious) positions were welcome. The range of authors, from Albert Deutsche and Albert Maltz, to Dorothy Thompson and Emerson Fosdick, was impressive.[89] In spite of all of these efforts, though, Coughlin continued to promote his policies until 1942, when he agreed to be silenced by the Catholic Church rather than face a criminal indictment on charges of subversion for his attacks on Roosevelt and the government. His official silencing did not end the tendency within the civil rights community to equate certain brands of religious expression with domestic and international fascism, however. During the war years, as Detroit was transformed into the "Arsenal of Democracy," the presence of religious fundamentalists and supposed fascists would occupy a good deal of the Left's time and energy.

"FORDISM IS FASCISM"

In its pre–World War II antifascist and antiracist campaigns, Detroit's labor–civil rights community attacked not only the Detroit Police Department and Father Coughlin but also the Ford Motor Company. Henry Ford's anti-Semitism and racial paternalism had been well known since the 1920s. For six years he financed and made editorial contributions to the notoriously anti-Semitic *Dearborn Independent,* a paper that ran scads of articles proclaiming the superiority of the "Anglo-Saxon-Celtic peoples," on the one hand, and the degeneracy of the Jews on the other. If there was any "strange unrest" and militancy among African Americans, the *Independent* unfailingly claimed it was only because "Bolshevik Jews" were using them as "a tool" to destroy the country. Resurrecting the "Protocols of the Elders of Zion," much as Coughlin's *Social Justice* had done, Ford carried on his own personal campaign against the "International Jew."

Many older Detroiters recall instances of Ford's "fascist tendencies" emerging during the 1930s, with his acceptance of the Nazi Iron Cross of the German Eagle cited as final proof of his sympathies.[90] Indeed, more than any other cause during the period extending from the Great Depression to the nation's entrance into World War II the UAW's drive to organize Ford—the last anti-union holdout after GM and Chrysler signed agreements with the UAW—served as a focal point for the various factions within the city's Left community, uniting antifascists with pro-labor and civil rights activists from a range of backgrounds and organizations. The struggle to unionize Ford became, in essence, a proving ground for the entire early civil rights movement in Detroit.

As early as 1936 the prospect of an open shop at the massive River Rouge plant, which employed over 9,800 Black workers (or 12 percent of the plant's workforce), was a source of racial, ideological, and class tensions.[91] Yet, even as traditional race improvement organizations such as the NAACP and the Urban League began to shift toward a more pro-union attitude on the national level, their executive committees in Detroit refused to forget the "debt" that African Americans supposedly owed to (Uncle) Henry Ford. When the CIO began massive organizing drives in the steel, auto, and manufacturing industries, the national NAACP gave its cautious endorsement, but the local NAACP refused to follow its lead. Although a small cadre of pro-union activists pushed for greater receptivity of industrial unionism, the majority of the Black middle class—like a majority of Black workers themselves—remained at best aloof and at worst hostile to the early UAW.

This old guard was not entirely unified, however. Some NAACP and Urban League leaders, such as Geraldine Bledsoe and Beulah Whitby, both of whom were members of Plymouth Congregational, were pro-union, as was insurance company executive Louis Blount, a former president of the local NAACP who maintained close ties with the BTWTA. Carlton Gaines, president of the BTWTA, remained "on the fence," and even the *Detroit Tribune* avoided taking sides. Working-class Blacks were equally divided. Few African American workers participated in the now famous sit-down strikes against the automotive industry in 1936 and 1937 against GM and Chrysler, mostly because they remained unsure and cautious about the new union's promise of equal treatment.[92]

The pros and cons of union affiliation, and the question of whether the new CIO unions would be better and less racist than the old AFL ones, were hotly debated in Detroit area barbershops and beauty salons, in bars, on street corners, and around kitchen tables. Hundreds of men and women became ardent supporters and organizers in the new union, but the bulk of Black workers adopted a very practical wait-and-see attitude. Many, like Hodges Mason, a Black auto worker employed in area plants since the 1920s, had studied the older craft union's dismal treatment of African Americans and as a consequence were initially "very anti-union." Yet Mason, who had come to Detroit from Atlanta, Georgia, in 1926, was eventually "so inspired" by the conduct of CIO-affiliated unions that he became an organizer and even compared the union to Christ for its efforts toward the salvation of Black workers.[93]

It was not until 1937, however, when the national convention of the NAACP was held in Detroit and labor organizers were invited to speak, that the issues of race and unionization came to a head in a more public way. Roy Wilkins, executive secretary of the national NAACP, arranged for a session on labor issues featuring Paul Kirk, a Black auto worker and communist labor organizer; John Davis of the National Negro Congress; and Homer Martin, a white UAW organizer who would go on to a rather checkered career. The panel was rounded out by remarks from John Dancy, the still very pro-Ford head of the Detroit Urban League.

When Fr. Everad Daniel and other ministers linked to the alliance between Ford and select Black ministers got wind of these plans, they launched a vigorous counteroffensive against the inclusion of labor radicals and even brought pressure to bear on the local NNC's Rev. G. W. Barber to renege on the offer of his church, Ebenezer AME, as the site for the proceedings. When these efforts failed, the group threatened a boycott. But the debate proceeded as planned, with Davis and others arguing for support of the UAW on the grounds of Black economic self-interest and Homer Martin, a former Baptist preacher, injecting an evangelical appeal. Martin assured the crowd that for the UAW interracial industrial unionism was both practical and moral. Comparing the UAW to Christ, he said: "I come to you tonight representing the poor, the oppressed and the exploited people, both colored and white. . . . The elimination of prejudice against the Negro is to me a definite part not only of a wise labor movement . . . [but] of Christianity itself."[94]

In the wake of a three-day fight over whether to endorse the UAW (which was finally done, albeit in a cautionary way), the tensions between the priestly and prophetic aspects of the church came to the fore. On the one hand, Father Daniel, along with Reverend Bradby and others, denounced the UAW and the national NAACP from both press and pulpit. The "arrogance" of Martin's Christ-UAW analogy simply provided more fuel for their fire. On the other hand, in the pages of the NAACP's *Crisis* magazine and other Black publications, pro-union advocates attacked the alliance between the ministers and the company. Of Daniel and others, Roy Wilkins wrote, "The spectacle of poor preachers, ministering to the needs of poor people whose lot from birth to death is to labor for a pittance, rising to frenzied, name-calling defense of a billionaire manufacturer is enough to make the Savior himself weep." In response, Father Daniel warned, "We can't afford to have Ford close down on us" and castigated the national office of the NAACP for not minding its own business. Although many Black workers probably identified with Daniel's question "Where would we go?" the national office continued its battle with the Detroit ministers.[95] It was in this sense that the question of "true" versus "false" religion entered the debate about workers' rights, unionization, and the political interests of African Americans.

Because of the close connections between Black ministers and the Ford Motor Company, the religious issues involved in unionizing Ford could not be easily dismissed. The alliance led many to ask, with the Rev. Horace A. White, "Who owns the Negro church?" The juxtaposition of White's prophetic question with Daniel's more cautious and priestly one nicely captures one aspect of this difficult debate. But White and other pro-union activists were also well aware that the company's influence extended far beyond the churches. Indeed, Henry Ford was as supportive of the Republican Party as he was antagonistic to unionization, and he used his influence over Black ministers, businessmen, and civic leaders to create an informal political machine. For example, the company oversaw the organization of Republican Clubs and Loyalty Clubs, in which membership was less than strictly voluntary. According to Christopher Alston, these clubs were yet another manifestation of Ford's power. To illustrate this point, Alston relates the plight of Willis Bradford, a Black worker and member of the Thirteen Men Committee (a Democratic organization), who lost his job after he refused to transfer his affiliation to one of the company-sponsored Republican groups.

AFFIDAVIT
I, Willis Bradford . . . was called into the Employment Office by Mr. Donald Marshall on or about February 19th or 20th, 1940. Our conversation was as follows: Mr. Marshall asked me what club I was a member of. I told him that I was a member of the "Thirteen Men Committee," a Democratic organization. Mr. Marshall said that he had organized the Wayne County Voters Association. . . . Mr. Marshall asked me how long I had been employed by the Ford Motor Company. . . . He then asked me if he and the Ford Motor Company had always treated me right . . . [and] said that if I wanted to keep my bread and butter and if I wanted to continue working for the Ford Motor Company I had better connect up.

Three weeks later, according to Bradford, he was laid off because "I was a member of a Democratic organization."[96]

This attitude was hardly confined to Ford's dealings with Black workers. As one observer noted, "In the fall of 1937, the Bill of Rights was also partially suspended in Dearborn when the Company-controlled City

Council banned all leafleting around the Rouge plant."[97] Regardless of race or ethnicity, workers were routinely fired for even discussing the merits of unionization inside or outside of the factories. When one thousand pro-union Ford workers marched in the 1937 Labor Day parade, they wore masks to conceal their identities. There was good reason for the masks, as one Black worker found out two years later. "In 1939 when I was marching in the Labor Day parade," recalled Shelton Tappes, a foundry worker and member of the local NNC. "I had my Ford badge pinned to my lapel. And as I got to the Fox Theater, a man stepped out from the curb and took a good look at my badge. . . . The next day I found myself fired."[98] Most of the reprisals were carried out by Ford's Service Department, which was assigned the task of psychologically, and at times physically, assaulting workers suspected of "radical activities." The National Labor Relations Board repeatedly cited Ford's militaristic practices, ruling that the company was engaged in a "war" against its employees' right to self-organization, but the company simply ignored it.[99]

In response to these conditions, the Civil Rights Federation launched a "Fordism Is Fascism" campaign, and enlisted the aid of the National Conference for the Protection of Constitutional Liberties in a nationwide boycott of all Ford products. Calling for "Human Rights—Not Fordism," the CRF proclaimed, "Our job is to make Ford's fascist island of Dearborn submit to democratic American principles."[100]

The anti-Ford campaign was widely supported; no major faction of the city's Left remained aloof from the ensuing struggle. With resentment growing, by 1940 the UAW felt strong enough to launch a drive to break the power of the company. Under the direction of Mike Widman, the UAW recruited one thousand volunteers and a staff of seventy full-time organizers, including veteran Ford workers such as Bill McKie and Veal Clough and younger workers such as Shelton Tappes, the foundry worker fired after marching in the 1939 Labor Day parade.

The battle to organize Ford has been described in detail elsewhere. Some aspects of the campaign are worth repeating, however, especially the efforts of the union to ingratiate itself with the Black community. For instance, when the Booker T. Washington Trade Association (hardly a hotbed of radical pro-unionism) staged a "75 Years of Negro Progress Exposition," the union arranged for Hodges Mason and Black communist Luke Fennel to man a CIO exhibit.[101] Much of the initial organizing occurred secretly within the plants and local communities—in homes, in small meeting halls, during social events, and in churches. Alongside organizing committees for Italian and Polish workers, a Negro Organiz-

ing Committee that included Joseph Billups, Walter Hardin, Chris
Alston, Leon Bates, Clarence Bowman, Veal Clough, and Sheldon
Tappes was established. The group immediately laid out a plan of action
and enlisted the aid of the local NNC, to which many on the Organizing
Committee belonged, as well as the support of community activists,
including Reverends Hill and White, John Miles (Hill's assistant pastor),
Father Dade, state senator Charles Diggs, Louis Martin (the editor of the
Michigan Chronicle), attorney C. LeBron Simmons, and others.

A number of women also became involved in the effort. "We brought
Negro women into the organization," remembered Rose Billups, who
organized the Women's Auxiliary for Local 600,

> because the wives were afraid the husbands, the Negro husbands,
> would join the union and lose their jobs, so we had to go in, individ-
> ually, even if we couldn't get them in. . . . Each woman used to bring
> in one member, two members, because I was promising that no one
> would know but myself. I used to go to the saloons, in the alleys to
> meet the Negroes. . . . They gave me their dues, and I used to bring
> them to Mike Widman.[102]

The Negro Organizing Committee, along with the Polish Committee, and with the aid of the entire civil rights community and groups
such as the IWO, kept up a constant barrage of anti-Ford and pro-union
propaganda. Christopher Alston published a number of special issues of
Ford Facts devoted to Black workers.

Meanwhile, the Left factions within the Polish community—the
other major ethnic group represented at the Rouge plant—rallied
behind the UAW. The People's League of Hamtramck, with the backing
of individuals such as Stanley and Margaret Nowak and Mary Zuk, and
groups such as the Polish National Alliance and the Polish Lawyers Society issued a manifesto denouncing Henry Ford as a fascist and friend of
Adolph Hitler and characterizing the unionization of the company as a
necessary step in the preservation of democracy.[103]

The moment of decision came on April 1, 1941, when Service
Department chief Harry Bennett forced eight men out of the rolling
mills, and fifteen hundred workers initiated a sit-down strike in response
that eventually grew large enough to paralyze the entire complex.[104] In
a matter of hours fifty thousand men were refusing to work or leave the
facility, and on April 2 the union called for a march out of the plant. An
estimated ten thousand picketers massed at strategic points; only about
fifteen hundred to two thousand workers remained inside the plant as

strikebreakers. Many of those still inside were Black workers, and when the company went on the offensive these Black employees became a key component in Ford's anti-union strategy. Don Marshall, among others, was sent into Black communities to address "Back-to-Work" rallies, which represented a major threat to the success of the strike and the tenor of race relations in the city. The 1939 Chrysler strike had been a dress rehearsal for this moment. Then, too, the company had attempted to generate a back-to-work movement among Black workers—a movement that would have surely led to intense racial violence. Then, too, Black workers were caught between rival factions: the UAW-CIO and the UAW-AFL, the latter headed by the same Homer Martin who had caused such a stir at the 1937 NAACP convention by comparing the union to Christ and whose organization now called for Black workers to return to the plants.[105]

In 1941, along with the back-to-work rallies, ministers sympathetic to Ford opened their pulpits to Marshall and other company spokespersons. Marshall worked hard in these forums to disparage the union, even using a bit of class baiting to dismiss "the various doctors, ministers, dentists and other near-professional men of the race who are ranting over the radio and riding in union cars to exhort the Negro to follow them."[106] Marshall's suggestion that the activities of pro-union middle-class Blacks were driven by a desire for status augmentation, and not an identification with the interests of workers, probably found a receptive audience.

Among those "men of the race" speaking on the radio and riding in union sound cars were Reverends Hill and White, both of whom used their authority as ministers to appeal to Black workers. According to veteran organizer Bill McKie, "Charles A. Hill, prominent Negro minister, who had been active all along in helping to organize Ford, stood for a solid day outside the foundry gates, his voice booming over the concrete walls asking the men inside not to fear the men outside, but to drop their fear and walk out, as brothers."[107] By the end of the month the strike was drawing to a close, and Ford finally capitulated to the presence of a union, though not necessarily the UAW. The next big push for the city's civil rights community, therefore, was to prepare for the National Labor Relations Board election to be held on May 21, 1941. At that time workers would be called on to decide which union would be authorized to bargain in their name.

Once again, members of the city's Left took to the airwaves, the newspapers, and the pulpits to ensure a favorable outcome for the UAW-CIO as opposed to the company-backed UAW-AFL. The NNC sent its members out to canvass for the UAW-CIO. State senator Diggs, in tandem with state senator Stanley Nowak, issued a joint statement appealing to both Black and Polish workers, while a series of pro-CIO editorials were run in the *Michigan Chronicle*. Ironically, the UAW-CIO won by a margin so wide that the votes of Black workers, many of whom supported the company-endorsed union led by Homer Martin, were not really crucial to the outcome. Yet, as labor historians August Meier and Elliott Rudwick note, the "long-range developments" indicated that the union's efforts to recruit Black workers had not "gone for naught."[108]

First, the UAW's efforts, where Black workers were concerned, had helped prevent wholesale strikebreaking, which could have led to riots, loss of life, and calls for the National Guard to end the strike by force. Second, the UAW-CIO's attention to Black workers gave valuable organizing experience to a number of unionists and community activists working with the organizing committees. The Black leaders that came of age during World War II and assumed control of the Black rights agenda did so, in part, on the basis of lessons learned doing union work. Third, the battle to unionize Ford decreased the company's influence and, as a result, strengthened the leftist labor–civil rights community. The Ford strike, that is to say, endowed the Left with a standing it would not necessarily have had otherwise in either the Black community or the city's ethnic enclaves. Moreover, this struggle prepared the civil rights community for the battles that lay ahead as the United States entered the war.

For Reverend Hill and his allies in organizations such as the Civil Rights Federation, the National Negro Congress, and now the huge and powerful UAW-CIO Local 600, the war years would prove critical to the development of political radicalism and civil rights activism in Detroit. A "new crowd" of activists, one aligned with the Left (especially the CP and its front groups), the Democratic Party, and the UAW-CIO, had finally begun to come into its own. During World War II, these activists effectively shifted the terrain of Black politics in Detroit.

THREE

EXPLOSIVE FAITH

The Politics of Religion in the
Arsenal of Democracy

"In recent times," wrote Louis E. Martin, editor of the *Michigan Chronicle* and a careful student of local politics, in January 1944, "there has been increasing friction between the two old American traditions, one which is essentially liberal and democratic and the other patently reactionary and anti-democratic." He continued:

> In perhaps no other great American city does this conflict come into sharper focus than in tumultuous Detroit. Even before the war this city was notorious for its union struggles and sit-down strikes, for its booms and depressions, for its industrial prowess and its almost vulgar vitality.[1]

When Martin penned this piece for the *Crisis,* he, like other prominent members of Detroit's civil rights community, was feeling chastened by the tensions and sporadic violence that plagued the city (and the nation) throughout World War II. By the end of the war, Detroit had experienced racially motivated skirmishes in its overcrowded residential neighborhoods, its high schools, its recreational spaces, its factories, and in a riot during the summer of 1943 that claimed 34 lives. Martin struggled to define what these episodes meant in terms of the city's past, present, and postwar political future.

Martin located the source of the violence in the "patently reactionary and anti-democratic" traditions identified with religious demagogues such as Father Coughlin, Gerald L. K. Smith, and J. Frank Norris, all of whom found fertile soil for their racist, anti-Semitic, and antilabor views in the social and economic dislocation created by the war; in the "poor leadership" provided by city officials such as Mayor Edward J. Jeffries Jr., who lacked the political will and moral fortitude to deal with the city's racial, ethnic, and religious tensions; and in the "restive, unassimilated masses of industrial workers" among the nearly five hundred thousand men, women, and children who had migrated to the Detroit metropolitan area during the war, many of whom "had to work out some practical pattern of life and make awkward adjustments to one another and all this in a brief period of time."

On the other side of Martin's equation—among the essentially liberal and democratic traditions—stood the civil rights community, including interracial groups such as the Civil Rights Federation, which confronted the city's social and political ills with direct action and mass pressure; "strong religious forces" comprising progressive Protestants, Catholics, and Jews and their organizations, "which profess interracial goodwill"; and, most important, organized labor or more accurately those union officials who supported the Black civil rights agenda over the protests of the rank and file.

Martin's analysis of these conflicts and coalitions, categorized into a "liberal" Left and "reactionary" Right, serves as a starting point for investigations into how the war influenced the tenor of civil rights activism in Detroit. A close understanding of the personalities and political theologies of both the reactionaries (Smith, Norris) and progressives (Williams, the People's Institute of Applied Religion) enables us to appreciate how religious beliefs and manifestations of faith were invoked on both left and right in a battle for the hearts and minds of Detroiters and the very soul of the city.

HILL, THE HOME FRONT, AND THE "DEMOCRATIC LEFT"

As Louis Martin suggested, on the eve of America's entrance into World War II Detroit's Left community was made up of labor unions and union officials, race improvement agencies, civil rights organizations, and, although Martin omits any direct mention of it, the Michigan Division of the Communist Party (MDCP). With the successful unionization of Ford Motor Company, Local 600, representing over sixty thousand members, became one of the largest and most progressive locals in the nation. The foundry, where Ford employed many of its African American workers based on company ideas of inferiority and social control, became a particularly influential base of union power, so much so that for the next decade Local 600 was to be a center of civil rights militancy and a virtual training ground for Black activists.[2]

George Crockett, an African American attorney who first came to Detroit from Washington, DC, in 1944 on behalf of the Fair Employment Practice Commission (FEPC) and subsequently went to work for the UAW, was essentially correct when he observed that it "was in the trade union movement that Detroit's Black leadership got its start in politics. They learned their political ropes in being elected or influencing the elections of union leaders, and from that they went out to organize the community."[3] The foundry unit sent more than a score of Black delegates to every UAW convention and provided at least half of all Black staff members hired by the UAW. With strategic input from Shelton Tappes, who was elected recording secretary in 1941, and foundryman Horace Sheffield, as well as Black unionists such as Christopher Alston, Arthur McPhaul, Dave Moore, and Nelson Davis, Local 600 provided time, money, and human resources for a series of civil rights mobilizations throughout the war years.

Local 600 was also a stronghold of the Communist Party, which had a decisive influence on its development. The River Rouge plant was "one of the few workplaces in the country where Communists, black or white, could proclaim their political allegiance without immediate persecution."[4] Copies of the *Daily Worker* were sold and read freely, and such "radical" ideas as racial and gender equality were discussed openly in meetings and the local's newspaper and publications. Further, there was a "special relationship" between Blacks and the CP. Inside the union, prominent party members such as Nat Ganley consistently supported the demand for a Black seat on the International Executive Board—a measure denounced in some quarters as "reverse discrimination"—and for the upgrading of Black workers. In return Black unionists, with a few exceptions, tended to back the left-of-center coalition headed by R. J. Thomas and George Addes in the factional fights that often pitted the CP against such anticommunist antagonists as the Association of Catholic Trade Unionists and Walter Reuther's UAW. Outside of the union, Black activists (and the civil rights community in general) found the party a willing participant in many, though by no means all, of the era's civil rights struggles.[5]

With the cause of industrial unionism now an established fact, Black unionists and their pro-union allies were accorded a new level of respect within the Black community. As the civil rights agenda shifted to focus on the social and economic plight of African Americans,[6] and as Black militants became increasingly vocal about the lack of democracy and freedom on the home front, activists such as the Rev. Charles Hill were able to extend their field of influence within the city's Left. Hill in fact became part of a cadre, based in the union movement and the orbit of the CP, that engaged in a barely muted struggle with the generation of community leaders that had achieved prominence after World War I and before the UAW's 1941 victory over Ford. Although the Ford-aligned minister Father Daniel had died in 1939, many others from this generation remained skeptical, if not openly hostile, to the radicals, especially those associated with the communists. Throughout the war years, both groups publicly appealed for unity while often working behind the scenes to increase their own influence.

The election for president of the Detroit branch of the NAACP at the end of 1942 was indicative of this ongoing tension. The local race pitted Hill against the incumbent, Dr. James J. McClendon, who had served as branch president since 1938. A native of Georgia and a graduate of Meharry Medical College, McClendon had remained studiously uncommitted in the debate over Black support of the UAW, and throughout his tenure as head of the Detroit branch he had tended to focus more on discrimination in public accommodations than in factories. The race was therefore widely viewed as a "contest between important political factions," with McClendon cast as the defender of a liberal strategy that eschewed radicalism and Hill as the representative of labor and militant progressives, especially those aligned with the Local 600 and the National Negro Congress.[7]

At no point in the campaign, however, was Hill publicly accused of being a communist. His platform is best described as pro-labor and broad based. Convinced more than ever that "the future of the Negro is tied up with the future of labor," he called for an extension of the recently formed cooperative relationship between the NAACP and labor organizations, especially the UAW. He also called for an increase in direct involvement by the NAACP membership. "I want to see the NAACP run by its members in regular membership meetings, and functioning through broad committees and neighborhood chapters. . . . I want to see the executive board include representatives of all groups. It must be inter-racial," he told the *Michigan Chronicle,* which devoted extensive coverage to the race, much of it with a pro-Hill bias.[8]

Hill ran a credible albeit slightly disorganized campaign, with the NNC's C. LeBron Simmons and the UAW's Shelton Tappes providing vigorous and vocal support. Equally vigorous but better-organized support was thrown behind McClendon by a politically diverse constituency that included the Rev. Horace White and Beulah Whitby, Reverend Peck and Carlton Gaines of the Booker T. Washington Trade Association, and Reverend Bradby, who, rumor had it, "instructed" his large congregation at Second Baptist to cast its ballots for McClendon. In fact, in the aftermath of the election, the Hill camp lodged complaints about the nominations and vote-tallying process and charged that the election was rigged because the vast majority of the approximately thirteen hundred members present were McClendon supporters and members of Second Baptist. Hill, who was defeated by an overwhelming margin, tried to stay above the fray.

The loss did not deter him from seeking other outlets for his political theology of community activism.[9] Still preaching a gospel of social and economic justice, Hill appeared to be everywhere at once on the city's home front. "There [was] always something going on all the time," he recalled, and "we just [didn't] have any rest." The war itself was emotionally draining. Like thousands of other parents, Reverend Hill and his wife Georgia bid a tearful farewell to their oldest son, Charles Jr., an auto worker and part-time law student, as he left home to join the armed forces. He enlisted in August 1942 and served with distinction in the Fifteenth Air Force Division (the Tuskegee Airmen), receiving three Battle Stars, the Air Medal, and two Bronze Oak Leaf Clusters.[10] At the same time, Reverend Hill's conventional ministerial duties were as pressing as ever. There were weddings to perform and eulogies to deliver, babies to bless, sick congregants to visit, and a church to continue to build and expand. He still occasionally made pancakes on Saturdays for the neighborhood children.

But Hill's role in the Ford strike had thrust him into the limelight of citywide oppositional politics. Having developed his view of religion as "a man's job" in the midst of the first world war, he now sought to apply that lesson during the second. His view of leadership was fairly straightforward: "Anytime a person accepts leadership, he has got to have the courage of his convictions. If he will have the courage . . . he will keep on and ultimately find that there are many others willing to join."[11]

Hill remained critical of ministers who would not take stands on important issues. Moreover, his "earthly piety" and no-nonsense style of activism, coupled with his ability to at least appear to avoid the factionalism that periodically flared up between leftists and more moderate liberals, gave him a reputation that few others could match. Jack Raskin, who took over the helm of the local Civil Rights Federation in 1940, recalled that Hill was "somehow separate from" the factionalism and personality politics that often hampered the effectiveness of the city's civil rights community and that he was perceived as "sort of a neutral kind of person."[12] Hill was not in fact a neutral person, although he did tend to be nonconfrontational. "And then he had another very cute saying," another local radical, Eleanor Maki, remembered, "about people who criticized him for supporting the left wing, and he said every time he saw a bird flying, he could see very well that it had a right wing and it had a left wing, and he couldn't see how it'd be able to keep going if it didn't have them both."[13] For both pragmatic and moral reasons, Hill cast his net widely.

While he often framed his activism and his political statements in a religious context, he was well received by those with a decidedly secular worldview. It seems that Hill's political ecumenicalism was equally applicable to the religious and nonreligious. For him, one of religion's jobs was to speak to the nonreligious in a language that they could understand and connect with on a moral and humanistic level. Hence Maki's comment that Hill was one of the few preachers "I could ever sit and listen to comfortably."[14] Many of the organizations in which Hill held leadership positions during the war revolved around single-issue initiatives that gave rise to a series of citizens' committees. Unlike more formal organizations that required membership dues, constitutions, and bylaws, citizens' committees were ad hoc political associations that nonetheless maintained close ties with the more stable groups and institutions that comprised the organizational network of the civil rights community. Along with the NAACP, the UAW, and the CP, the backbone of that community was the local branch of the National Negro Congress and the indigenous Civil Rights Federation. Both groups were founded in the mid-1930s, and both had animated Hill's idealism.

Reverend Hill had been head of the CRF's Negro Department since 1938, and his personal and political ties to the group strengthened during the war when he became a fixture on its Steering Committee. In 1941 the CRF underwent an internal shake-up. The Rev. Owen Knox resigned his directorship, and Jack Raskin became executive secretary. Knox, a white Methodist minister whom Hill had come to respect, was a committed pacifist whose opposition to U.S. involvement in World War II had, in the wake of Hitler and Stalin's nonaggression pact, placed him in temporary agreement with the Communist Party. Knox knew there was a CP presence within the CRF (the party was listed as a supporter on the CRF's letterhead) and the National Federation for Constitutional Liberties, the CRF-like national organization of which he became chairman in 1940. But when Germany invaded Russia and the American communists threw themselves into the war effort some voiced the suspicion that Knox's continued opposition to the war was a cover for his anti-Semitism. Publicly, at least, Knox blamed the "strong Russian sympathies" of both organizations for his resignation.[15]

Hill and the small core of committed activists at the CRF were apparently less concerned than Knox about communist opportunism and tended to support the war. Whether this was because of a directive from the Comintern is open to debate, as is the question of exactly how many members of the CRF's Executive Committee were also members of the CP. What is clear is that throughout the early 1940s the CRF expanded in size and increased its influence in the city's civil rights community.

Raskin's ascendancy helped fuel this process. He was the first head of the CRF who had not been a member of the clergy, and unlike Reverends Bollens and Knox he came from a working-class background. He was also the first Jewish head of an organization based, to some degree, in Black and Jewish communities. By one estimate, nearly 50 percent of the group's core membership (no more than twelve hundred at its height) were either Blacks or Jews, and the group's Executive Committee embodied roughly the same proportions.[16] Raskin's parents were refugees from czarist Russia who immigrated to Detroit around the turn of the century. Born in 1913 and raised in Detroit, Raskin went straight from high school into the factories, where he became involved in union activities during the Depression. He joined the CRF as a volunteer in 1938 after visiting his brother, Dr. Morris Raskin, who worked in the UAW's medical department. His brother's office was in the Hoffman Building, down the hall from the CRF's tiny headquarters, and Raskin was there during a particularly violent strike, which was met with a great deal of police brutality. People were bringing injured workers into the medical offices, and the CRF was taking statements. "And I became, well, sort of emotionally involved, and became interested in the CRF at that time."[17]

Raskin appears to have had even more of an interest than his predecessors at the CRF in the demands of African Americans, and he threw himself and the CRF more and more into the struggles of the city's Black population. He saw a basic affinity, an ideological kinship, between working-class Blacks and Jews; as a result he helped move the organization, during World War II, toward a more explicit focus on "the elimination of anti-Semitism and prejudice against the Negro people."[18] For Raskin, this was one way to continue the federation's tradition of positioning itself well to the left of both the Jewish Community Council and the NAACP.[19]

The desire to offer a radical alternative to more traditional organizations remained equally important to the NNC, whose national body continued to have internal difficulties of its own. As was the case with the CRF, many of these difficulties were directly related to the presence of and fears about communists. And, again like the Civil Rights Federation, tensions within the NNC were heightened because of changes in the CP line. When the NNC held its third national meeting in 1940, any speaker, including A. Philip Randolph, who was not sympathetic to the new CP position against the "imperialistic war" raging in Europe was booed and shouted down. When Randolph linked the Soviet Union with other imperialist and totalitarian nations, the first exodus, led primarily by white delegates (presumably CP members), began. As he stressed the loyalty of African Americans to the United States, and assured the audience that in any conflict between the United States and the Soviet Union Blacks would side with their country, even more delegates left the hall. Randolph ended his controversial speech by urging that the NNC remain controlled by Blacks and dedicated to their struggles, with a leadership "free of intimidation, manipulation or subordination, with character that is beyond the reach of the dollar . . . a leadership which is uncontrolled and responsible to no one but the Negro people."[20]

Almost immediately after the meeting, Randolph was denounced as "a traitor," a "red-baiter," and "a frightened Negro bourgeoisie." His resignation, due to "Communist infiltration," caused quite a stir; many of the group's former supporters followed suit, and a number of local branches of the NNC did not survive. The Detroit branch was weakened, but it managed to weather the storm.[21] Moreover, the widespread view of the NNC as communist dominated did not deter Reverend Hill and many of his colleagues. There were a number of possible reasons for his decision to stick with the NNC and, by extension, to remain within the orbit of the CP. Unlike Randolph, who, as a member of the Socialist Party, had opposed the CP since its inception, Hill was not invested in the long-standing ideological battles that had fractured the Left. Nor did Hill appear to have had Randolph's burning desire for organizational control or his commitment to all-Black and Black-led organizations. Hill's decision to stay with the NNC (and the CRF) may also have been related to timing and circumstance. The changes in the CP's position from the Popular Front to revolutionary fermentation and back again were contemporaneous with the battle to unionize the Ford Motor Company—a circumstance that may have provided an extra impetus to place unity and pragmatism over the machinations of the distant Comintern. Despite the internal difficulties of the national organization, the Detroit

NNC, as noted in the previous chapter, played an important role in mobilizing support for the UAW within the African American community, and it was likely for this reason that Hill had assumed the helm of the local chapter by 1942.

Finally, Hill may have been influenced by a certain amount of naïveté, on the one hand, and the pull of friendship and personal affinity on the other. When Hill became chair of the Detroit NNC, his young friend and protégé, Coleman Young, became executive secretary (before being inducted into military service), and many of the men and women he had been allied with remained active members. It was, in short, a community of like-minded activists. The local branch of the NAACP remained as suspicious of the NNC as ever, but in an atmosphere of increased racial tension the NAACP and the NNC worked together on a number of occasions in the early 1940s.[22] Navigating between the NAACP and the NNC, Hill used both groups—along with his church and the CRF—as a base of operations for his activism throughout the war years.

As with many African American activists operating within the orbit of the CP, Hill may have had personal reservations about Randolph's resignation from the NNC and his call for an all-Black mobilization, but he did not fail—in defiance of the CP's position—to support Randolph's newly formed March on Washington movement (MOWM).[23] Perhaps more than any other single event during the 1940s, the nationwide mobilization for the march set the tone for contemporary civil rights activism. Louis Martin called it a "classic example in recent history of the effectiveness of the mass demonstration technique," a technique that has its "ultimate base" in the theory that "the inherent sense of justice of the American people when sufficiently aroused will not countenance the persecution of the Negro."[24] Initiated in July of 1941, the MOWM was a national mobilization organized to bring one hundred thousand Blacks to the nation's capital to protest economic and social injustices and demand federal action. It was to be an all-Black movement for two reasons: first, to keep the MOWM free of communist contamination; and, second, to give African Americans across the nation a better sense of their own agency and power.[25]

Toward this end, the national organization was to provide an overarching framework for the march, with the movement's core contained in local branches in various cities. On June 7, the MOWM reported active branches in Kansas City, Saint Paul, Saint Louis, Chicago, Buffalo, Newark, Jersey City, Asbury Park, Westchester County, New York, Philadelphia, Baltimore, New York City, Richmond, Atlanta, Tampa,

Savannah, Jacksonville, Washington, and Detroit. The MOWM received a great deal of support in Detroit, and Reverend Hill, among others, including Reverend White and Father Dade, devoted a large portion of his time to soliciting funds and marchers, arranging transportation, and preparing for a simultaneous march to be held in Detroit. Reverend White, whose politics seemed to be increasingly aligned with Randolph's, was especially active.[26]

Whether the MOWM would have been able to mobilize one hundred thousand Black marchers was and is debatable. There is some justification for viewing it as a "magnificent bluff." Although the march was eventually called off, or rather delayed (for some twenty-two years as it turned out), after President Roosevelt issued Executive Order 8802, the MOWM was significant for a number of reasons—first and foremost for the existence of 8802 itself. The executive order outlawed discriminatory hiring practices in the defense industries, government agencies, and job-training programs for defense production. It also established the Fair Employment Practice Commission as an investigative agency. While the FEPC had few powers of enforcement and was terribly understaffed throughout its existence, it did have the power to expose discrimination via public hearings that garnered national and international media attention. For many aggrieved Black workers, the FEPC was also one of the more viable mechanisms for redress. Moreover, just as the Wagner Act became the Magna Carta of labor organizing and legitimized the right to unionize, Executive Order 8802 upheld the demand for a new class of rights—fair employment.[27] Thus, the definition of what constitutes a "civil right" became even more expansive.

Characterized as the first significant federal policy to address the concerns of Black Americans since the Emancipation Proclamation, Executive Order 8802 (and the FEPC), like the Wagner Act (and the National Labor Relations Board), also strengthened the idea that the state was the final arbiter of minority rights. As A. Philip Randolph was fond of saying, "All roads led to Washington."[28] From 1941 on, the need to maintain pressure on the government and provoke its decisive intervention remained an important strategy for activists. By borrowing from the direct-action, mass-pressure techniques of the CIO-led union movement, the MOWM was, at the same time, an important bridge between labor activism and civil rights. As was the case with many progressive labor leaders, especially those with ties to the Left, Randolph and the MOWM adopted the same theory of power that had given the CIO many of its early victories. "Power and pressure do not reside in the few, the intelligentsia," Randolph maintained. Instead, power and pressure "lie and flow from the masses." Power, for Randolph and like-minded activists, was an "active principle of only the organized masses" when they are united for a definite purpose. Thus, the "Call to Negro Americans to March on Washington for Jobs and Equal Participation in National Defense" read, in part:

> Dear fellow Negro Americans, be not dismayed in these terrible times. You possess power, great power. Our problem is to hitch it up for action on the broadest, daring and most gigantic scale. In this period of power politics, nothing counts but pressure, more pressure and still more pressure, through the tactic and strategy of broad, organized, aggressive mass action behind the vital and important issues of the Negro. To this end we propose that ten thousand Negroes MARCH ON WASHINGTON FOR JOBS IN NATIONAL DEFENSE AND EQUAL INTEGRATION IN THE FIGHTING FORCES OF THE UNITED STATES.[29]

This is not dramatically different from the strategy advocated by theologian Reinhold Niebuhr in his seminal 1932 text *Moral Man and Immoral Society*. Therein, the theologian, whose first parish appointment was in Detroit, argued that the liberal overreliance on personal conscience and "social goodwill" was obsolete and ineffective. In the future, he wrote, reform movements would have to incorporate a "measure of coercion" and force if they hoped to succeed. Individual men and women may be swayed by moral arguments, Niebuhr declared in an implicit critique of the excessive optimism of the old social gospel, but an organized force only yielded power to an equally organized force.[30]

Even though the FEPC represented only a partial concession to the MOWM's demands, in both strategy and outcome, the movement signaled a new era in Black political protest—one squarely rooted in the tactics of mass pressure on state agencies, direct action, and moral suasion to bring about economic justice and industrial democracy. The use of labor unions, especially union locals, along with other mediating structures such as churches, clubs, and race organizations, to mobilize large numbers of people in order to cajole or threaten federal agencies into action would become the major strategy of civil rights activists throughout the remainder of the twentieth century. The demand for fair employment legislation and additional FEPCs within states, cities, and labor unions, would become equally characteristic of postwar protest.[31]

Randolph attempted to keep the MOWM alive after the cancellation of the march, but the group never achieved either a sustainable mass base or an organizational structure sufficient to make this truly possible. Ideologically, however, Randolph continued to play a leading role in shaping the debate about civil rights struggles. During a 1942 MOWM convention held in Detroit, he stressed the need to see a national march as just one of the options available to activists. Calling attention to "the strategy and maneuver of the people of India with mass civil disobedience and non-cooperation," he proposed that these techniques could also be applied in America "in theaters, hotels, restaurants, and amusement places." On this score, the religious-political leader Mahatma Gandhi and the political theologian Reinhold Niebuhr were in complete agreement. By echoing both, Randolph gave a philosophical and spiritual framework to the course of civil rights protests being carried on in Detroit and elsewhere.[32] In Detroit, the MOWM—along with its tactics and ideology—was duly incorporated into the general tenor of civil rights militancy and melded into a growing series of interlocking organizations. The question of an alliance between African Americans and whites and between liberals and radicals was also incorporated. This, too, would become a prominent and often contentious feature within Black protest in the second half of the century.

If Randolph and the MOWM provided a philosophical framework for activists, the war provided the urgency. After the bombing of Pearl Harbor, local activists applied pressure politics both locally and nationally. Like African Americans across the nation, Detroiters joined the *Pittsburgh Courier*'s call for a "Double Victory"—victory at home and victory abroad—and increased militancy within the context of national loyalty. Having "closed ranks" during World War I, few were prepared to sacrifice their rights again in the name of national unity. When a Black man was savagely beaten and lynched in Silkeston, Missouri, a few weeks after Pearl Harbor, the *Chicago Defender* offered a second slogan: "Remember Pearl Harbor and Silkeston too."[33] "The very character of this war," read an editorial in the *Michigan Chronicle,* which avidly supported the *Courier*-inspired campaign, "a war for freedom, for democracy, for liberation, has of necessity produced profound changes in our own thinking and has accelerated the hopes of all of us for a new America and even a new world."[34]

While some religious figures opposed America's entrance into the war on pacifist grounds, Reverend Hill did not. He urged an all-out attack on the "Nazi juggernaut" before it reached the Western Hemisphere and, like Louis Martin and others, was equally enthusiastic about attacking the racist juggernauts at home.[35] In Detroit, this offensive posture meant a concerted effort to secure fair employment, adequate housing, and alleviation of the racial and religious tensions dividing the city. In each area, and throughout each domestic battle, the civil rights community was drawn closer together, in some ways, and pulled farther apart in others. Summing up the civil rights activism in wartime Detroit, the *Chronicle's* Martin could write: "In few cities have mass demonstrations been used so effectively as in Detroit in the last six years. The Negro leadership and the rank and file citizens march and picket as a matter of course today."[36]

There was much to picket and march about. Discriminatory practices in the auto industry during the conversion to war production had been a serious topic during the year before America's entry into the war. With the bombing of Pearl Harbor and the enactment of Executive Order 8802, the issue of fair employment became one of the most salient matters confronting the city's civil rights activists. Conversion to defense production, which relied more heavily on skilled workers in traditionally white jobs, rendered many of the jobs that Blacks had been restricted to unnecessary. Even in the plants where Blacks had achieved a measure of seniority, white workers with less seniority received a disproportionate share of upgrading. Unemployment, too, continued to be a pressing issue. Nationally, the percentage of Black workers involved in manufacturing and industry, having grown from 6.2 percent in 1910 to 7.3 percent in 1930, had, by 1940, reached a new low of 5.1 percent. In Detroit, Black male unemployment rates still managed to exceed the average jobless rate by three times. For Black women, the situation was equally tenuous. In a striking reversal of its earlier policy, the Ford Motor Company virtually ceased the recruitment and hiring of Black men—and continued to refuse to hire Black women—even in the midst of a labor shortage.[37] Hence the shortcomings of the national FEPC had swiftly become apparent.

In response, activists in Detroit organized two FEPC-inspired groups: the interracial Metropolitan Detroit Council on Fair Employment Practice (MDCFEP) and the predominantly Black Citizens Committee for Jobs in War Industry. The histories of both groups reveal important aspects of the city's early civil rights community. The MDCFEP, for instance, grew out of a long-standing tradition of informal lunchtime conversations at the cafeteria of the Lucy Thurman branch of the YWCA, located in the heart of the east-side Black community on St. Antoine street. Geraldine Bledsoe recalled that "this was a very famous period for Lucy Thurman because [we] used to have a meeting there almost every day at lunchtime; we'd be meeting to discuss what new issues there were, what the strategies were, what needed to be done." The chief problem with this approach was that it often excluded members of the working class or anyone else whose job precluded these casual "working" lunches. For people like Bledsoe, who had gone from being a placement officer in the Michigan Unemployment Commission to state supervisor of Negro placement in 1941, a lunchtime meeting was simply a matter of scheduling. For someone with a factory job, this type of flexibility was rare.[38]

But the history of the MDCFEP is not just a story about subtle class bias in protest organizations. It is also a story of activism spawned as much by the strengths of the federal FEPC as by its weaknesses. A discussion of both, along with the continuing problems of fair employment in the city and the region, was the topic of the lunchtime meeting in the spring of 1942 that led to the formation of the Metropolitan Council. A small coordinating committee was set up, and within a month's time the group had representatives from over seventy organizations. The council was interracial and interfaith, with Edward W. McFarland, a professor of economics at Wayne State University, serving as chairman. Drawing on the moral authority of church and temple, Reverend Hill, along with Rabbi B. Benedict Glazer, Fr. J. Lawrence Cavanagh, and Dr. Thoburn Brumbaugh of the Detroit Council of Churches, served as vice chairs.

The Executive Board was rounded out by Zaio Woodford, a white feminist attorney associated with the Detroit Federation of Women's Clubs; Geraldine Bledsoe; Gloster Current of the NAACP; Jack Raskin of the CRF; and fifteen others representing labor and civic groups. The overall aim of the council was to "assure the full utilization of the local labor supply in the war effort, using every worker at his highest skill level." They understood that the mere five officials in the Detroit FEPC office were insufficient for the task at hand and viewed themselves as a supplement to the government agency. At the same time, the MDCFEP *superseded* the terms of the president's executive order by adding sex to the list of discriminatory practices that needed to be addressed.[39]

Throughout the war years members of the council handled complaints and heard charges. Working in small groups, they interviewed and pressured personnel managers and corporate presidents. Funded by the War Chest of Metropolitan Detroit, the group maintained a small staff for these and other purposes. Acting as a clearinghouse for information, the Metropolitan Council also engaged in educational activities to sway public opinion and increase understanding among interracial groups. It supported legislation to implement fair employment practices and assisted employers and unions in developing a sound policy for integrating members of minority groups into industry.[40] By August 1943 the group had agreed to refer all cases to the FEPC, which had established a subregional office in the city, and thereafter limited its activities to non-referral cases from August 1943 to August 1945. During its existence, the Metropolitan Council handled just under one thousand cases involving more than seven hundred companies and was able to adjust 58 percent of them.[41] The organization would also prove instrumental during postwar efforts to make the FEPC permanent and seek fair employment legislation in both Michigan and Detroit.

The second group, the Citizens Committee for Jobs in War Industry, was also characteristic of wartime activism in Detroit. The citizens committee had a less formal structure than the MDCFEP, but it, too, worked in the area of fair employment. Established by Reverend Hill, with support from Black union leaders in Local 600 and members of the NNC, it was an umbrella group spanning the ideological spectrum of the city's African American activists from the Booker T. Washington Trade Association and the Detroit Urban League to the Detroit National Negro Congress and the local NAACP. Gloster Current, a militant in his own right, served as the group's recording secretary, while first Mamie Thompson, the NAACP's treasurer, and later Raymond Hatcher of the Detroit Urban League handled the finances.[42] Like the Metropolitan Detroit Council, the citizens committee worked in tandem with the national FEPC's Detroit investigators, securing the "loan" of Ray Hatcher for the task of gathering actual cases of discrimination and turning them over to official FEPC investigators.

While the MDCFEP adopted a more mechanistic approach and received municipal funding, the citizens committee sought to function as a mass protest and pressure group, aspiring to be the "main instrument for exerting . . . pressure upon federal government, city government, unions and plant management" and to be "an example of the 'Double Victory' they [Blacks] want to see as the outcome of this war."[43] It was also, unlike the MDCFEP, predominantly African American and very much in the spirit of Randolph's MOWM, especially in its attempt to keep the group Black led and directed.

The citizens committee adopted a broad perspective in the fight "against refusal to hire persons of minority races, religions and nationality groups," but nonetheless it managed to reserve special consideration for the plight of African American workers. Under the principle that "segregation is discrimination," it maintained a high standard for what constituted fair employment and fought against the creation of special segregated divisions in plants. Committee members, for example, were particularly worried that the recent appointment of an African American to the personnel department of the Briggs Manufacturing Corporation "may mean the beginning of a policy of segregation" and planned to send a delegation to Briggs to discuss the issue. They were dedicated, as one statement put it in January 1943, to the "integration of Negroes into their jobs and into the unions." Moreover, they advocated direct representation of Blacks on the War Manpower Commission, for the passage of a Michigan State FEPC bill, for mass demonstrations against employers who discriminated, and, finally, for the "mobilization of the Christian Church in behalf of the anti-discrimination fight."[44]

Why the committee viewed fair employment and nondiscrimination as a religious issue, or at least an issue around which religious bodies and communities should organize, is an interesting question. Certainly, both the Metropolitan Detroit Council on Fair Employment Practice and the Citizens Committee for Jobs in War Industry incorporated interfaith religious leadership and participation, including Black and white churches, the Detroit Council of Churches, the Catholic Youth, the Congregation of Beth-El, the Jewish Community Council, and the Association of Catholic Trade Unionists, among others. And discrimination on religious grounds, especially toward Jews and Catholics, was among the practices that they fought against. (And this with good reason: of the 355 cases of alleged discrimination based on religion filed with the FEPC from July 1943 through June 1944, a significant proportion involved people of the Jewish faith, followed by Seventh Day Adventists, Jehovah's Witnesses, and Catholics.)[45] Still, there is a suggestion of a *particular* duty on the part of the religious. Part of this duty, at least on the part of Catholics toward Blacks, is captured in a statement released by the National Catholic Welfare Conference at the direction of archbishops and bishops in 1943.

"We owe these fellow-citizens," the statement says of African Americans, "who have contributed so largely to the development of our country, and for whose welfare history imposes on us a special obligation of justice, to see that they have in fact the rights which are given them in our Constitution." These rights include not only political equality, "but also fair economic and educational opportunities, a just share in public welfare projects, good housing without exploitation, and a full chance for the social advancement of their race." Such sentiments were viewed as consistent with the church's social teachings enshrined in documents such as *Rerum Novarum* and Pope Pius XII's encyclical *Sertum Laetitae* (1939), which deals explicitly with "special and considerate care" toward "neighbors of the Negro race." White ethnic lay Catholics, including many Detroit area Poles, often took a very different position on their

Negro neighbors, but the moral tone set by the Catholic hierarchy—on issues ranging from fair employment to national health care—was indicative of the shared morality of many members of the city's civil rights community. Moreover, it helps to explain why groups such as the Association of Catholic Trade Unionists, along with the local diocese in general, were important members of that protest community.[46]

Guided by this (holy) spirit, the citizens committee and the MDCFEP struggled to bring the federal FEPC to Detroit for a series of public hearings on the vexing situation in Detroit's industries, especially at the Ford Motor Company. After months of negotiations involving numerous trips to Washington, DC, to meet with federal officials—"I was going to Washington all the time," remembered Hill—the groups had to turn to other means. This was especially true for the citizens committee and its efforts around African American women. Black women faced more obstacles to securing industrial employment than either Black men or white women. Although Detroit was experiencing an acute labor shortage, the labor pool created by African American women, approximately twenty-eight thousand potential workers, went relatively untapped. Black women, then, constituted the most neglected source of nondomestic labor. Of the 389 Detroit-area plants surveyed by the War Production Board, only 74 employed Black women, whereas 239 used female laborers.

Even when Black women did find jobs in plants they were generally excluded from the more profitable skilled jobs for which white women were being trained and were relegated instead to positions as janitors and matrons.[47] As historian Jacqueline Jones points out, the majority of Black women "measured the impact of the war on their own lives primarily in terms of the quality of their jobs and living quarters." Challenging the "Rosie the Riveter" stereotype, which held that women worked only for patriotic reasons, she quotes Lillian Hatcher, a union activist and one of the first African American women hired above the service level in Detroit's auto industry.

> I was working not for patriotic reasons, I was working for money. . . .
> And I really needed that money, because my son was wearing out corduroy pants, two and three pair a month, gym shoes and all those other things my daughters too had to have. . . . And our house rent . . . we had to save for that . . . and keep the light and gas.[48]

Although many Black women were barely staying afloat economically, the drive to place them in industrial employment represents one of the few times that Hill and his predominantly male colleagues directly addressed the particular concerns of working-class women and took direct action on their behalf.

Black women themselves used every available avenue to secure fair and gainful employment. As Nancy Gabin demonstrates in her study of women in the UAW, African American women appeared more willing than men to utilize the power of the state and the union hierarchy to crack the barriers that confronted them—perhaps because of the resistant nature of those barriers. Many more women than men lodged complaints with the FEPC, and the first FEPC probe into the situation in Detroit specifically addressed their concerns. In the process, argues historian Megan Taylor Shockley, they "transformed their relationship with the state" and "redefined citizenship during and immediately following World War II by basing it on their real or potential contributions to the wartime state." They also became more prominent within the city's civil rights community. The drive to secure positions for Black women was a protracted battle, which began with negotiations with top company officials and ended with pickets and public protests.[49]

The citizens committee, with the aid of Black unionists in Local 600, manned picket lines at the plants and produced educational handbills. They also attempted to involve the federal government, with Reverend Hill leading delegations to persuade officials with the FEPC and the War Manpower Commission to intervene on behalf of Black women. By February, the citizens committee could claim victory, as sixty-eight women were hired at the Rouge plant and slower gains were being made at the Willow Run plant near Ypsilanti. Still, by 1943 African American women were only about 3 percent of the female industrial workforce. Although these protests led to some concessions by industry, and helped to generate support for the formation of a Woman's Bureau in the UAW in 1944 with Hatcher as codirector, the record of the Left community and the unions in addressing the concerns of Black women was a mixed one.[50]

The struggle to bring more African American men and women into the defense industries did increase the public profile of the city's Left-labor activists, helping to establish fair employment in terms of both race *and* gender as a major civil rights issue. It was, as we shall see, the chief motivation behind an April 1943 joint NAACP-UAW demonstration held in downtown Detroit's Cadillac Square—a prime downtown site during the early 1930s for marches and rallies of the unemployed—and the issue provided a point of convergence for a Black united front. This is not to say that the tensions were erased, however. Following Hill's defeat in the election for the presidency of the Detroit NAACP—the largest branch in the nation throughout the war years—McClendon moved to marginalize him. While he continued to give some public support to Hill and the Citizens Committee for Jobs in War Industry, at the same time McClendon effectively triangulated the committee by bringing Black unionist Walter Hardin, who also served as head of the UAW's Inter-racial Committee, onto the NAACP's board and making him cochair with Prince Clark of the branch's Labor Committee.

Drawing the NAACP and the UAW closer together would render the citizens committee redundant, even though the NAACP's Labor Committee was not without problems. As Gloster Current suggests in a July 1943 letter to Walter White, the group's constitution is "not clear on what a labor committee is to do, nor has the National Office, seemingly, given much thought to fully incorporating labor into its program." Finally, the Executive Board decided to no longer handle the group's finances, a move that, as Meier and Rudwick suggest, "delegitimized the Citizens Committee's operations among the mainstream of the black community. . . . Yet for a few brief moments it had brilliantly articulated black protest against race bias in Detroit's war plants and Hill himself remained a figure to be reckoned with."[51]

The committee's brief and brilliant activism not only solidified Hill's place within the city's civil rights community; it also contributed to the earning and purchasing power of the Black working class. The housing situation in Paradise Valley, as the thirty-four blocks of the city's east-side ghetto was still commonly known, was bad and getting worse as each year brought more and more Black migrants to the city in search of work and opportunities. Even as the rapid increase in population brought more squalor and misery to the neighborhood, the increase in earning potential fueled Black businesses, the underground economy of numbers runners, the building funds of churches, and the coffers of the entertainment industries. All of this made life in Detroit's African American communities a little more bearable. Musicians and singers, such as blues vocalist John Lee Hooker and saxophonist Yusef Lateef, worked in the factories by day and in small clubs in Paradise Valley by night. The Forest Club, Club 666, Brown's Bar, and the Paradise Theater, along with the Blue Bird on the west side, were patronized by working-class men and women. "Detroit had Ford and Chrysler as well as Studebaker and Packard plants," recalled one of the city's local musicians. "Black folks was coming up from the South and getting hired, and making a lot of money in those factories. Motown had a lot of folks." Years later this would still be the case: "Folks would work in the factory but would go and record for Berry Gordy"[52]

According to another local artist, Roy Brooks, "it was a whole social thing going on. . . . Music had a lot to do with it." The music produced and performed there embodied the struggles of the clientele, as southern gospel and blues traditions mingled freely with the fast pace of industrial life set against the backdrop of the assembly line.[53] Many of these clubs also drew an interracial crowd and were frequented by members of the Left. Going to black-and-tans (integrated clubs) was part of the culture of local members of the Left community.[54] In a sense, the clubs became part of the movement culture in Detroit in both direct and indirect ways. Man cannot live by protest alone. Churches provided solace and spiritual communion on Sunday mornings; clubs and cabarets spoke to the soul in a different way on Saturday nights. Some institutions aligned with the civil rights community gave local musicians another outlet with which to hone their skills and earn a little extra money. Musicians recall getting gigs at Detroit Urban League and NAACP affairs, and "in the churches you could perform—like St. Stephen, Hartford Baptist, and so on." Moreover, some local activists were themselves talented musicians. Gloster Current was a jazz pianist and director of the Gloster Current Orchestra, which played in area clubs. Future activist the Rev. Albert B. Cleage Jr. also had a small band that was able to secure a few bookings.[55] Hence, it is difficult not to see the cultural industry in Detroit as an integral part of social activism. It was a tradition that would continue to express itself over and over, from the performances of gospel singer and rhythm and blues artist Aretha Franklin in her father's church in Detroit to the explosion of Motown Records on the cultural (and political) scene.

CONFRONTING THE REACTIONARY RIGHT

As significant as these cultural and political developments were, they did not lessen (and probably increased) the level of ethnic and religious tension in Detroit. Union officials and civil rights activists, members of the Catholic hierarchy, and others may have taken a forthright stance on equality, but for a large segment of the white working class such proclamations and resolutions were essentially meaningless. Intense economic competition and the social distance between racial and ethnic groups often took precedence over ideological statements about the "Brotherhood of Man" and "Solidarity Forever." These tensions were compounded as more and more southern whites flocked to Detroit. The flowing waves of migration among African Americans have received far more attention by scholars, but the "Great White Migration" was equally important in reshaping the city. From 1940 to 1943, more than fifty thousand additional Black southern migrants arrived in Detroit; during the same period half a million southern whites followed a parallel path along the railroad tracks and Interstates 65 and 75.

The white migration began during World War I, hit its peak in the years between 1945 and 1960, and continued through the 1970s, leaving the South with a net decrease of almost five million people by 1960. Hailing from the lowlands and highlands, from the rural Appalachian Mountains and more urbanized areas such as Birmingham, Alabama, southern migrants were actively recruited during both world wars by industrialists in the Midwest, especially Illinois, Indiana, Ohio, Wisconsin, and, of course, Michigan. Only the Far West—the destination of the Joad family in *The Grapes of Wrath,* a novel and film that played a prominent role in creating the cultural iconography of the "Okie" migration—received more white southern men, women, and children. Detroit, too, had long been a popular destination for migrants. By 1930, the city had attracted over 66,000 white southerners, compared to close to 50,000 in Chicago, 30,000 in Indianapolis, 11,000 in Hamilton, Ohio, and over 8,000 in Flint, Michigan, where 60 percent of all southern migrants were white. Along with Flint, Detroit was very popular among migrants from Arkansas, followed by Tennessee and Kentucky.[56]

While many among this early wave of migrants returned home during the hardships of the Depression, the floodgates had reopened by the late 1930s and early 1941. This much larger secondary influx corresponded with the drive for industrial unionization and helped to solidify the stereotype of the southern "hillbilly" as a hardworking, hard-drinking "redneck" who was determinedly antiunion. It was a stereotype generated in part by industrialists, who seemed to favor the "less militant" southerner over the "more radical" white immigrant or native-born northerner. Part of this mixture of fact and fiction was captured in a 1935 *Nation* article by Louis Adamic.

> These hill-billies are for the most part impoverished whites, "white trash" or little better, from the rural regions. The majority of them are young fellows. They have had no close contact with modern industry or with labor unionism—this, of course, is their best qualification. Their number in Detroit is variously estimated as between fifteen and thirty thousand, with more coming weekly, not only in company-chartered buses but singly and in small groups on their own hook, for no one has a better chance of employment in Detroit these days than a Southerner of unsophisticated mien. . . . These workers are happy, are . . . much "safer"—for the next few

months anyhow, while big production is on—than local labor, poisoned by the ideas of unionism and perhaps even more dangerous notions.[57]

It is true that many of these newly arriving workers had not been involved in the struggles for industrial unionism that had created a sense of working-class solidarity. It is also true that many white southerners, much like their Black counterparts, were initially wary about the merits of unionization and thus tended to remain aloof. Yet, as historian Peter Friedlander notes in his study of the development of the UAW, their level of activity in the nascent union did eventually increase, and once converted to the cause of unionism they rarely backslid. Moreover, while the racism and conservatism so endemic to white southern culture remained a problem inside the racially, ethnically, and culturally diverse UAW, some of the men and women who migrated north had participated in union struggles in southern industries such as mining and textiles and they brought these experiences with them.[58]

By 1941 estimates placed the white in-migration to Detroit at over seventy-five thousand, with a housing vacancy rate of only 0.4 percent, which meant that clashes over housing in wartime Detroit were inevitable. The average migrant during this period had traveled roughly 340 miles to get to the city. Forty-one percent were from rural areas, 21 percent were last involved in agriculture, 68 percent were in Detroit for the first time, 10 percent were unemployed, more than 50 percent were alone, approximately 33 percent were living in a separate dwelling, over 50 percent were doubling up with others, and 10 percent were living in trailers and motels. Overall, these wartime migrants were younger than their predecessors; most dramatically, the proportion of white southern migrants in the labor force rose from 57 percent in prewar Michigan to 67 percent in wartime Detroit. Almost overnight, Detroit was transformed into a "boomtown" without the resources to accommodate the increase in population.[59]

Although many migrants traveled alone, they brought with them a distinctive culture that contributed to "a new cultural and ethnic mix that distinguished Detroit from New York and Cincinnati from Boston."[60] They brought with them a worldview rooted in a "plain-folk culture" of honor and dogged independence that emphasized "hard work and plain living [and] promised deliverance from the forces of power, privilege and moral pollution." They established neighborhoods throughout the city and developed cultural institutions as rich and varied as those simultaneously flourishing in Paradise Valley. As James

Gregory rightly observes in his study of transplanted southern culture in the Far West, it was also a culture structured by the twin pillars of the church and the saloon, two seemingly polarized elements in Protestant life. Drinking, hard drinking, in the South was often an act of defiance, but, Gregory writes, "it was a kind of ritualized, guilt-ridden defiance which in the end reinforced the religious-based moral codes." It was, he continues, part of "the large rhythm of sin and repentance that tied together this culture of moral opposites."[61]

This sense of eschatological rhythm captures a central feature of the lives of southern exiles struggling to sing familiar songs in a strange and often cold land. The songs themselves were an important contribution to the urban cultural mix of Detroit. The distinctive sound of "hillbilly" music was created within the southern diaspora by folk musicians who traveled from Florida to Ohio, Indiana, and Illinois before and during World War I and was propagated by radio programs such as *National Barn Dance* out of Chicago and by jukeboxes in local saloons wherever migrants settled. One popular song played repeatedly in Detroit area bars and social clubs catering to the white southern population was Danny Dill and Mel Tillis's "Detroit City," whose lyrics wailed:

> Home folks think I'm big in Detroit City.
> From the letters that I write they think I'm fine.
> But by day I make the cars, by night I make the bars.
> If only they could read between the lines.

As was the case with African Americans' blues songs, the hardships of life in Detroit's factories and neighborhoods figure prominently in a number of hillbilly ballads of heartache and homesickness, loss and disappointment.[62]

The other major way of dealing with feelings of cultural vertigo and personal insecurity was provided by religion and the hundreds of small churches that were interspersed with bars and music venues. Historians of religion in America have generally located the roots of the so-called postwar religious revival in the social dislocation engendered by the war years. But if it makes any sense at all to speak in terms of revival then it was not located in the mainstream Protestant congregations, which experienced a decline during the Depression and afterward. Rather, the revival was located in the rise of Holiness and Pentecostal churches and a variety of "free" Baptist congregations founded by southern whites (and Blacks) in overwhelming numbers in urban centers such as Detroit.[63] Perhaps because many migrants expected to return home after a brief sojourn up North, large and established churches with white southern congregations were fairly slow to develop. At the same time, established Northern Baptist churches were often unwelcoming and the styles of worship much more constrained and formal than in the South.

Moreover, the 1850s split between that Northern Baptist Convention (which became increasingly liberal) and the Southern Baptist Convention (which became increasingly conservative) could still be felt theologically and culturally. For many, the sheer variety of religious groups and institutions was overwhelming. "There's so many different denominations," one migrant recalled. "Southern people went to a Baptist or Church of God or Methodist type of church. . . . But so many northern people are Catholic people, an awful lot of them, so there's an awful lot of Polish people in Detroit"—not to mention the thriving chapter of the Nation of Islam and an array of sects and cults. Hence, for migrants in wartime Detroit, small storefront congregations and the services of "factory preachers" were a welcome alternative.[64]

The common observation that wartime Detroit had become part of a "Bible Belt" was not far off the mark as the city experienced a religious explosion that attracted national attention. "Since Pearl Harbor," a writer for *Collier's* magazine observed of the rise of small storefront and basement churches, "Detroit has become the scene of a greater American Armageddon."[65] By one account, "over 1,000 little church communities have been set up. . . . [The] bond with their preachers and little storefront and basement churches is about the only real tie for tens of thousands of uprooted families."[66] Although the existence of close religious ties, transplanted and transformed in a new urban environment, belies any simplistic understanding of "uprootedness," these small congregations, with their charismatic pastors, did help smooth the process of social adjustment for many believers.[67]

For Detroit's civil rights community, the existence of these churches was not an inherent problem. True, they grated on the nerves of more progressive, mainstream clergymen, who tended to equate fundamentalism with backward, conservative political views. But what concerned leftists the most was what they perceived to be the connections between these small churches, ethnoreligious bigotry, and racism in the automobile industry and the unions. "One of the best holds of the big executives on the life of the community is their influence through the local churches," stated a 1943 survey of religious and ethnic tensions in the city. Composed by a five-person research team that conducted nearly three dozen interviews between September 10 and September 30, it was meant to be a confidential report on the conditions facing civil rights organizations such as the Civil Rights Federation and the Jewish Community Council. As such, the "Survey of Religious and Racial Conflict Forces in Detroit" provides a virtual road map through the various sources of reaction in the "cauldron" of Detroit, with special emphasis on the "3,500 fundamentalist clergymen in Detroit," who, the authors believed, "look to the company for jobs and subsidies to help their storefront and basement churches."[68]

The accuracy of these numbers, and of the extent of any direct dealings between industry executives and these churches, should be questioned. On the one hand, there was a deep cultural and probably class bias against southerners and fundamentalists, who are often referred to as "primitive" and characterized as mindless followers of powerful men. On the other hand, there was an equally deep political bias against Detroit area auto executives, who the survey described as the most reactionary, antisocial, and uncooperative group of industrialists in the country. The policies of the notoriously anti-Semitic Henry Ford and the existence of an alliance between Black ministers and Ford in the 1920s and 1930s provided a precedent for the collusion of religion and industry, but there was a tendency to play rather fast and loose with the equation of fundamentalism and a reactionary politics in the service of big business. And yet there was some reasonable cause for concern. Gerald L. K. Smith, for example, proudly admitted that he "came so completely into the confidence of Mr. Ford that he specified: 'Everyone who sold merchandise to the Ford Motor Company contributed to [Smith's] Christian Nationalist Crusade.'"[69] Similar claims were made by and about the Rev. J. Frank Norris, who tended to huge flocks of followers both in Fort Worth, Texas, and at Detroit's Temple Baptist Church, of which he became pastor in 1934.

Although not well known today outside of fundamentalist circles, during the 1940s Norris was one of the most prominent and controversial ministers in the nation. Reverend Hill saw him as the civil rights community's "worst enemy," working hand in glove with the automotive industry to recruit Southern Baptist preachers to act as both rabble-rousers and pacifiers. "Norris gives these fundamentalist preachers their line here," Hill said. "He helps them get money from the bosses" and ties in their activities with "several Klan outfits."[70] Norris was indeed a powerful figure and a commanding orator possessed of a fire-and-brimstone style and a set of political positions that were as proindustry as they were anti-Black and anti-Semitic. Reverend Hill seemed very deliberate in his choice of the term *fundamentalist* as opposed to *evangelical* to describe Norris, as if he, as an evangelical, did not want the two confused.

There is a saying that a fundamentalist is simply an evangelical who is angry about something. Norris was angry. He was angry about "modernism," that is, the need to make adjustments to the modern world, especially what we would now call secular humanism. He was angry about theological liberalism, particularly those forms codified within the social gospel. He was angry about Darwinian theories of evolution, the application of higher criticism to the Bible, and the rejection of the Bible's inerrancy.[71]

Reverend Norris accepted the position in Detroit and shuttled back and forth between his two large congregations out of a desire, in part, to do battle with the Northern Baptist Convention. As a nominal Southern Baptist and, more important, as a fundamentalist—in fact he helped to spread the fundamentalist doctrine across the South and throughout the nation—Norris, who was born in Dadeville, Alabama, in 1877, adhered to a strict faith that viewed itself as being at odds with modernism in general and liberal theology in particular. A firm believer in biblical literalism and dispensational premillennialism,[72] Norris saw the hand of God bringing history rapidly to an apocalyptic close. Although the end was near, he nonetheless tirelessly preached the obligation of all true Christians to fight a host of threats to the faith and the American way of life, including modernism, communism, Jews, labor radicals, and any form of race mixing.

Temple Baptist, which Norris promptly removed from the Northern Baptist Convention when he assumed the pastorate, consisted mostly of transplanted southerners pulled north by opportunities in the auto industry. Temple, which was located on Fourteenth Street at Marquette, had roughly 800 members when Norris arrived in 1934. Two years later he reported an increase of over 4,000 new members at both churches, and after five years Temple alone had added another 6,193 souls. By 1946, the combined membership of Temple in Detroit and First Baptist in Fort Worth was 25,000.[73] By the 1940s Reverend Norris was a nationally known figure with perhaps the largest following of any American minister, making him something of a precursor to the pastors of today's megachurches. From his pulpits and a radio broadcast on Detroit's WJR, as well as in the pages of his paper, *The Fundamentalist* (with a circulation in Detroit and across the South estimated at around 40,000), Norris continued to preach a message of antimodernism, anticommunism, anti-Semitism, and anti-Black racism. He struck up a friendship with Father Coughlin, believing that fundamentalists had more in common with the

Catholic Coughlin than the "modernist machine Baptist." He was also popular with a number of the city's industrial leaders, including presidents and vice presidents of General Motors, Chrysler, and Ford.[74]

In the sections of the "Survey of Religious and Racial Conflict Forces" devoted to Norris, the authors note that he had "built up a religious community that rivals Father Coughlin's" and had the advantage of being "independent of denominational control," which meant that there was "no bishop to silence him." The survey also raises a number of claims (some made by Norris himself) that he received funding from area industrialists to expand the properties associated with Temple Baptist and to travel throughout the United States and Europe. Viewing Detroit as a major site in the struggle between "concentrated heavy industry and organized labor," any hint of a relationship between industrialists and figures such as Norris seemed indicative of the battles still to come. "It should not be taken as an indication of class-war mentality by the writer to note the fact [that] in Detroit the big executives are expecting an eventual knockdown and dragout fight against organized labor," they wrote. While some of the "older industrialists" believe it possible "to kick the unions out and restore the open shop," the more "realistic" executives expect "Detroit management to regain a dominant position and put the unions in a very subordinate position." In light of this inevitable confrontation, the industrialists "find it more useful to plan their labor strategy now and to begin gathering about them the kind of hard-talking and hard-hitting stooges (G.K. Smith, Frank Norris et al.) who can wage the eventual fight." For many within the civil rights community this was precisely the problem.[75]

There was a war to win—at home and abroad. When considering these fundamentalist congregations, the implication always (and at times unfairly) pointed in one direction: fascism. Antifascism, it should be recalled, had been the rallying cry for the civil rights community from at least 1935 onward. The existence of a series of fascist dangers—the police department, the Black Legion and the Klan, Father Coughlin and the Ford Motor Company—was a central part of the community-building process, and the CRF continued to keep records on the various hate groups that sprung up in and around the city. These antifundamentalist/antifascist sentiments persisted as Norris and Smith came to replace Coughlin as the city's leading religious demagogue to fear and revile after he was finally silenced by the Catholic Church in 1942.

The path that led Gerald L. K. Smith to the city in 1939 was long and indirect, taking him from the Midwest to the South to Detroit. Born in February 1898 in the small hamlet of Pardeeville, Wisconsin, roughly thirty-five miles south of Madison, Smith and his family were heirs to the spirit of independence and self-reliance of the midwestern pioneer. The son and grandson of Disciples of Christ preachers, he was also heir to a frontier faith, one that rejected the man-made and therefore hopelessly artificial creeds and denominational structures of Presbyterians, Methodists, and other mainline churches. Known variously as "Christians," "Churches of Christ," and "Disciples of Christ," the Disciples of Christ was founded in 1831 with the ultimate goal of transcending the factionalism of the Protestant faith and restoring the pristine, primitive church of the New Testament. As restorationists, they held the Bible to be an unambiguous guide for contemporary belief, practice, and organization. Unlike the brand of fundamentalism practiced by Norris, the Disciples generally opposed a "settled clergy" and discouraged even the taking of the title Reverend, which might explain why Smith found it so easy to drop once he left the official ministry. The Disciples were also loosely structured, requiring few creedal obligations and maintaining a diversity of views on the relationship between God and man.[76]

Theirs was not an emotional, spirit-infused style of worship. Rather, it was highly rational and even legalistic in approach. It was not, Smith recalled, "one of those excitable fundamentalist outfits where you could substitute groans and amens for a clear-cut discourse."[77] At the age of twelve he publicly confessed his faith in Jesus, preached a small sermon to his parents, and set about devoting his life to the ministry, taking seriously the restoration of "New Testament" religion. Having previously accepted pulpits in Illinois and Indiana, in 1929 he took a position at the Kingsway Christian Church in Shreveport, Louisiana, where he eventually met the politician Huey "the Kingfish" Long, the man who changed his life. Smith's association with Long was strange and intense. He was a self-described "hero-worshipper" who left the formal ministry to carry on a "ministry of truth to the people" as an organizer for Long's Share Our Wealth campaign—a populist Depression era movement that centered on a guaranteed annual income. Smith was so enthralled by Long that rumor had it he slept curled up at the foot of the Kingfish's bed.[78]

When Long was assassinated in September 1935, Smith delivered the eulogy to 150,000 mourners at the open-air funeral in Baton Rouge. Long's death left Smith rudderless and in search of a constituency. Given that Smith, like Coughlin (and Norris), had come to reject Franklin Roosevelt and vilify the New Deal, it is not surprising that he eventually washed up on the shores of Detroit and joined Coughlin in the failed anti-Roosevelt presidential campaign of William Lemke. He was also drawn to the city by promises of money and support from

Horace Dodge and other local businessmen. Although relations between Smith and Coughlin soon soured, Smith found Detroit, with its influx of migrant workers from the South and the rural Midwest, a congenial location and set up shop. He organized his Committee of One Million (he boasted of a membership of three million, but it was probably far fewer than even the one-million goal) and was "on the air every Sunday night naming all the Communists in the CIO." "WJR," he later recalled, "went out thousands of miles. You could even hear it in New Orleans." His following continued to grow as the United States, much to the dislike of his America First Party, entered World War II.[79]

No sooner had Coughlin's *Social Justice* ceased production and circulation than Smith's paper, *The Cross and the Flag*, made its appearance. While he tended to be much more obsessed by the specter of the "international Jew," his political theology was tinged with anti-Black racism. In one issue, he wrote:

> I know of no self-respecting person in the city of Detroit who is opposed to Negroes having every modern facility necessary to make them comfortable and to assist them in a desire to be progressive. But most white people will not agree to any of the following suggestions: (1) Intermarriage of blacks and whites; (2) Mixture of blacks and whites in hotels; (3) Inter-relationships between blacks and whites in a school system; (4) Wholesale mixture of blacks and whites on streetcars and on trains, especially where black men are permitted to sit down and crowd close to white women and vice versa. I have every reason to believe black women resent being crowded by white men on streetcars and elsewhere; (5) Permitting mixtures of blacks and whites in factories, especially where black men are mixed with white women closely in daily work.[80]

Of course, Detroit was filled with white workers who hardly needed any prodding from religious figures such as Smith and Norris. But, true to form, the civil rights community tended to focus on the dark side of fundamentalism, so much so that for local activists fundamentalism as fascism became the cause of almost every racial disturbance in the city, from racially motivated hate strikes in the plants to the controversy over government housing projects and the 1943 riot. If, as one observer put it, "Detroit was ripe for a socially conscious religious movement" during World War II,[81] it was also true that the city was a prime site for a religious war as battle lines were drawn over jobs, housing, and race mixing.

Intertwined with the dynamics of race, national origin, class, and the social distance between groups, housing had long been a touchy subject in Detroit—and would remain so well into the 1960s. Restrictive covenants, the racism of the Federal Housing Administration (FHA), which allowed Blacks to build homes in relatively few areas, and at times racially motivated violence had kept most of the African American population crowded into a few localized sites. Although the boundaries of the heavily congested east-side ghetto had expanded over the years and Blacks had begun to move to the west side of the city, Black migrant war workers faced a devastating housing shortage. "In spite of the fact that the Negro population has expanded from 135,000 persons in 1940 to approximately 185,000 in 1944," Shelton Tappes reported in his 1944 address to the Wayne County CIO Housing Conference, "it can definitively be stated that by no means has the availability of housing been proportionate to this population increase." As a result of legal and illegal restrictions, Tappes concluded, "Negroes must either pay excessive rentals for overcrowded quarters, or . . . live in dilapidated areas so unsafe or unsanitary that they are unfit for human habitation."[82] Rent strikes and protests filed with the city's Fair Rent Committee had done little to alleviate the housing problem, and it became clear that some sort of governmental intervention was necessary.

In September 1941, a temporary housing project for African American workers bearing the name of Sojourner Truth was constructed by the Detroit Housing Commission (DHC) and financed by the Federal Housing Administration. Black activists and their white supporters had hoped that the project could be used to break down segregation. Yet both the FHA and DHC had an explicit policy against "any attempt to change the racial pattern of any area in Detroit" since such an action "will result in violent opposition to the housing program."[83] Given the choice between segregated housing and no housing at all, a coordinated movement to challenge the status quo would have to wait. Unfortunately, even segregated housing did not sit well with whites in the neighborhood. The area's Polish residents, quipped Reverend Hill, thought that Sojourner Truth was a Polish woman. Realizing their "mistake," the project soon became embroiled in a seven-month-long controversy.[84]

The Sojourner Truth housing controversy, in which Reverend Hill played a leading role, was more than a battle over Black occupancy of defense housing.[85] Placed in a broader context, the controversy was also about the racial, ethnic, and religious tensions that afflicted the city throughout World War II. It was, as Coleman Young put it, "a microcosm of all the indigenous issues that plagued Detroit—the severe housing shortage, the competition between blacks and immigrants, the polarizing agenda of the left wing and the right, and the chronic insensitivity of the United States government."[86]

At the outset, however, the site seemed ideal. It was some distance from the main African American district on the city's lower east side but only three or four blocks from a Black middle-class community called Conant Gardens where nearly 125 Black families resided. Between Conant Gardens and the project, approximately 50 Polish families lived intermixed with a few Blacks. Both of the public schools in the neighborhood were racially and ethnically mixed. Moreover, in the past the relationship between Blacks and Poles, the city's two largest cultural minorities, had been relatively good. State senators Stanley Nowak and Charles Diggs, for instance, had run joint campaigns in city elections, and both were elected to represent districts with Polish and Black residents. Still, the DHC was met with a storm of criticism from residents led by Congressman Rudolph G. Tenerowicz, Joseph Buffa, an Italian American realtor, and Fr. Constantine Dzink, a Polish Catholic priest—who wanted to exclude non-whites altogether.

Father Dzink, who was also interviewed by the authors of the 1943 "Survey of Religious and Racial Conflict Forces," was in effect a Polish Catholic version of Gerald Smith and Frank Norris. He is described as "an aged, bald, Polish peasant" who has "power without a show of force" and regularly gives "'instructions' (not sermons) to his obedient Poles at five Masses each Sunday morning." Throughout the interview, Dzink continuously referred to "niggers" and the growing alliance between Blacks and Jews: "And now here in Detroit . . . we have the Jews and Niggers making a combination," he is quoted as saying. "The Niggers are trusting the Jews and giving up their money to them and defending them and voting for them. Nobody ever votes for a Jew except another Jew or a Nigger." As men of the cloth, Dzink, Frank, and Smith each latched onto racial and ethnic fears and then legitimated these fears by endowing them with a quasi-divine character. For each, the dictates of God and country rendered race mixing a dangerous practice.[87]

Citing the damage to property values and fear for the safety of "our white girls," an association—the Fenelon–Seven Mile Road Development Association, a white citizens committee—was formed. The association met weekly at Dzink's St. Louis the King parish church, located on St. Louis Avenue in the heart of a large Polish neighborhood, to hear speakers (including priests), and plan strategy.[88] Their persistence paid off. In the first in a series of reversals, the Federal Housing Administration turned the project over to whites. Immediately, the Black community, aided by the national offices of the NAACP and the Urban League, swung into action, and the controversy gave rise to a Black citizens committee. The committee was organized by the Rev. Horace A. White, who was the only African American member of the Detroit Housing Commission, State senator Charles Diggs, Louis Martin, J. J. McClendon, and Gloster Current of the NAACP, as well as attorney C. LeBron Simmons and Reverend Hill. Hill was elected as chairman, with Simmons serving as treasurer.[89]

As with the Citizen's Committee for Jobs in War Industry, which would be organized subsequently, the Sojourner Truth Citizens Committee reveals the degree to which coalition politics, organized around a single issue, was a real possibility in wartime Detroit. The committee arranged for mass meetings every Sunday at various churches to distribute information and raise funds. Its activities were supplemented by almost daily lunchtime meetings at the Lucy Thurman YWCA. Eventually, every major institution, organization, and socioeconomic class in the Black community was represented. Support from white leftists and liberals was a bit lacking at first, but as the controversy heated up the committee began to take on an interracial character. Jack Raskin and the CRF helped with legwork, strategy, and publicity. Using the mimeograph machine at the CRF office, they kept the community informed by producing a weekly newsletter, and details of the controversy were reported in the city's Black papers. While the majority of the members of Jewish community maintained a very low profile, "considerable financial assistance" was given by Jewish merchants led by Samuel Liebermann of the Jewish Community Council. To counter the inflammatory pronouncement of racist demagogues, Dr. Henry Hitt Crane, the noted pastor of the Central Methodist Episcopal Church, served on the Steering Committee and "spoke courageously before congregants, councilmen and irate white protestors."[90] Pressured by the foundry men of Local 600, particularly Horace Sheffield and Shelton Tappes, the local protested, manned picket lines, and donated large sums of money. Financial assistance from these sources, coupled with plate passing at weekly mass meetings that attracted over three thousands persons at their height, gave the committee an operating budget of over six thousand dollars—funds held and guaranteed by the Detroit NAACP.

Reverend Hill spoke at many of the mass meetings and large rallies held throughout the summer of 1942 and accompanied the interracial delegations that met with local, state, and federal officials. Geraldine Bledsoe, one of the dozens of women who became involved in the controversy, remembered Hill as being "in the forefront of it all. . . . We'd go out to the Sojourner Truth grounds and stand upon trucks and make speeches. . . . And he [Reverend Hill] really did give his, you know, enormous part of his physical strength, an enormous part of his economic resources as well."[91] With the involvement of prominent clergymen and the utilization of churches as meeting sites, the fight to save the Sojourner Truth homes for Black occupancy took the form of a religious crusade. "God give you courage to stand for the right you will be rewarded with the faith and support of the people," read a telegram Geraldine Bledsoe sent to Mayor Jeffries's office. Louis Martin, who was a Catholic, urged other Catholics and the archdiocese to support the citizens committee. Even a telegram from the secular-minded Jack Raskin begins with congratulations extended by "my church and organization."[92] For Reverend Hill, this religious bent was even more pronounced. "I believe," wrote Hill to a fellow clergyman who suspected that the Sojourner Truth committee was part of a communist plot "to expose the damnable hypocrisy of white America and the white Christian church, so-called—which cries 'Let us be brothers and have unity,' and yet fosters and harbors the best instrument that denial has to prevent the kingdom of God coming here on earth, which is racial hatred through the claim of white supremacy."[93]

Hill was careful to frame his and the committee's demands in terms of morality, justice, and loyalty to the nation and its principles. The Sojourner Truth controversy was, according to Hill, "a crisis of all America," and in this vein he reached out to the loyal and patriotic Polish Americans living near the Sojourner Truth homes. "Our enemies are the same," he declared, "Hitler hates both of us."[94] Hill was well aware of the positions in favor of Black occupancy that had been taken by Polish friends and fellow activists such as Stanley Nowak and his wife Margaret, as well as the outspoken and uncompromising Mary Zuk. In fact, Hill's view appeared to rest on the idea that no individual or group willing to give time and energy to the fight should be excluded.

The committee was victorious, but the price of victory was violence. As the first group of Black workers attempted to move in, they were met with over a thousand angry whites armed with clubs and knives. Although neither side involved in the controversy needed any outside encouragement, the white citizens committee blamed the violence and disruption on a communist conspiracy to stir up race hatred while Hill and the civil rights community put the blame on domestic fascists, religious demagogues, and the KKK. Once again, the connections between the KKK and fundamentalist demagogues (with anti-Black Catholics lumped in for good measure) were repeatedly invoked as a cause for unrest.

CLAUDE WILLIAMS COMES TO TOWN

Although the bigotry and episodes of violence in wartime Detroit had myriad causes, members of the city's Left remained fixated on what they perceived to be the religious roots of racism. Left-labor activists took every opportunity to denounce divisive religious figures such as Gerald Smith, J. Frank Norris, and their followers, but none of their efforts made much of a dent in either Smith's or Norris's popularity. The problem was that all of their activities took place almost exclusively on the level of negative propaganda. Rarely did they attempt to reach the thousands of the city's evangelical and fundamentalist believers directly in a language to which they could relate. The deficiencies in this tactic were finally addressed in the spring of 1942 when another potential solution to the perceived fundamentalist problem presented itself. In early May, just months after the violent scuffle generated by the Sojourner Truth housing controversy, Detroit's civil rights community was augmented by the arrival of Claude C. Williams, a southern white minister who preached a radical gospel inspired as much by Marx and Lenin as it was by Christ. Accepting a position as "minister of labor" for the Detroit Presbytery, Williams soon became involved in local political struggles. Just as the CIO and UAW deployed workers as organizers able to reach other workers, the Left welcomed Williams as a white religious southerner able to reach other white religious southerners. Along with many of the members of the civil rights community, Williams was convinced that the "500,000 uncritical ex-rural people who have come to Detroit . . . provide fertile soil for all who would sow 'Divide and Conquer' seeds of hate."[95]

Williams was no stranger to Detroit and acclimated quickly. He had first visited the city in the fall of 1941 as a speaker at an event organized by the CRF's Professional League for Civil Rights, when he probably met Hill for the first time, and he had a warm relationship with the Rev. John Miles, who was Hill's assistant pastor at Hartford Avenue Baptist. Miles was "an old colleague of Tennessee days" whose antiracist work with Williams had once led them to be run out of Chattanooga. He also came to know Stanley and Margaret Nowak, Maurice Sugar, and the other members of the civil rights community. "Claude Williams is living proof to many people that the church can be interested in the people and in the problems of labor and people generally," wrote Stanley Nowak in

1944. "He has made those most neglected and ignored by the church feel that the church is for them, too, and that there is a brotherhood, a living, vital brotherhood in the church today, that is above color and labels.[96]

Williams's ties to Reverend Hill were especially close. Not only did Hill literally thank God for Williams's work in Detroit, but the two men remained friends even after Williams returned to the South.[97] When he was defrocked in the mid-1950s for his "communistic" leanings and unorthodox theology, Hill reordained him at a ceremony performed at Hartford.[98] The two ministers shared a number of views, but, unlike Hill, Williams developed a highly intricate political theology and left behind a rather lengthy written record. Although his stay in Detroit would prove to be brief, Williams's sojourn is well worth considering for what it reveals about the nature of the relationship between religion and left-oppositional politics during the war.

Williams's background made him ideal for the task at hand. Born in 1895 to a family of tenant farmers in the hills of Weakley County, Tennessee, Williams was raised in a strict, fundamentalist household. A respect for the often unyielding land and a pious belief in the promise of Heaven and the fear of Hell structured his early life. Indeed, Williams's reflections on his fundamentalist upbringing and early education offer some insights into the general nature of these beliefs.

> I entered the ministry in 1921, because I felt that God had called me to preach the Gospel. I believed that there was a literal burning Hell of Fire and Brimstone and that there was a beautiful, pleasant, joyous Heaven. I believed it. And I loved people. . . . And I didn't want people to go to Hell. So I entered the ministry to save their souls. . . . The evangelical emphasis was the heart of all of my messages.[99]

After completing his religious training at Bethel College, a small seminary run by the Cumberland Presbytery, Williams married Joyce King, a Bethel missionary student from rural Mississippi. With Joyce, he accepted the pastorate of a cluster of Presbyterian congregations in middle Tennessee, where the two were warmly received.

Williams's evangelicalism remained, but the context was gradually altered as he began to rebel against the strict fundamentalism of his youth. The pietistic view of God and Christianity that he and Joyce were given as a birthright was increasingly brought into question as the young couple began to explore the central themes of modern religious thought. When Williams discovered Harry Emerson Fosdick's *The Mod-*

ern Uses of the Bible in 1927, he called it a "turning point" in his life. Like other theologians and practitioners of a militant social gospel, Fosdick counseled his readers to ignore biblical literalism (and apparent factual inaccuracies) and focus instead on the revolutionary potential of Christianity. Following this advice led Williams away from a conventional church ministry and toward a new struggle with the meaning of religion and its application in everyday life and politics. Taking a leave of absence from his congregation, he enrolled in the Rural Church School at Vanderbilt University where he participated in a series of summer seminars taught by Alva W. Taylor, who, like Fosdick, had adopted a perspective on the role of religion in modern society inspired by the social gospel. Williams credited both men with aiding him in the removal of "theological debris" from his understanding of Christ and His teachings.[100]

Williams also credited other students at Vanderbilt—especially Don West, Miles Horton, Howard Kester, and Ward Rogers, all of whom would become deeply involved in socialist, trade union, and civil rights work in the South—with helping him to see the connections among race, gender, class, and economic exploitation within the context of American capitalism.[101] By the time he left Vanderbilt, Williams had already developed an "unorthodox" view of the Bible and Christianity. The differences between him and Reverend Hill in this regard are instructive. In Hill's preaching style, for instance, political affairs and social commentary were generally appended to the beginnings and ends of his sermons. "The meat of his sermons" recalled the Rev. Charles Adams, Hill's protégé and the current pastor of Hartford, "did not seem to me to be titled in the direction of his ideological commitments." Rather, he tended to focus on the exegesis of biblical themes and stories and the application of moral and spiritual—as opposed to overtly political—teachings. I have suggested throughout that Hill's politics was very much rooted in his religious commitment to social justice, but there was, as Adams observed, a sort of theological separation between his sermons and his activism. Unlike Hill, who arguably never lost his evangelicalism or his conservative understanding of the Bible, Williams infused theology with politics and social commentary at every turn.[102]

Moreover, Williams was dedicated to stripping away much of the supernaturalism associated with religion. Thomas Jefferson famously created a revised version of the Bible by literally cutting away the references to miracles and other "irrational" and "unbelievable" passages. Williams did this and more—he transformed Jesus into the very human leader of a class-conscious revolutionary movement aimed at destroying "fascist" Rome. This, Williams argued, was a more authentic vision of

Jesus, one that could be fruitfully juxtaposed with the obtuse "Christ-centered" theology of Saint Paul. Such views, coupled with his growing affinity for labor unions, his attacks on segregation—not to mention his smoking, drinking, and swearing—precipitated his removal from his position at the church in Paris, Arkansas, where pictures of Eugene Debs, Lenin, and Jesus (his three heroes) adorned the parsonage walls. In the following years, Williams traveled throughout the state organizing hunger strikes, working with the Southern Tenant Farmers Union (STFU) and laying the foundations for what he envisioned as "a mass people's movement."[103]

The cumulative result of Williams's efforts was the People's Institute of Applied Religion. The genesis of the institute was the Sunday evening "Philosopher's Club" sessions held in the Williams home in Paris, Arkansas, where Claude and Joyce were sent in 1930 to serve a small Presbyterian mission church and where the young couple threw themselves, body and soul, into efforts to organize mine workers with an eye toward joining the United Mine Workers of America. The Sunday sessions were a regular feature of church life, involving open and wide-ranging discussions of religion, politics, and culture. As Williams traveled across the state to other mining regions, similar "socio-Christian forums" were established. It was through this kind of religious and political work that Williams first came to the attention of prominent theologians such as Reinhold Neibuhr and sympathetic religious laypersons such as Norman Thomas, who sent his regards as "a former Presbyterian minister and as a Socialist." From his post at the Union Theological Seminary, Neibuhr offered more than his regards. He also sent financial and spiritual support, the former through the auspices of the seminary and its Fellowship of Christian Socialists and the latter through a sporadic correspondence that lasted several years.[104]

Even after Williams was forced to leave Paris in 1935—decamping first to Fort Smith, Arkansas, where he was jailed for three months for participating in a demonstration by unemployed workers and tried for heresy by the Presbytery, and then to the relative safety of Little Rock, where he and Joyce became heavily involved in the STFU—they continued to devote themselves to worker education and organizing in a religious context. It was in Little Rock that Williams got his first major opportunity to truly test some of his developing ideas of how to use the Bible as a foundation for political transformation, as his work with the STFU encouraged him to set up a school—the New Era School of Social Action and Prophetic Religion—to train grassroots organizers. Further, by 1938 he had taken over the directorship of the state's most notable labor school, Commonwealth College (founded by utopian socialists in the 1920s), which allowed him to use his work with sharecroppers as the field program of the institution. At Commonwealth, Williams collaborated with a local artist, Dan Genin, to develop charts and visual aids that demonstrated Williams's political interpretations of biblical themes and passages. The charts from this period were simple line drawings in black and white, such as one called the Divine Triangle, in which Love, Hope, and Faith were juxtaposed with Individualism and equated with the Religion of the People using plus and minus signs to express the relationships: Love, Hope, and Faith minus Individualism equals Religion of the People.[105]

This productive period in Williams's life did not last long. Sectarian conflict within the STFU, primarily between socialists and communists, led to his expulsion from the board, and he subsequently resigned from Commonwealth. In the aftermath of disappointment and potential defeat, he persevered by transforming the New Era School into the People's Institute of Applied Religion. Formally organized in 1940, the PIAR was the culmination of years of practical work as an organizer among both rural farmers and industrial workers whose perceptions of life were deeply rooted in religious belief. In its initial years, it worked closely with the sharecropper movement and the emerging activism of the CIO in the South, for which it received union support and praise. The PIAR also received support from Niebuhr and Harry Ward, as well as organizations such as the Methodist Federation for Social Action, the Church League for Industrial Democracy, and especially the National Religion and Labor Foundation, whose executive secretary, Willard Uphaus, was a friend of Williams's. Liston Pope, a student of the role of religion in the Gastonia strikes in textile mills and author of *Millhands and Preachers,* was on the board in the early 1940s.[106]

In terms of practical programs, the PIAR sponsored three-to-ten-day institutes for roughly fifty people equally divided between Blacks and whites and men and women. The participants were generally drawn from members of the clergy and lay preachers because, as Williams put it, "[T]hese were people who had some tendency toward leadership." These leaders were "the toiling Negro and white preachers, exhorters, deacons and teachers among the mass religious movements, denominations and sects." Using scripture, songs, prayer, and the increasingly elaborate visual aids designed by Williams, the PIAR attempted to *supplement* religious piety with a conscious critique of the social system and its failings. "We were realistic," Williams explained years later, "or at least we tried to be."

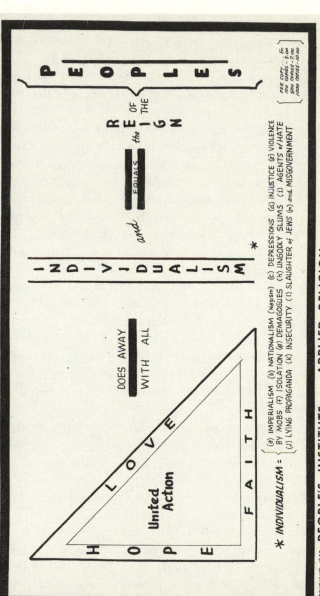

THE DIVINE TRIANGLE

SCRIPTURE: I COR. CHAPTER 13

TEXT: NOW ABIDETH FAITH, HOPE, LOVE, THESE THREE ; BUT THE GREATEST OF THESE IS LOVE.
I COR. 13:13

PEOPLES

R
E OF
the N THE
G
I

EQUALS

and

I N D I V I D U A L I S M

*

DOES AWAY
WITH ALL

L O V E

United
Action

H O P E

F A I T H

* *INDIVIDUALISM =* { (a) IMPERIALISM (b) NATIONALISM (Nazism) (c) DEPRESSIONS (d) INJUSTICE (e) VIOLENCE
BY MOBS (f) ISOLATION (g) DEMAGOGUES (h) UNGODLY SLUMS (i) AGENTS of HATE
(j) LYING PROPAGANDA (k) INSECURITY (l) SLAUGHTER of JEWS (m) and MISGOVERNMENT }

• COPYRIGHT 1942 PEOPLE'S INSTITUTE of APPLIED RELIGION - 313 S.E. FIRST ST. - • EVANSVILLE • INDIANA

PER COPY 5c
100 COPIES - 3.00
500 COPIES - 7.00
1000 COPIES - 10.00

"The Divine Triangle" chart, People's Institute of Applied Religion, 1941 (Claude C. Williams Collection. Courtesy of Walter P. Reuther Library, Wayne State University.)

We discovered that the fact that people believed in the Bible literally could be used to an advantage. . . . Being so-called fundamentalists, accepting the Bible verbatim, had nothing whatsoever to do with a person's understanding of the issues that related to bread and meat, raiment, shelter, jobs and civil liberties. Therefore, our approach was not an attempt to supplant their present mindset, but to supplement it with a more horizontal frame of reference. And we found that supplementing and supplanting turned out to be the same thing."[107]

In this way, the PIAR worked to influence religious leaders—and, by extension, those who looked to them for guidance and reassurance—to renounce the sin of ultraindividualism, racism, sexism, and ultimately the capitalist system as a whole.

A PIAR report from the fall of 1941 describes several institutes held in Cotton Belt places such as the Missco, Arkansas, federal farm; Longview, Texas; Hayti, Missouri; and Osceola and Carson Lake, Arkansas. The work of these institutes was carried out by a group of colleagues who joined the organization shortly after its formation, including the Rev. Owen H. Whitfield, a Black Missouri preacher and codirector of the PIAR; Williams's brother Dan, himself a sharecropper and preacher in Missouri; the Rev. A. L. Campbell, a white preacher and dynamic organizer from Arkansas; Don West, who had studied with Williams under Alva Taylor at Vanderbilt; Harry and Grace Kroger; and others. Thus, by the time Williams was invited to Detroit in the spring of 1942, he could boast of a substantial organization with a two-year track record of success.[108]

In his correspondence with the Rev. Henry Jones prior to his arrival in Detroit, Williams claims to be thoroughly convinced of two things: first, that to do anything about the growing intolerance in America "we must do something among the people whose economic conditions and lack of understanding have made them intolerant"; and, second, that the international situation and conditions at home "provide an ideal opportunity to launch an all out offensive for justice and goodwill among these people through prophetic religion." In this regard, his decision to follow the waves of southern migrants to the Arsenal of Democracy is understandable, especially given his belief that these migrants "constitute the balance between democracy and fascism, being potentially the democratic instruments for a just society and potentially the shock troops for an unjust society"—between, that is to say, the two traditions that Louis Martin claimed structured the tensions in America and wartime Detroit.[109]

When Claude Williams arrived in Detroit, he found many willing allies, including Reverends Hill and Miles, who were supportive of the PIAR's work among "factory preachers." Williams immediately grasped the importance of the men, and occasionally women, who worked in the factories during the week and ministered to the spiritual needs of tiny congregations in storefronts and basements on Sundays, as well as those who set up makeshift altars and held services in the plants themselves. He was particularly interested in the Pleasant Valley Tabernacles, which, as he explained to the authors of the "Survey of Religious and Racial Conflict Forces," began in the Ford plants and were "in most of the large plants," including "very large well-supported Tabernacles in Department 71 of the Dodge Truck Mound Road Plant, in the DeSoto Gun Plant, and in the Dodge Main Plant." The report summarizes "Congregations of these Tabernacles comprise, in addition to fellow workers, company officials and their white collar workers, plus the munitions workers from the Southern Baptist churches."

> The pastors are usually ignorant and often almost illiterate. These pastors of the basement churches preach and pray for their college-bred bosses, company officials, and favorite stenographers. They must be laughing up their sleeves. Of course the preachers are flattered and are given good enough collections to keep the little basement churches going.[110]

These shop preachers were the PIAR's chief target audience. One prominent recruit, Virgil Vanderburg, an African American shop preacher and worker employed by the Packard Company, strove to implement the institute's teaching—its belief that "the starting point of learning is at the level of the known"—at his Packard plant. Beginning in February 1943, he told an audience at a PIAR event, "we gathered the names of and made acquaintance with some twelve work-a-day preachers" at the plant. This group served as "a nucleus" for PIAR recruitment and training and allowed them to steadily increase their in-plant network of "Negro and white brothers in the ministry." "At present," Vanderburg proudly related, "there are twenty religious meetings in Packard each week at the noon hour" and the number of "listeners at the Thursday and Friday meetings combined far outnumbered the attendance at the monthly Packard Local union meetings."[111]

Such laudable efforts to fight fire with fire, did not prevent the outbreak of hate strikes at Packard touched off by the upgrading of Black workers. On June 3, 1943, twenty-five thousand white workers walked out and many milled around the gates of the plant listening to local members of the KKK deliver anti-Black diatribes. A frantic UAW president, R. J. Thomas, had to threaten the men with the loss of their jobs to get them back to work.[112] As Williams observed in a 1943 article entitled "Hell Brewers of Detroit," an "exposé" of religious fascist and racist demagogues in the city, Detroit seemed headed for a major racial and religious explosion. And Williams, personally, seemed headed for a showdown with Gerald Smith.

Smith was featured prominently in Williams's article, as he was in the Civil Rights Federation's pamphlet "Smash the Fifth Column" and the 1943 survey, which quotes him extensively. In response, Smith contacted the Presbyterian hierarchy and demanded that Williams be silenced. Years later Smith was still angry, calling Williams a "fraudulent clergyman" who was as "completely in the Communist apparatus as a man could be."[113] Throughout the summer of 1943 Smith distributed copies of a "confidential" report on Williams, detailing his "subversive" activities in the South and the city to members of the local Presbytery along with a variety of local religious figures—including, oddly enough, Reverend Hill. The feud between Smith and Williams lasted for years, even after Williams left Detroit.

Throughout the spring and summer the city remained as much a study in contrasts as Smith and Williams. On the one hand, the UAW and NAACP worked together to bring ten thousand of their members to Cadillac Square to protest racial discrimination in Detroit area plants. On the other hand, hate strikes and periodic violent flare-ups seemed to portend a darker future. Speaking at the rally at Cadillac Square, Walter White added his voice to a growing chorus of foreboding. "Let us drag out into the open what has been whispered throughout Detroit for months, that a race riot may break out here at any time." "The ugly truth," agreed the Association of Catholic Trade Unionist's *Wage Earner*, "is that there is a growing, subterranean race war going on in the City of Detroit which can have no other ultimate result than an explosion of violence, unless something is done to stop it." "Detroit," warned a writer for *Life* magazine, "Is Dynamite."[114]

The short fuse was finally lit on Sunday, July 20, 1943, when over ten thousand residents crowded onto Belle Isle, the city's island park, seeking relief from the heat. Fights broke out across the park, escalating throughout the day, and rumors swiftly spread throughout the city's downtown neighborhoods. Many residents of Paradise Valley heard and believed that a white mob had thrown a Black woman and child—in some versions a pregnant Black woman—off the wide stone bridge that joins the island to the city. In other neighborhoods, the rumor was that a Black mob attacked a white woman. In any case, by 11:00 p.m. some five thousand people were battling along the expanse of the bridge while the violence spread to the city proper.

Throughout the night, roaming white mobs attacked Black residents, while the looting and burning continued nearly unabated. Representatives from the civil rights community, including Reverends Hill and White, Father Dade, Jack Raskin, and the UAW's R. J. Thomas, among others, gathered at the Lucy Thurman YWCA for a strategy meeting with Mayor Edward Jeffries, who was denounced by the assembled group for his inaction. After nearly twenty-four hours of violence and chaos, the governor proclaimed a state of emergency and the mayor took to the airwaves to plead for calm. By this time, nearly 75 percent of the city had been affected by the riot, sixteen transportation lines were cut off, the Fire Department was struggling to contain multiple fires, and city hospitals were operating at full capacity. After almost two days, federal troops entered the city and forcibly cleared the streets; shortly thereafter, President Roosevelt signed a proclamation placing Detroit under federal martial law. By the time order was restored, thirty-four people had been killed (twenty-five African Americans, seventeen of whom were killed by the indiscriminate shooting of the police into buildings and crowds around Hastings Street), more than seven hundred people had sustained injuries, over two million dollars' worth of property had been destroyed, and a million man-hours had been lost from war production. Overall the city was deeply scarred both physically and psychologically.[115]

Everyone seemed to have a different and often conflicting story about who or what had caused the riot. The mayor's office, in a "white paper," held African Americans and their Left and liberal white allies responsible and attempted, in the eyes of the civil rights community, to whitewash the whole affair. In response, union officials (including UAW president R. J. Thomas), city councilman and former UAW organizer George Edwards, the NAACP, the NNC, the Urban League, the International Labor Defense, the National Lawyers Guild, the Association of Catholic Trade Unionists, and the Communist Party, among others, joined a coalition that spanned the left, right and center of the city's civil rights community and called for a grand jury investigation into the riot and its aftermath. Leftists tended, by and large, to place the blame on the KKK, Father Coughlin, J. Frank Norris, Gerald Smith, and other "hell brewers" in the city. Others, as a writer for the *Detroit News* recorded, blamed southern whites, who "have come here in vast numbers, bringing with them their Jim Crow notions of the Negro." One of the stranger rumors blamed a shadowy organization, the Development of Our Own, founded by Satakata Takahashi (his real name was Naka Nakane), who represented himself as a major in the Japanese army dedicated to assisting African Americans in the fight against white supremacy.[116]

Reverend Hill, for his part, split the blame among southern whites, religious demagogues, and "jitterbugs": a reference to the unconventional style adopted by Black and white youth in Detroit (and other cities) during the war. Hill saw no larger social or cultural meaning behind the zoot suit or its place in Black urban youth culture. While he always took a special interest in the welfare of young people, he had little respect for this type of cultural politics. During the riot he had had a run-in with the jitterbugs in the form of a rock thrown at his head through a car window. "Oh my God, we got the wrong man," the youths are reported as saying—evidently because of his light complexion they thought he was white. The young men apologized profusely and offered to drive him home. Hill was fine except for "a great big hickey on the back of his head about the size of an orange." "A peculiar thing," he recalled, is that "when I came on the [white] area, they threw rocks at me; so I got them from both sides."[117]

Thousands of stories make up what historian Dominic J. Capeci Jr. calls the "layered violence" that affected the city and its residents in myriad ways. In one small but interesting footnote to African American radical history, one of the young men caught on the bridge between the island and the city was a Black southern migrant and autoworker (and Local 600 member) named Robert F. Williams. Inspired by the militancy of Black UAW members, he penned a piece for the *Daily Worker* in which he promised to one day return to the South and launch a movement for Black freedom and dignity. Years later, he would do precisely that as head of the Monroe, North Carolina, NAACP and an advocate of armed self-defense. In an instance of at least this little corner of history coming full circle, his uncompromising example, his 1962 book *Negroes with Guns,* and articles published in his *Crusader* magazine would inspire a generation of Black radicals in Detroit in the early 1960s.[118]

On a larger level, the riot changed everything and nothing. In an effort to stem the tide of criticism, Mayor Jeffries hastily organized an interracial committee on race relations, to which Hill was appointed, although it had little real power. This maneuver became yet another reason for the civil rights community to work for Jeffries's defeat in the upcoming elections. Since his election in 1939 Jeffries had maintained strong support within the Black community, but his handling of the riot, as well as his order against interracial housing, had tarnished his reputation and encouraged African American voters to back the labor slate. "We shall support the labor slate because we believe that the Negro people and organized labor are committed in theory and practice to democratic ideals which must be upheld at all costs," wrote Louis Martin.[119] Unfortunately, this strategy backfired and Jeffries was able to turn the animus of the Blacks and the civil rights community to his advantage.

Throughout the campaign, Jeffries attacked the "un-American" cabal of union officials and their Black allies and was widely accused of opening the door "for the Klan, for pro-fascists, the Smithites, and all other reactionary elements in the population."[120] Nonetheless, Jeffries painted his political opponent, Judge Frank Fitzgerald, as a puppet of the UAW and repeatedly used the alliance between Blacks and the UAW to ignite racial fears. "Arrayed against me," Jeffries proclaimed, "are groups demanding mixed housing—the mingling of Negroes and whites in the same neighborhoods. . . . The Negroes of Detroit, in the primary, voted against me almost unanimously. I take it, therefore, that my opponent must have promised to make mixed housing the policy of his administration if elected."[121] The Jeffries campaign set a pattern in municipal politics that was to endure for the next two decades. On the one hand, his negative attacks brought the identity of interests between African Americans and union officials into clearer focus. In 1943 and thereafter, Black districts voted overwhelmingly for the labor slate. Such levels of support had not been the norm previously. On the other hand, the politics of race, labor, and Red baiting proved successful in unifying conservatives and reactionaries while splitting the vote of the union's white rank and file.

All the elements of what would emerge as a pattern dominating postwar politics in the city were in place on November 4 as nearly four hundred thousand citizens went to the polls. Jeffries was reelected by a comfortable margin of thirty-five thousand votes. Fitzgerald carried all of the African American districts, as well as the city's west side, where a number of UAW members resided, while Jeffries racked up landslide victories in outlying, low-income white districts, which were also heavily populated with UAW members. For the union and the civil rights community, the election was both the embodiment of Detroit's postriot problems and an important political lesson. The need to obtain political power and representation within municipal government became a leading priority, especially for the Black community. All prior attempts to get an African American elected to the Common Council had failed, including the 1943 campaign of attorney Edward Simmons. Renewed efforts to do so became more pressing than ever, and the man chosen for the job would be none other than Reverend Hill. As World War II drew to a close, the civil rights community could only look forward and wonder and fret and hope and pray about the future. It was already clear, however, that Red and race baiting would become a key factor in the ongoing struggle between the two American traditions.

FOUR

TO FULFILL
YESTERDAY'S PROMISE

Anticommunism and the Demise
of the Early Civil Rights Community

> Our great city of over two million people made a mighty contribution
> during the war years, as the arsenal of democracy, toward the defeat
> of mankind's enemies. Today the anxious hope of our citizenry is
> that our fond city will show the way of fulfillment of yesterday's
> promise to the people of economic security, expanding prosperity,
> cultural enrichment and strengthened democracy.
> —Rev. Charles A. Hill (1945)

Detroit's civil rights community entered the immediate post–World
War II period as a well-organized, if not always successful, center of
social protest. The war had provided a context in which demands for
civil rights and social justice, particularly for African Americans, could be
framed within a language of national defense, antifascism, and the
spread of democratic principles. The war years had also presented a
number of practical challenges that had helped to solidify a movement
culture, deepening the community's resolve to continue to work for
meaningful social change. Like most Americans, members of the city's
civil rights community mourned the death of President Roosevelt and
joined in the celebrations on V-E Day and V-J Day. They welcomed home
sons and husbands, friends, comrades, and lovers.

They were, again like most Americans, apprehensive about the future—about the new president, Harry S. Truman; about the possibilities of a return to depression and unemployment; and about the new world emerging from the death and destruction of a war ended by the unleashing of atomic power. But these apprehensions were mixed with hope and determination that the promise of American democracy could now, perhaps, finally be fulfilled, especially since the evils of European racism had been exposed and discredited. If a fascist regime premised on notions of racial superiority and domination could be defeated abroad, then its counterpart in the United States could likewise be dismantled.[1]

The Detroit Council of the National Negro Congress reflected the general tone of postwar activism in the city in the summer of 1945. The 112 delegates attending the NNC's "Plan for Victory and Peace" conference discussed and supported resolutions on full employment during and after reconversion, on integration of the armed forces, on abolishing the poll tax, and on the advantages of an even stronger Black-union alliance to achieve greater representation in municipal government.[2] Throughout the immediate postwar period, Detroit's civil rights community fought against a gathering storm of conservatism and repression. Both the institutions and individual members of the city's Left engaged in various efforts to save the New Deal coalition and, as the Rev. Charles A. Hill put it during his first campaign for a seat on the city's Common Council, "to show the way of the fulfillment of yesterday's promise."[3] To do so meant a struggle, both locally and nationally, against the forces arrayed against them. Nationally, congressional electoral gains by conservative Republicans and Democrats had created a powerful coalition that was vocally opposed to extending the more progressive measures of the New Deal and acting on the demands of cultural and political minorities. By 1948, most communists and fellow travelers within the CIO's member unions would be purged (the process was nearly complete by 1952); the Progressive Party, which backed Henry Wallace against Truman in the politically decisive—and divisive—presidential campaign of 1948, had suffered a stunning defeat; and organizations such as the NAACP, the Americans for Democratic Action (ADA), and the Association of Catholic Trade Unionists had promulgated a series of explicitly anticommunist policies.

The split between liberals and leftists had become irreversible.[4] On one side stood liberal anticommunists, who supported Truman and his cold war policies of containment; on the other side stood a much-beleaguered Communist Party accompanied by activists, such as Reverend Hill, who were for various reasons unwilling to denounce the party and its front organizations. Stanley Nowak, whose support for Wallace gave the government yet another reason to try to deport him, articulated the Left's domestic- and foreign-policy critiques of Truman and the emerging anticommunist status quo when he pointed out that "just two years after the close of the war which was to defeat fascism and clear the road for social progress . . . we find reaction sweeping our land, the rights of labor being destroyed, civil and democratic rights trampled upon, and an alarming clamor for war against our allies and friends, the Slav nations."[5]

Rejected by liberals, the city's Far Left was rendered all the more vulnerable to McCarthyism.[6] Under these circumstances, leftists redoubled their efforts to protect civil liberties, especially their own, and extend civil rights, attempting throughout to shore up their depleted numbers. The NNC, for example, had merged with the International Defense League, the National Federation for Constitutional Liberties, and in Detroit the Civil Rights Federation to form the national Civil Rights Congress, whose Detroit chapter was among the strongest in the nation. "The Civil Rights Congress shall be broadly based on the people of the United States," stated the resolution of incorporation adopted at the group's initial meeting, which was held in Detroit in May 1946, "and to that end shall take into membership all individuals willing to support its program, shall establish branches throughout the country and arrange for unification, affiliation or cooperation with existing groups and organizations to achieve maximum unity and effectiveness in carrying out its programs." Although its executive board included such well- known liberals as Mary McLeod Bethune and Dr. Benjamin Mays, the president of Morehouse College, the government wasted little time in branding this new organization as "one of the most dangerous front groups in the nation."[7]

Through the CRC and other groups, such as the Michigan Progressive Party, the Left carried on its battles for a permanent Fair Employment Practice Commission on the federal level and a state FEPC within Michigan. It sought guarantees for fair housing and battled anti-civil-liberties legislation such as the Taft-Hartley Act, the Smith Act, and a proliferation of municipal loyalty oaths. It also fought an impressive number of individual cases of police brutality and misconduct. These measures offered a significant but ultimately temporary bulwark against the destructive forces of anticommunism. By the early 1950s, the city's Left community was forced to adopt an almost wholly defensive posture. The processes through which the city's Left went from a dynamic local movement to an increasingly marginalized collectivity make for a complex and often dramatic story of national, state, and local repression, as well as liberal anticommunism—all of which narrowed political alternatives not just in Detroit but throughout the nation.

It is also a story of the personal toll that the cold war took on the public and private lives, on the friendships and loyalties, of activists who were forced to defend themselves and their politics. Indeed, friendship played a large role in the decline of the Detroit Left. What a party, a union, or a civil rights agency says publicly does not always correspond to the actions of its individual members; interpersonal relationships are always more fluid and complicated than a party line. That is to say, individuals active in the city's civil rights struggles did not necessarily end long-standing friendships because of political differences. The warm ties of comradeship, affection, and in some cases love were a source of comfort for the men and women who found themselves increasingly under attack. Equally important was the sustaining political faith of local activists who, faced with public accusations of betrayal and perfidy, stuck to their convictions and principles. Finally, it is the story of a liberal-labor coalition that guided much of the city's civil rights activism in the late 1950s and early 1960s when the nation witnessed the dramatic appearance of a southern-based movement.

CANDIDATE HILL

The tragic events that culminated in the racially motivated riot of 1943 continued to shape the context of political activism in the postwar period. The problems of inadequate housing, employment discrimination, police brutality, and de facto racial segregation were as pressing as ever. As a result, "intelligent political action" was widely deemed to be the "next step" for the city's civil rights community. "We must not merely defeat those bigots in office," urged Louis Martin in a *Michigan Chronicle* editorial, but

> we must take positive action on behalf of candidates who are dedicated to the welfare of the whole community, candidates who will stand up and fight for justice for all regardless of color. Neither the housing issue nor any other political issue will be justly resolved until the overall majority of Detroit organizes its political strength and takes affirmative action in behalf of good government for all the people.[8]

Although Martin alluded to coalition politics as good government for all people, Black Detroiters viewed gaining representation, particularly on the city's Common Council, as an especially pressing political necessity.

There were hopes of re-creating the success of activists in New York, where Black communist Benjamin Davis had been elected councilman in 1943—the same year in which Adam Clayton Powell Jr. left the council to run for Congress—and where in March 1945 Governor Thomas Dewey signed a state FEPC law, the first U.S. law prohibiting employment discrimination in the private sector. Black Detroiters could also look to nearby Cleveland, where an African American city councilman had recently been elected.9 In urban communities across the nation, the goal was to secure a voice in local decision making. This was an even more difficult task in Detroit than in most places, with the exception of the South, because Progressive reformers in the early twentieth century had eliminated the city's ward system and replaced it with nonpartisan, citywide elections. Instead of a system in which each ward elected its own councilman, Detroit's Common Council was reduced to nine members elected at large.

Although this reform had been initiated in the interests of "good government," African Americans had long suspected that its real purpose was to diffuse their potential political power. Hill, believing that these changes had been made because "the Negro was becoming so well organized," worked for the resumption of the ward system, "just like we have districts for Congress or in the Legislature." "We worked to get re-districting, and to go back to the ward system," Snow Grigsby, founder of the protest-oriented Civic Rights Committee in the early 1930s, concurred, "because we found, in an election, that councilmen lived way out in areas too far away from the people . . . [and there was] no councilman down in the inner city where one is needed. . . . We tried for many years to get this set up in wards, but people [in power] didn't go for it. . . . [I]f we had the ward system, we would have enough in there who would have some voice in the Common Council."10

Hill, Grigsby, and others who were critical of the at-large council did have a point. While the Black vote was largely responsible for the election of Charles C. Diggs to the state Senate in 1934, and the Rev. Horace A. White in 1944, they had been unable to place an African American candidate on the city's council. While the percentage of Blacks in the city's population had risen from 9.2 percent in 1940 to 12.9 percent by 1944, even if every eligible Black voter supported a single Black candidate under the at-large system, that candidate would still have needed an additional eighty thousand votes to secure ninth place—the cutoff for election to the council. Hence, the only way African Americans could achieve an electoral victory was through an alliance with other political forces.11 The 1943 mayoral race, in which Blacks and unionists

attempted to defeat the incumbent, Edward Jeffries Jr., had already laid
the foundation for a Black-labor alliance in electoral politics, and in
1945 both groups sought to build on this foundation to promote a
strong labor slate.

The 1943 municipal elections were a turning point in local politics.
They were nastier than any local electoral battle previously waged in the
city and were tainted with a level of racism not seen since the mayoral
election of 1924, when Klansman Charles Bowles narrowly missed being
elected as a write-in candidate.[12] The way the 1943 elections devolved
was also surprising. Mayor Jeffries had been elected in 1939 with a sizable portion of the African American vote in part based on the popularity of his father, Judge Edward Jeffries Sr., within the city's Black communities. Regarded as "an old-time liberal and a friend of Negroes and
labor," the senior Jeffries was known for his fair treatment of Black
defendants, including James Victory, the African American World War I
veteran whom Maurice Sugar defended in 1935. The younger Jeffries
retained the fairly high level of Black support that flowed from his
father's goodwill until he announced a policy that left intact the "racial
characteristics" of any neighborhood where wartime housing projects
were to be built. The "white paper" he issued after the 1943 race riot,
which blamed the violence on Black leaders and victims, only made matters worse.[13]

Jeffries was thus regarded as weak and ineffectual in 1943, and he
trailed his chief opponent, Judge Frank Fitzgerald, in the primary by
over thirty-eight thousand votes. Remarkably, Jeffries even lost the districts around the Sojourner Truth housing project, as he was seen as
being "too friendly" toward the project's Black residents, who had begun
to occupy homes there despite violent efforts to keep them out. Facing
what looked like the end of his political career, Jeffries launched a
vicious campaign of race and labor baiting unparalleled in the city's history and successfully rode a wave of fear and resentment back into office.

It was in the wake of this still superheated environment that Reverend Hill announced his candidacy for the Common Council in 1945.
A series of March "caucus" meetings were held among select Black lead-
ers and their white allies, including businessman Fred Allen; Fr. Malcolm
C. Dade of St. Cyprian's Episcopal Church; the Rev. Horace A. White,
the pastor of Plymouth Congregational Church and a member of the
Detroit Housing Commission; Josephine Belford of the Democratic Fed-
erated Clubs; Louis C. Blount, general manager of the Great Lakes
Insurance Company and president of the Booker T. Washington Trade
Association; Gloster Current and Dr. J. J. McClendon of the NAACP;

attorney C. LeBron Simmons of the NNC; Snow Grigsby; deputy labor commissioner and former Garveyite Joseph Craigen; Jack Raskin of the CRC; the Rev. John Miles, by then copastor of the Detroit Council of Applied Religion; and Reverend Hill.

For the most part, Hill's support was based in the same intergenerational and inter-ideological group that frequented the noontime "roundtable" at the Lucy Thurman branch of the YWCA. His wider constituency, however, was probably the most diverse to come together in Detroit any time before or since. All agreed that the stakes were high enough to call for an expedient alliance, but finding one candidate on whom everyone could agree was not easy. Charles C. Diggs would have been ideal, but a 1944 graft conviction precluded this possibility. Two other likely candidates, Reverend White and L. C. Blount, both declined to run. There was a good deal of support for Hill before the meeting, especially among unionists, and he gradually emerged as a consensus candidate. Although there were worries that Hill's "communistic leanings and association with the left-wingers" would lose him the support of the more conservative wing of organized labor, most agreed that his "integrity and leadership" endowed him with the potential to appeal to all Detroiters. "We've heard the familiar charges of communism," one of Hill's advocates declared. "We've heard that label so often that it is meaningless. We aren't interested in a Negro who is too conservative. We want Hill."[14]

The only significant challenge to Hill's candidacy came from Edward A. Simmons, an attorney who had run reasonably well in the 1943 primaries. Seeking a second bite of the apple, Simmons had been drafted to run in early April by a small group of supporters led by prominent local Democratic Party operatives Joseph Cole and Emmett Cunningham— the same group that had previously called for Reverend White's removal from the Detroit Housing Commission. Simmons attracted only lukewarm support, however. He was seen as too friendly with Jeffries, who had appointed him to (and ousted Hill from) the Mayor's Interracial Committee after the 1943 elections, and too uninvolved in the campaigns against police brutality and for open housing. Editorials in both the *Michigan Chronicle* and the *Detroit Tribune* urged Simmons to withdraw. Finally, on May 5, the *Chronicle* published an open letter from Simmons, throwing his support behind Hill "in the interest of racial unity."

"Last week," the *Chronicle* subsequently editorialized, "community leaders representing different schools of political thought buried their differences and dedicated their energies to the Councilmanic campaign of the Reverend Charles A. Hill."

Considering the personal ambitions and the variety of views of the local leaders, this is no mean achievement. The leadership squabbles among Negroes are always a little ridiculous when you consider the common contempt in which the leadership is held by the night-shirt crowd across the color line. Now that the tempest in the tea-pot has subsided a major job awaits."[15]

It was indeed a major job. Reverend Hill's participation in the 1941 Ford strike, along with his involvement in the Citizens Committee for Jobs in War Industry and the Sojourner Truth Citizens Committee, gave him standing as a committed activist and community leader. It also helped that he was then vice president of the Metropolitan Council on Fair Employment, a broad interracial coalition.[16]

Hill aspired to be "The People's Candidate." His platform was designed to appeal to Blacks and members of the working classes. He promised, for example, to act on fair employment legislation and to cut the "red tape" and derogatory "hounding" of welfare recipients. He attacked the city's transportation and sanitation services as a "shame to our great city" and vowed to improve these services in all areas of Detroit, "especially the low income neighborhoods." In Hill's campaign literature and speeches, he often introduced a class—as opposed to a race—dynamic, constantly stressing the need for improvement for people in all neighborhoods, "not only the privilege [sic] group."[17]

Of course, Hill's very presence made race even more of an issue in the city's already racially divisive elections. Not only was he the only Black candidate in the council race, but he continuously raised the issues of police brutality and segregated public housing—the third rail of Detroit politics. Hill and his supporters felt that a Black presence on the council would help break the stalemate on the housing question, which they saw as the root cause of many difficulties for the city's minority population. They looked again to the example of Benjamin Davis, a New York politician who had recently introduced a measure denying tax exemptions to projects sponsored by any housing, insurance, or redevelopment company that directly or indirectly discriminated on the basis of race, color, or creed.[18]

Hill's platform was made up of a mixture of contentious issues, and there is every reason to believe that his supporters hoped that his being a man of the cloth would give his candidacy an extra boost. At the close of World War II, Hill's church, Hartford Avenue Baptist, had the largest Black Baptist congregation on the city's west side, and ground had recently been broken with much fanfare for an extension of its physical

plant. For most ministers the primary sign of success were an acknowledged ability to preach well, attract a good choir, and build up one's
church. Hill was, accordingly, extraordinarily popular with his congregants and the church's deacons and trustees.[19] Hartford's size and reputation, coupled with its members' loyalty to their pastor, endowed Hill
with a strong base of personal and institutional influence. His involvement in professional associations, particularly the Detroit Council of
Churches and the interracial Baptists' Ministerial Alliance, which represented over 198 Baptist congregations in the area, was of equal importance: Hill's three-year stint as chair of the DCC's Interracial Committee,
in conjunction with his alliance membership, increased his chances of
gaining much needed interracial support in the city's religious communities.

Ministerial supporters opened their churches to Hill and members of
his campaign committee and plugged his campaign during Sunday services. "For the first time in 9 or 10 years," remarked a prominent clergyman at a Hill campaign meeting, "I prefaced my sermon to the congregation asking them to get out the vote." "I believe," he continued, that
"we have the greatest opportunity for the issues are clear and the time
and tide in our favor."

> The first thing we did was to try and get the people to register before
> saying anything about personalities. We don't tell them how to vote
> but we tell them how we are going to vote. We are behind the slate
> you are putting out.[20]

The slate in question was the result of the Black-labor alliance. At the
same time that the Black leadership was working behind the scenes to
select a candidate, the CIO's Political Action Committee (CIO-PAC) was
haggling over its own endorsements. It was rumored that the committee
was considering a deal with Mayor Jeffries, whom the UAW had opposed
since 1943 and whom African American leaders refused to support.[21] It
was not until May, when Richard T. Frankensteen, a handsome and athletic vice president of the UAW, announced his candidacy, that the
Black-labor alliance regained its stride. By the end of the month, the
CIO-PAC, with the backing of the Hill for Council Committee, endorsed
Frankensteen for mayor along with three candidates for the Common
Council: George Edwards, an incumbent; Tracy Doll, executive secretary
of the CIO-PAC, and Reverend Hill.[22]

Once the endorsements were locked in, both groups turned to the
practical matters of registering voters and devising strategies to combat

the race and labor baiting that had defeated the emergent coalition in 1943. The CIO-PAC spent more than one hundred thousand dollars and organized nearly five hundred precincts throughout the city in the third attempt by unionists to elect a mayor and the first to elect one of their own. The CIO-PAC also loaned four international representatives to the Hill committee and set up four campaign offices in African American neighborhoods in order to get out the crucial Black vote.

In order to help defray the cost of Hill's campaign, the CIO-PAC published joint campaign literature urging residents to support the entire labor slate. The Hill committee also received donations of time and money from most segments of the civil rights community, including Ford Local 600; the Michigan Citizen's Committee, a liberal organization formed in 1944 to reelect Roosevelt; the Wayne County Democratic Committee (even though the election was nominally nonpartisan); the CRF; the NAACP; the NNC; and the Michigan Division of the Communist Party. Neither Frankensteen nor Hill openly welcomed the CP's support, but the existence of a Left coalition that included the CP attests to the lingering influence of Popular Front politics in postwar Detroit; such a coalition would be nearly impossible just three or four years later.[23]

In addition to running a campaign, Hill and his supporters were forced to take the ideological offensive against the expected race and Red baiting. The Hill committee and the CIO-PAC planned for the worst. Strategy sessions were held nearly every day at Lucy Thurman, and both the Hill committee and the CIO-PAC endorsed a resolution from the Detroit Council of Churches urging candidates to refrain from inflammatory campaign rhetoric about race, religion, and nationality. The Hill committee was especially careful to stress the breadth of its candidate's platform. Under the slogan, "Elect a Man Who Will Represent All of the People," Hill's campaign focused on jobs, police brutality, housing, transportation, sanitation, and union rights.

Hill's campaign continuously emphasized the interracial nature of the candidate's support by highlighting endorsements from prominent white figures such as the Rev. Henry Hitt Crane. "Hill's campaign is assuming the proportion of a gigantic community-sponsored movement," Fred Allen, Hill's campaign manager, stated. "It is interracial in character and bids fair to place the first Negro in the Common Council in the history of Detroit."[24] This evident interracialness was not a uniform phenomenon, however. "What I found out in most cases," recalled Reverend Hill, "was that when [a white cocandidate] came to Negro groups, he would lift me very high; but he was very, very quiet when we went to white groups. That happened in so many cases."[25] This was clearly the case with Frankensteen, who was hardly a fiery radical. As a writer for the leftist magazine *PM* noted, the mayoral candidate's strategy was to "placate any fears of householders and other solid citizens that he is not a safe man to be mayor." This was especially true with regard to the issue of open housing.[26]

In the end, all this careful emphasis on racial cooperation could not prevent the general election campaign from taking a nasty turn. Both Hill and Frankensteen did well in the first round of voting in August, and the entire labor slate advanced to the second and final round in November. Frankensteen led in the August primary, with 41 percent of the vote to Jeffries's 34 percent, while Hill ran a strong ninth in the council race. The *Michigan Chronicle* celebrated Hill's unprecedented victory with a banner headline: "Hill Sets an Election Record." But with his position once again threatened, Mayor Jeffries went on the offensive.[27] He branded Frankensteen a hostage to "alien" powers that wanted to use Detroit as "a spring-board, as a jumping-off place—for their revolutionary crusade." "If they can seize Detroit," Jeffries warned, "the industrial metropolis of the nation, they figure all other industrial communities will follow suit. Thus, they reason, they can in time knit together a political empire that will rule the United States." He even went so far as to read from an issue of *Political Affairs,* a publication of the Communist Party, attempting to show that Frankensteen's campaign had used the text as a political manual.[28]

Local newspapers, particularly those serving small communities in and around Detroit, picked up this theme in pro-Jeffries editorials and advertisements. "Communism has entered this political campaign," stated an advertisement in the *Detroit News.* "November 6th is not just another date on the calendar," warned the *Home Gazette,* a paper catering to the city's northwest side: "It is a date with destiny. Voters who want to see the hands of Russian Quislings kept out of managing Detroit will be aroused to help get out the American vote . . . to defeat all Quislings and Communist Fronters."[29] Hill, who was branded as one of the "most active Communist front figures in all America," was implicated along with the rest of the labor slate. "Exposing Rev. Hill" was the banner headline of an article that listed Hill's political "offenses": his chairmanship of the local NNC, his membership in the old Civil Rights Federation, and his defense of members of the Young Communist League who were expelled from the University of Michigan for "subversive" activities in 1940. Hill was also accused of being a "fellow plotter" with the CP's Ben Davis. Overall, the *Home Gazette* felt its readers had been duped in the

August primaries: "[M]any whites voted for him on the assumption that he would be a reliable and responsible representative of the negro population. HIS COMMUNISTIC ASSOCIATIONS THROW A NEW LIGHT ON HIS QUALIFICATIONS."[30]

Despite all efforts to prevent the use of Hill's presence on the labor slate to ignite racial fears, the Jeffries forces organized a concerted effort to label the labor slate as overly friendly to the campaign for fair and interracial housing—even though Frankensteen attempted to keep this troublesome issue at arm's length. Anonymous cards appealing to Black voters and supposedly printed by the Frankensteen campaign were circulated to convince voters that "White Neighborhoods are again in Peril." In another representative instance, Jeffries blatantly asked listeners at a rally whether they "want a Sojourner Truth housing project in their neighborhood." As far back as the 1920s, Detroit had a housing shortage. No additional housing was built during the Depression, and a brief building spurt in the late 1930s was cut short by World War II. Seen in light of the city's nonintegration policy and the existence of some 150 white "improvement associations," the housing shortage among Detroit's African Americans seemed intractable. Hill's support for integrated housing was treated by Jeffries's allies as a problem of cosmic proportions. Any mention of open-occupancy laws was greeted with so much contempt and hostility in white neighborhoods that this issue, more than any other, probably accounted for the labor slate's defeat at the polls.[31]

Religion was also used to divide the labor coalition. While religion and politics had always overlapped in Detroit, faith became an issue in the 1945 campaign in new and troubling ways. Frankensteen was accused, alternatively and ironically, of being a radical Jew, an anti-Semite, and an ally of Fr. Charles Coughlin. On the one hand, Frankensteen fell victim to a well-organized "whisper campaign," particularly in the city's Polish neighborhoods, suggesting that the candidate, a native-born white Episcopalian whose name was misspelled and mispronounced as Franken*stein* in the rumor mongering—was Jewish. At the same time another local paper published Frankensteen's favorable comments about Father Coughlin—made in the early 1930s when Coughlin the populist was influential in drumming up support for Frankensteen's fledgling union, the Automotive Industrial Workers' Association (AIWA)—alongside Coughlin's later anti-Semitic editorials. The effect of this dishonest juxtaposition was to suggest that Frankensteen was a "disciple" of the present-day, reactionary Coughlin.[32]

Hill experienced problems of his own. While few seemed to question the merits of having a clergyman on the Common Council, Hill's ministerial credentials were questioned because of his radical politics. There is little doubt that at least part of the animus against Hill issued from Gerald L. K. Smith and his followers. Hill had had a run-in with Smith in 1943 over Hill's association with Claude Williams, who had left Detroit and returned to the South at the end of 1944, and they had denounced each other in a private exchange of letters about Williams's "communist" leanings. The disagreement had gone public in the form of a dispute over how to interpret a Langston Hughes poem entitled "Goodbye Christ." Hughes's poem opens:

"Listen, Christ
You did all right in your day, I reckon—
But that day's gone now"
They ghosted you up on a swell story, too
Called it Bible—
But it's dead now.
The popes and the preachers've
Made too much money from it.
They've sold you to too many

Kings, generals, robbers, and killers—
Even to the Tzar and the Cossacks,
Even to Rockefeller's Church,
Even to the SATURDAY EVENING POST.
You ain't no good no more.
They've pawned you
Till you've done wore out.

Goodbye,
Christ Jesus Lord God Jehova,
Beat it on away from here now.
Make way for a new guy with no religion at all—
A real guy named
Marx Communist Lenin Peasant Stalin Worker ME—

I said, ME!

Originally published in the *Negro Worker* in 1932 while Hughes was in Russia, it was republished in Smith's *The Cross and the Flag* and widely circulated as part of his Christian nationalist crusade. The poem, which Hughes sought to repudiate years later, would haunt him for the rest of his life, as figures such as Smith used it for their own designs.[33]

In an exchange of letters carried in the *Michigan Chronicle,* Smith challenged Hill, "as a minister of the gospel," to make anything "good out of the poem." Insisting that the issue had nothing to do with race, he warned Hill about the "bootlicking politicians and patronizers of the Negro" who simply flatter Blacks because it is "smart politics." Smith, on the other hand, promised only the unvarnished truth. In his reply, Hill never really dealt with the implications of Hughes's poem. Instead, he defended Hughes by insisting that he was no more a communist than Smith himself and that the Christ Hughes was saying goodbye to is "the Christ held up by the white supremists" and those who have "no concern for the brotherhood of man." Hill concluded his letter by hoping for the day when Smith and others like him would come to challenge the "anti-Christian, anti-democratic forces by insisting that all barriers that divide men because of race, creed or national origin be broken down, and that the Kingdom of God shall become a reality here and now."[34]

That day did not come in 1943, nor did it come in 1945, when Smith joined the forces arrayed against Hill to discredit him and the rest of the labor slate. Always an avid anti-Semite, and even using Judaism as an indictment of non-Jewish targets, Smith insisted to a crowd of listeners that his endorsement of Jeffries had nothing to do with Frankensteen's "Jewish" background. An editorial in the ACTU's *Wage Earner* quoted Smith conflating Judaism and communism by instructing his followers to oppose Frankensteen and the labor slate on the grounds that "Stalin should not name the mayor of Detroit." In the end, negative campaigning about the dangers of Blacks, Jews, communists, and radical unionist political power won the day. Jeffries was reelected with a margin of sixty-five thousand votes, and three of the CIO-backed candidates for the council, including Reverend Hill, were defeated. But the news was not all bad. Frankensteen garnered 44 percent of the total ballots cast, including 61 percent in Polish working-class neighborhoods and 75 percent in Italian precincts, and over 90 percent of African American votes. The wards dominated by Irish and southern whites proved to be the toughest nuts to crack, with the CIO winning less than half of the votes cast in these areas.[35]

Although the defeat was that much more painful after the great promise of the primaries, neither the UAW nor Hill withdrew from the political arena. Despite repeated accusations of communist sympathies, Hill rode a wave of popularity in the Black community to the presidency of the Detroit NAACP. It was a personal triumph. He had worked with the local NAACP for close to two decades, and his relationship with the organization had often been strained. His 1942 attempt to win the presidency, with the backing of Black labor radicals who wanted to push the organization in a more democratic and militant direction, had not gone well. While some saw the election as a mere clash of personalities, it also represented a clash of political orientations.[36] Although Hill won the NAACP elections in 1945, the old divisions and tensions persisted.

Hill appointed left-wing unionists such as Sam Sage of the Wayne County CIO Council to the NAACP Executive Board and attempted to give the branch's working-class base more input. He also insisted that the branch undertake more direct-action protests rather than relying solely on legal tactics. This is not to say that the group's legislative strategy was neglected, however. Hill was careful to monitor the branch's four ongoing restrictive covenant cases. The first, *Sipes v. McGhee,* was argued all the way to the Supreme Court under his watch, and the four cases would all be consolidated, along with cases from other parts of the country, in the court's 1948 landmark *Shelley v. Kramer* decision, which found discriminatory covenants unconstitutional.[37] But Hill's connections to the Left hampered his effectiveness at the NAACP. "Rev. Hill had come in for criticism by leaders in the NAACP for his apparently close liaison with leftwing elements," reported the Association of Catholic Trade Unionists' *Wage Earner,* and his defeat for reelection at the end of the year was regarded as an important part of the national office's attempts to save local branches from being "captured" by communists.[38]

Although he held the presidency for only one year, Reverend Hill mentioned his position proudly on all of his campaign literature when he again ran, unsuccessfully, for Common Council in 1947, 1948, and 1949. Hill was never elected to the Common Council and was never again able to put together as broad a coalition as he had in 1945, although future Detroit mayor Coleman Young, who frequently served as his campaign manager, certainly tried. With Young often at his side Hill became a perennial candidate for whom the act of campaigning was as important as the increasingly remote possibility of winning. Following the precedents set by local politicians such as Stanley Nowak and Charles Diggs Sr. (and by his son, Charles Diggs Jr., with his 1951 election to the state House) Hill made his campaigns part of the larger struggle for rights and social justice. At various times, he promised to work for general improvements such as slum clearance and low-income housing; at others, he explicitly focused on minority issues such as discrimination in life and automobile insurance and "the reign of fascist-like and police terror" in the city, during which Hill demanded the removal of police chief " 'shoot first' Harry Toy."[39]

Although Hill did not engage as often in cultural politics, at least in the contemporary sense of the term, he did campaign for the signing of Black baseball players to the Detroit Tigers.[40] Detroit had a considerable number of Black baseball fans, many of whom supported the Brown Bombers, a Negro League team financially backed by Joe Louis, but the Detroit Tigers' racist hiring policies were a sore spot. When the major leagues finally began integrating in 1946, the Tigers were the second-to-last team to sign African American players. Both the team and the stadium became symbols of racism. Hill and others fought long and hard against the owner's discriminatory policies, and when the Tigers' first Black player, Ozzie Virgil, stepped onto the field in June 1958, Blacks turned out in large numbers for the occasion. Virgil, who was also the first Dominican player in the major leagues, was generally described as a "mediocre" player, but that day, to the surprise of everyone, he went five for five.[41]

His advocacy for integration of professional baseball didn't place Hill too far outside the liberal political mainstream. Yet some of the positions he adopted reveal the extent to which he remained involved in Left politics. When the city first proposed a Loyalty Amendment, which would require all city employees to sign a noncommunist oath, Hill worked for its defeat as part of his 1949 Council campaign. Arguing that those "forces who use violence to blot out democracy are the very ones who yell loudest for pledges of 'loyalty,' " he denounced the measure as part of Detroit's "witch-hunt."[42] More broadly, Hill also campaigned for the banning of the atom bomb and for the promotion of world peace. A man of the cloth urging peace was not unusual. But the specifics of Hill's position placed him in direct opposition to the Truman administration's foreign policy and in line with the pro-Soviet Left.[43]

Recalling his close friend Stanley Nowak's criticism of Truman's fight against international communism, Hill signed a 1949 petition to ban the use of militarized atomic power without the authorization of the United Nations. The reverend was apparently unconcerned that both the Soviet Union and the American Communist Party supported the measure. Hill also joined Nowak and others in their campaign to stop the rearming of West Germany because "the Soviet Union, Poland, Czechoslovakia, Bulgaria, Romania and Albania stated jointly that they will not tolerate the re-arming."[44] He also continued his association with the Detroit branch of the Civil Rights Congress, which was among the most active and important CP front groups of the late 1940s and 1950s.[45]

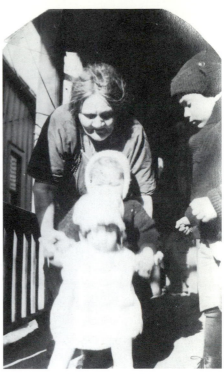

The Rev. Charles A. Hill and
Georgia (Underwood) Hill, circa 1925.
(Courtesy of Bruce and Beth Morrow and family.)

Mary Lantz Hill with grandchildren, circa 1929.
(Courtesy of Bruce and Beth Morrow and family.)

The Jay Street house occupied by Mary Lantz Hill and Charles A. Hill.
(Courtesy of Bruce and Beth Morrow and family.)

The Rev. Charles A. Hill with daughter Roberta at her wedding, 1946.
(Charles A. Hill Papers. Courtesy of the Bentley Historical Library, University of Michigan, reproduced by permission of Bruce and Beth Morrow and family.)

The Rev. Charles A. Hill at his desk, 1940s.
(Courtesy of Walter P. Reuther Library, Wayne State University.)

The Rev. Charles A. Hill and Paul Robeson, 1948.
(Courtesy of Bruce and Beth Morrow and family.)

The Cleage family in front of its Scotten Street home, circa 1930. *Left to right:* Henry, Louis, Pearl, Barbara, Hugh, Gladys, Anna, Albert Jr., and Dr. Cleage Sr. (Courtesy of Kristin Cleage Williams.)

Albert B. Cleage Jr. and Doris (Graham) Cleage with daughters Kristin G. (about five) and Pearl M. Cleage (about three), circa 1951. Dr. Cleage Sr. is in the background on the porch. (Courtesy of Kristin Cleage Williams.)

Freedom Now Party candidates during the 1964 election campaign. *Left to right:* Loy Cohen (secretary of state), Dr. James Jackson (lieutenant governor), the Rev. Albert B. Cleage Jr. (governor), and Milton Henry (Congress).
(Photo by William Smith, reproduced courtesy of Kristin Cleage Williams.)

The Rev. Albert B. Cleage Jr. speaking to an overflow crowd in Detroit's Cobo Arena during the 1963 Walk to Freedom rally.
(Courtesy of Walter P. Reuther Library, Wayne State University.)

The Rev. Albert B. Cleage Jr. in front of the Shrine of the Black Madonna Bookstore and Cultural Center, Detroit, circa 1970s.
(Detroit News Collection. Courtesy of Walter P. Reuther Library, Wayne State University.)

The Rev. C. L. Franklin greeting a member of his congregation, undated.
(Courtesy of Walter P. Reuther Library, Wayne State University.)

Canon Malcolm G. Dade with
portrait by local artist DeVon
Cunningham, circa 1983.
(Courtesy of Margaret J. Dade
and family.)

America First Party rally, 1943. Gerald L. K. Smith appears at center.
(Gerald L. K. Smith Collection. Courtesy of the Bentley Historical Library, University of Michigan.)

The Rev. J. Frank Norris preaching on Belle Isle, Detroit, 1938.
(Detroit News Collection. Courtesy of Walter P. Reuther Library, Wayne State University.)

Walk to Freedom march on Woodward Avenue, Detroit, 1963, with Dr. Martin Luther King Jr.
(Tony Spina Collection. Courtesy of Walter P. Reuther Library, Wayne State University.)

George Crockett and Coleman A. Young at Detroit HUAC hearings, February 1952.
(Detroit News Collection. Courtesy of Walter P. Reuther Library, Wayne State University.)

Carl Winter, pictured under arrow, at Leon Mosely protest rally, 1948.
(Detroit News Collection. Courtesy of Walter P. Reuther Library, Wayne State University.)

RED BAITING THE FEPC TO DEATH

The Communist Party's support of Hill and his bids for Common Council was subjected to thorough scrutiny in the press and was thus certainly common knowledge. It is difficult to know what effect, if any, this fact had on Hill's standing within the Black community. Surely it helped that Reverend Hill linked his various Common Council campaigns to what became the last major mobilization initiated by the city's early civil rights community, namely, the demand for a city and state fair employment practice act. The idea of fair employment as a civil right was born out of the work of A. Philip Randolph and the March on Washington movement, which had prompted Roosevelt to issue Executive Order 8802. The federal Fair Employment Practice Commission established by that order had always been limited in its scope to industries contracting with the federal government for wartime production. Once the war ended, the FEPC, like many other New Deal agencies, was attacked by a conservative coalition of Republican and southern Democratic congressmen. Nationally, activists coordinated a campaign to "Save the Federal FEPC," but once Congress discontinued its appropriation, many activists turned their attention to efforts on the local and state levels.

The initial campaign for a Michigan FEPC was spearheaded by the state branch of the Civil Rights Congress. Hill devoted a great deal of time to the cause. In 1945 and 1946, several FEPC bills were introduced into the Michigan legislature by pro-labor politicians, including Stanley Nowak. Although these bills faced no open opposition from either party, they were all killed in committee, largely as a result of lobbying efforts by the conservative Michigan Manufacturers Association. In the fall of 1946, the Michigan CRC turned instead to the use of initiating petitions as a political strategy. Attorneys Ernest Goodman and C. LeBron Simmons, who were associated with both the CRC and the National Lawyers Guild, discovered a provision in the Michigan Constitution that mandated legislative action within forty days on any petition signed by 8 percent of all those casting votes in the most recent (in this case 1946) election for governor. If the legislature were to reject, amend, or fail to act on the measure, it would automatically be placed on the ballot.[46]

There were certain risks attendant on the use of this loophole. On the one hand, activists could use the drive to collect petition signatures as a way to pursue their goal of educating people about employment discrimination. This approach called for a top-down planning strategy that then had to be implemented on the grassroots level and was seen by its supporters as the only way, however slim the chances for success, of forcing the state to adopt fair employment legislation. On the other hand, naysayers warned that, even if enough signatures could be collected within the limited time allotted, voters might still choose to kill the model bill when it appeared on the ballot. Even the sympathetic Gloster Current considered such a strategy to be "ill-timed, ill-considered and dangerous."[47]

Obviously, no one could guarantee the outcome. Although the initiating-petition provision had been on the books since 1913, it had never been used. "It [the initiative petition for a state FEPC] will be the first time in the history of Michigan," stated an editorial in the *Plymouth Beacon*, "that the people will seek to enact legislation over the heads of the representatives."[48] It was, agreed the Rev. Charles A. Hill, a "highly democratic procedure," one rooted in "the great traditions of our nation." In a rhetorical flourish, Hill insisted that the ideals for which "the Revolution, the Civil War and the Second World War were fought" were all embodied in the campaign for equal job opportunities.[49] Armed with this new strategy, the CRC sought the cooperation of over three hundred Michigan-based organizations, "embracing every sector of the people."

In an article for *Jewish Life* assessing the aftermath of the petition drive, Reverend Hill wrote:

> The idea for the petition campaign had originated with the Civil Rights Congress, and a conference prior to the collection of signatures had been under the exclusive sponsorship of the Congress. But it was agreed that the issue of FEPC was so broad, and the possibilities for united action so great, that it was essential to include all organizations in the state in the circulation of petitions. At the conference, therefore, the committee was broadened to include all interested organizations. All groups in the community, political, religious, labor and radical, became active in the campaign. The Jewish people, the Negro people, Protestants, Catholics, professionals and workers entered the competition to turn in the most signatures. It was a demonstration of the unity of the people.[50]

Unity, or at least cooperation, was necessary to collect the 133,328 signatures needed (the goal was set at 200,000, just to be on the safe side) in the short weeks from early September to December 15, 1946, which was designated as Bill of Rights Day.

Hill was appointed chairman of the Committee for a State FEPC,

which helped orchestrate the massive effort. His own participation
tended to emphasize the duty and responsibility of the religious. "You
couldn't go to church on Sunday," recalled one member of Hill's congregation, "without having signed one of those forms for fair employment." Under Hill's supervision, Hartford was established, along with
the offices of organizations such as the NAACP, Local 600, the American
Jewish Congress, and the Masonic Lodge (St. John's), as an official Petition Collection Center.[51] Attempting to capitalize further on the moral
authority of the pulpit, Hill organized a group of more than twenty leading clergymen, including Fr. Malcolm Dade of St. Cyprian's, the Rev.
T. T. Timberlake of the Detroit Council of Churches, and the Rev. J. H.
Howell of St. Stephen AME, to issue a "Thanksgiving Statement for the
Committee for a State FEPC." Connecting "our Pilgrim Fathers" and the
freedom to worship with the "freedom for men of all races, tongues, and
kindred to work according to their skills," the group urged every citizen
to "take seriously the meaning of this national day of Thanksgiving [and]
to sign one of the FEPC petitions as a positive act of faith in the future of
our country as a bulwark of freedom."[52] The committee also managed to
secure the support of prominent political figures, including Mayor Jeffries, who declared an "FEPC Day" during the petition drive, and Walter
Reuther, who was in the process of solidifying his position at the top of
the UAW.[53]

High-minded ideals, religious commitment, and seemingly broad-
based support did not prevent internal tensions and fissures from emerging within the FEPC coalition. The coalition could not escape the factionalism that was becoming more and more pervasive within the Left in
general. The Communist Party's active and open participation was the
central source of contention. Early on in the petition drive, the *Wage
Earner* warned that communists and communist sympathizers were trying
to "capture" the campaign.[54] Local activist Geraldine Bledsoe recalls that
before this time anticommunism "was a sort of muted thing." She
assigned the breakup of the FEPC coalition, however, to the increasingly
vocal "struggle over the ideology of communism."[55] More specifically,
the presence of communists in the coalition hastened a divergence of
opinions regarding the most appropriate course of action once the petitions had been gathered and submitted.

The CP, along with Hill and other CRC activists, viewed the initiative
petition as a way to force the legislature to act, or, barring that, to place
their FEPC proposal on the ballot and let the voting public have the final
say. According to the more moderate factions, particularly those associ-

ated with the NAACP, the Jewish Community Council, and the Association of Catholic Trade Unionists, such "faith in the people" was sheer folly. Instead of pressing for a vote—a daring plan considering the beating that the labor slate had taken in recent elections—the moderates preferred to use the petitions as leverage in the state legislature, an equally daring move, considering the strength of antilabor voices in the state House and the intense lobbying of the Michigan Manufacturers' Association.[56]

There was nothing necessarily communistic about the petition, but it was soon defined as such by liberals. As a result, the formerly inclusive Committee for a State FEPC was split in two as the campaign moved from the collection of signatures to the building of legislative support. Thus, in early January 1947, the Michigan Council for Fair Employment Legislation was formed "to rally the widest possible . . . liberal support" as opposed to the "narrow sponsorship" of the committee. The CRC and CP were pointedly excluded from the new group, and Bishop Francis J. Haas, a former chairman of the federal FEPC, was selected as honorary chair. Headed by George Schermer, director of the Mayor's Interracial Committee, and Oscar Cohen of the Jewish Community Council, the Michigan Council immediately voted to pull out of the CRC-backed committee. More dramatically, it decided to openly denounce the rival group. The campaign ended with the city's civil rights activists divided and the petition nullified on a legal technicality.[57]

Reverend Hill and others could still hope that "the people will finally wield unity that will result in the establishment of FEPC in Michigan and elsewhere." But unity—a concept to which much of the Left continued to cling—was becoming ever more difficult to achieve. The groundwork had already been laid for the final round of factional fights within the civil rights community, fights that would influence the direction of civil rights activism for the next decade. Calls for "unity among all progressive forces" fell on increasingly suspicious, and even hostile, ears.

By the end of 1947, the liberal Michigan Council for Fair Employment Legislation was still fighting for a Michigan FEPC. In response to the "tremendous impact" of the release of a report by Truman's Committee on Civil Rights, entitled *To Secure These Rights*, the group decided to broaden its agenda and change its name to the Michigan Committee on Civil Rights just in time for the messy election season of 1948, in which civil rights activists would become embroiled in factional fights between and among Democrats, Progressives, Republicans, Dixiecrats, liberals, conservatives, and Communists.[58]

PROGRESSIVE ACTS OF FAITH
Henry Wallace and the 1948 Campaign Season

I have stated elsewhere that red-baiting has paid and is paying great dividends. While masses of the people have been distracted by carefully manufactured "red menaces" the reactionaries have taken control of the government, inflation has continued its spirals upwards, and our major economic and social problems have intensified.[59]

—Henry A. Wallace, 1948

The internal difficulties hampering Detroit's civil rights community have to be seen in a broad national (and international) context. The national mood that made the original federal Fair Employment Practice Act and Commission possible was in retreat as a new conservatism enveloped American political culture. Businessmen and industrialists, who had lost the faith of working people during the Depression, were restored to a position of respect during World War II, and the Republican Party was increasingly successful at the polls as the nation set about the task of restoring "normalcy" and enjoying prosperity. That this quest for normalcy included a seemingly reactionary desire to curb the power of labor unions and silence the Left—particularly those organizations with actual or supposed ties to the Communist Party—was one of the tragedies of the postwar period.

The consequences of this new conservatism for Detroit's civil rights community were extreme, as each of its major institutional components—labor unions, civil rights organizations, and the Communist Party—came under attack from the government and cold war liberals. Normalcy dictated not only that labor unions enter into a cooperative association with the government bureaucracy—a process begun during World War II—but also that any area of potentially "subversive" opinion or action be contained and eventually destroyed. This "domestic containment," the counterpart of President Harry S. Truman's foreign policy to isolate and limit the threat of international communism, created a climate in which any "inappropriate" (i.e., communistic) demand for civil rights was regarded with circumspection.[60]

With postwar strikes sweeping the nation, labor unions were viewed as increasingly unmanageable. The no-strike pledge enacted during World War II was effectively nullified by a restless workforce. In 1946, nearly 4.5 million people in various industries and occupations went on strike, demanding wage increases to compensate for wartime sacrifices and inflation. Some 116 million workdays were lost—four times as many as during the 1937 sit-down strikes—and the long-standing ties between the CIO and the Democratic administration were strained to the breaking point.[61] The bitter 103-day strike led by Walter Reuther against General Motors was, at the time, part of the largest strike wave (1945–46) in the nation's history.

The GM strike began nearly three weeks after Richard Frankensteen's defeat in the mayoral elections, and, because the UAW demanded a pay increase without a corresponding increase in the price of automobiles, it was an assault on the status quo. (Reuther's "anti-inflation" strategy had the full backing of neither the CIO nor the government, and the UAW was forced to settle for a lower pay increase than it had initially sought with no mention of automobile prices.) Overall, the strike wave ran counter to the administration's policy of domestic containment. Truman took drastic steps in response, temporarily nationalizing packinghouses, railroads, and coal mines in order to forcibly end strikes. He also threatened to draft defiant railroad workers into the army and fined the coal miners' union 3.5 million dollars for refusing to abide by the government's back-to-work order. By reviving the old tactic of blaming worker activism on the unhealthy influence of the Communist Party and its sympathizers, conservative politicians refashioned their battle against the postwar strike wave into a new front in the war against domestic subversion.[62]

The Labor-Management Relations Act of 1947, better known as the Taft-Hartley Act, was Congress's response to the nation's "labor problems." Designed to "emancipate union and non-union workers from the tyranny of racketeers and the treason of Communist labor leaders" and to avoid or at least minimize "industrial strife," Taft-Hartley, passed over President Truman's veto in June 1947, was above all a congressional attempt to keep the peace and domesticate unions. The law outlawed the closed shop and granted other favorable advantages to management. Moreover, the National Labor Relations Board was prohibited from dealing with any union whose local, national, or international officers had not submitted an affidavit swearing that he or she was not "a member of the Communist Party or affiliated with such party, and that he does not believe in, and is not a member of or supports any organization that believes in or teaches, the overthrow of the United States Government by force or by any illegal or unconstitutional methods."[63]

Although progressive unionists opposed Taft-Hartley, most labor leaders eventually capitulated and signed the anticommunist affidavits. Walter Reuther, for example, was critical of the law's ability to undermine the power of unions but used the anticommunist provisions to rid the UAW of communists and sympathizers, many of whom happened to be his rivals. Reuther's high-profile role in the GM strike, coupled with his attacks on communists associated with his rival, George Addes, and the left-of-center caucus, secured his election to the UAW presidency in 1946. Over the next three years, anticommunist sentiment, and particularly its manifestation in the Taft-Hartley Act, facilitated Reuther's assault on the Far Left.[64] Reuther's rise to power influenced not only the course of labor activism in the city but also the nature of the relationship between African Americans and the UAW. Ironically, many of his actions reinforced the government's desire to contain the radicalism of Blacks and workers. They also hardened the split in the city's civil rights community.

Reuther's anticommunism, which was supported by the UAW's right-of-center coalition—including socialists, Trotskyists, and the Association of Catholic Trade Unionists—won him a decisive victory. Although Reuther was a socialist who had once harbored some sympathy toward the CP and the Soviet Union, he was willing to engage in Red baiting as a means to an end.[65] As a result, dozens of union officials who had been central to the Left-labor community in Detroit were expelled. Maurice Sugar, a member of the International Labor Defense and the National Lawyers Guild and the union's legal counsel since 1936, was fired, as was Black attorney George Crockett, director of the UAW's first Fair Practice Committee and one of the most outspoken critics of discrimination inside the union. Crockett and Sugar later joined with Ernest Goodman to form the city's first integrated law firm, one of the first in the nation, which defended many within the Left community during the Smith Act trials and the period before HUAC. (Years later, augmented by younger attorneys, the firm would also come to the defense of the New Left.[66])

Within Local 600, activists such as Shelton Tappes, who lost his 1945 campaign for reelection as recording secretary, adapted to the confines of liberal anticommunism and signed a loyalty affidavit. Christopher Alston, Arthur McPhaul, Dave Moore, and others with strong ties to the CP lost their positions altogether. The Reutherites' efforts to control Local 600 did not end there, however. Throughout the late 1940s and early 1950s, Reuther and his supporters took dramatic measures to keep Local 600 in check, including placing it under the administrative control of the UAW's Executive Board.[67]

Many activists remained within the union and continued the struggle for union democracy and racial equality as best they could. Black unionists such as Horace Sheffield, Robert "Buddy" Battle, and Nelson Jack Edwards had been more or less loyal Reutherites for years. They had always opposed the "manipulation of the left-wing" and the "yoke" of the CP and would form a key contingent in the liberal-labor coalition that emerged to carry on the struggle in the late 1950s.[68] Meanwhile, others who were ousted from the UAW and the CIO sought alternative avenues for their civil rights activism. It was in this environment that the Progressive Party was organized as a third-party challenge to the Democrats (and liberal anticommunism) and the Republicans (and conservative anticommunism). Leftists within the civil rights community in Detroit supported the Progressive Party and its presidential candidate, Henry Wallace, from the start. Reverend Hill, who had closely followed the reversal of fortune experienced by his friends and political allies in the left-of-center UAW coalition, attended the Progressive Party's founding convention in Philadelphia in 1948 as a member of the party's National Committee; subsequently, he also became a cochair of the party's Michigan Division.[69]

Hill was among the "60 leading [African American] ministers" who traveled to Philadelphia to express their support for Wallace's candidacy, and he was duly named to the nominations committee. Hill predicted that "the Progressives' forthright stand on segregation will win the overwhelming majority of the Negro vote" and justified his support of Wallace in both racial and religious terms. Agreeing with the other clergymen in attendance that religion "does not exist in a vacuum" and that one's stand on pressing issues such as "peace, democracy and abundance" was the test of a "truly moral and devout man," Hill insisted that neither the Democrats nor the Republicans "afford the church-goer any hope." Both, he continued, advocated "pro-fascist standards" and "violate[d] all the precepts of the believer."[70]

The Progressive Party was in a sense the last major attempt to save the New Deal coalition. Wallace had been both Roosevelt's vice president and his secretary of agriculture. Although he was wary of Communist Party support, both Wallace and the party felt that he, not Truman, had the right to the mantle of the New Deal. To Hill and others, Wallace seemed just the sort of morally devout man the nation needed.

Progressive strategists sought to make their party a grassroots movement with broad appeal; dubbed "Gideon's Army," it took on a pronounced religious tinge. The platform that emerged out of the 1948 convention, for instance, concluded: "Under the guidance of Divine Providence, the Progressive Party, with strong and active faith, moves forward to peace, freedom, and abundance." Wallace himself borrowed freely from the texts of the Old Testament prophets in speaking, for example, of the day when men shall "beat their swords into plowshares and their spears into pruning hooks." Along with an appeal to Providence, the party's platform also included a strongly worded critique of Truman's policy toward international communism, a promise to use the power of government to create sixty million new jobs, an attack on discrimination in all areas of social life, and support for fair employment practices.[71]

Born in 1888 on a farm in central Iowa, Henry Wallace was the progeny of hardworking farmers and devout Presbyterians; his father was a United Presbyterian minister. Wallace was also imbued with a touch of mysticism and wore the markings of a man engaged in a lifelong spiritual quest. Having been raised in the United Presbyterian church, Wallace passed through a skeptical phase during college, attended Roman Catholic services for a time, and finally found a spiritual home in the high Episcopal church. Throughout, he honed a political philosophy as informed by scientific rationalism as by the social gospel and midwestern populism. In a series of addresses delivered at the Chicago Theological Seminary and the Federal Council of Churches in the early 1930s while he was still Roosevelt's secretary of agriculture, Wallace demonstrated his talent for mixing politics, economics, and religion and his understanding of the necessarily cooperative relationship between church and state. "It is the job of Government, as I see it," he proclaimed, "to devise and develop the social machinery which will work out the implications of the social message of the old prophets and of the Sermon on the Mount; but it remains the opportunity of the Church to fill men's hearts and minds with the spirit and meaning of great visions."[72]

Hill certainly shared these sentiments and stuck with the Wallace camp even after the Democratic Party adopted its own civil rights plank—in part out of fear that Wallace would otherwise capture the Black vote—and even after Strom Thurmond led his renegade Dixiecrats out of the Democratic Party to create a third-party challenge from the right. Although Wallace and Hill had much in common when it came to political theology, as well as foreign and domestic policy, it is difficult to know exactly why Hill continued to support Wallace even after it was clear that the Progressive Party's campaign was a lost cause.

Hill obviously believed that Wallace would be better for the Black population, the working class, and the Left than either Truman or Thomas Dewey, who ran on the Republican ticket. But he never explained what he meant by his statement that both the Republicans and the Democrats advocated profascist standards. Still, a number of possibilities can be inferred. First, it may have been the case that Hill had been preaching unity of all progressive forces for so long that unity, which implied the inclusion of communists, took precedence over everything else. Second, it may have been the case that Hill was, like the CP, truly concerned about Truman's policies toward the Eastern Bloc on the foreign stage and the containment of labor at home. In his own 1948 campaign for Common Council, Hill stated that he was pro-Wallace and against the Marshall Plan. As Stanley Nowak, who was running on the 1948 Progressive Party's ticket for the state Senate, put it during a joint appearance with Hill, "The issue in this campaign, of war or peace, fascism or democracy, free labor or slave labor under the Taft-Hartleyites, an end to Jim Crowism, reduction of prices and return to price control, seemingly do not interest the back-room shaffters of the state Democratic party clique."[73] In Nowak's telling, the issues are merged and inseparable, and only an untainted third party could properly address them. The threat of Thurmond and the Dixiecrats—and what, after all, would have been so new about such virulent forms of southern racism?— was an insufficient reason to return to the Democratic fold.

Finally, Hill might have felt not only the pull of politics but, once again, of friendship as well. He had accepted the chairmanship of a political organization, the Michigan Progressive Party, to which most of his closest friends belonged, including Nowak and Coleman Young. At least initially, the new party's platform and its presidential candidate were attractive to workers and minorities. All of the "good people" appeared to be pro-Wallace. When Wallace made an appearance in Detroit soon after he announced his candidacy in December, 1947, some thirteen thousand people paid to hear him speak. The advance ticket sales were so great that his local sponsors had to move the affair to the city's Olympia Stadium. Presidents of local unions and units in the area formed an Auto Workers National Committee for Wallace, and pro-Wallace committees were convened in a number of local unions, including Ford Local 600.[74]

Local activists such as Hill, Nowak, and Young, who had been recently elected director of organizing in the ideologically divided Wayne County CIO, all ran for local office on the Progressive Party ticket, and activists associated with the Civil Rights Congress created Wallace for President Committees throughout the city's communities. Yet on Wallace's second campaign visit to Detroit in the late summer of 1948 the city's pro-Wallace groups couldn't even muster 450 people to attend. In the months between Wallace's two visits, anti-Wallace forces had managed to isolate the Progressive Party outside of the political mainstream. The liberal attack was spearheaded by the CIO, Americans for Democratic Action, and the NAACP, which joined forces to frame

Wallace as "soft on communism," and the Progressive Party as the latest "communist front" bent on destroying the American way of life. The CIO urged its members not to support Wallace because such support threatened to divide the Democratic Party and facilitate a Republican victory. The CIO-PAC, which had been so supportive of Hill's candidacy in 1945, now went to great pains to ensure that all member unions and their locals understood the dangers represented by Wallace and the Progressives.[75]

The UAW's Executive Board denounced the Progressive Party as "a Communist Party maneuver designed to advance the foreign policy interests of the Soviet Union at the expense of democracy and freedom throughout the world." The ADA, for its part, released a four-hundred-page "exposé" of Wallace and his supporters. Worrying about Black Wallace supporters, or indeed anyone sympathetic to his brand of "communism," the NAACP also joined the anti-Wallace crusade. In Detroit, the ADA forces, which included Fr. Malcolm Dade, Rabbi Leo Fram, the Rev. Robert Bradby Jr. (who in many ways followed in the footsteps of his father, Robert Bradby Sr., who had died in 1946), Walter Reuther, Dr. James J. McClendon, Edward Swan (a former chief FEPC examiner for Michigan and the new executive secretary of the NAACP), and Paul Weber of the ACTU, as well as former members of the Left community such as George Edwards, organized around anticommunism and the defeat of the Progressives.[76]

This division in the Left community, which had been growing ever since the campaign for a state FEPC, broke wide open during the annual Labor Day parade in 1948. The remnants of the once vital left wing of the civil rights community was led down Woodward Avenue by Wallace, but his presence was overshadowed by President Truman, who chose Detroit's Cadillac Square as the site to kick off his reelection campaign. "The breach within the CIO was on public display that afternoon," recalled Coleman Young, "as the Reuther caucus paraded on the square behind Truman while the leftists and Progressives peeled off in another direction to rally on behalf of Henry Wallace." The Wallace campaign and the Progressive Party were, according to Young and others, ill-fated from the start. Young's own attempt to run for the state Senate on the party's ticket was, he stated, "the biggest mistake of my life . . . [for] it took me fifteen years to rehabilitate my position with the Democratic Party."[77]

At least Young, who would become not only a state senator but also the first Black mayor of Detroit, was able to eventually "rehabilitate" himself politically. Many of his associates were not so fortunate. Reverend

Hill's support of the Progressive Party—even after Wallace's defeat—cost him any chance, however slim, of winning a long-desired seat on the city's Common Council; it also seriously damaged his 1951 bid for Congress.[78] Within the Black community, Hill's church, Hartford Avenue Baptist, was known as "that Red church," although the majority of his congregation remained devoted. Hill continued to work around the Red label, but it did tarnish his hard-earned status as a tireless fighter for civil rights and social justice.

The anti-Wallace crusade could be seen as a foundational moment in the solidification of a liberal-labor coalition. This coalition had its basis in the old labor–civil rights community, but it pointedly excluded those, such as Reverend Hill, who remained in the CP's orbit. In a sense, anticommunism served the same unifying function for liberals as antifascism had for leftists during the Popular Front years. Furthermore, anticommunism probably hardened the identity of interests on both sides of the ideological divide. As members of the liberal coalition grew together, politically and ideologically, local members of the Progressive Party and the old Left community were wedded to one another by even stronger ties—ties formed not only through long-standing relationships but also through the shared experience of defeat. Responding to the negative publicity that Wallace supporters received at the hands of the conservative *Detroit News,* which published a list of "Reds for Wallace," Wallace himself called it "an honor list, with my good friend the Rev. Charles A. Hill; that progressive union leader George Addes; and that outspoken worker for the people, State Senator Stanley Nowak."[79] That must have offered some comfort. It is worth remembering, however, that the publicly drawn ideological lines were by no means always observed in the personal and social lives of local activists. By the 1960s, flexibility, which had long been a distinctive trait of the city's political mobilizations, would begin to reassert itself. There were certainly important divisions, but few were ever quite as starkly drawn as they may have seemed from the outside.

But the liberal anti-Wallace forces in Detroit were emboldened by their victory; their liberal anticommunism had found an even greater audience. The era of the united front was over, and ideological tensions within the Left played out repeatedly on the terrain of social activism. Of course, this contest between ideologies and organizations was hardly limited to Detroit but left its stamp on the civil rights movement nationally as well. When the NAACP organized its national civil rights mobilization in the fall of 1949, CP-aligned Left organizations and individuals were barred. When William Patterson, the chairman of the National CRC, protested his group's exclusion and appealed to the unity of all progressive forces, the NAACP turned him down in a scathing three-page reply written by Roy Wilkins. "In the present Civil Rights Mobilization we have no desire for that kind of cooperation, or that kind of unity," the letter stated.

> We do not believe it will contribute to the success of the campaign. On the contrary, we believe it will be a distinct handicap. The organizations sponsoring this Civil Rights Mobilization are seeking the enactment of civil rights legislation to the end that minority groups may be more fully protected in their rights under the American constitution and the American concept of democracy. We do not believe in light of the consistent performance of the Civil Rights Congress and its associates, that this is their end objective. This was the basic consideration in the decision not to list the Civil Rights Congress as an organization to be invited to cooperate.[80]

Like many anticommunist liberal groups, both nationally and locally, the NAACP and its allies latched on to the proposition that communists and their organizations must be disassociated from "legitimate" civil rights mobilizations. Whether this was true due to the political climate of the times, and if so to what degree, remains debatable.

The mobilization was a positive endeavor, but it is difficult to ignore the confusion over communism behind the scenes. The NAACP had already taken measures to exclude the Civil Rights Congress. Under orders from the CIO it also excluded the United Electrical Workers (a CIO member), as well as ten other unions under investigation for being "communist dominated" and therefore politically compromised. Moreover, it rejected out of hand the demand that Congressman Vito Marcantonio, one of the most consistent fighters for civil rights legislation in the House, be allowed to speak as a representative of the hated Progressive Party. To further guard against communist infiltration, all delegates were required to obtain certified advance credentials, which were authenticated by representatives of the NAACP, the CIO, the ADA, the American Jewish Committee, and other staunchly anticommunist organizations.

The differentiation between valid and nonvalid credentials was made almost capriciously. In one case, all the delegates from the New York City NAACP, whose president had photocopied his signature for the credentials of hundreds of attendees, were initially barred. The decision was not reversed until Adam Clayton Powell Jr. intervened. In another case, a wife was allowed in while her husband, a trade unionist from a politically suspect union, was not. The fact that many of those who were assigned to control admission were white did not help matters. "You people can afford to pick and choose who's going to fight for civil rights," a member of one group of Black delegates was reported to have said, but "[t]he fight is too tough for the Negro people for us to be so choosy."[81]

Nonetheless, the NAACP succeeded in bringing over four thousand people to Washington, DC, in February 1950, to press for civil rights legislation. In Detroit, over one thousand people gathered to hear Roy Wilkins and give local delegates a big send-off.[82] The mobilization, as one slightly disgruntled leftist commentator put it, "turned out to be a powerful outpouring of the determination of the Negro people to win civil rights despite possible embarrassment to either the Truman administration or the bourgeois and social democratic leaders of the over 50 'non-communist' organizations which reluctantly called the Mobilization."[83] The exclusion of the CRC and other radicals was an affront to William Patterson, however, who stepped up his critique of the NAACP and its liberal allies. Patterson hoped that his position against the NAACP would "certainly be a guide to action on a local scale."[84] Jack Raskin, head of the Michigan CRC, was less convinced. Tension between Raskin and the national office of the CRC had been developing for some time, and this conflict probably had something to do with his resignation as executive secretary in 1950.

Raskin's tenure as head of the organization had been mixed. The dedicated activist had established a wide network of contacts, most of which he committed to memory. He liked to get things done but was not fond of writing reports to the national office. He had the ability to work on many issues simultaneously, but his lack of organization could be frustrating to his coworkers. As Anne Shore, who left New York to become secretary of the Michigan branch around 1947, put it, the office was "a mess." "There is a fine potential here," she related, "but it is so amorphous that it drives me crazy. The hundreds of contacts we have all seem to be in Jack's head." Still, Raskin's dedication to the cause of civil rights, civil liberties, and antiracism led him to make enormous sacrifices. His CRC salary was always small, too small to support his wife and their young child, and Raskin resigned in late 1950 for "personal reasons"—even though he believed that the push for his resignation was influenced by the CP's desire to have an African American in this key leadership position.[85]

Sometime between the end of 1950 and the summer of 1951 Raskin was replaced by Arthur McPhaul, a Black communist and auto worker who had recently lost his job at Ford's River Rouge plant. Born in rural Georgia, McPhaul came to Detroit from Oklahoma with his family during World War I. The son of an outspoken Methodist minister, McPhaul was introduced to racial segregation at an early age. He later recalled that "it wasn't much better in Detroit than in the South, not a lot." He began working at Ford in 1935, and became a volunteer organizer for the UAW soon after. Like many others, he saw a direct connection between union organizing and civil rights and affiliated himself with both the NNC and the Civil Rights Federation. He also came to know Reverend Hill, whom he described as "one of the outstanding black leaders of that period" and whom he admired for Hill's commitment to "speaking out on issues that affected not only black people, the black community, but all poor people." Although there was certainly a great deal of anticlericalism in radical circles and a tendency to think of religion as "the opiate of the masses" and of ministers as ineffectual, McPhaul attended services at Hill's church with some frequency. The two men eventually became close friends and allies.[86]

So McPhaul was no stranger to the Left community when he took over Raskin's position at the CRC, nor was he a stranger to its racial dynamics. Patterson and others at the national offices insisted that African Americans be elevated to positions of authority on the local level, but, as McPhaul realized, such a policy rankled even "the best white people." True, some Blacks associated with the civil rights community could not seem to recall much racism in its ranks. "I don't get any feeling that there was any domination by whites," recalled Geraldine Bledsoe. "I was caught up in the middle of much of the civil rights movement, and I would say there were more whites than Negroes, but I would say they walked pretty much side by side." For the most part, Hill concurred. McPhaul tells a different story: "I guess it was part of the racist system in which they live. . . . I had a running fight all the time with Anne Shore. . . . I want to say I have a great deal of respect for her, but she was still full of chauvinism. Just could not accept leadership from a black person."[87] McPhaul's experiences left him bitter and disillusioned about the capacity of whites to thoroughly dedicate themselves to antiracism, but he was just as likely to find fault with African American liberals, not to mention conservatives.

Despite his criticisms, McPhaul never lost faith in the organization that he guided through its final years. His tenure as head of the local branch was an active one. In the early 1950s, the Left community was forced to divide its time between mobilizing on civil rights issues such as fair housing, fair employment, and police brutality on the one hand and the defense of civil liberties, and by extension their own political viability, on the other. While the CRC insisted that "in spite of all the hysteria being put in the papers that we are on the subversive list, we have plenty of support, not with the big shots but with the Negro and Jewish people we have a big circle of friends," community activism was becoming increasingly difficult.[88] As historian Ellen Schrecker notes in her study of McCarthyism and the American communist movement, the financial and human cost of defending members and sympathizers was exorbitant. "The struggle to fend off the government's onslaught turned the party and its adjunct organizations into self-defense groups," she writes, "preoccupied with fundraising and legal strategies."[89]

The result was a mixture of offensive and defensive tactics, of civil rights and civil liberties—*especially* civil liberties. The CRC worked on a wide and impressive variety of cases, including that of Lemas Woods. Woods was a private in an all-Negro army unit stationed in the Philippines who was accused of murder. Hastily sentenced to death by a military court, he sent a farewell letter to his father. The senior Woods, a member of UAW Local 208, spoke to his shop steward about his son's situation, and the steward referred him to the CRC. During the campaign to reverse Woods's death sentence and secure him a new trial the CRC distributed over thirty thousand leaflets and held dozens of community meetings in churches and other venues around the city. They took the case on in April 1946; in August 1947, after a new trial held at San Francisco's Presidio, Woods was found guilty only of involuntary manslaughter. His sentence was eventually reduced to eighteen months.[90] Much the same mixture of legal strategy and community activism was on display when the CRC mobilized around the shooting death of Leon Mosely, a fifteen-year-old African American boy who was beaten and then shot by police.

On the night of June 4, 1948, a police cruiser fell in behind Leon Mosely, who was allegedly driving in a "suspicious" manner. A pursuit began and was swiftly augmented by reinforcements. Several shots were fired during the chase, and Mosely drove the car, which turned out to be stolen, into a tree. According to witnesses, the police pulled Mosely out of the car and began to pummel him. Mosely either broke loose or was deliberately allowed to "wobble down the street," but in either case he was shot in the back and killed. The incident joined a long list of community complaints against the police and Police Commissioner Harry S. Toy. A Joint Committee for Justice for Leon Mosely was quickly set up, headed by the Rev. T. S. Boone, of King Solomon Baptist Church, and Coleman Young, with representatives from the CRC, the CP, the CIO Council, the UAW, and even the NAACP and the Michigan Committee on Civil Rights. Hundreds attended the young man's funeral, and days later thousands participated in a march to City Hall to demand action. Acting on behalf of the family, CRC attorneys pressed for and finally received a coroner's inquisition, which would investigate whether the officers involved had committed a crime and then make a recommendation to the Prosecutor's Office. The inquisition found unanimously that the shooting was "unwarranted and unwise" and that the two officers involved were culpable.[91]

The demonstrations continued, and the pressure eventually forced the Prosecutor's Office to act. Unfortunately, instead of issuing a warrant against the two officers for a felony, the prosecutor sought only a manslaughter warrant for one officer and none at all for the other. Commenting on this mixed success, Reverend Hill reminded his allies that "the fact that any type of warrant was issued against a police officer is a direct result of the organized protests and demonstrations of an aroused community." While he expressed regret at the weaker manslaughter charge, it was progress nonetheless, "for this is the first time that we have been able to get a verdict of any kind." Hill incorporated the case into his Common Council campaign and the Joint Committee for Justice kept up the pressure, only to be thwarted in the end by a recalcitrant Commissioner Toy, who refused to have the officer arrested.[92]

Attorneys Ernest Goodman, George Crockett, C. LeBron Simmons, and others associated with the legal staff of the Michigan CRC and the National Lawyers Guild spent a tremendous amount of time and effort on cases like those of Lemas Woods and Leon Mosely. They typically worked on a pro bono basis, and the resources that the CRC and community groups could generate were always spread thin. They were spread even thinner when the Left was forced to defend itself in cases such as that of the "Michigan Six," in which six members of the Michigan Division of the Communist Party faced trial for alleged violations of the Smith Act. This was only the first in a series of state-sponsored trials and hearings that would decimate the Communist Party and its sympathizers in Detroit and across the nation. In the words of Joseph Starobin, the foreign editor of the *Daily Worker,* the party became "at least a case of civil liberties, at best an object of sympathy, but no longer a power."[93] Much the same could be said for most of the men and women who had dedicated a portion of their lives to Detroit's early civil rights movement.

HUAC
The Un-Americans Come to Town

With the Korean War heating up, Detroit, still a center of defense industry production, was beginning to receive a great deal of attention from the government's subversive hunters. It was in this politically charged environment that the House Un-American Activities Committee set up shop and held hearings in the city in 1952. "The Un-Americans are sent to Detroit," warned Arthur McPhaul, "to put the 'fear of God' into the people. . . . [T]heir side show can prove exceedingly damaging to organized labor and the struggle for complete equality for the Negro people."[94] The cumulative effect of the hearings was indeed damaging, both politically and personally. McPhaul found himself a chief target of investigation. When he refused to turn over the records of the Michigan CRC, he was convicted of contempt. Ernest Goodman and George Crockett fought the conviction all the way to the Supreme Court, but ultimately lost, and McPhaul served nine months in prison in 1959.[95] He was just one in a long list of activists who were called before the committee. Eleanor Maki, one of the founding members of the old Civil Rights Federation, was also summoned. She treated Detroiters to some sensational newspaper coverage when she disappeared for two weeks before finally appearing in front of the committee,[96] after which she lost her job in the Detroit public school system, which had a loyalty oath of its own.

Coleman Young's testimony made him an instant celebrity in the city's Black neighborhoods for chastising the committee's counsel, a Virginian named Frank Tavenner, and the committee head, Congressman John Wood of Georgia, for mispronouncing *Negro* as *Nigra*. Recordings of his belligerent testimony on the "un-Americanness" of the proceedings against people who had been engaged in the struggle for Black rights were widely circulated. Reverend Hill was also called. While he refused to answer most questions on Fifth Amendment grounds, he did manage, despite the advice of his attorney, George Crockett, to get in a few verbal jabs. In response to the suggestion that he had been "used" by communists "for their own purposes," he replied that "the Bible is my only guide." "Do you mean," countered the senator, "that the Bible influenced you to sponsor a banquet for two Communists?" At another tense moment, Congressman Donald Jackson (R-CA) remarked with some asperity: "It is bad enough that a man should commit treason by joining the Communist Party. But for a minister, a wearer of the cloth, to aid and give comfort to communism is to compound that offense by including the Almighty God is his treason."[97]

The exchanges between Hill and the congressmen caused quite a stir in the Black ecclesiastical community. Once again, the "proper" role of churches and clergy, where and with whom they should stand, was avidly debated in Detroit. While most observers seemed to take offense at Congressman Jackson's remarks, their responses to the hearings were otherwise mixed. The Detroit edition of the *Courier* interviewed twenty-seven local pastors about Hill's testimony. Fifteen supported him outright, five did so with reservations, two condemned him, and an additional five had no comment. The strongest statement of support came from the young Reverend Albert B. Cleage Jr., who had just taken up his first pastoral appointment in Detroit at St. Mark's Community Church. "I have absolute confidence in the Reverend Hill's integrity, loyalty and Christianity, and I am much more willing to accept his definition of God's position on race prejudice, segregation and discrimination than I am of the House Committee on Un-American Activities," he told the paper.[98]

Horace White, once a political ally of Hill's and a mentor of Cleage's, was especially harsh in indicting his old compatriot. White characterized Hill as a communist "dupe" and well-meaning but naive. The third of the trio of pro-labor Black ministers, Fr. Malcolm Dade, who served on the city's Loyalty Investigating Committee, raised similar questions about Hill's political sympathies.[99] In fact, Dade claimed that his "feelings had been [so] aroused by the *hostility to the committee*" in Hill's testimony that he felt compelled to walk into the Federal Building and deliver a prepared statement to Chairman John Wood. "The disparaging remarks expressed yesterday by a clergyman . . . make imperative a statement by a minister of the Gospel of Christ of the true feelings of the Negro religious community regarding communism," the statement read. Dade wanted to make it as clear as possible that neither he, the Episcopal Church, nor Blacks in general had any doubts that "communism is most devilish. . . . For deep in the very marrow of the Negro's bones and roots, is a sincere love for God and a tested loyalty to his country." At any time when the nation's security is threatened, he assured the committee, the African American "closes ranks with his fellow Americans."[100]

There were some who felt that Dade and White had betrayed Hill, especially given their shared past of political militancy. Since the NAACP's Edward Turner had already strongly denounced the CP on behalf of both the NAACP and "the race" in his testimony before the committee, one wonders why Father Dade felt it necessary to add his own rebuke. But all three men seem to have been doing what they believed to be right, not only for themselves but for the larger communities they were dedicated to serving. Dade and White represent a road—a safe, liberal path—that Hill could have taken but did not. Although White died in 1958, Dade went on to enjoy a full and rich career as a well-respected pastor. In 1962 he was elected as the only clerical member of the Michigan State Constitutional Convention, and he served by appointment on a variety of city commissions from the 1940s until his retirement in 1972.[101]

Hill's reputation was once again damaged by this testimony but not destroyed. He maintained his position at Hartford, and no coordinated attempt was ever made to oust him. Young emerged from the hearings as a folk hero; recordings of his testimony were made, sold, and exchanged throughout Black Detroit.[102] The other men and women who were called included Stanley Nowak, who was nearly deported as a result; C. LeBron Simmons; Arthur McPhaul; and five members of Local 600 (Jack Conway, William Hood, John Gallo, David Moore, and Nelson Davis) who were subsequently fired and struggled for years afterward with damaged reputations and difficult work situations.[103]

It is not clear whether the government had an explicit strategy for destroying Left organizations and activists by forcing them into costly and prolonged legal defenses, but this was certainly one of the greatest successes of McCarthyism. When Black attorney and longtime NNC member C. LeBron Simmons was asked by an interviewer whether any significant questions had not been asked or answered in their session, he replied: "Yes, you did not ask me what it [my activism] cost me."[104] The costs for some were very high indeed. George Crockett served four months in prison for contempt of court in his defense of eleven CP leaders tried under the Smith Act in 1949. "When you come out of prison, people don't line up to have you represent them," he later remarked.[105] By 1956, activists such as McPhaul, who was soon to be jailed as well, were working on a voluntary basis, the funds of the Michigan CRC having been depleted by the cost of defending communists and suspected communists.

Likewise, the Michigan branch of the American Committee for Protection of Foreign Born, which had fought the deportations of radicals, was barely solvent. All of the HUAC proceedings were public, and the media coverage wreaked havoc on the social fabric of the city. One contemporary observer helpfully pointed out that "any social historian anxious to get the 'feel' of dark epochs like the Salem Witch-Hunt or the Stalin purges in Russia [could find] fertile soil in this tense, febrile city since the opening of the hearings by the congressional Committee on Un-American Activities last week."[106]

Sensational stories filled the major newspapers. In one auto plant, the wife of an accused "Stalinist" was driven from the plant, with newspaper men "egging on the workers for 'some action shots.'" Individuals were attacked on streets and in front of their homes. A prominent radio commentator and a well-known businessman both issued public statements after receiving death threats because people with names similar to theirs had been identified as communists.[107] The "Great Fear" had come to Detroit, but even as the HUAC hearings destroyed reputations and weakened political associations the adversity also strengthened the personal ties between activists. When Hill's oldest son, Charles Jr., was nearly drummed out of the air force reserves on charges of communist sympathies because it was reported that he read the *Daily Worker*, drove his father around town, and had attended a social gathering at his father's house, members of the Left community rallied to the young Hill's defense. "It was the only time I remember being afraid," recalled Charles Jr., who flew with the fabled Tuskegee Airmen. His sister Roberta and brother Lantz were similarly harassed.[108] George Crockett, Maurice Sugar, Ernest Goodman, and C. LeBron Simmons sacrificed careers spent defending wealthy clients, and their firm barely stayed afloat in its early years. "We didn't make much of a living during the McCarthy period," remembered Goodman, "but it was a hell of a practice."[109]

"Seeing that there was no venturing into the mainstream," recalled Coleman Young, "I pulled back and took refuge among one of my own." Having few other options, he and Jack Raskin opened a dry-cleaning business on Livernois Avenue on the city's northwest side (where a freeway stands today), "hoping that there was a living to be made on the shirts and slacks of Progressives and Communists." Discussions once held in union meetings, churches, and community forums continued, with such vitality that people complained "they couldn't get their pants back because we were always arguing about Wallace or Truman or DuBois." "I was a hell of a spotter," Young insisted. "It's just that there wasn't much of a call for politically enlightened spotters in those days." The social ties that had sustained the core members of the civil rights community did not disappear; people attempted to nurture them as best they could. The annual Buck Dinner, a tradition started by Maurice Sugar in the early 1930s, remained a cultural institution in Detroit's leftist movement culture. It provided an opportunity for activists and old friends to socialize, and it was also a venue for fund-raising for the defense committees of individuals and organizations. (The Buck Dinner continued, becoming in later years a source of funding for New Left activism in the 1960s.) "We stuck close to our friends," said Young. "Through it all we had a pretty good time together for a battered group of political misfits, which says something about misery and company."[110]

In one of the odder instances of an activist being persecuted for his or her views and activities, Claude Williams, who had transferred the home base of his Institute of Applied Religion from Detroit to Birmingham, Alabama, after 1944, was tried by the Presbyterian church for heresy. Williams was repeatedly accused of communist subversion by such prominent Red baiters as Gerald Smith and Elizabeth Dilling, and the Detroit Presbytery, to which Williams still technically belonged, along with the National Council of the Presbyterian Church, had finally had enough. Although the committee assigned to the case dropped the charge of communism on the grounds of insufficient evidence, they did find him guilty of heresy for his distinctive brand of politically charged theological innovation. He was officially defrocked and expelled—the only such case in the twentieth century. Hill's decision to reordain Williams as a Baptist preacher at a 1965 ceremony at Hartford—a move it was thought would help Williams's work with a new generation of southern civil rights activists—was a highlight in the two men's friendship.[111]

Although the early 1950s was a dark time for leftists such as Claude Williams, Charles Hill, and thousands like them in Detroit and across the nation, the city's Left community did not merely fade away. Reverend Hill remained a consistent voice for the civil liberties of all Americans, particularly those whose political affinities lay with the radical Left. He continued to use his church as a "free space" for organizing and exchanging ideas. Old friends and allies with national reputations, including Paul Robeson, Claude Lightfoot, and Ben Davis, were always welcome at Hartford Avenue Baptist. Hill merely insisted that members of his congregation transcend rumor and come and find out for themselves what such men had to say.[112] "Reverend Hill's church was one of the few places that Paul Robeson could come to Detroit and have a concert and go away with some money to help him live, really, during that period when he was denied places to give concerts in this community, as well as communities all over the country," recalled Geraldine Bledsoe in a story that was often repeated. "Reverend Hill's church was one church that was always open to him. And this was characteristic of his [Hill's] position in all of these matters."[113] In fact, Hill became so close to Robeson politically that at least one researcher identified him as "the leader of this group" of Robeson's followers.[114]

Reflecting the tenor of the times, Hill opened his church to a variety of cultural and political programs that often centered on Africa, Cuba, or the Soviet Union. Robeson's performances were always billed as cultural evenings, as were the cultural bazaars, discussions, and presentations of films. Many of these events were organized by another good friend of Hill's and Robeson's, Erma Henderson, a young Black woman who became involved in the Progressive Party, the Council on African Affairs (which was also an important concern of Robeson's and Hill's), and the fight for the Sojourner Truth Housing Project. Like Coleman Young, Erma Henderson eventually rehabilitated herself politically. She would go on to win and then hold a seat on the Common Council for over a decade.

Although his reputation had been sullied by the HUAC hearings, Hill continued to support the activities of older civil rights organizations such as the Civil Rights Congress, as well as newer ones such as the National Negro Labor Council. But realistically Reverend Hill's moment as the man "around whom the world of Negro activism turned" was at an end. There was a general recognition that the labor movement, which had provided such an important base for his activism, was becoming an increasing liability in the Black struggle for social and economic liberation. As the UAW became an institution to fight with *and* against, Hill found himself an ever more marginal player in the struggle led by Coleman Young and the other Black unionists associated with the NNLC.

In 1953, the Rev. Charles A. Hill celebrated his fiftieth birthday and his thirty-third year at Hartford. With what one author described as a "high, balding brow and copper skin," he was now a grandfather. Beyond his duties to his congregations, which were always demanding and important, Hill's activism was focused less on Detroit and more on national and international causes, including the American Committee for Protection of Foreign Born and the American Peace Crusade, which opposed American involvement in Korea. Both groups were eventually classified as subversive communist fronts by the government. Certainly, Hill's church remained a place where various ideas were discussed, but the locus of activism was shifting. It was a phase of civil rights activism of which Hill was certainly supportive but to which he was not central.[115]

IN THE SHADOW OF THE COLD WAR

In the shadows of the cold war, domestic anticommunism, and the raucous abundance generated by the nation's postwar economic boom stood thousands of Black workers who had lost their all too brief foothold in American industry. The government's attempts to silence "dangerous Reds" and free the nation from subversive influence did not visibly improve the lives of Black workers. Blacks had made important gains in Detroit's industries in the 1940s, but they were still largely confined to domestic labor in downtown office buildings and nonskilled labor in the plants and on construction sites. Based on the argument that whites would not accept close contact with Blacks, they were also barred from employment as delivery truck drivers and in the service departments of companies such as Michigan Bell. Nor could they secure employment in many of the city's retail stores. While Black industrial workers were attempting to hold on to the gains made during World War II and the Korean War, the boom and bust cycles that structured employment in the auto industry—along with the harsh processes of deindustrialization—hit African American workers, and especially Black women workers, the hardest.[116]

Unemployment in Detroit's African American community was by most estimates at least double the average for whites in every recession of the 1950s, and the same was true in Black communities across the nation. Yet the union movement put forth few coherent programs to deal with these racial disparities and their effects. Frustrated with this reticence, radical Black unionists, hamstrung as they were by the Red label, nonetheless took matters into their own hands; the NNLC grew out of the local activism of Black, and some white, unionists, particularly in Detroit and Harlem. In Detroit, Coleman Young and William Hood, the recording secretary of Local 600, were the driving force behind the creation of the Greater Detroit Negro Labor Council, which merged with other local councils in 1951. Although the Negro Labor Councils, much like the Jewish Labor Council and the ACTU, were union based, they had the support of community activists such as Hill and Erma Henderson, as well as national figures such as Adam Clayton Powell and Paul Robeson, who sang and addressed the crowd at the NNLC's founding convention in Cincinnati in 1951.

"We approached Cincinnati in two capacities, basically," Young explained, "as Negroes and Black people, and as trade unionists. And we dedicated ourselves to a dual role: to bringing democracy to a trade-union movement . . . and using that trade union base to move the trade-union movement and our white allies within it into the liberation struggle for Black people, with a primary concentration on economic issues."[117] The conditions facing Black women and southern workers received a great deal of attention at the founding convention and from the national body throughout its existence. "We need not continue to be driven backwards on the South," declared Black unionist Viola Brown, who reported on Black oppression in the South at the convention. "We need not let the South remain an unorganized base for us, and an organized base for reaction and fascism. We in the South believe that a force can be made . . . if together, North and South, we begin to make it."[118]

As part of its "Gateway to the South" mobilization, the NNLC fought to make sure that African American workers got a fair share of the jobs in new Ford and General Electric plants opening in Louisville, Kentucky. The campaign was spearheaded by the Louisville chapter of the NNLC. Coleman Young, along with Nadine Baxter and other Detroiters, went to Louisville to protest the discriminatory practices at the Ford plant; both Young and Baxter were arrested. Back home in Detroit, what was left of the Left within Local 600 demanded that the UAW get involved in the situation in Louisville. Under the continuous assault of "advertisements, protests, demonstrations, and legal action," both Ford and General Electric were forced to comply with the NNLC's demands. The group also managed to secure small but significant victories for Black women.[119]

At the founding convention, over a third of the delegates were Black women. Octavia Hawkins, a Chicago garment worker and member of the Amalgamated Clothing Workers Union, served as its first treasurer. The body adopted a resolution calling for "job opportunities for Negro women throughout industry, in offices, department stores, public utilities, airlines, etc."; for the organization of domestic workers, "both North and South"; for job training and upgrading for women; and for "the right to play a leadership role in government, industries and the unions, based on demonstrated ability and willingness to give leadership in family and other struggles." This emphasis on Black women in itself represented a significant advance. Throughout its existence, the old civil rights community tended to submerge gender issues under those of race and class. The resulting myopia is epitomized in comments such as this one from Charles Hill: "I never made appeals on behalf of Negro women, only women." In contradistinction to such attitudes, the NNLC attempted to articulate and mobilize around the specificity of interlocking forms of race, class, and gender oppression.[120]

This resolution was behind the NNLC's decision to confront the Sears and Roebuck Company, which had a robust policy of racial discrimination. Picket lines were set up outside of Sears stores in Cleveland, Detroit, Newark, Philadelphia, Saint Louis, and Chicago, the site of the company's headquarters. After long negotiations and much agitation, practically all Sears outlets outside of the Deep South had come to terms with the activists by 1954. As part of its southern campaign, the NNLC also targeted southern factories that employed high percentages of Black women; in 1953, for example, it sponsored a strike among Louisiana sugar workers. In Detroit, the labor council, which included unionists such as Nadine and Willie Baxter, Chris Alston, and Harold Shapiro, as well as community activists such as Ernest Goodman, Hill, Erma Henderson, and Nadine Gordon (the Detroit correspondent for the *Detroit Courier*), concentrated its efforts on a new mobilization for municipal FEPC legislation.[121] Back in 1946, the Left community had turned to the initiative petition to force action on fair employment legislation; in 1951, the Detroit Negro Labor Council used the same strategy on the municipal level. And once again the campaign to secure fair employment legislation was ensnared in factional fights. As the Detroit council began its petition drive, liberals associated with the NAACP, the Jewish Community Council, the Detroit Interracial Committee, and Catholic organizations concentrated their efforts on persuading the city's Common Council to enact the legislation and thereby defeat the "Reds."[122]

To ensure the defeat of the petition drive of the Detroit NLC's, the liberal coalition also stepped up their anticommunist crusade. The Michigan Committee on Civil Rights (MCCR), a liberal umbrella group that grew out of the older, anticommunist Michigan Council for Fair Employment Legislation, referred to the Detroit NLC's backing as the "kiss of death" for FEPC legislation and reaffirmed its opposition to that group, for "posing as friends of FEPC this group consists almost entirely of people expelled from the CIO for Communist sympathies." Speaking on behalf of the UAW, Walter Reuther called the petition drive an "irresponsible Communist-inspired approach" that was "not cleared with the UAW-CIO." Along with seven other international officers, Reuther issued a directive to local unions calling upon auto workers who had signed the petition to withdraw their signatures.[123] Thanks to this confusion, the petition and its model FEPC ordinance were successfully kept off the ballot.[124] The liberal coalition was no more successful in its policy of suasion than the Detroit NLC had been with its petition campaign, but at least the liberal coalition could deflect attention away from its own shortcomings by exposing the "communists." Detroit and the state of Michigan would have to wait until 1955 before FEPC legislation was finally enacted.[125]

The experiences of the Detroit NLC were not dissimilar to the experiences of the NNLC overall. While the group could claim small successes, it could not withstand the anticommunist assault from liberals, unions, and the government. In 1956, the NNLC was placed on the U.S.

attorney general's subversive list and investigated by the Subversive Activities Control Board (SACB). Instead of fighting an expensive legal battle, the NNLC voted to disband. Council secretary Coleman Young spoke for many in the old Left community when he issued the following statement after destroying the group's records.

> In surveying this situation, the leaders of the [NNLC] came to the conclusion that we would not dissipate the energies of our members attempting to raise the tremendous sums of money required to go through the SACB hearings, and at the same time, jeopardizing their personal well-being when the freedom struggle is at its present height.[126]

The idea that the NNLC could operate under the fetters of anticommunism was improbable from the beginning. Like so many other left-wing efforts organized to secure the socioeconomic and civil rights of Blacks, the NNLC did not survive the cold war. And yet it did succeed in raising, once again, certain issues—about the failure of the labor movement to deal with its internal racism and employment discrimination, about the inseparable relationship between race and gender; and about the need for Black self-determination in the context of coalition building—that would structure the course of civil rights activism in Detroit over the next two decades and beyond. By the end of the decade, a younger cohort of activists would begin to ask the same questions and devise new political strategies. Many of the older activists, such as Reverend Hill, whose politics had been shaped by the Depression, World War II, and the difficulties of the postwar period did not manage to adjust to the "new mood" of Black political radicalism in the late 1950s and the 1960s; others, such as Christopher Alston and Coleman Young, did. It was the latter group that bridged the gap between the early civil rights community and the later one that rose and took its place as a new local movement with its own cultures of protest and struggle and its own complex ties to religion and faith.

FIVE

THE FREEDOM STRUGGLE
NORTH AND SOUTH

Coalition Politics and the
Foundation of a Second
Civil Rights Community in Detroit

"I think we overestimated the potential support of the trade union move-ment," Coleman A. Young lamented years after the National Negro Labor Council had been hounded out of existence in the late 1950s, "and underestimated the necessity of rooting ourselves in the ghetto." We needed," Young continued with the clarity of hindsight,

> in retrospect, it seems to me, a more even-handed approach . . . and we had an unrealistic concept of how far the trade union movement would go without organized pressure and support from the black community. We were "'way out in front.'" Life took care of that. When the man cracked down we didn't have but one place to go and that's back to the ghetto.[1]

Young was not the only person to journey back to the ghetto. An entire cohort of Black activists felt it could no longer rely on a labor movement that was increasingly bureaucratic and recalcitrant about the racism in its own ranks. Nor could these operatives continue to rely on the Communist Party, which, along with most of its "front groups" (such as the Civil Rights Congress) had been driven underground by the anticommunist crusade.[2] More broadly, Young's assessment also reflected some activists' growing skepticism about the viability of coalitions formed with leftist and liberal white allies.[3]

The events that unfolded in the South during the early years of the modern civil rights movement offered a model for collective action and self-determination within African American communities at large. There was a sense that what was being done in the South out of circumstance and necessity could be implemented in Detroit by design. It was this sense that fueled the rising popularity of Black nationalism in some Detroit activist circles during the late 1950s. In Detroit, Black nationalism came to stand for a "political return to the ghetto" and the principles of grassroots community organizing. But the idea itself, however defined, was not new. Detroit had a strong and vibrant chapter of Marcus Garvey's UNIA dating back to the 1920s and played host to the nascent Nation of Islam, whose Temple #1 was constructed there. Although Black nationalism was opposed by activists such as the Rev. Charles A. Hill, it eventually became, in a sense, Detroit's "other" social, political, and cultural tradition—one that younger activists would eagerly tap into.

Detroit's new articulation of Black nationalism was driven not only by the conservatism of the labor movement and the narrowing of political alternatives under McCarthyism but also by dramatic changes in the city's social and economic landscape. The 1950s were hard on the city and its residents. If there was any truth in the old saying that "as goes Ford, so goes Detroit," then things were not going well. After the loss of profitable defense contracts from the Korean War, area plants scaled back production and laid off thousands of workers. Smaller concerns, such as Hudson and Packard, were unable to compete in the new marketplace and ceased production altogether. It was not until the mid-1960s that the industry would experience an upswing in the bust-and-boom cycle. The processes of decentralization, implementation of new technologies, and suburbanization of the white workforce combined to transform the industry and the city.[4] Industrial decentralization and the movement of plants to the suburbs and other areas of the country began in earnest in the 1950s. As an example, in 1941, the year of the crucial Ford strike, the automaker's massive River Rouge complex had employed eighty-five thousand workers. By 1957, due to automation and decentralization, only forty thousand workers remained.[5]

Automation was supposed to increase efficiency at the point of production, but it came at an enormous cost for unskilled workers. The jobs that had provided a point of entry into the industrial workforce for first-

generation Europeans and later for Black Americans were in short supply. African American workers were confined to unskilled positions during the twenty years from 1940 to 1960, not only in the automotive
industry but in other occupations as well. Nearly two decades of struggle
for fair employment practices had culminated in the Michigan Fair
Employment Act of 1955. Yet in 1960 nearly 70 percent of all Black male
laborers were *still* classified as unskilled factory operatives, service workers, or day laborers, exactly the same percentage as in 1940. In 1950,
Black families' average income was 76 percent of that of white house-
holds; by 1960, the number had fallen to an even more dismal 52 percent.[6]

As contributors to family earnings, Black women continued to lag
behind men. The employment opportunities for women were greatly
diminished in general throughout the 1950s, as Black and white women
were forced out of industrial jobs gained during World War II. Although
the UAW had a special Women's Bureau to deal with issues of work and
gender, the union was disinclined to fight for the retention of its female
members.[7] Wanita Allen, a young Black woman and former domestic
worker, was hired at Ford's River Rouge plant during the war and then
was laid off in 1945. "After a taste of a decent job," Allen later remarked,
"to go back to housework [was] just almost impossible." Divorced and
with a young daughter to provide for, she had few alternatives. Although
women workers did make steady gains throughout the 1950s (33 percent of women age fourteen and older worked outside of the home by
the end of the decade), six out of every ten Black women workers were,
like Allen, employed in domestic and service jobs. Only 20 percent of
Black women worked at the more profitable jobs available in industry,
sales, or office work, compared to nearly 60 percent of white women.[8]
Detroit also suffered through four major periods of recession in the
1950s, further aggravating the effects of gender and race discrimination
in the workplace and union halls. As a result, unemployment at the end
of the decade hovered at 10.2 percent overall and 18.2 percent for
African American men and women. The situation was even worse for
young workers, with unemployment among those age sixteen to twenty-
nine ranging from a high of 76 percent to a low of 21 percent, depend-
ing on whether the assessment was based solely on conditions in Detroit
or in the entire metropolitan region.[9]

The construction of an extensive highway system around and
through the city during the postwar period—unaccompanied as it was by
the creation of a modern mass transit system (a deficit that plagues
Detroit's workers to this day)—quickened the suburbanization of the

city's native white and ethnic white population, which followed the industrial exodus. During the 1950s, over 350,000 white and white ethnic, mostly young families made the transition from city to suburb in pursuit of their own American Dream: home ownership, good schools, a nearby shopping mall, and racial and class homogeneity. Since most of Detroit's suburban areas initially barred Blacks, Latinos, and in some cases Jews, it was the non-white and multiracial poor who were left behind in the inner city. At the same time, more Blacks were making the transition from the South to urban areas such as Detroit. Black southern workers, who were pushed out of the rural South by the introduction of more efficient farming technologies and the transition to less labor-intensive crops such as timber and feed, were attracted to Detroit by the illusion of better employment opportunities and less systematic discrimination. The illusion proved powerful, even at this late stage; during the 1950s, 'Detroit's African American population grew from 303,000 to 487,000, or 29.1 percent of the city's total. White and white ethnic out-migrants and Black in-migrants effectively passed each other coming and going.[10]

Not everything associated with this transformation of the city was bad. In fact, an old joke circulates among some older Black Detroiters about standing at the city limits and waving a cheerful good-bye and good riddance to departing whites, especially the transplanted southerners. The numerical increase of the non-white population translated into impressive gains for Black politicians. Blacks were elected to the Detroit School Board, to other administrative positions, and, as was the case for attorney George Crockett, to key judgeships. By the mid-1960s, a total of ten Black state legislators had been elected, including Coleman A. Young, who had by now managed to rehabilitate his reputation in Democratic circles. Largely due to the existence of Detroit's two large Black congressional districts, Michigan was also the only state to send two African Americans to Washington as members of its congressional delegation. Finally, in 1957, Black attorney William T. Patrick Jr. broke the racial barrier to the city's Common Council—the goal that had eluded Reverend Hill for over a decade and the Black community for even longer.[11] Patrick was followed in 1965 by the Rev. Nicholas Hood, who always fully acknowledged the role of Hill, Reverend White, and others in laying the foundation for his achievement. Straddling the pulpit and the podium, Hood served as senior pastor of Plymouth Congregational until 1985 and maintained his council seat until he retired in 1993.[12]

Meanwhile, suburbanization reduced some of the city's racially based housing tensions, as primarily middle-class Blacks moved into the Twelfth Street area, which was previously occupied mostly by Jews. Blacks also began to move into other parts of the city. The rate of Black home ownership, which was always relatively high in Detroit, nearly doubled, exceeding 40 percent by the mid-1960s. "Detroit was not unlike Chicago or Harlem where there was a concentration of Black people," observed a local activist. "But Detroit was unique in terms of the geographical patterns of how we lived—significantly homes, a basement, a back yard." It is no small matter, for instance, that Motown Records was founded in a privately owned residence on West Grand Boulevard: "Our homes were points of congregation. That gave us a certain control and development that likely triggered the later development of Motown," recalled the label's founder, Berry Gordy. The struggling young company's location gave its early recordings a distinctive flavor. "Motown was a family, right from the beginning," Gordy remembered, "living together, playing together, making music together, eating together."[13]

Still, the majority of Blacks suffered in inadequate housing. Many of the young artists who found a surrogate home and career at Hitsville, USA, had been raised in the city's deteriorating projects, and the majority of the private housing available to minorities remained substandard. Of the eighty-seven thousand new housing units built between 1940 and 1952, for instance, only 2 percent were available for Black residents. Restrictive covenants had been ruled unconstitutional in 1948, but the efforts of white residents to bar Blacks, coupled with the discriminatory policies of banks and the Federal Housing Administration, worked against African Americans' quest for better housing.[14]

The city instituted a series of slum clearance plans throughout the 1950s and 1960s. Initially, these programs, which were supposed to be offset by the construction of new, low-income housing, did not seem like a bad idea. "Raze the Slums," had been a liberal rallying cry since the early decades of the twentieth century. Reverend Hill had supported the idea in his 1940s Common Council campaigns, and the issue was a perpetually popular one within the city's Left community. In practice, however, the slum clearance program did more harm than good. By the 1950s, the Black population was finding out that "urban renewal," as the saying went, really meant "Negro removal." Across the country, urban renewal policies destroyed African American neighborhoods. Little or no effort was made to relocate the displaced. The Detroit Plan for urban renewal was conceived under Mayor Jeffries in 1946 but was implemented in 1950 under a new mayor, Albert Cobo, who actively opposed public housing.[15]

Although nearly two thousand Black families were quietly displaced in the clearance of some 129 acres of Black Bottom in the oldest core of

Paradise Valley, Cobo studiously ignored the plan's already vague requirement to replace the lost homes with new low-income dwellings. When the first housing project on the cleared land was finally erected in 1958, rents were four to ten times higher for the middle-class residents of the site's new Lafayette Park development than they had been when the area was still a slum. The same sequence was repeated throughout the city's older core areas, as urban neighborhoods gave way to luxury apartments, highways, industrial parks, and medical complexes. In the midst of this massive redevelopment drive, which spanned the period from 1956 to 1966, only 758 low-income units were constructed.[16]

The result was even more overcrowding, unsanitary conditions, and vice in the few besieged neighborhoods that remained. In a broader sense, the city also lost its centers of culture and community. Black Bottom was, as Coleman Young put it, "a thrilling convergence of people, a wonderfully versatile and self-contained society. It was degenerate, but not without a lofty level of compassion. It was isolated, but sustained by its own passion. It was uneducated, but teeming with ideas. It was crowded, but clean. It was poor, for the most part, but it was fine."[17] While readers might question Young's rather rosy memories, many older Detroiters would likely agree with his sense of loss over the reduction of a wide array of vital Black businesses, including jazz clubs, restaurants, and barbershops, as well as homes and churches, to piles of rubble. In the end, slum clearance, for the most part, merely reproduced what it was supposed to destroy.

Many Black Bottom refugees resettled in and around the Twelfth Street district (north of Grand Boulevard between Linwood and Hamilton Avenues), which had recently served as a haven for Black middle-class homeowners. Neat single-family homes with front lawns and backyards were arrayed along either side of Twelfth while the avenue itself was lined with crowded, increasingly dilapidated apartment buildings interspersed with mostly Jewish-owned stores and businesses. The neighborhood's Jewish population, which had been located in the Hastings Street area until World War I and the influx of African Americans into the city, once again found itself living on the front lines of a Black "invasion."

As older Jewish and other white residents fled the neighborhood, rents skyrocketed while maintenance and services declined. The area's very modest African American population in 1940 had grown by 1950 to over one-third non-white. By 1960 the area had become overwhelmingly Black, with only 3.8 percent white residency. It's density of over twenty-one thousand persons per square mile was more than twice that of the city's other neighborhoods. Pimps, prostitutes, and numbers runners followed their lower-class Black clientele, and the Twelfth Street commercial strip from West Grand Boulevard to Clairmount Avenue soon replaced Hastings as the center of both high and low Black nightlife. This "east-side invasion" bred class resentment among middle-class residents struggling to maintain their hold on the neighborhood.[18]

The brutal processes of urban renewal also provoked the city's clergy, and especially the Rev. Nicholas Hood, to a new wave of activism. Hood was a newcomer to Detroit. Born in Terre Haute, Indiana, and educated at Purdue University and Yale Divinity School, he pastored New Orleans' Central Congregational Church from 1949 to 1958. During his tenure there he significantly improved the church's physical plant, installing central air-conditioning just before his departure to the relief and delight of his congregants. He also threw himself into the nascent civil rights movement, working with the local NAACP, helping to found the New Orleans Improvement Association (established on the model of Montgomery, Alabama's association), and participating in the founding of the Southern Christian Leadership Council. Hood was called to Detroit in the fall of 1958 by the members of Plymouth Congregational as a replacement for the Rev. Horace White, who died in February of that year. The congregation was doubtless attracted by Hood's similarity to White. Both men were well educated and well spoken, and both were inspired to liberal activism by the dictates of the social gospel. In fact, as a divinity student at Yale, Hood had studied under Liston Pope and H. Richard Niebuhr, Reinhold Niebuhr's brother. And Hood found White's legacy a "natural fit." Taking after his predecessor, Reverend Hood was dedicated to the notion that "The soul cannot be saved without saving society."[19]

Plymouth, located at the intersection of Garfield and Beaubien Streets, was situated in the midst of the old decaying center of Paradise Valley, a society in need of a lot of saving. "It was right in the heart of the slums," Hood recalled. "There was prostitution; Hastings was right around the corner." And yet he also saw a great deal of potential. After praying about it and consulting with his wife and children, Hood agreed to relocate. Two years into his new ministry, Reverend Hood opened the pages of the local newspaper only to discover that Plymouth was part of a 450 acre plot to be cleared during a new wave of urban renewal. To make matters worse, the plans called for the removal of all the neighborhood's Black churches, while leaving white religious institutions intact. In response, Hood pulled together a coalition of clergymen, from the pastors of large established churches such as Plymouth to the ministers of small storefront churches, and created, in 1961, the Fellowship of Urban Renewal Churches "for the purpose of trying to get the city to change its policy to allow Black institutions to remain in the neighborhood." By then, the Cobo administration (1950–57) had been replaced with that of Mayor Louis C. Miriani (1957–62), who was not inclined to cut deals with the fellowship; several displaced churches were forced to sue for the right to buy land within the proposed renewal area.[20]

The rebuff from the mayor's office encouraged the fellowship's ministers to unite with labor and civil rights activists against Miriani, who had never been popular among the Black population. This seems to have been one of the first times that storefront preachers, who lacked the class and social status of their more established counterparts, were included in any sort of political coalition. When the liberal Jerome P. Cavanagh was elected mayor in 1962, the fellowship justifiably claimed part of the credit. "Overnight," remembers Hood, the policy was changed. "Well, that showed me the power of politics," he reminisced. Impressed by this experience, Hood ran for Common Council, unsuccessfully, in a special election in 1964 and then successfully in 1965.[21]

His position at the pulpit, in the community, and on the council made Reverend Hood a prominent member of the city's liberal coalition. He continued his housing ministry at Plymouth, eventually working directly with the office of Housing and Urban Development (HUD) to create the Medical Center Court, a twenty-acre, 230-unit development that was the first low- and moderate-income project built in the city since World War II. Unlike city-sponsored urban renewal programs, the Medical Center Court plan allowed some of the area's displaced residents to return to the neighborhood after the complex was opened in 1963. The center was also one of the first housing projects to be sponsored by a church, at a cost of three million dollars. As part of his efforts to "humanize urban renewal," Hood also arranged for Plymouth to be relocated to a spot just a few blocks from its original location (which became a parking lot for one of the area's new hospitals). It was moved to the corner of Warren and St. Antoine, right across the street from Bethel AME, one of the oldest Black churches in the city, which was also able to remain in the area as a result of the protests.

Despite such important victories, local, state and federal governments were painfully slow in addressing the new realities in the inner city. In the expanding economy of the "Affluent Society," poverty and structural racism were not supposed to exist outside of the "backward" South. Nicholas Lemann exaggerates only slightly when he points out that "anyone working, during the late 1950s and early 1960s, on the assumption that a Northern racial crisis was on the way had ventured into daring, avant-garde intellectual territory."[22] Although Detroit eventually played a large role in the nation's war on poverty, few of the city's mayors or the state's governors offered constructive plans to deal with urban decay or racial and socioeconomic inequalities until the 1960s. The UAW had failed in each of its attempts to elect one of its own as mayor, and the Common Council was severely polarized on racial issues. Cumulatively, political, spatial, social, and economic shifts forced activists to devise new strategies in pursuit of civil rights and social justice. These new strategies would be devised by men and women who formed a second civil rights community, the center of a new local movement in Detroit.

Although some of veterans of the old NNLC and the Civil Rights Congress were able to bridge the generational gap, the first- and second-wave communities had their own distinctive characters. They share certain "family" resemblances but were also characterized by important differences in context, organizational structure—particularly institutional and noninstitutional loci—and ideology. Yet, like its earlier counterpart, the later community found its moral center, to some degree, in Black churches that were hospitable to its movement culture. The Christian faith and the conservatism of certain clergymen were often subjected to scathing critiques, but some young activists did accept spiritual solace, and political direction, from one minister in particular, the Rev. Albert B. Cleage Jr., whose Central Congregational Church (later the Shrine of the Black Madonna) was located on Linwood at Hogarth, near Twelfth Street. Here, again, the shift in the city's political geography from the east side to the northwest was evident. Central Congregational was just down the street and around the corner from New Bethel Baptist, which was pastored by the Rev. C. L. [Clarence LaVaughn] Franklin, yet another Black preacher who would soon leave his mark on Detroit.

By transforming Central Congregational into a "free space" for Black militants of diverse political persuasions, and by translating his own political theology into the language of the Black liberation movement, Cleage served a function in the later civil rights community similar to that provided by the Rev. Charles A. Hill in the earlier period. Indeed, Hill's relationship with Cleage offers one lens through which to view the relationship between the two communities. Their often-public theological and political disagreements helped to define the differences between two periods of Detroit activism and the role of religion in each.

The later community and its movement culture did not spring into existence fully formed, however. The two protest centers were separated by a lull in the cold war, the rise of the southern civil rights movement, and continued negotiations among labor, liberal, and leftist activists in Detroit and across the nation. It was a period in which the labor-liberal coalition, having succeeded in marginalizing the Communist Party and its political milieu, dominated oppositional politics.

In the years between the Montgomery Bus Boycott and the passage of the Civil Rights Act, this often troubled coalition shaped the tenor of activism in northern centers such as Detroit. Although self-styled militants would eventually denounce the liberal coalition for its "gradualism" and "middle-class orientation," it was an important point of reference for the development of those same militants' political consciousness. It was also a significant force in its own right. As Reverend Hood put it, "I was not as 'radical' as Hill, White or Dade, and surely not Albert Cleage; but there are many ways in which to accomplish the goal of FREEDOM." He continued,

> I come out of the freedom movement in the South (New Orleans), and we used the method of the "good guys" and the "bad guys" all working to win the goal of desegregation. I was the one inside negotiating with the power structure and my friends were on the outside protesting. This method worked all over the South, so I brought this technique with me to Detroit, and in six years I was elected the second Black councilman in the modern history of Detroit.[23]

Hood also worked with the NAACP, serving from time to time on its Executive Board, and was appointed to the Detroit Commission on Community Relations (DCCR). Like the stories of other individuals and organizations of the period, Reverend Hood's experience offers insights into the strengths and shortcomings of a liberal coalition that felt it had the right to a seat at the negotiating table. Hood's story also exemplifies some of the ways in which clergymen continued to struggle in search of a role in local activism.

ROSA PARKS, THE AFL-CIO, AND THE LIBERAL-LABOR COALITION

In retrospect, the divisions within the national liberal-labor coalition were due not only to strain in the alliance between African Americans and the CIO but also to timing and circumstance. On December 1, as the Congress of Industrial Organizations and its longtime rival the American Federation of Labor were meeting in separate conventions to put the final touches on a merger agreement, a Black southern seamstress, Rosa Parks, was refusing to move to the "colored" section at the back of a Montgomery, Alabama, city bus. Her ensuing arrest was not Parks's first act of political resistance but just the latest in a string of protests that had structured her entire political life. She had served as secretary of the local NAACP since 1943 and was a supporter of the Brotherhood of Sleeping Car Porters. Ms. Parks was arrested and jailed for her supposed offense on the bus. Five days later, as the CIO and the AFL were holding their first joint convention as the newly formed AFL-CIO, the Montgomery Bus Boycott was kicked off with a mass rally in one of the city's Black churches.[24]

The creation of the AFL-CIO and the start of the Montgomery Bus Boycott naturally affected the course of civil rights activism in Detroit, as elsewhere. The National Negro Labor Council, with its strong Detroit council, approached the union merger cautiously while simultaneously celebrating the boycott. "December 5th will be an historic date for American Labor," the NNLC wrote in an open letter to the AFL and the CIO.

In combining their 15 million members into a new labor organization, the AFL and CIO took a long and significant step toward the realization of one of labor's most cherished objectives—the unity of all who labor under the banner of a single mighty union. But while the council "hail[ed] present developments toward labor unity because of these positive potentials . . . and because of the specific impetus that labor unity could give to the centuries old struggle for the Negro people in America for Full Freedom," the new union's commitment to racial equality within its own ranks was not, the council warned, "automatic or built-in." "In fact, as the merger provisions now stand," the NNLC suggested, "there is every reason for grave concern." Contrasting the Supreme Court's 1954 rejection of separate but equal in *Brown v. Board of Education* and the leaden pace of unionization in the South, the NNLC took great pains to demonstrate the weakness and inadequacy of the union's "mealy mouthed language" on Black civil rights.[25]

The AFL-CIO's statement against racial discrimination was indeed mealymouthed. The leadership's rhetoric opposed racism in its member unions but refused to bar AFL craft unions, some of which had a long and ongoing history of excluding Blacks. Moreover, the delicately brokered agreement contained no mechanism for sanctioning unions that continued their racist practices, whether formal or informal. The maintenance of unity between the relatively progressive CIO and the relatively conservative AFL required that such controversial issues be handled carefully. This sometimes meant minor concessions to Black demands. A. Philip Randolph, of the Brotherhood of Sleeping Car Porters, for instance, was elected to an AFL-CIO vice presidency; and a special Civil Rights Department was created with initial support from Randolph and the NAACP.[26] At the same time, the AFL-CIO's new Executive Board remained silent on the yearlong bus boycott in Montgomery. Even the boycott movement's public appeals to morality failed to prick the conscience of the board, whose members refused to endorse either the 1956 National Day of Prayer or the 1958 Prayer Pilgrimage for Freedom to the nation's capital to demand civil rights legislation. On issues of economic justice, the Executive Board's responses ran the gamut from silence to outright hostility.[27]

Although such inconsistencies made it clear from the beginning that the newly merged union was going to be at best a diffident ally, the demand for economic justice—a central concern of Detroit's labor-based civil rights movement—united southern and northern struggles in the mid-1950s. Indeed, the Montgomery Bus Boycott (and Baton Rouge's bus boycott three years earlier) should be seen in the same light as urban Black boycott movements that had been used in such places as Detroit, New York, and Chicago since the 1930s. The old slogan "Don't buy where you can't work" was translated by Montgomery activists into "Don't ride."

In his first speech after he agreed to lead the bus boycott, and in his later assessment of the boycott in *Stride toward Freedom* (1958), Dr. Martin Luther King cited the historical precedent of the labor movement and its importance in his own efforts to secure economic justice. "Labor unions can play a tremendous role in making economic justice a reality for the Negro," King wrote. "Since the American Negro is virtually nonexistent as the owner and manager of mass production industry, he must depend upon the payment of wages for his economic survival." Nearly 1.3 million African Americans belonged to the member unions of the AFL-CIO, he pointed out, meaning that only "combined religious institutions" could claim greater Black membership. As such, King insisted that the labor movement take a leadership position in civil rights struggles. "The Negro then has a right to expect the resources of the American trade union movement to be used in assuring him—like all the rest of its members— of a proper place in American society. He has gained this right along with all the other workers whose mutual efforts have built this country's free and democratic unions."[28]

The conjuncture of the civil rights and economic justice movements greatly influenced the early years of the modern civil rights movement in the South, which was overwhelmingly working class. The Highlander

Folk School, which was organized by southern labor activists in the 1930s (many of whom were rooted in the same spiritual and ideological soil as their comrade, Claude Williams), was dedicated to the education and mobilization of southern Blacks and whites. Seasoned activists such as Rosa Parks and Ella Baker had worked with Highlander for years, and the school became an important site of activism during the modern civil rights struggle. Meanwhile, King and other southern activists joined their northern counterparts, including A. Philip Randolph and the Brotherhood of Sleeping Car Porters, as well as leftists in the NNLC, in demanding that the AFL-CIO abolish discrimination in its member unions and shops.[29]

The connections between race and economics were embodied in the presence of labor–civil rights activists such as Rosa Parks, E. D. Nixon, and Bayard Rustin, to name just a few of the most visible figures associated with the southern-based movement. Nixon, one of the organizers of the bus boycott, worked with Parks and members of the brotherhood, and was a local official of the old AFL. Rustin had been a member of the Young Communist League in the 1930s, a youth organizer for the 1941 March on Washington movement, and a cofounder of the Congress for Racial Equality (CORE). He had successfully incorporated the Gandhian philosophy of nonviolent direct action into the first Freedom Rides staged by CORE in 1947, and when he got word of the Montgomery situation he traveled south to meet King and get in on the action.[30] A similar identity of interests was also at work in the North in cities such as Detroit. Much of Detroit's history of civil rights activism had been linked to labor and working-class issues. Furthermore, a number of Black workers had been involved in both northern and southern struggles, and for many of these workers the South was still home.

A sizable percentage of Detroit's African American population had migrated to the city from Mississippi, Alabama, and Georgia; travel back and forth between home and adopted home was easy and consequently common. As a result, many Black Detroiters developed a transregional consciousness. Transplanted southern Blacks followed the southern struggles with great interest, contributing funds, favorable publicity, prayers, and in some cases direct action. When the brutal murder of Emmett Till, a fourteen-year-old African American youth from Chicago, hit the national press in 1955, complete with gruesome photographs, Blacks across the nation were outraged. Like their southern counterparts, northern Black politicians, including Detroit's Charles C. Diggs Jr., who had taken over his father's seat in the state legislature, traveled south to witness the trial of Till's murderers. The Detroit community, like those of other cities, held rallies and fund-raisers in support of Till and his family.[31] Snow Grigsby, whose career as a local activist stretched back to the early 1930s, had been making the North-South circuit since the 1940s, protesting southern injustices on behalf of the NAACP. Charles Denby, a Black auto worker who came to Detroit during World War I, developed relatively close ties to the small Detroit section of the Socialist Workers Party, and had been active in various aspects of the labor–civil rights struggle, returned home in 1955. "I decided to go to the South," he wrote in his autobiography, "when so many new developments were taking place among the Blacks." He went to offer his services as an activist and organizer, voicing his personal critique of Walter Reuther and members of the AFL-CIO hierarchy, who either openly opposed the boycott or remained silent.[32]

The North-South connections worked in both directions. The promise of industrial employment and a better life had lured Ernest C. Dillard away from Alabama, and Dillard (not a blood relation to the author) arrived in Detroit in June 1938 with approximately five dollars, a borrowed suitcase full of possessions, and a supply of syrup sandwiches. "It was the next day after Joe Louis won from Jim Braddock. I left the night of the fight," he recalled. He celebrated the Brown Bomber's victory in Detroit "since down there we couldn't talk about black folks knocking out white folks, not even in a mixed group." His wife, Jessie Mae Dawson, whom he had married on Christmas Day, 1934, at the Hutchinson Baptist Church in Montgomery, Alabama, and their two children, Marilyn and Ernie Jr., joined him eleven months later.[33] Jessie Dillard became a central figure in her new city's block club organizations and in the local ACLU. Ernie Dillard shared his wife's interests and also became active in UAW politics (in Local 51 at the GM Fleetwood plant) and the NAACP's fight to break down restaurant discrimination.

Like Charles Denby (the pen name of Simon P. Owens), Dillard was active in the Socialist Workers Party until, as a member of the so-called Cochranite faction led by Bert Cochran, he broke with the party around 1953. Dillard later enjoyed a long career as a frequent contributor to the Cochranites' *American Socialist* magazine. Although he and his wife remained in Detroit for most of their adult lives, physical distance did not dissipate their ties to the region they still considered home. In 1956, Dillard organized a small committee to fund the publication of his anti-segregation pamphlet "An Open Letter to the White People of Mississippi." As a UAW local officer, he continued to insist that the nation's "most progressive union" take a more aggressive stance in support of southern Blacks. In both direct and indirect ways, the southern struggle framed Dillard's activism in Detroit.[34]

TULC AND THE LIBERAL-LABOR COALITION

While Blacks in Detroit certainly supported the southern struggles, there was a recognition that Blacks in northern centers faced a different set of circumstances. Blacks in Detroit could vote, but they were still forced to contend with police brutality and discrimination in housing, employment, restaurants, and shops. "Black Detroiters," as one observer put it, "didn't compare their lot in life to Black Wattsites, Black Harlemites or Black anywhere else. Black Detroiters compared their lot in life to white Detroiters."[35] And compared to those white neighbors African Americans in the city had worse jobs, worse homes, worse schools, more unemployment, less political representation on the local level, and a more circumscribed range of personal and collective freedoms. In response to these problems, the ongoing Black freedom struggle witnessed the growth and consolidation of two major focal points—or local centers—that directed and coordinated activism in the decade between 1957 and 1967.

The first of these centers of activism was the liberal-labor coalition, which had grown out of the Black-union alliance during and after World War II and whose history I have already begun to sketch around figures such as the Rev. Nicholas Hood and issues such as urban renewal. For the most part, this group was dominated by the generation of activists that had worked with, and then against, the old Left community. The UAW, widely regarded as one of the most progressive unions in the nation, was involved in the coalition along with the NAACP, Black churches, the Jewish Community Council, the ACLU, the Detroit Urban League, the Detroit ADA, the Michigan Committee on Civil Rights, and other civil rights organizations that had managed to survive the HUAC trials.

There were, however, observable generational differences. The new liberal-labor coalition had no core institution comparable to the Communist Party, which had once so effectively held together a wide network of organizations and individuals. The union, having lost some of its moral authority, fulfilled this function as best it could with assistance and prodding from the NAACP and Detroit CORE, both of which lacked a mass base. The Detroit NAACP had gone from being the largest and most aggressive branch in the country, with 25,000 members during

World War II, to only 5,162 members in 1952, partly as a result of the organization's adoption of a less confrontational approach. The Detroit branch of the Socialist Workers Party was relatively small and did not have the capacity to function in the same way the Michigan Division of the CP had at its height.[36] Once archenemies, the MDCP and the Detroit NAACP now found themselves in a simultaneous decline.

The massive drives to unionize Black, white, and white ethnic workers, which had given rise to the early civil rights community, were no more. It was the unique concentration of industry that had fostered a many-sided Left in the city in the first place. While industry's presence in Detroit continued to fuel labor activism, unions gradually became something to fight *against*. Activists often found themselves in search of other means through which to protest and apply pressure. At times they were forced to go over the heads of the unions (to federal agencies such as the U.S. Civil Rights Commission), to undercut them (by appealing directly to the rank and file), or to circumvent them (through contacts with the NAACP and other community-based organizations). At still other times, frustrated activists tried to blast right through the wall of union indifference by means of open confrontation. The situation was not without its ironies. For instance, Black unionists had once denounced the NAACP for not taking a strong stance on labor questions, but after the AFL-CIO merger it was the NAACP's Labor Committee, headed by Herbert Hill, that played a major role in critiquing the unions.

In 1957, Black unionists, including Horace Sheffield, Ernest Dillard, and Robert "Buddy" Battle (who, incidentally, was the second husband of Coleman Young's first wife), along with Willie Baxter and Nadine Brown of the then defunct NNLC, formed the Trade Union Leadership Council (TULC), which was intended to make up for the UAW and NAACP's failures to address the needs of Black workers. For the most part, the TULC, which later formed an affiliation with the Negro American Labor Council (NALC), A. Philip Randolph's new "Negro caucus" in the AFL-CIO, continued where the NNLC had left off, despite the groups' ideological differences.[37]

These differences were of long standing. The TULC was formed around a core of longtime Reutherites, who had opposed the Addes-Thomas-Frankensteen caucus that was once been so supportive of Black demands. Some TULC members had ties to the SWP and harbored bitter memories of being denounced, as Sheffield put it, as "black fascists by these people." "Look," he continued, "every twist and turn that the Communist Party made, they made it too." Having survived and supported the Communist purges, such individuals were now forced to work within the same kinds of constraints they had one imposed on their Communist colleagues.[38] The irony is that the TULC later launched campaigns on some of the very same issues—especially the need for a "Black seat" on the UAW's International Executive Board—that the CP-backed factions had once fought for and that Reuther-aligned Black unionists had been called on to oppose.[39]

The TULC described itself as "a non-partisan and non-profit organization devoted to the struggle of all people, for first class citizenship, full freedom, and unrestricted equality in every aspect of the political, economic, and social life of America." Recognizing the historical affinity between African Americans and the unions, the TULC pledged itself to "create a better understanding and more wholesome relationship between the Negro people, and the labor movement."[40] It worked, that is to say, within the existing paradigm of civil rights protest. The TULC was as cognizant as any other organization in the city of the significance of Black churches, and it incorporated a director of religious affairs into its leadership structure from the very beginning. The group was also active in a range of cultural activities, especially the promotion of Negro History Week, and in efforts to educate society about Negro history and culture in general. Its agenda did not, however, include a call for Black nationalism.

Ernest Dillard, for one, was of the opinion that "the last thing blacks need to do [is] to go on a corner and start hollering, 'Black! Black! Black!'" Similarly, Battle and Sheffield publicly disagreed with the Rev. Albert Cleage about the viability of an all-Black slate of candidates in the 1962 elections. Cleage "supported an all-black slate," explained Sheffield, "and, hell, we said, 'that's crazy.' We supported an integrated slate—we had a Polish candidate, we had a Jewish candidate. In that respect we were bound to be in conflict." It was hardly the last time these men and their organizations would clash.[41]

While the TULC was not terribly different, ideologically, from the NAACP, it did provide a more congenial home to unionists. The TULC's Freedom House became the center of social life in certain activist circles. Although the organization's inner sanctum was accessible only to members and their guests, an array of leftists and liberals frequented its popular bar area. "There is a discussion of ideas," Sheffield explained at the time, "and we have the price of drinks as low as we can. Every Saturday we have 400 to 500 people here that socialize, dance, have drinks, etc—this is how we keep the doors open."[42] Coleman Young, for example, did not have a very good political relationship with the TULC but could often be found at the Freedom House bar drinking and swapping stories. After he regained his status in the Wayne County AFL-CIO and ran for elective office, he often relied on the grudging support of TULC members. Other older leftists, such as the CP's Christopher Alston and Ernest and Jessie Dillard, who were associated with the SWP and its splinter groups, also participated in the social life of the TULC and contributed to its activities. If people knew about Dillard's SWP affiliations, and certainly many did, no one ever harped on the matter publicly.[43] "Party lines" were often blurred in the social circles of Detroit activists.

The TULC considered itself a militant organization, especially where racial discrimination in the unions and the building trades was concerned, and its members often worked with the NAACP and the liberal-labor coalition to achieve its goals. Both organizations participated in a series of confrontational boycotts and picket lines that benefited their middle-class and working-class constituencies. Given the lack of opportunities for training and career advancement in the Black community, both groups focused on creating opportunities for skilled workers.[44] They shared many objectives and even some of their members. Willie Baxter, for instance, was the head of TULC's Civil Rights Department and also served on the Executive Board of the Detroit NAACP. TULC members Horace Sheffield and Ernest Dillard had worked with the NAACP for decades. The two groups grew even closer once the TULC decided to drop its policy of excluding nonunionists.

One of the most successful (nonunion) joint activities conducted by members of the TULC, the NAACP, and others was a protest against restaurant discrimination. In the mid-1950s, Ernest and Jessie Dillard, along with James Boggs, yet another transplanted southerner with ties to the SWP, helped to form the Discrimination Action Committee within the NAACP. It was the first organized group to systematically deal with the widespread discrimination in the city's restaurants. Dillard wanted "to do a little something" in Detroit, as he said a few years earlier when he addressed a SWP meeting on the "Negro Question." During that forum, he spoke of the need to reassess the NAACP. It was not so much the NAACP that "had changed," he said, but the nature of civil rights struggles, especially in the South. "If we got a good ear to the ground we might be able to do a little something," he told his audience, "in connection to making friends and influencing people. That is, in direct contact." As Boggs recalls it, he and Dillard "called ourselves infiltrating the NAACP."[45]

Dillard sought to revitalize the organization's Detroit office by embracing direct-action techniques. The Discrimination Action Committee's principal mission had been to target restaurants, but its scope was later broadened to include roller rinks, bowling alleys, bars, hotels, and other entertainment and recreational venues.[46] The committee's style was simple. Members met every Friday night to identify restaurants with histories of discrimination against Black patrons; "sandwiched" or interracial teams of volunteers then entered these establishments and sought to be served. "We didn't have any money," recalled Arthur Johnson, who became the executive secretary of the NAACP in 1949, "so we got the cheapest thing on the menu."[47] If service was denied—thereby violating the Diggs Law, which prohibited racial discrimination—the police would be called and charges brought. The courts were a last resort if no agreement could be reached through other means.

Much of this activity involved local union officials—Black, white, and Jewish—and rank-and-file members, who often drew a direct, albeit imperfect, analogy between picketing and sit-downs in restaurants, on the one hand, and the sit-down strikes during the early years of the CIO on the other. Oscar and Dolores Paskal, both of whom were unionists, secular Jewish socialists, and members of Detroit's CORE, related much of their early involvement in breaking down restaurant discrimination to the workplace, principally the need to lunch near downtown offices. Similarly, Ernest Dillard recalled loosely organized "attacks" on restaurants and bars around the plants where he and James Boggs worked involving coworkers: "you know, just ordinary folks offended by overt racism."[48] Ethel Schwartz, a Jewish office worker, says that "she merely went to lunch with some colleagues from the Office Professional Employees Union." The interracial group just "happened" to go to Sero, a restaurant in downtown Detroit that did not serve African Americans. Schwartz, who had been involved with the Unemployed Council in the 1930s, downplayed her involvement. But as Black worker Dave Moore, who met her in the 1940s, notes, "Ethel led the fight. . . . She organized a picket line right around the restaurant. The picket line grew and grew. After a couple of days, it just got so that no one went in there."[49]

This activism was often countered by restaurant owners' efforts to make their food and beverages inedible to their interracial would-be clients. And neither the police department nor the courts always fulfilled their obligations under the state Civil Rights Law. "All that shit is true," concurred Marilynn Adams, a young Black woman who worked at the law firm started by Ernest Goodman and George Crockett and who became the first TULC secretary. Adams remembers bouts of physical illness after being served tainted food and being chased by policemen hostile to their activities. Adams, whose family had been members of Reverend Hill's Hartford Avenue Baptist Church since the 1920s, was not "risking her life," as young people were in the South. But she was "deeply moved" by the southern struggles and wanted to get involved with similar activities in Detroit. She was just one of the innumerable young people whose political lives were structured around the NAACP, their churches, and organizations such as the TULC—and later groups such as CORE, which was revitalized in the early 1960s.[50]

Marilynn Adams's position in the TULC office also introduced her to a broad range of labor issues. Her father had been employed in the automobile industry since the Depression, but her knowledge of union politics had until then been primarily secondhand. For Adams and others her age, the introduction to union politics was not marked by the optimism of the 1930s and early 1940s but by resentment bred by the often strained relationship between the UAW and minority workers. After nearly twenty years, Black workers were still not being upgraded and trained in skilled trades, and the UAW had yet to elect a Black representative to its International Executive Board. The demand for a Black member on the board, which was once dismissed as a communist ploy, was now dismissed as "reverse Jim Crow." African American workers had gotten a foot on the bottom rung of the ladder but in the majority of cases were unable to climb any higher.

When the U.S. Civil Rights Commission held hearings in Detroit in 1960, the UAW was confronted with hard facts about its failure to address the hopes and aspirations of its Black membership. According to testimony given before the commission, much of it by Horace Sheffield, only 1 percent of tool and die makers were Black, 1 percent of structural workers were minorities, 1 percent of carpenters, 2.1 percent of electricians, and 5.2 percent of mechanics or job setters were non-white. The numbers were not much better in city plants. There were only 341 Black workers in skilled positions at the Big Three automakers' plants out of a total skilled work force of 15,550. Few young Black workers were allowed into apprenticeship programs, and Blacks in management were almost nonexistent.[51]

When Herbert Hill, the Jewish head of the national NAACP's Labor Committee, released his assessment of the first five years of the AFL-CIO, it revealed the same pattern nationwide. Hill's report charged that the union was more concerned with creating "a liberal public relations image" than attacking internal and external discrimination. The testimony of unionists such as Sheffield and Battle before the Civil Rights Commission, alongside Hill's report on internal racism among AFL-CIO member unions, expanded the already substantial rift between Blacks and the union.[52] The TULC's mild critique of the UAW's racial practices gave way to angry demands. In 1957, the TULC could praise the labor movement for being "far in advance of the rest of the community in the fight against discrimination" while noting that some of its member unions had barely began to take up the struggle. But by 1962 their criticisms took on a harsher tone, focusing on the movement's duplicity and paternalism. "The old clichés, the syrupy sentiments are no longer saleable. The pious platitudes about patience and fortitude we leave to the Uncle Toms," read an open letter printed in the *Vanguard,* the TULC's official publication, edited by Ernest Dillard. "A man either has full equality or he doesn't—there is no satisfactory twilight zone between."[53]

The union met these criticisms with hostility. Although its Executive Board had never seemed rankled by the existence of the Association of Catholic Trade Unionists and the Jewish Labor Committee, the TULC and NALC were denounced in the old anticommunist language of "dual unionism" as threats to movement unity. When A. Philip Randolph insisted that the color line be eliminated in member unions—a position wholly consistent with the AFL-CIO's statement against discrimination— George Meany, long-time head of the AFL and subsequent president of the newly merged union, personally accused him of arrogance in presuming to speak for all Black workers.[54] Back in the 1940s, the Rev. Horace A. White had complained that the union movement, particularly the UAW, had usurped the Black church's moral authority in the flowering of civil rights activism; by the 1960s, it was patently clear that the unions had ceded the high ground.[55]

The political alliance between Blacks and labor, which extended back to 1943, also showed signs of strain when the TULC flexed its independent political muscles by backing an unknown—Jerome P. Cavanagh—in the mayoral election against the UAW-supported incumbent, Louis C. Miriani. Like his predecessors, Miriani had lost favor in the Black community by insisting that all of the city's problems could be solved through increased law and more order and by sanctioning a police crackdown in African American neighborhoods. The police department, which was 96 percent white, declared open season on "suspicious" minorities, and its efforts resulted in mass arrests, legally questionable detentions, and beatings. While the ACLU and the NAACP, whose executive secretary, Arthur Johnson, had been stopped and searched without cause, protested Miriani's crackdown, the real upheaval came during the mayoral campaign. Executives within the TULC, who, like Horace Sheffield, were also UAW staff officials, found themselves in a tight spot: their allegiance to the union (and their jobs) required them to support Miriani, but their allegiance to the city's African American communities required that they oppose him.

The TULC directorate chose to oppose the union. Marilynn Adams recalls Black unionists dropping off boxes of Miriani campaign literature in one part of the TULC's Freedom House and taking Cavanagh literature out the back door. Launching a "5 plus 1" campaign, they held massive voter registration drives and fund-raisers for Cavanagh and five Common Council candidates, including Black attorney William T. Patrick, an incumbent, and block club organizer and Wayne State University sociology professor Mel Ravitz, a newcomer. With the help of the TULC and the Black community's anger at Miriani, Cavanagh, the thirty-one-year-old longshot, staged the greatest political upset in many decades of Michigan politics. He carried 85 percent of the Black vote and 56 percent of the total; William T. Patrick, Mel Ravitz, and three other TULC-supported liberals were also either elected or reelected to the council.[56] Horace Sheffield reaped praise for helping to engineer the victory, as did Black ministers led by the Rev. Stephen Spottswood, pastor of the Metropolitan AME Church and a relative newcomer to the city. As chairman of the Political Affairs Committee of the Interdenominational Ministerial Alliance, Reverend Spottswood prevailed upon other ministers, including Reverend Hill (with whom he had worked closely), to support Cavanagh. Spottswood's decision to campaign vigorously for the young challenger grew out of a conversation with Sheffield after the two men had watched Cavanagh make his initial bid on television.[57] It was merely the first of many joint electoral partnerships between the TULC and the ministerial alliance.

Anyone fond of historical parallels would appreciate the basic similarities between Cavanagh's victory and the victory of Frank Murphy nearly thirty years earlier. Both men appealed to and won support from similar social groups—Blacks, the poor, and ethnic workers. Both men were also Catholics who supported the church's more progressive positions on social action. Murphy promised a "new era in the Tabernacle" of city government, while Cavanagh advocated a heightened sense of decency, especially with regard to race relations. Both mayors also insisted that the federal government play a central role in finding solutions to urban problems. Frank Murphy was pro–New Deal before there was a New Deal, and Cavanagh spearheaded the federally financed War on Poverty programs in Detroit. Between July 1, 1962, and August 1, 1967, Detroit received more than $230,422,000 from the government's coffers. Even with the infusion of government monies, Cavanagh, much like Murphy, found that the city's financial woes impeded his efforts to make good on his campaign promises.

Cavanagh did, however, appoint more African Americans to administrative positions than had any previous mayor, and he won the gratitude of Black Detroiters by appointing George Edwards, a former UAW organizer, city councilman, and Michigan Supreme Court justice, to be the city's new police commissioner. Together Cavanagh and Edwards promised to revamp the Detroit Police Department and "teach the police they didn't have a constitutional right to automatically beat up Negroes on arrest."[58] After the riots in 1943, Edwards had pointed to the "open warfare" between the police and Blacks as one of the city's leading sources of unrest. In 1961, he still believed that "Detroit was the leading candidate in the United States for a race riot."[59]

Thus, the 1960s opened on a relatively optimistic note for the liberal civil rights coalition. The TULC was just reaching what would prove to be its peak of thirteen thousand registered members, and many civil rights activists felt that the new mayor was willing to take progressive action to alleviate the city's tensions. Southern sit-ins and Freedom Rides were attracting national attention and galvanized northern communities into action. Residents of Detroit participated in the southern struggle in a number of ways. Some, such as Walter Bergman, a teacher, union activist, and member of CORE, participated in Freedom Rides; others such as Viola Liuzzo, the wife of a Michigan Teamster official and member of the local SWP, joined in the voter registration projects. Their involvement came at a high price, though. Bergman was nearly beaten to death, and Liuzzo was killed in Alabama by the Ku Klux Klan.[60]

Less dramatically, Detroit took part in a series of boycotts against national chain stores such as Woolworth, whose regional southern outlets practiced racial discrimination. Picket lines, "manned by 100 students, trade unionists, and sympathizers," were set up around Woolworth stores downtown, as well as on the city's east side and in the university towns of Ann Arbor and East Lansing, in a show of solidarity "with southern Negro students who sparked a wide-spread movement against Jim Crow practices in Dixie lunch counters operated by Woolworth Corp."[61] The TULC orchestrated the collection of funds, food, and clothing to ship south for distribution in its own version of "strike relief." The southern struggle was invoked time and time again as a way to mobilize support for hometown political projects. "No one in their right mind would deny that had Dr. Martin Luther King and the Montgomery Bus boycotters failed in their historic struggle," read a representative TULC flyer urging support for William T. Patrick and Mel Ravitz in the 1961 Common Council elections, "the cause of freedom in America would have been seriously retarded." The elections themselves became part of Detroit's new "Operation Freedom."[62]

This overwhelming sense of optimism was propelled by the pulse of the upbeat Motown sound. "The trappings of a new age were all around the city," wrote Coleman Young, with Motown's recordings "tapping into the indigenous rhythms and prodigious resources [and] remaking the image of the Motor City with sweet and funky urban music by the likes of the Supremes and the Temptations and the Four Tops and Marvin Gaye."[63] "I was influenced by the Motown sound," says JoAnn Watson, longtime executive director of the Detroit NAACP. "Much of the music was a real anthem for many of us."[64] But Motown's musical optimism was also cited by the national media in their efforts to create a falsely harmonious image of the city. Almost overnight, Detroit became a "model city." According to the *National Observer,* earnings were up, unemployment was down, and slum clearance had made Detroit a more livable city. In the realm of race relations, a reporter for *Fortune* was positively effusive.

> Detroit has acquired freshness and vitality. . . . Accustomed to years of adversity, to decades of drabness and civic immobility, Detroiters are naturally exhilarated. . . . Of all the accomplishments in the recent history of the city, the most significant is the progress Detroit has made in race relations. The grim specter of the 1943 riots never quite fades from the minds of the city leaders. As much as anything else, that specter has enabled the power structure to overcome tenacious prejudice and give the Negro community a role in the consensus probably unparalled in any major American city. . . . Negroes are sufficiently well organized socially and politically to have elected a member of the Detroit common council in a city-wide election. They have also elected three local judges, ten state legislators, and two congressmen (Michigan is the only congressional delegation in Washington with two Negroes.)[65]

These were important gains. But the focus on high rates of home ownership, employment gains, and the number of Blacks elected to public office obscured the deep structural problems still plaguing the city's working-class and lower-class residents. Activists critical of the liberal coalition felt that these economic and racial improvements were not enough. This feeling was particularly strong among a number of young activists who eventually joined forces and went "back to the ghetto," as Coleman Young once phrased it. This group was to form the core of the second of the city's new movement centers.

BACK TO THE GHETTO

Opposition to the labor-liberal coalition prompted the development of an alternative center of protest in early-1960s Detroit. This center is harder to define than the liberal-labor coalition that coalesced around the TULC and NAACP, but is in some ways more dynamic and intriguing for its fluidity. Unlike the liberal coalition, this second group did not automatically regard the trade union movement as an ally and was relatively uninvested in the specifics of liberal anticommunism. Moreover, its institutional loci were more dispersed and community based. Like the early civil rights community, this alternative center was interracial, though less so by the end of the 1960s than in its early days. For many young people coming of age at the time, neither the TULC nor the NAACP or CORE seemed quite radical enough; they felt a need to seek out alternatives. It was among these young activists that Black nationalism, linked to the class struggle in Detroit, the nation, and the world, would find its most receptive audience.

The nascent Black nationalist center was comprised of young workers and students who were as invested in the southern struggle as were their older counterparts. Many were the sons and daughters of unionists. Some gravitated toward individual members of the SWP and the party's Friday evening Labor Forums. Others were greatly influenced by independent Marxist thinkers such as Grace Lee and James Boggs. Still others were high school and college students disaffected with the status quo but who had yet to gravitate toward any particular ideological position. As one of these activists, Mike Hamlin, put it: "During the period from 1957 to about 1965 many young blacks, black workers in particular, in northern cities like Detroit found themselves greatly frustrated, alienated and disaffected by the conditions facing us."[66] For all of their diversity of background and experience, Hamlin's portrait is broadly accurate. Certain themes emerge again and again from group members' biographies: a working-class background, involvement in the southern civil rights movement, a sense of alienation, and a desire to act.

"My family," said Dan Georgakas, a Greek American activist who later chronicled the struggles of his friends and allies in the League of Revolutionary Black Workers, "was horse collar, New Deal Democrat and very pro-union, in Detroit mostly meaning the UAW." The UAW was so prominent in Detroit that "even as a child you were drawn into union politics at family picnics on Labor Day," recalled General Baker, whose family migrated to Detroit from rural Georgia in 1941. The Bakers made a home in the east-side ghetto of Black Bottom and "lived on the ups and downs of the auto industry like most working-class families in Detroit."[67] Like the Bakers, Mike Hamlin's family was composed of southern share-croppers who migrated to Detroit during World War II. While working on the loading docks at the *Detroit News,* Hamlin met two other future activists: John Watson, one of the hundreds of Black students at Wayne University (renamed Wayne State University in 1956); and Ken Cockrel, who went on to become one of the city's leading radical attorneys. Hamlin credits Watson with helping him channel his anger into constructive outlets. "I was angry," recalls Hamlin, "when I came back to Detroit in 1960 from the army."

> I was interested in terrorist kind of activity. It was a response to frus-
> tration. A lot of people at that time talked about kamikaze or suicidal
> attacks. You would end your pain and strike a blow. But then I met
> John Watson. . . . And [I felt] maybe there could be a greater impact
> by organizing people and focusing on the working class. It was
> through him that I began to understand classes and class society.[68]

Ken Cockrel also cited his friendship with Watson, along with his experiences at Wayne State, as important factors in the development of his political identity. Indeed, Wayne, which by the mid-1960s had more African American students than all of the Ivy League and Big Ten schools combined, was a central site of congregation and political education. Like the families of so many from his cohort, Cockrel's relatives worked in the auto industry and the service sector. When times got hard, they went on public assistance. As a result of two separate accidents only months apart, Cockrel had lost both of his parents when he was twelve years old. He lived with relatives until he dropped out of high school in his junior year and joined the armed services. After three years of army life and an honorable discharge, he decided to return to school. Although he lacked a high school diploma, administrators at Wayne allowed him to take an entrance examination, which he passed, and to enroll as a political science major. Cockrel became involved in Left political circles at Wayne, worked a number of odd jobs, and managed to complete both a bachelor's degree in political science and a law degree.[69]

Some of these young seekers, like Luke Tripp, another African American student at Wayne who entertained a youthful desire to blow up Mississippi, felt that religion was relatively unimportant to their political identity. Tripp was baptized a Catholic but preferred to think of himself as "a free thinker."[70] But, as in the early civil rights community, many of the new generation felt the need to translate their religious faith into political commitments and a more secular morality. This process of translation often involved leaving the institutionalized church in favor of a "revolutionary morality." "When I was eighteen I left the church," remarked Charleen Johnson, who became involved in community organizing and welfare issues. She left because she felt that the church inculcated a sense of powerlessness in its members' lives. For Johnson and others, religion was the "opiate of the masses," part of the system that must be opposed. "At the time we were entering into the sixties, the civil rights movement, and I got involved in the revolution. I was looking to overthrow the system."[71]

There was nothing novel about this tendency. Some segments of the clergy, particularly those disposed to a social gospel perspective, had long chastised the church for being insufficiently engaged in addressing social ills. It was certainly the nationalist-minded Rev. Albert Cleage's position that Black urban churches had failed to keep pace with the needs of their congregants and that these churches needed revitalization lest they become totally marginal to the life of the urban communities they were supposed to serve. The Black church, insisted an African American clergyman writing in the pages of the radical journal *Freedomways*, had been lax in its "moral responsibility" to set standards. "It is no secret," he wrote, "that the church has allowed the labor movement, NAACP, CORE, the entertainment world, and the world of sports to push ahead of it, all too often, in the struggle for freedom and equality."[72]

An impulse to leave the church was common among members of the city's second civil rights community. But it was far from universal. Socially concerned Catholics, for instance, found the climate in some parishes more hospitable to their ideas when Vatican II opened the church to the winds of change in the late 1950s and 1960s. This change built on Detroit's long tradition of Catholic activism, especially around the Catholic worker movement of the 1930s. Some priests, such as Fr. Clement Kern, had actually worked with the old civil rights community. While the second-generation movement was taking shape, Catholic activists, young and old, were taking steps to revitalize the church's Left, particularly around issues of racism and economic marginalization. "The

Catholic church did a good job on me," recalls Eleanor Josaitis, another young woman involved in community organizing. "Feed the hungry meant something to me even as a kid. I was always trying to figure out a way to translate the gospel message into my life. . . . [Then] came the civil rights confusion of our time. I became a follower of Dr. Martin Luther King."[73] Sheila Murphy Cockrel, the wife of Ken Cockrel, was also influenced by her Catholic background. "I grew up in the Detroit Catholic Worker movement," she reminisced. While she accepted her parent's religious values, she rejected their pacifism. Civil disobedience was for her an important political tool, but "not a stance about life." "I began working in '66 for the WCO [West Central Organization]," she continues, "which was the first citywide attempt at community organization that was rooted in the concept of self-determination, using the Alinsky model." Her parents were also active in the formation of WCO and served on its Board of Directors. It was during her WCO days that she met and married Ken Cockrel.[74]

Peggy Posa, a Protestant, also insisted that her "first introduction to the social-issue arena came from a strong religious background. The first issues I was actively involved in were the civil rights movement and the anti–Vietnam War activities." Posa worked with Ken and Sheila Cockrel and Mel Ravitz, who was a leading figure in the city's block club movement, in which religious institutions were often central.[75] Ravitz was born in New York City in 1924 but raised in Detroit. He had worked with the liberal coalition since the 1950s in organizations such as the NAACP, the TULC, and the small local chapter of CORE. In 1961 he, along with William T. Patrick, became one of the most liberal voices on the city's Common Council. Trained as a sociologist, he got his start in city politics in 1953 when he went to work for the City Planning Commission's crime prevention and neighborhood preservation program.[76]

In this capacity, Ravitz helped to lay the foundation for later groups such as the more militant and confrontational WCO. Organizing block by block in homogeneous areas, as well as interracial and interethnic ones, Ravitz, and later much of Detroit's block club movement as a whole, "made the alley the focus of our first action efforts to consolidate the thinking of the people of the neighborhood."[77] He also understood that churches, as social institutions rooted in the life of the surrounding community, were important sites for organizing block clubs and community associations. Throughout the 1960s, religious organizations remained a major source of funds for community activists. The WCO's first director, the Rev. Richard Venus, was a white clergyman, and religious bodies, including the Archdiocesan Solidarity Foundation and the Detroit Catholic Worker, as well as area churches and parishes, all contributed to the cause.[78]

While block clubs, made up primarily of home owners, were initially viewed as conservative, middle-class organizations, some did take on a more political bent. The change was supported and encouraged by the local NAACP and the Detroit Urban League,[79] which published their own newspapers and collectively defined problems and solutions. Eventually, a number of block clubs participated in the formation of greater neighborhood councils and transneighborhood associations. City officials witnessed the creation of a monster, as block clubs began to challenge urban renewal policies, contest the power of the school board, and oppose unpopular candidates for elected positions. Officials tried to have the block club program dismantled, but they failed; instead, the clubs became a fixture throughout the city and a frequent source of headaches for the local political establishment. The clubs' potential to effect social change attracted older activists such as Ravitz, Ernest and Jessie Dillard, and Reverend Cleage. Some future community activists, such as Rosa Sims, got their start within these same associations: "I owe a lot to my father. He was active in the community and was an officer in the block clubs. . . . I got directly involved in community work. I was president of the junior block club."[80]

Activists such as the Dillards considered their work with the block clubs to be one of the more concrete expressions of their socialism. Younger activists, inspired by Saul Alinsky and his "Back-of-the-Yards" crusade in Chicago, attempted to push the clubs in a more militant direction—one with a pronounced class basis. In Chicago Alinsky had developed a distinctive style of organizing groups once thought to be unorganizable. Consciously adapting the methods of the labor movement in the 1930s, Alinksy's own method was based on creating as much tension as possible and forcing city administrators to meet the demands of the disadvantaged. It is easy to see the youthful appeal of such a method, and generational dynamics produced both conflict and cooperation within block-club and community-based groups. As Sheila Murphy Cockrel put it, "As I grew older I began to see that my parents didn't fully understand that they had created a family with the inherent idea of class conflict."[81] Cockrel's assessment of the class and generational tensions within her family holds true, to a certain extent, for the entire civil rights community. Younger activists developed different ideas, strategies, and goals but were not fully divorced from the older generation of activists that had paved their way. When large segments of the city's New Left turned to community organizing in the mid- to late 1960s, the basic structure was already in place. The new cohort introduced its own methods and strategies, but it did not have to start from scratch.

Block clubs, and later community organizations such as WCO, were also central to women's activism. "In the block clubs," notes General Baker, "when you do alley cleanup, ain't but two men and all the rest is women."[82] The women who tell their tales tend to mention religion far more often than their male counterparts, and those who turned toward community organizing at the grassroots level were overwhelmingly female. While Baker, along with Luke Tripp, Mike Hamlin, John Watson, and others, got more involved in labor organizing during the late 1960s, creating the Dodge Revolutionary Union Movement (DRUM) and the League of Revolutionary Black Workers, their female counterparts tended to focus on welfare rights, tenants' rights, and antipoverty campaigns. Marian Kramer, who was married to General Baker, worked with block clubs, the WCO, and the Westside Mothers, a welfare-rights group initially organized by the Detroit CORE. "A lot of social struggles were right there in the community," notes Kramer, who had been influenced by her work in the South with the Student Nonviolent Coordinating Committee. "Women had developed a lot of skills and were becoming central in the organizations."[83]

This is not to suggest that gender roles were carved in stone. Women were also active in male-dominated groups such as GOAL, the Freedom Now Party, and the League of Revolutionary Black Workers. On the other side of the equation, some men certainly participated in the block club movement. Waymon Dunn, an older Black resident, served as the head of one of the city's largest confederations of block clubs, and younger male activists such as Baker and Cockrel organized and directed neighborhood clubs. Male activists were also involved in the activities of the WCO and similar groups. Yet gender roles were a source of tension within the movement. "We were forceful, but we were played down," insists Kramer. "There were people like Arleen, Gracie, Cass Smith, myself, Edna Watson," she continues.

> We endured a lot of name calling and had to fight male supremacy. Some would call us the IWW: Ignorant Women of the World. I was thought of as one of the grouchiest women. In meetings, we attempted to form a Black Liberation party, there was debate [about] where the struggle had to be. One faction said that the forces should

be in the plants, at the point of production. I said, "Yes, but all those men got to come back into the community; they live somewhere. We've got to be organizing in both places.[84]

The articulation of a firm position on gender and class by women activists differentiated the later movement center from its earlier civil rights predecessor. Although the earlier movement recognized the necessity of "organizing in both places," there was a qualitative generational difference. Certainly women were involved in the early movement. Rose Billups, Geraldine Bledsoe, Eleanor Maki, Vera Vanderberg of the NNC, Zaio Woodford of the League of Women Voters, and the women of the NNLC, among others, often marched on the front lines of political mobilization, but "women's issues" never achieved the centrality they obtained in later years. While there was a great deal of women's activism around the edges of the early movement—meat boycotts, the activities of the Housewives League of the Booker T. Washington Trade Association, sit-down strikes and walkouts in traditionally female industries such as cigar making—the core organizations tended to be male dominated. The National Negro Labor Council was really the only earlier group to demonstrate a clear understanding of the relationships among class, race, and gender and to take account of these interlocking forms of oppression in their protests.

But by the 1960s a new pattern was emerging. The political consciousness of this new generation of young men and women had been formed in the matrix of a new set of familial experiences, by the violence that menaced the southern struggle, and by their exposure to changing cultural trends. This consciousness crystallized in myriad small discussion groups and associations. Interpersonal ties were crucial. "We would gather in each other's homes and talk about what kind of activity we could develop in Detroit around the edges of the civil rights movement," remembered Mike Hamlin. Recognizing a debt to people outside of their own modest ranks, the newcomers turned to older activists such as James and Grace Lee Boggs. "Jimmy taught and reached a lot of people," says General Baker. "Early on, if you wanted to deal with problems as an auto worker, you were separated from history. Unless someone gave you continuity, some history, you were on your own. Jimmy tried to give us that direction."[85]

If cross-generational influence was indeed key to the development of political radicalism in 1960s Detroit, Grace Lee and James Boggs personified that influence. Married in 1954, they were a dynamic team grounded in leftist politics. James Boggs had come to Detroit from Bessemer, Alabama, in 1937 after hoboing around the country. He landed a job as a production worker at Chrysler and became a union organizer. Actually, he recalls with a grin, he became a "union thug": "We used to say we went out and recruited people into the union, but we really just used to beat them up until they joined."[86] His position at the Chrysler plant brought him into contact with the small group of Trotskyists active in and around the Socialist Workers Party. Through his association with the SWP, he was able to study at the party's Third Layer School in New York City, where he also met his future wife, Grace Lee.

Born in Providence, Rhode Island, Grace Lee was the daughter of Chinese immigrants. She had earned a doctorate in philosophy at Bryn Mawr in 1940 and became interested in radical politics and the Black struggle after leaving Philadelphia for Chicago. There she organized tenant groups and lectured for socialist and communist groups throughout the city's Black communities. She also worked as a local organizer for A. Philip Randolph's 1941 March on Washington movement.[87] It was in Chicago that Lee first became aware of the Trotskyists and one of the movement's leading theoreticians, West Indian Marxist C. L. R. James. She became a close friend of James and collaborated with him on a number of scholarly works. Although they parted company in the early 1960s, the Boggses played an important role in introducing their mentor to young radicals in Detroit.

Born in Trinidad in 1901, C. L. R. James had risen through Marxist and Pan-Africanist circles in Britain to become an important figure in international Trotskyism. Traveling to the United States in 1938 for a short speaking tour, the young activist wound up staying for fifteen years. During his residence in the States, which included time spent in Detroit during World War II, James moved in and out of the Socialist Workers Party and eventually formed his own wing of the movement,[88] the so-called Johnson-Forest tendency, which was led by James (whose party name was Johnson), Raya Dunayevskaya (whose party name was Forest), and Grace Lee.

Like their movement's founder, Leon Trotsky, the members of the Johnson-Forest tendency were bitterly anti-Stalinist and critical of oppressive conditions within the Soviet Union.[89] But whereas Trotsky, and much of the SWP hierarchy, held that the Soviet Union had devolved into a "degenerated" worker's state due to the rise of the Stalinist bureaucracy and could be reformed by a political revolution, other segments of the movement put forth a much harsher critique. For the members of the Johnson-Forest tendency, Stalinism was not an aberration or a devolution from a more authentic bolshevism. Instead, it was

the logical outcome of the revolutionary vanguard party's transformation into an all-encompassing power fused with the state. Soviet workers
were no better off under this system of "state capitalism" than their
Western comrades were under "private-property capitalism."[90]

The opposition of an evolutionary understanding of Soviet development against Trotsky's de-evolutionary one held important implications
for revolutionary parties outside of the Soviet Union. Drawing inspiration from the American scene, as well as his own studies of anticolonial
struggles in Africa and the West Indies, James and his group cautioned
against any vanguard party that promised to provide "enlightened leadership" to the "backward masses." According to James and others in the
Johnson-Forrest tendency, the opposite was true: even in the Russian revolution, the proletariat "taught and disciplined Lenin and the Bolsheviks
not only indirectly but directly."

> The Bolsheviks learned to understand the vitality and creative power
> of the proletariat in revolution. . . .The proletariat repeatedly led the
> Bolsheviks and gave Lenin courage and wisdom. Between 1890 and
> 1921 the interrelation between leader, party, class and nation was
> indivisible. . . .With the proletariat or against it, that is the future of
> every modern nation. What was the secret of Lenin's greatness is that
> he saw this so clearly because this choice was the inescapable product
> of the whole Russian past.[91]

The upshot of this reformulated Leninism was that no revolutionary
party could hope to lead the masses without taking part in a dialectical
interaction recognizing the creative power and dynamic spontaneity of
the proletariat. Without a flexible and democratic interaction, vanguard
parties, regardless of their good intentions, risked the danger of limiting
the working class's revolutionary potential and distorting their own
goals.

Most important, James and the members of the Johnson-Forrest tendency located the sources of American revolutionary potential in the
social and cultural milieu of the working class, as well as in the particular
struggles of women and African Americans. In his studies of African
American history and culture, James attempted to incorporate the per-
spectives of these groups, and of other diasporic peoples, into a more
humanistic theory of revolutionary Marxism. Because he saw race and
class as part of the same dynamic, James was able to make significant contributions to Marxist thought in this area. "Let us not forget," he cautioned fellow party members,

that in the Negro people there sleep and are now awakening passions of a violence exceeding, perhaps, as far as these things can be compared, anything among the tremendous forces that capitalism has created. Anyone who knows them, who knows their history, is able to talk to them intimately, watches them in their churches, reads their press with a discerning eye, must recognize that although their social force may not be able to compare with the social force of a corresponding number of organized workers, the hatred of the bourgeois society and the readiness to destroy it when the opportunity should present itself, rest among them to a degree greater than in any other section of the population in the United States.[92]

Although he was not then well known in Detroit or indeed in the United States, James's ideas and writings trickled down to American radicals through his associates and ex-associates. James did not, however, give much sustained attention to African American and working-class religious sensibilities; he did not see religion as a factor in the vitality and creative power of these communities. In fact, in a later essay he noted that while living in the United States he had "no idea that this kind of community could be built in the southern Black Churches; but of course, this was the source of Dr. King's power." He went on to suggest that a similar inattention to religion's potential among "certain people who are revolutionaries" was a major problem for revolutionary parties. Although there was nothing in James's approach, particularly toward the cultural realm, that actually precluded the incorporation of oppositional religious ideas and practices, it was left to his followers, especially Grace Lee and James Boggs, to write about religion's potentially revolutionary role in movements such as Albert Cleage's Black Christian nationalism.[93]

After ten years of working with the SWP, C. L. R. James could claim that he and other members of the Johnson-Forrest tendency "always found [ourselves] closest in theory and practice to rank and file workers" and that their 1951 break with the party had freed them "to make this social milieu the basis of our whole existence."[94] Unfortunately, James's deportation from the United States as an undesirable alien in 1953 hampered the group's development. For a time he did manage to keep in close contact with Dunayevskaya, the Boggses, and others, and he continued to contribute essays to the group's newspaper, *Correspondence*, edited by James Boggs, which was published in Detroit after the group left the SWP. He also contributed to a number of the tendency's ancillary projects such as the publication of Charles Denby's *Indignant Heart* and a series of inexpensive and accessible paperbacks on topics ranging from the reflections of working women to student rebellions and factory life. Many of these small books, along with political tracts, newsletters, and pamphlets, were sold or given away in Black and working-class neighborhoods.[95] Meanwhile the group strove to increase the level of intellectual debate and exploration within Marxist circles, for example, by publishing the first American edition of Marx's *Economic and Philosophic Manuscripts of 1844,* in which themes of alienation and consciousness loom large.[96]

Yet, because of internal disputes and the pressures of McCarthyism, the small group eventually broke apart. In 1955, Raya Dunayevskaya led her own breakaway faction organized around the philosophy of Marxist-humanism and the publication *News and Letters.*[97] By 1961, James and Grace Lee Boggs had also broken with C. L. R. James, depleting the ranks of the old Johnson-Forrest tendency.[98] The Boggses rejected James's view that the proletariat was the only group able to create the impetus for social reorganization and argued instead that the bulk of the U.S. working class was not only "backward and bourgeoisified" but also a "vanishing herd" diminished by the technological transformations of capitalism. While the Boggses maintained their belief in the revolutionary potential of African American workers, they increasingly focused on third world revolutions as the force that would destroy capitalism. Their emphasis on revolutionary and anticolonial struggles in Africa, China, and Cuba—which were also a focus of the SWP—placed them closer, ideologically, to younger, New Left radicals, whose interests the Boggses encouraged.[99] But the couple's rejection of the working class as the primary revolutionary agent drove a wedge between them and C. L. R. James. The deported radical retorted with a warning to anyone who disagreed with his view of the proletariat, declaring that "we are enemies, outspoken and relentless."[100]

Given James's affinity for American Black nationalism and pan-Africanism, his harsh critique of his former colleagues is a bit puzzling. Indeed, James, more than anyone else, was responsible for the Socialist Workers Party's efforts to support Black workers' entry into the vanguard of revolutionary struggle, and even after he broke with the party his ideas on the subject continued to exert a great deal of influence.[101] For example, in his early defense of the Nation of Islam, George Breitman, a white American Marxist, continuously referenced the SWP's statement "Negro Work," which was written in part by James. Guided by James's example, Breitman produced some of the earliest favorable articles on Malcolm X and the Nation of Islam to appear in almost any national publication.[102]

Like James and Grace Lee Boggs, Breitman was an important link in

Detroit's pattern of cross-generational connections. He had been a member of the SWP since the mid-1930s and was sent to reorganize the Detroit affiliate in 1953 after nearly 40 percent of its membership was expelled for disregarding party discipline. James and Grace Lee Boggs had already broken with the local SWP, and internal splits and external political repression had left the group with no more than ten members. Working closely with his wife Dorothea, along with Frank and Sarah Lovell and Evelyn Sell, Breitman converted the group's Friday Night Forum into a tool for discussion and recruitment, and he continued to oversee the forum from 1954 until he left Detroit in 1967. A former editor of the SWP's *Militant,* Breitman was largely responsible for giving the paper the distinction of being the only white publication to embrace the Nation of Islam and its brand of Black nationalism. Although African Americans did not join the SWP in large numbers, the *Militant,* along with publications produced by the Boggses, was fairly widely read. Indeed, the forum and the *Militant* deeply influenced a number of young activists.[103]

In retrospect, attendance at the forum appears to have been something of a prerequisite for later activism, and it is important to acknowledge this non-CP Left tradition in the city's radical history. The forum had been bringing together activists and intellectuals from throughout the city and across the nation since 1954. Ernest Dillard often presented lectures there, as did older Detroiters such as the Black communist Christopher Alston. There is even reason to believe that the Rev. Charles A. Hill may have attended a few of the sessions.[104] The forum was, as one observer put it, "a real institution in Detroit." Young Detroiters such as General Baker, Mike Hamlin, Dan Georgakas, Edna Watson, and Luke Tripp all attended the Friday sessions. Through the influence of the forum and their own small discussion groups, as well as the guidance of local radicals such as James and Grace Lee Boggs, these young activists became engaged by the early 1960s in a number of philosophical and ideological debates about national and international political struggles. At least three issues seem to have been foremost in the thinking of these nascent militants: nonviolence as a strategy in the civil rights struggle; the importance of Black nationalism; and the revolutions in Cuba, Africa, China, and elsewhere.

The debates over nonviolence were particularly heated. General Baker noted that the "polarity" of violence or self-defense and nonviolence was "constantly debated" in the Black community. Although we have come to portray this debate, somewhat generically, as a dispute between Reverend King and Minister Malcolm X, it is more properly defined in places such as Detroit as between Reverend King and southern self-defense advocate Robert Williams. While it is not clear whether Williams's experiences as a worker at Detroit's River Rouge plant and as a member of Local 600 during World War II were well known on the national level, he was embraced as an important local figure. Whereas King understood nonviolence as philosophically necessary and tactically desirable—a choice, almost a religious calling, that entailed inner transformation and physical commitment—Williams advocated a more "flexible" approach that incorporated self-defense. He wrote:

> My only difference with Dr. King is that I believe in flexibility in the freedom struggle. This means that I believe in non-violent tactics where feasible. . . . In civilized society the law serves as a deterrent against lawless forces that would destroy the democratic process. But when there is a breakdown of the law, the individual citizen has a right to protect his person, his family, his home, and his property. To me this is so simple and proper that it is self-evident.[105]

Williams was not advocating random acts of violence but individual acts of resistance, which, when coupled with mass mobilizations in North and South alike, would boldly challenge the white power structure. Williams was concerned, moreover, that pure nonviolence was too much to ask, that it would, by necessity, exclude all those unwilling or unable to practice the necessary discipline of body and spirit.

Williams organized "rifle clubs" during the 1950s, for which he was forced out of his post as head of the Monroe, North Carolina, NAACP. If his call for armed self-defense irritated the national hierarchy of the NAACP, his sympathies for the Nation of Islam and the Cuban revolutionaries made his relationship with the organization all the more tense. As historian Van Gosse points out in his study of Cuba, the cold war, and the rise of the New Left, Williams was one of the earliest Black American supporters of Castro and the revolutionary struggles in Cuba, and his "partisanship for Castro helped insert the Cuban revolution into the black political debate." Drawing on religious symbolism, perhaps to rival his political adversary, Reverend King, Williams characterized Cuba's example as "the new Sermon on the Mount . . . a pilgrimage to the shrine of hope."[106] Williams's support of the Cuban revolution and his critique of the dominant philosophy of the southern civil rights movement placed him, albeit uneasily, in league with Left organizations such as the Socialist Workers Party. The SWP was supportive of Williams's philosophy, and the party's paper carried highly favorable reviews of his activities.[107] When Williams was forced to flee the United States after being charged with kidnapping a white couple during a particularly violent confrontation between Freedom Riders and local whites in Monroe in 1961, the SWP aided his escape through Mexico to Cuba, where he was given asylum.

"The Socialist Workers Party had played a major role in the events in Monroe, North Carolina," writes Conrad Lynn, a Black attorney and former Communist Party member with complicated ties to the SWP.[108] Lynn, who had been a close friend of Williams for years, acted as his legal counsel and assisted the SWP in forming defense committees for him across the country. From his self-imposed exile in Cuba, Williams published his *Negroes with Guns* and an occasional newsletter—all of which won converts among young activists suffering from a sense of alienation. Williams's book was "popular early reading" for a number of young radicals in Detroit: "We were able to get our hands on *The Crusader,* a publication that Robert Williams printed from Cuba. . . . He had a shortwave radio program on Friday nights called 'Radio Free Dixie,' that you could pick up from Havana."[109]

The SWP's association with Black activists such as Robert Williams, Conrad Lynn, and journalist William Worthy (who defied U.S. travel bans first to China and then to Cuba) should be viewed as part of the party's effort to link international revolutionary struggles with the fight for African American liberation. If the defense of the Cuban revolution represented one axis of party activity, then the defense of Williams and the party's growing interests in the revolutionary potential of Black nationalism represented another. Indeed, the party's support for Williams was reinforced by an increasing interest in the Nation of Islam and Malcolm X. Lynn notes that "the SWP had begun to see the revolutionary implications of the Black Muslim movement with the rise of its latest spokesperson, Malcolm X."[110] All of these connections, which were being made on a national and international level, filtered down to local activists in Detroit in myriad ways. This is not to suggest that young Black nationalists necessarily needed the SWP, but the party did manage to pull together a number of diverse ideological tendencies.

Black nationalism was definitely "in the air" in Detroit and other Black communities throughout the nation; the SWP was simply a contributing factor to its popularity. General Baker had just enrolled at Highland Park Junior College in 1959 when he "discovered" Malcolm X. "I was hit," he recalls, "with the question of how the Black Muslims existed all this time and I didn't know about it," especially since they were "fathered" in Detroit and Malcolm X and Elijah Muhammad were very much in the news. Herb Boyd, who had graduated from high school in that same year, was also becoming interested in the Nation of Islam. For Boyd, the acquaintance came through a combination of (white) media hysteria over the NOI and local Black Muslims selling copies of its chief organ, *Muhammad Speaks,* door-to-door. Boyd was invited to the local mosque and later became a "stone Malcolmite." His involvement in the Nation of Islam, along with his love of jazz and his reading of Black writers such as Richard Wright, gave Boyd a cultural perspective on Black life and struggle; his association with James and Grace Lee Boggs, as well as with local Black nationalists such as Richard and Milton Henry, who would go on to found the Republic of New Africa, helped to shape his "first political perspective."[111] This blending of political trends was far from unique; any number of activists could have told a similar story.

The SWP's forums, along with its informal discussion groups, gave young militants a social space where they could hash out their views on Robert Williams and Cuba, Black nationalism and the Nation of Islam, and a range of other issues. The explosive combination of personal experiences and political ideas fueled the search, as General Baker put it, for "something to do around the edges of the civil rights movement."[112] This movement in the United States would also come to be suffused with an international perspective. If Black nationalism was in the air, then so was worldwide revolution. Although Mike Hamlin and others eventually found that they had to go beyond the SWP and "create a new method of dealing with exploitation and oppression," the forum, and the influence of the Boggses, did help to advance a broader perspective on political struggle. The Soviet Union had a place in the hearts and minds of many activists from the old Left community, but among this new generation the Soviet Union was displaced by an interest in Cuba, China, Africa, and of course Vietnam.

Meetings and discussion forums on the status of the Cuban revolution were held throughout the city. Many of them were sponsored by the SWP, whose local paper, the *Michigan Militant,* carried a series of articles under banner headlines such as "Cuba—a Happy Land" and "Hands off Cuba." Moreover, the party was a key player in the organization of the Fair Play for Cuba Committee, the major pro-Cuba political group in the United States.[113] In a sense, Cuba was this generation's Spanish Civil War—an international event opposed by the U.S. government with both national and international implications. Cuba's guerrilla warriors had the same sort of romantic appeal that Spain's partisans offered nearly three decades earlier. This appeal was heightened by Castro's apparent success (even after he admitted that he had not established a workers' state) and the U.S. government's fear of communism. Supporters of the Cuban revolution and opponents of U.S. foreign policy led delegations to Cuba in defiance of the government's travel ban. Adam Clayton Powell Jr. led one such group; General Baker, Luke Tripp, Charles Simmons, and Charles "Mao" Johnson, another young Black activist, were part of a local contingent that made the same journey. "I had read Che Guevara, Fidel Castro's *History Will Absolve Me,* and Franz Fanon's *Wretched of the Earth,*" recalled Baker, "but I still went to Cuba with a half-baked outlook and no set theory. . . . Going to Cuba was a real sobering experience and a real turning point in my life."[114] "Cuba," says Gloria House, who worked for years with SNCC in Alabama before she returned to Detroit, "was a major turning point for me, or more of an affirmation of my vision of what life could be about."[115] The Cuban revolution, along with the Cultural Revolution in China and the anticolonial uprisings in Africa, would continue to exert influence on the tenor of radicalism in Detroit for many years to come.

By the mid-1960s, all of these diverse ideological trends were beginning to converge in a heterogeneous community of young activists who were as inspired by revolution in Cuba and other parts of the world as they were by the southern and northern civil rights movements. It was not always an easy fit, and by the end of the decade irreconcilable differences would manifest themselves. In the meantime, though, they looked for intellectual and personal guidance wherever they could find it: in the SWP, in the writings of Robert Williams, in the Nation of Islam, and in the ideas and activism of local figures such as James and Grace Lee Boggs and the Rev. Albert B. Cleage. What many of these intellectual and political approaches had in common was a shift away from, or rather beyond, the conventional understanding of rights and justice. By expanding the language of rights to include both personal and social transformation, their efforts laid the intellectual foundation for a far greater challenge to American society.

Reverend Cleage's activism and his distinctive political theology, which was in itself a redefinition of the social gospel, were an important part of this trend. By the mid-1960s, Cleage had emerged as a leading figure within radical circles, voicing a Left, and decidedly Black nationalist, critique of Detroit's liberal-labor coalition. Cleage, whose denunciations of the philosophy and strategy of nonviolence grew louder every year, had ties to the local SWP, the Nation of Islam, and the general collective of opponents to America's Cuban policy. As such, he managed to attract a fairly large following among the city's young militants, as well as among members of the old Left. Cleage's personal transformation from a middle-class NAACP activist to a middle-class radical mixing Christianity with Black nationalism is an intriguing story in its own right. Given his high profile within the movement, it is well worth exploring the details of his political biography before considering his role within the new civil rights community.

SIX

BLACK FAITH

The Rev. Albert B. Cleage Jr.,
Black Christian Nationalism, and the
Second Civil Rights Community in Detroit

By the late 1960s, the Rev. Albert B. Cleage Jr. had become a leading figure in the movement to link African American religion and Black theology with Black nationalism and Black power. He was, notes theologian James H. Cone, "one of the few black ministers who has embraced Black Power as a religious concept and has sought to reorient the church-community on the basis of it."[1] He was also one of the most controversial religious activists to appear on the national scene in the midst of the "long hot summers." For Cleage, who disputed nonviolence's value as either a political strategy or a philosophy, the urban rebellions of the late 1960s were just a "dress rehearsal" for the real revolution yet to come. Violence was undesirable but necessary if rapid change was to be achieved. It was the duty and destiny of the Black church to serve as the cornerstone of the new Black nation that would emerge. In preparation, Cleage used his own church and congregation to inaugurate the Black Christian nationalist movement. "We reject the traditional concept of church," Cleage explained in his 1972 book *Black Christian Nationalism: New Directions for the Black Church.*

In its place we will build a Black Liberation movement which derives its basic religious insights from African spirituality, its character from African communalism, and its revolutionary direction from Jesus, the

Black Messiah. We will make Black Christian Nationalism the cornerstone of the Black man's struggle for power and survival. We will
build a Black communal society which can protect the minds and
bodies of Black men, women and children everywhere.[2]

Cleage had not completely rejected the notion of racial integration
early in his career during the 1950s. He began his clerical service as a
local activist struggling to win converts, both religious and political. A
minister, organizer, and ideologue, over time Cleage helped to define
an emergent Black nationalist perspective within the city's civil rights
movement. Both inside and outside the movement, Cleage was commonly regarded as an enigma: a Christian minister who contended that
almost everything about traditional Christianity was false; a Black nationalist who by outward appearances could "pass" for white; and a self-styled
champion of the poor, the marginal, and the dispossessed with impecca-
ble middle-class credentials. Few commentators and even fewer critics
failed to mention Cleage's light skin color in particular.

Grace Lee Boggs, for example, describes Cleage as "[p]ink-complex-
ioned, with blue eyes and light brown, almost blonde hair" (his eyes were
in fact gray). His first biographer, journalist Hiley Ward, a religion writer
for the *Detroit Free Press* in the 1960s, contends that Cleage's light com-
plection left him with "a lifelong identity crisis."[3] Ward, who seems
obsessed with Cleage's coloring, describes the reverend's mother, Pearl
Reed Cleage, as white in appearance with very thin features: "My grandmother was a Cherokee Indian," he quotes her as explaining, "my father
was a mulatto, and my mother was a very fair lady." The rumors that Pearl
Reed Cleage forbade her seven children to play with children who were
visibly darker than they, and that the Cleage family was (as the *Michigan
Chronicle*'s Louis Martin asserted) "the fair mulatto type, not too interested in unions," seem to be the products of unjust presupposition and
bias.[4]

Friends, family members, and associates at the Shrine of the Black
Madonna have described the role of race, class, and family in Reverend
Cleage's life very differently. According to his sister, Barbara (Cleage)
Martin, "we never passed. We never even tried to pass." Martin recalls
her mother giving lectures on Black history at nearby Wingert Elementary School; other sources cite Pearl Cleage's efforts to get the Detroit
Board of Education to hire Black teachers and provide a decent education to Black children. Similarly, their father, Dr. Albert Cleage Sr., is
described by his children and family friends as a dedicated "race man,"
who, though not a member of the UNIA, was sympathetic to Garveyism.

According to an official publication of the shrine, these "early impressions of racial pride and civic duty influenced young Cleage's thinking and shaped his outlook on life." Both versions of the early raw materials that helped to form Reverend Cleage probably contain a mixture of truths, falsehoods, evasions, and misunderstandings.[5]

Cleage himself has left a scant written record on the question, but his statements and pronouncements make it clear that he regarded intraracial color stratification as a manifestation of what he called "the declaration of Black inferiority." He seems to have simply accepted as axiomatic the idea that "we are all colors. . . . We are mixed up with everything under the sun, but we are all black."[6] "You can mix all the hues of the rainbow," he said on another occasion, "and if at the end you add a little Black, you are Black. Black is not only beautiful, Black is powerful!" While the color of God was not a subject on which he tended to linger, he did periodically extend his reasoning to the godhead. If, as Genesis tells us, man is made in the image of God, Cleage suggested, then we must look at man to see what God looks like. Since there are "black men, there are yellow men, there are red men, and there are few, a mighty few white men," then God must be "some combination of this black, red, yellow and white." Since, further, under American law "one drop of black makes you black," then at least under the standards established in the United States "God is black."[7]

FIRST SON

It is interesting to speculate about the degree to which Cleage's theological reasoning is rooted in his own autobiography. His political theology changed (he would probably have said it evolved) over time, and he seems to have been in constant dialogue with his past—rejecting some elements and embracing others and subtly re-creating himself in the process. Some of the aspects of his life that strike us as contradictory and paradoxical were, for Cleage, opportunities for personal, political, and spiritual reflection and growth. If this is the case, then the only way to understand Reverend Cleage's political theology is to start with his biography.

Fortunately, Cleage's early life is relatively well documented. He was undeniably the product of a very close-knit family, the eldest of the four Cleage boys and three girls. The family traced its roots as far back as Athens, Tennessee—the small town to which his grandfather, Louis, an ex-slave, had drifted after the Civil War. It was there that Louis met and married Cecil, an ex-slave fathered by her white owner. Reverend Cleage's father, Albert Buford Cleage Sr., was the youngest of Louis and

Cecil's five sons, born and educated in Tennessee and later trained as a physician at the Indiana School of Medicine, where he received his medical degree in 1910 and then interned at the city hospital. Albert Jr. was born in Indianapolis one year later in June 1911. When the opportunity to establish a private practice in Kalamazoo, Michigan, presented itself, Dr. Cleage and his wife Pearl moved the family north. The senior Cleage was well regarded in Kalamazoo, where he served as the town's only Black doctor; but Detroit, a larger city with more opportunities, was where the family chose to settle for good.[8]

Dr. Cleage readily integrated himself into the life of Detroit's expanding Black community, becoming a charter member of St. John's Presbyterian Church, active in the St. Antoine (segregated) branch of the YMCA, and a founder of Dunbar Hospital, the city's first Black health care facility. Frustrated by the difficulty of obtaining treatment even at those Detroit hospitals that would admit African Americans, Cleage and a small group of his fellow Black physicians founded Dunbar Hospital in the city's St. Antoine district in 1918. Dunbar received funding from the Community Chest Fund, a public charity, and in its first five years cared for over three thousand patients. In 1928, the hospital moved to a larger, adjacent facility capable of keeping up with the high demand for its services. The decision to found a Black hospital was not uncontroversial. Some in the community, such as Snow F. Grigsby, believed that to do so was to admit defeat in the fight to desegregate the city's hospitals. Grigsby, the founder of the Civic Rights Committee, denounced the Dunbar plan as a "'Jim Crow' set up." Dr. Cleage, however, regarded the establishment of Dunbar Hospital as the most practical and expedient means of providing Black health care, as well as training and employing Black doctors and nurses.[9]

Dr. Cleage's educational attainments and social activities earned him ready admittance into the city's African American elite. His ideas seemed to be in line with the ethic of collective self-help and community building that guided local activism in the years before the Depression, unionization, and world war so altered the political landscape. He built up a thriving private practice and established a good reputation in Republican circles, founding a Black Republican club in the 1920s. In 1930, he was actually appointed to the position of city physician by Charles Bowles, a white Republican mayor widely reputed to have close ties to the Klan—an accomplishment for which Reverend Cleage remembers being congratulated with fairly regular beatings from his classmates on the way home from school.[10] As the city sank into the pit of the Great Depression, and the Black presence on the city's welfare rolls rose to a staggering eighty percent of the total, Dr. Cleage was hired at a salary of $3,000 per year—an income and resulting social status that placed his family way above the norm. As a result, and unlike Charles Hill, Albert Cleage enjoyed a relatively stable childhood marked by all the benefits of the middle-class environment his parents were able to provide.

The Cleages' elevated social status did not, however, fully protect them from the ravages of racism. On the one hand, they owned their own home in the west-side Tireman neighborhood (a roomy house with a sizable porch on the corner of Scotten Street and Moore Place, a block from Hartford Avenue). And Dr. Cleage's practice catered not only to Black patients but to white ethnic ones as well. "I'd go with him [on house calls] many a time," Reverend Cleage told his biographer, "on Sunday afternoon through Polish, Irish, and other districts, and people would call out and hold up their babies which he had brought into the world and say, 'See how much they like you.'"[11]

On the other hand, Cleage records painful memories of racism, especially at the schools that he and his siblings attended, including Wingert Elementary and Northwestern High School. Barbara Cleage Martin noted that her brother was not allowed to work on the school newspaper because of racial prejudice and that while classroom seating for white children was alphabetical Black children were relegated to the back rows. Years later, when he took on the School Board over its complicity with racist practices, Reverend Cleage would make reference to these experiences—in many ways carrying on the fight started by his own mother.[12]

It is also certain that Albert Cleage Jr. and his siblings were devoted to their mother, who doted on them even as she ruled the household. Pearl Cleage oversaw every aspect of the children's lives, from their schooling to their choice of playmates. All of her children were educated in public, and predominantly white, schools, and she remained on guard for any evidence of educational discrimination. She also saw to the children's religious education, "schooling him [Albert Jr.] in the exercise of faith," writes biographer Hiley Ward.[13] Dr. Cleage had always been reasonably active at St. John's, but young Albert had an especially strong ecumenical bent and seems to have been particularly drawn to churches and ministers with a strong interest in young people. In 1928, while still at Northwestern High School, Albert Jr. became the chairman of the Youth Group at nearby St. Cyprian's Episcopal, which was pastored at the time by Fr. Malcolm Dade. Later, during his years at Wayne University, Cleage became the unofficial youth pastor at Horace White's Plymouth Congregational and director of the Plymouth Youth League. Rounding out his association with Detroit's trio of activist Black ministers, Cleage attended various events and meetings at Reverend Hill's Hartford Baptist and later claimed that Hill was one of the two men who had most forcefully shaped his ministerial life.[14]

The other was the Rev. Horace White. Cleage was very active at Plymouth and once dreamed of succeeding White as pastor. White seems to have influenced the young Cleage's interests not only in the ministry but in social work as well. As an accredited psychiatric social worker at the University of Michigan, White had helped to found the Lapeer Parents Association, the first of a series of organizations incorporated under the Michigan Association for Retarded Children, and Cleage himself later majored in psychology at Wayne University and worked for a time as a city social worker.

Like the young Reverend Hill, Cleage took an indirect path to the ministry. From 1929 to 1931, he ran a booking agency for small musical combos, including the jazz band put together by Gloster Current, then executive secretary of the local NAACP. Cleage also tried his hand at a career as a drummer. In both of these capacities, he spent a great deal of time in the small jazz and blues clubs of Paradise Valley—early experiences that probably account for his continuing interest in jazz as a distinctively Black cultural product.[15]

The course of his formal education proved equally erratic. Cleage attended Wayne sporadically from 1929 to 1938, leaving at one point to attend Fisk University for less than a year before returning home to his close-knit family. During these educational wanderings he studied with some of the nation's leading sociologists, including Donald Marsh at Wayne and Charles S. Johnson at Fisk. After returning to Detroit, Cleage also took a position as a caseworker for the Detroit Department of Health until he became too discouraged with the "band-aid" approach of social services.[16] By the time he gave in to the call of the ministry and entered the seminary at Oberlin College in 1938, Cleage was already steeped in sociology, social psychology, and at least an outsider's view of the traumas of urban life, particularly its effects on children.

There is a suggestion in Cleage's reminiscences that he felt religion and political struggle would be more effective in fighting those traumas than social work. As he would later characterize it, "I was a sociologist and a psychologist before I became a religionist, so I had more to unlearn! I went into the church because I could not see anything that you could do for Black people with white-oriented sociology and psychology, but it still had to be unlearned."[17] While at Oberlin, Cleage worked for two years as a student pastor at Painesville, Ohio's Union

Congregational Church, where he created a smaller version of the sort of comprehensive youth ministry that he would later sustain throughout his ministerial career. When he received his degree in divinity in 1943, it included, significantly, an emphasis on religious education.

For all of his grounding in practical concerns, Cleage also acquired a reputation among his peers as an intellectual. He was a voracious reader, more interested, he once said, in reading books than actually acquiring degrees.[18] And the approach that he evolved over the years to theological questions integrated both intellectual and pragmatic dimensions, incorporating but also reaching beyond the social gospel perspective deployed by his role models, Reverends Hill and White. During his time at Oberlin, for example, Cleage began to blend his interest in religious education with an exploration of theological neo-orthodoxy. The neo-orthodox theology of Reinhold Niebuhr and German theologian Karl Barth had become extraordinarily popular in American seminaries of the late 1930s and early 1940s, and Oberlin was no exception. Neo-orthodoxy was seen in these spiritual communities as a realistic remedy to the excessive utopianism of the social gospel, dismissing as unrealistic the social gospel's conception of human nature and its suggestion that the Kingdom of God could be created on earth. Since God's will could not be fully comprehended due to the limited capacity of man, the neo-orthodox camp claimed, His Kingdom simply could not be man-made.[19]

Even as he was absorbing the lessons of neo-orthodoxy, Cleage was also developing a fascination with the darker side of existentialism captured by John Paul Sartre in plays such as *No Exit*. In Cleage's mind, the two strains of thought naturally merged. While the social gospel saw human nature as essentially good and society as radically reformable, neo-orthodoxy emphasized the inherent sinfulness of men and women and the essential immorality of societies and social groups. Social relations were particularly problematic, given their roots in inequality and coercion, masked by pernicious ideologies such as racism, ethnocentrism, and xenophobia.[20] This fit neatly with the lessons of existentialism. "This creating hell for each other," said Cleage, in reference to *No Exit*, "is terribly true, though people wish to think something else." God does not operate *deus ex machina:* "nobody is really outside to straighten out the situation if people themselves do not do something."[21]

Cleage's experiences as a caseworker in 1930s Detroit may have contributed to this view of social problems as too intractable to be resolved by moral suasion alone. "I read Niebuhr for a time, especially as an antidote to the social gospel," Cleage said. "Horace White was essentially social gospel, which had little connection with reality. It was utopian, full of action but not much realism." Similarly, Cleage could say that while he admired the "radicalism" of Reverend Hill's politics the problem was that he "would become evangelical on Sunday morning."[22] Healthy realism for Cleage meant meeting power with power, the sort of realism necessary for revolutionary struggle. In this aspect, at least, Cleage resembled A. Philip Randolph during his call for the (first) March on Washington in 1940. But over time Cleage's stress on realism would become the basis for his religious and political critique of Martin Luther King's second March on Washington in 1963.

"We've got to make sure the definitions of human nature and society are both sound," Cleage argued. "This was the problem of Dr. King. He was not realistic. You can hope for change, but it must be predicated on reality, not what we dream of." Cleage suggested that all of the "white liberals," who were more enamored of King's dream than of reality, "ought to all go back and read Niebuhr because they react when you say all whites are part of immoral society."[23] While Cleage was certainly critical of King's political and philosophical intentions, he was not so adverse to the unintended consequences of King's activism. In a powerful sermon preached just days after King's assassination in 1968, Cleage noted that every time King staged a nonviolent, peaceful campaign the nearly always violent white reaction "enabled us to see white people as they really are. All the dreams and myths that we picked up in our churches . . . disappeared, because in these confrontations we began to see white people unmasked." To this extent, Cleage credited King with helping to speed the creation of a Black nation. Across the country, those who reacted with anger and violence to King's murder, those who "marched, the people who looted, and the people who burned were in a deep sense," Cleage concluded, "his [King's] disciples."[24]

When Cleage was ordained in 1943, his emerging political theology was still largely an academic matter, and his articulation of Black nationalism lay more than a decade in the future. But even at this early stage his experiences essentially confirmed his theological outlook. Cleage was ordained and married in the same year, to Gladys Graham, whom he had met at Plymouth Congregational. (The Cleages divorced in 1955 after having two children, Kristin and the poet and playwright Pearl.) At age thirty-two Albert Cleage Jr. began his ministerial career in earnest, accepting his first pastorate at the Chandler Memorial Congregational Church in Lexington, Kentucky, where he passed an uneventful year before receiving a call to serve as interim copastor of the Fellowship of All Peoples in San Francisco. Cleage had been recommended for the new position by Charles S. Johnson of Fisk, and he agreed to serve until

Howard Thurman, the noted Black theologian, could finish his term at Howard University. Cleage's time with the fellowship was short but instructive. The fellowship, like all of the other "all peoples" congregations that appeared during the 1940s, was based on the assumption that interracial brotherhood could be hastened by breaking down the racial barriers between Black and white Christians.[25] When Cleage arrived, the recently formed congregation numbered about fifty members. But if the young pastor arrived with an open mind, he soon soured on the fellowship's interracial makeup. Looking back on the experience, he later denounced the notion of an interracial church as "a monstrosity and an impossibility." "I've had a lot of experience with white people in church," Cleage remarked during one of his later sermons, "and usually white people don't understand black people even though they go under the banner of being Christian."[26] Cleage saw an artificiality in the style and substance of fellowship worship and a lack of concrete involvement in social problems. He was particularly annoyed with his white copastor's (Alfred G. Fisk, a Presbyterian professor of philosophy at San Francisco State University) avoidance of such issues as Japanese internment and the treatment of Black soldiers and war workers. The two men also found themselves at odds over their theological focus. While Fisk preached the glories of Heaven on alternate Sundays, Cleage gave them Hell. When Howard Thurman arrived to take up his post, Cleage quickly departed.[27] Although their paths crossed only fleetingly, any connection between Cleage and Thurman is suggestive.

By the early 1940s, Howard Thurman was probably the most celebrated African American theologian and mystic in the nation. He had already made a pilgrimage to India to meet with Mohandas K. Gandhi and Rabindranath Tagore, the poet of India, who, Thurman wrote, "soared above the political and social exclusiveness dividing mankind" and moved "deep into the heart of his own spiritual idiom and came up inside all peoples, all cultures, and all faiths." Much the same can be said of Thurman himself. Inspired by Tagore, the American composed his own poetic excavations of inner spirituality, hope, sorrow, and the will to love.[28] As his poetry and prose make clear, Thurman considered mysticism not an introverted rejection of the social world but rather the path to a more profound engagement with society and an avenue for social change.[29]

Born in Dayton, Florida, on November 18, 1899, Thurman was reared by his grandmother, a former slave, who taught him to read from the Bible, out loud, and encouraged the development of his intellectual and spiritual gifts. Educated at Morehouse, Columbia, and the

Rochester Theological Seminary (an intellectual center of the social gospel), he accepted his first pastorate position in Oberlin, Ohio, in the late 1920s—a full decade before Cleage traveled there to study at the seminary. Thurman became a prominent leader in youth movement circles and a sought-after speaker on the YMCA lecture circuit, particularly among interracial audiences. In the late 1920s he was appointed to the board of the pacifist Fellowship of Reconciliation (FOR), the organizational progenitor of CORE. A strong advocate of theological training at Black colleges, Thurman served as a professor of religion and director of religious life at Morehouse and its sister school, Spellman College, from 1928 to 1932, after which he became a professor of Christian theology at Howard University and later the first dean of Howard's Rankin Chapel.[30]

It was following on this impressive list of achievements that Thurman decided to accept an invitation from Albert Fisk and A. J. Muste to the copastorate at the Fellowship of All Peoples. While Cleage denounced the idea behind the fellowship as a nightmare, Thurman wrote that an interracial church was "a dream which has haunted me for ten years." All Peoples was very much in keeping with the senior theologian's dedication to what he called "a creative experiment in interracial and intercultural communion, deriving its inspiration from a spiritual interpretation of the meaning of life and the dignity of man."[31] This experiment was necessary, in Thurman's view, for the full flowering of democracy. In this belief, at least, Thurman was closely aligned with advocates of the social gospel such as Reverend Hill.

And yet, despite the obvious differences, there are also very interesting similarities between Thurman and Cleage. Both men, for instance, drew a careful distinction between Christianity, on the one hand, and the religion of Jesus, on the other, believing the former to be a corrupting influence on the latter. In his best-known book, *Jesus and the Disinherited* (1949), Thurman insists that we examine the "religion of Jesus" against the backdrop of the historical Jesus in order to "inquire into the content of his teaching with reference to the disinherited and the underprivileged." For Thurman, the three most important facts about Jesus, the man, was that he was a Jew, poor, and a member of a despised and marginal minority group. In a sentiment that was later echoed in Cleage's political theology, Thurman lamented the severing of Jesus from Israel and the Old Testament from the New. "How different might have been the story of the last two thousand years on this planet grown old from suffering," he writes, "if the link between Jesus and Israel had never been severed!"[32] Cleage was equally disparaging of any attempt to place the New Testament above the Old and insisted on a political and familial link stretching from Abraham through Moses, the Prophets, and Jesus. All were members of the Black Nation Israel, which the Lord promised to make holy and great. In their attempts to preserve and high-light the religion of Jesus, both men were also leery of (Thurman) or even downright hostile toward (Cleage) the Apostle Paul.

This aversion to Paul is, like the conflation of Jesus and Moses and the stress on the Old Testament, a fairly common historical tradition in African American Christianity. Thurman's grandmother had him read the Bible out loud—with the exception of Paul. Having been enslaved, she explained, she had heard enough about the apostle's justifications for the peculiar institution; now, free, she felt no need for further expo-sure to his writings. Cleage, too, held Paul responsible for just about everything that had gone wrong with the religion of Jesus, the Black Mes-siah; it was Paul who had introduced the emphasis on individual salva-tion and created a bastardized religion, Christianity, suitable for white Rome and the gentile world. In perhaps an overly dualistic formulation, Cleage asserted that "white Christianity" was based in the New Testa-ment, in the Epistles of Paul, where a "faith in universal brotherhood" was offered as an "escape from the guilt of white racism." On the other hand, Cleage said, Black religion was essentially based on "the Old Tes-tament concepts of the Black Nation Israel" and the collective struggle for liberation. Accordingly, Cleage's sermons were filled with allusions to the Exodus and the ethical pronouncements of the prophets.[33]

In later years Cleage would pull away from the limelight to build the Black Christian nationalism movement and, like Thurman before him, would turn to poetry to capture his own mystical experience of the divine. In a Thurmanesque move, Cleage came to see the experience of God and love as the basis of revolutionary transformation and a program of self- and communal actualization as ultimately more important than institutional strategy and tactics. In one of his poems, "The Messiah," written in the 1980s, one can clearly see the merger of Cleage's two phases. In the first stanza the narrator has awakened to the realities of Blackness that surround him but has not yet learned the true path to enlightenment.

I am Black,
I am Oppressed
And I seek to end my oppression.
I would strike out against it,
But I can neither understand it
Nor face it.

Certainly I must change
Both myself
And the society in which I live
But the nature of change evades me,
And all of my efforts have been in vain.

In the second stanza, the narrator has made an important discovery and
been transformed. The "I" has become "we."

As we feel today,
So men felt 2,000 years ago
Until a child
Created out of the very substance of God
Discovered his inner Divinity
And changed the world.
Who can foretell the birth of one
Who is to be anointed Messiah,
With power for the powerless,
Healing for the sick,
And Liberation for those in chains?
'What I do ye can do, and even more.
The Kingdom of God is within you.'
So every town and Ghetto
Is Bethlehem.
And every child born of a Black Madonna
Is a new MESSIAH . . .
Only waiting to discover
His inner Divinity.[34]

This transformation was still unimaginable at the time of Cleage's
departure from All Peoples. For the time being, he crisscrossed the
country, accepting the pastorate of Chandler Congregational Church in
Lexington, Kentucky, where he remained for less than a year, and then
returning to California to enroll in the graduate program in visual education at the University of Southern California's cinema department.
Always keenly interested in education, Cleage was hungry to explore the
potential visual techniques in religious education. More pointedly, he
was interested in religious filming, "in trying to find a way to touch the
black man en masse." Taking technical classes in cinematography during
the day (including a seminar with Cecil B. DeMille), at night Cleage
returned to the familiar terrain of jazz clubs, this time as a photographer.

He also preached throughout the surrounding area and developed a network of contacts in the radical intellectual and religious communities around Hollywood. Unfortunately, filmmaking soon proved too expensive a pursuit, and the doctoral course work too time consuming, and he left the program toward the end of 1944.[35]

Once again Cleage turned to the ministry, accepting the pastorate of the 124-year-old St. John's Congregational Church in Springfield, Massachusetts, in 1945. It was there that he first used his religious position as a springboard for political activism. During his five years at St. John's, Cleage served on the Executive Board of the local NAACP, as well as its Legal Redress and Housing Committees. He was also simultaneously involved in the Roundtable of the Conference of Christians and Jews, the YMCA, and the American Red Cross. While he was locally regarded as an outspoken or even blunt opponent of police brutality, employment discrimination, and racial segregation in public housing, none of his activities at this time placed him outside the mainstream of post–World War II civil rights activism.

Cleage's engaging personality and preaching style, as well as his successes in increasing membership and the value of the church's property, fueled his reputation as a pastor. Under these circumstances, it seemed only natural that he would also be involved in civil rights work. But his future radicalism was clearly incubating, and when Hiley Ward interviewed some of Cleage's Springfield parishioners a few pointed out that he did not place much faith in local whites.

It appears that Springfield had a miniature version of the Ford–Black Ministers alliance, which had long dispensed employment opportunities in Detroit area plants. Cleage must have seen the basic similarities between this large patronage system and the smaller one in Springfield. Whereas Detroit's alliance was controlled by ministers such as the Rev. Robert Bradby of Second Baptist, Springfield's had been governed by the Rev. William N. DeBerry, Cleage's immediate predecessor at St. John's.[36] "DeBerry was a big black god and ran much of the town," recalled one older congregant. "You couldn't get a job washing dishes unless DeBerry said so." But the youthful Cleage took his predecessor on, launching an investigation into DeBerry's handling of the church's property and tax evasion that eventually resulted in a lawsuit. The church and the entire community were deeply divided over Cleage's challenge, and the young pastor made some powerful enemies. Once the suit was settled in Cleage's favor, however, he racked up a series of successes in helping St. John's to increase its real estate holdings and extend its outreach programs. One former congregant remarked that

Cleage "recognized and fought against the system by which whites controlled blacks," most likely a reference to the reverend's willingness to
challenge the Springfield city government's exclusion of Blacks from its
new public housing developments and to create new opportunities for
Black employment in downtown stores.[37]

The outward differences between Cleage and Reverend Hill were still
relatively minor at this point. Certainly there were theological diver-
gences. Cleage was critical of Hill's social gospel roots, while Hill was
clearly more comfortable than his junior colleague with the idea of an
interracial church, having in fact supported the establishment of an All
Peoples congregation in Detroit (a local religious institution that grew
out of the Rev. Claude Williams's People's Institute of Applied Religion).
And yet, if Cleage had been in Detroit at the time, there is a very strong
possibility that he would have embraced the same sort of activism
favored by Hill and the city's early civil rights community.

And Cleage did want to be back in Detroit. But it was not until 1950
that an opportunity presented itself. When the members of St. Mark's
United Presbyterian mission in Detroit began to seek a new pastor in that
year, a good deal of support was voiced on Cleage's behalf. Having
passed an examination conducted by the Presbyterian hierarchy, he
readily accepted the position. Finally, after years of crisscrossing the
country, Cleage was back home.

Things went well at first. Cleage joined the Detroit NAACP and was
put in charge of the organization's membership drive. A sermon he
preached on the evils of America's materialistic standard of values and
the lack of concern for "the teeming masses of our underprivileged
brothers" was well received and noted in the pages of the *Michigan Chronicle*.[38] Yet he once again found himself chafing at his congregants' "Sunday piety." Meanwhile, the Presbytery was doing everything in its power
to discourage Cleage's political activism in the local NAACP. Frustrated,
Cleage led a group of dissenters out of St. Mark's Presbyterian to form a
new congregation, St. Mark's Congregational Church. He clearly saw
this as not only a religious move but a political one as well. "It was never
my intention to destroy St. Mark's," he later mused.

> I have a lot of mixed feelings about that. I had a vision and strong
> feelings about what a church should be that had been developing for
> a long time. In Detroit, my ideas developed rapidly and the same
> thing probably would have happened no matter where I was. . . . It
> wasn't a big glorious thing. It was very difficult and emotional. I had
> friends and people of whom I was very fond at St. Mark's.

Lacking a permanent physical structure, the small congregation held services around the city until 1957, when it secured the former Brewster-Pilgrim Church in the Twelfth Street district, on Linwood at Hogarth Street, and adopted the name Central Congregational.[39]

For the first time, Cleage was given the opportunity to build a church from the ground up, giving it his own distinctive theological and ideological cast. Central's blend of theology, social criticism, and community organizing attracted a large following of young professionals and residents from the Twelfth Street district and across the city during the late 1950s. Reverend Cleage was particularly proud of his youth ministry, which was reported to be the largest such program in the area. "I believe I have been able to communicate with these young people," he remarked, "and know their problems."[40]

Kenneth Cockrel recalls that there was a fair amount of gang activity in the neighborhood around Central; there were "the Unos and the Shakers and the Chili Macs" while he was a student at Northwestern High School. Cleage "played a role" in deciding what kind and degree of police presence was necessary to control the gangs at Northwestern.[41] Central's growth was also fueled by its Parish Visitation Program. Reasoning that the "half a million Black people in the five-mile radius surrounding the church" were all part of Central's parish, and thus his congregation's responsibility, Cleage sent teams of congregants into the community to visit families and introduce them to the church's evolving mission. He also began to attract a core of activists who would later become influential in the theory and practice of a Black nationalist politics.[42]

CRITIQUING THE LIBERAL COALITION
The Origins of a New Protest Community

One of those who attended services at Central was attorney Milton Henry (later Brother Gaidi Obadele). Henry had come to Detroit from South Philadelphia by way of Pontiac, Michigan, where he had served six frustrating years on the City Commission. A World War II veteran and graduate of Yale Law School, Henry had moved to Detroit in the early 1950s and was soon followed by his brother, Richard (later Brother Imari Obadele), who worked for several years as a reporter at the *Michigan Chronicle* and as a technical writer at the U.S. Army Tank Automotive Center in Warren, Michigan. James and Grace Lee Boggs were also among the attendees at Central, as was Edward Vaughn, owner of Detroit's first Black bookstore (on Dexter Avenue) and later a political ally of Cleage's.[43] Cleage political views and expanded activism were finding a wider audience.

Even as he preached change from the pulpit and worked through the church, Cleage also made good use of the independent press, another traditional avenue for social influence in African American communities. In the latter half of 1961 Cleage, his siblings, and a few friends launched their own bimonthly newspaper, the *Illustrated News.* "Friends and associates decided to put out a good black paper," explained Cleage's sister, Gladys Evans, "more of a general newspaper but born of the idea to give an objective, intelligent outlook."[44] The reverend's brother, attorney Henry Cleage, served as the chief editor, while another brother, Hugh, a farmer, apprenticed himself to a printer in order to handle production. Once denied a spot on his school newspaper because of racial discrimination, Cleage now controlled his own outlet.

Printed on bright pink newsprint, with a free circulation of over thirty-five thousand (estimates range as high as sixty-five thousand), the *Illustrated News* was published from 1961 to 1965. During these four short years, the paper served as an important public platform for Cleage and his associates. Reverend Cleage, as a contributing editor, penned the majority of the articles, with contributions from his brother Henry and attorney Milton Henry and his brother Richard. The *News* was an outlet for emerging Black nationalism and a platform for often-virulent criticism of the racial status quo, as well as a community-organizing tool. Cleage's articles in particular were critical of the Black middle class and the liberal coalition, from which he took great pains to distance himself. Indeed, among his earliest contributions was a series of articles entitled "The Negro in Detroit," which targeted the shortcomings of the Black middle class with special scorn reserved for the Black clergy.

In a less than complex analysis of class stratification in African American communities, Cleage suggested that the desire for integration and white acceptance had left the Black middle class with "no critical facility . . . no real ability to evaluate the white community and select the good and reject the bad."[45] In Cleage's assessment, "authenticity" and true self-knowledge lay in the lower middle class—"the solid foundation of all Negro organizations"—which had little desire to fashion itself into a mere "replica of the white community." Because the Black working class had a structurally defined critical distance from the white mainstream, Cleage suggested that it was more organically connected to the cultural traditions that could sustain African Americans in the face of oppression. Cleage thus pitted his affinity with the lower classes against his own middle-class background on cultural grounds. He wrote with the authoritative tone of an insider who had repositioned himself on the outside, one who had achieved his much-valued critical distance not by circumstances of birth but by choice.

Christian themes of repentance and conversion played an important role in this discourse, which eventually led to the formulation of Black Christian nationalism. In order to fully embrace the Black church as the foundation of the Black nation, Cleage expected that the "guilty" would reorient their lives and, in effect, re-create themselves. They must declare, as he put it, that "I have been an Uncle Tom and I repent."[46] Clearly, in critiquing his upbringing Reverend Cleage was also questioning the one institution—the Black church—to which he had dedicated much of his life.

In this conceptualization of racially polarized class dynamics, Cleage argued that "the Negro church has prospered poorly in the North because it has been unable to relate the gospel of Jesus Christ meaningfully to the everyday problems of an underprivileged people in urban industrial communities." Because it had failed to tap into the authenticity of "the folk," the African American church had failed to keep pace with the community it served, becoming "lost in a sea of triviality and aimlessness." In what Cleage considered the worst-case scenario, some former congregants had turned their backs on the church while others had sought "integration" in small, ineffective, interracial churches.[47]

In a particularly introspective moment, Cleage later recalled his assertion that interracial churches were a monstrosity. What bothered him the most about these churches (which were never very prevalent and certainly never constituted a real threat to the Black church) was not that what "seemed like integration from a white person's point of view is not really integration."[48] Rather, he said, his animus was primarily cultural.

Years before Cleage fully articulated the political theology of Black Christian nationalism, the church had already become for him the repository of cultural authenticity. Loyalty to the Black church could only be rejected at one's peril. To put it another way, before he became a committed Black nationalist, politically, economically, and socially, Cleage was a cultural nationalist with a religious bent. In the late 1950s and early 1960s he could work toward integration but only as long as integration was tempered with a respect for cultural difference. Civil rights and social justice would be meaningless and empty, he suggested, unless they drew on the critical perspective and cultural authenticity typical of the lower classes, traits that had been abandoned by their middle-class peers. Culture was always central in Cleage's political theology. His early discussions of Black nationalism in the *Illustrated News* always came from a cultural perspective.

One particularly good example, again deeply related to his personal experience, is "Black Nationalism in Jazz," about a forum featuring singer Abbey Lincoln and her husband, drummer Max Roach, which had been staged at Central Church. That Cleage, who once had dreams of a musical career himself, staged such a forum highlighted his early interest in cultural struggles and struggles over culture. With Lincoln and Roach's release of their *We Insist: The Freedom Now Suite* in 1961, followed by Lincoln's *Straight Ahead,* the couple were causing a stir in the jazz world with recordings now deemed to be classics. At the time, they were denounced, primarily by white jazz critics, in the pages of *Down Beat,* assailed for "politicizing" jazz by introducing an "inappropriate" Black nationalist perspective. Rumors circulated that the two had intimate connections to the Nation of Islam. But Roach and Lincoln, seconded by Cleage, defended what their critics called "Crow Jim" (Jim Crow in reverse) on the grounds that jazz was "essentially a Negro musical idiom."[49] In his article on the forum, which had been attended by approximately one hundred people, Cleage called the event a "rather uncomplicated representation of the argument that the Negro must stop trying to look and act like the white man, and must begin to take pride in himself . . . in his color, in his hair, and his distinctive negroid features." "Even those who were not ready to follow her example," he said in reference to Lincoln's "natural" afro, "were forced to admit that 'Black Nationalism' looked good on Abbey."[50]

Although early on Cleage retained a blind spot when it came to the relationships among women, gender, and Black nationalism, his understanding of how culture did, and must, influence political struggles became more sophisticated over time. Years later, and in an almost Maoist vein, he wrote:

> Culture grows out of struggle. In China the Red Guards fought in the streets against those who were taking on Western ways, not because they thought Chinese people looked more beautiful in Chinese dress, but because they knew that Western ideas and dress were weakening the power of China. It was a power struggle. We have made an artificial separation between cultural revolution and the power struggle. They are more excited about culture than they are excited about the struggle for power, because it is easier to put on African clothes than it is to struggle and sacrifice.[51]

In 1966 and 1967, Cleage would again mobilize around these ideas by agreeing to become one of the sponsors (along with Vaughn's Bookstore and the Inner-City Organizing Committee) of Detroit's Black arts conventions, which held sessions at Central Congregational. Although older artists participated, including John O. Killens and Detroit's Dudley Randall (founder of the Broadside Press), the conventions were primarily oriented toward younger writers who had embraced various forms of Black cultural nationalism, including poets Larry Neal and Haki Madhubuti (formerly Don L. Lee) and activists such as Muhammad Ahmad (Max Stanford) of the Revolutionary Action Movement (RAM).[52]

In the pages of the *Illustrated News,* Cleage's cultural project coexisted with his political agenda. At every turn, Reverend Cleage distanced himself from the established Black leadership strata and the liberal civil rights coalition. Although he had served on the Executive Board of the NAACP in the mid-1950s, he came close to calling his former fellow board members incompetent on a number of occasions. His condemnation, strong as it sounded, was never total however. When a group of Black ministers started a selective-buying campaign in 1962—yet another reincarnation of the "Don't Buy Where You Can't Work" idea— he gave the loosely organized mobilization his full support, remarking that "Negro ministers" were finally becoming a "New Force in the Detroit community."[53] Similarly, although he was often critical of the TULC for its allegiance to the UAW, it was, in Cleage's opinion, "doing a tremendous job in the areas of trade unionism and policies." He even praised the Cotillion Club, a highly exclusive, middle-class Black organization, for "making major steps forward" on the problem of police brutality— perhaps because the group's president at the time was George Crockett.[54]

Still, Cleage tended to hold the infectious optimism of the early 1960s at arm's length. While he agreed, for instance, that "the Negro became the most potent political force in the city of Detroit" after playing a role in the election of Mayor Jerome Cavanagh (he even claimed part of the credit for Black voter turnout), Cleage stilled believed that "Our New Mayor Bears Watching." Never one to trust whites, regardless of how liberal they seemed, Cleage insisted that Cavanagh had not been made fully "aware of the role the Negro must play in this community."[55] The reverend had, at the same time, given considerable support to William T. Patrick in 1961 and, more controversially, to three (and only three) Black candidates for the state legislature in 1962: Russell S. Brown, Frederick Yates, and Charles Diggs Jr. He was widely denounced for his supposedly racist strategy of concentrating votes, or "plunking," by the Detroit Council for Political Education and the Fair Campaign Practices Commission among others.[56]

More specifically, Cleage focused his dissatisfaction on the public school system and urban renewal. Both of these important community issues exerted a disproportionate effect on the Black urban poor. In Cleage's view, the Detroit public school system was as segregated and inadequate as the one in Little Rock, Arkansas, and he used the *Illustrated News* to run a series of "exposés" illustrating this problem.[57] A number of the pieces were written by an anonymous teacher at Northwestern High, and it is interesting to speculate on whether Luke Tripp, one of the city's young Black militants and a swimming instructor at the high school, could have been Cleage's "mole." Cleage also penned a number of the articles himself. Drawing on his own experiences, he wrote that he had been "aware of the discriminatory practices of our public school system since I was a student at Northwestern High back in the 1930s." "Later," he continued, "I saw evidence of these practices while a student at Wayne and as a worker in the Department of Welfare. I left Detroit to continue my education. When I returned home ten years ago . . . I found that few of the discriminatory practices have been changed."[58]

The practices had not changed, but the context had, and the difference was dramatic. Whereas many of Cleage's troubles had resulted from being in a small minority of Black students within a primarily white school, in the 1960s Black students found themselves relegated to predominately Black and educationally inferior schools. The problems were the same, however—racially biased textbooks and teachers and administrators who ran the gamut from paternalistic to insensitive to outright racist. While Cleage tended to blame traditional race improvement agencies such as the NAACP and the Detroit Urban League for their failure to confront the situation, these groups were not really the problem. The true issue was the city's changing demographics. Even as "white flight" drained off the city's white middle-class residents from 1962 to 1966, the city's schools added almost twelve thousand students, more than half of whom were Black. Because of residential segregation, whole school districts became overwhelmingly African American, and because the entire system depended on an increasingly shrinking tax base of home owners, predominately Black schools became increasingly impoverished schools.[59]

Cleage's critique was not directed at the need for Black children to be educated in predominately Black schools, as his own negative assessment of being educated in a primarily white setting might suggest.

Rather, his contention was that Black students were being mistreated by white teachers and administrators and done a disservice by biased textbooks and inadequate facilities. At this point in his career, the solution Cleage was putting forth was still based on equity as integration. Years later, he would reorient himself toward the quest for equity as community control in which Black parents controlled education for Black students taught by Black teachers. This reorientation was not peculiar to Cleage but was part of a growing trend in the late 1960s and 1970s.[60]

Cleage was also quick to point out the Detroit School Board's inadequate response to these demographic changes and the financial crisis they produced. The board had adopted a bylaw in 1959 banning discrimination in all school operations and activities, but administrators played fast and loose with district boundaries, often transferring students to other districts in an effort to maintain segregation. Even the School Board itself had to admit to both "obvious laxity" and "insubordination" in enforcing its own policy.[61]

In Cleage's view, the board needed some prodding, and the opportunity presented itself in early 1962. Sherrill School, which was located on the southwest side of the city, had gone from majority white to majority Black in the 1950s; by 1962, it was 95 percent African American. More important, the quality of both its physical plant and its educational resources was clearly inferior to that of the city's white schools. Disputes over district boundaries and student transfers sent a clear signal to Sherrill parents that their school's administrators and the School Board were attempting to forestall desegregation. Frustrated over the inaction, a group calling itself the Sherrill School Parents Committee broke ranks with the Parent-Teacher Association and approached Cleage, who had been keeping up a constant harangue about school conditions. Cleage, along with Milton and Richard Henry, among others, had recently organized a new protest group, the Group on Advanced Leadership. An all-Black organization, GOAL was designed to be a "chemical catalyst" in the fight against bias. "A chemical catalyst speeds up the chemical reaction," Richard Henry wrote in the *Illustrated News*. "Similarly we will speed up the fight against bias."[62]

Cleage and GOAL viewed the Sherrill school predicament as one that was likely to spark the sort of chemical reaction they felt was necessary for change. But their position also drove a wedge between GOAL and the NAACP. Cleage claimed that he had "tried to convince the NAACP that action should be taken in this situation. . . . [a]lthough we felt an alert NAACP would have acted without having to be convinced."[63] Opposing the NAACP's decision to study the Sherrill situation, Cleage and GOAL

Group on Advanced Leadership (GOAL) pamphlet, circa 1964 (George Breitman Papers. Courtesy of Robert F. Wagner Archives, Tamiment Library, New York University.)

took matters into their own hands. Cleage became chair of the Sherrill
Parents Committee and launched a series of pickets and boycotts against
the school. Parents kept their children home and walked the line, joined
by a group of community activists and ministers, including the Rev.
Charles A. Hill, who was now in his late sixties but remained active in the
city's civil rights movement (in fact, when parents and students from
Northwestern High staged a similar boycott in 1962 the advance "strike
meeting" was held at Reverend Hill's Hartford Baptist).[64]

Dissatisfied by the results of their picket, GOAL attorney Milton
Henry initiated a lawsuit against the School Board on behalf of the
aggrieved parents. The suit, which was underwritten by the TULC and
guided through the legal process by George Crockett and his firm,
Goodman, Crockett, Eden and Robb, charged the board with systematic
mistreatment of Black students, a result of the "drawing, redrawing and
gerrymandering" of districts. The plaintiffs demanded an increase in the
number of Black teachers and administrators, as well as the removal of
textbooks presenting negative images of African Americans. The text-
book issue was particularly close to the heart of GOAL president Richard
Henry, who in 1963 lodged a formal complaint with the School Board
against his son's eighth-grade text for its failure to acknowledge the contributions of African nations to world civilization. GOAL threatened a
citywide boycott on this issue as well, and the School Board relented,
adding two supplementary chapters to the texts.[65]

The NAACP initially maintained a polite distance from the Sherrill
dispute, although it did eventually support the lawsuit.[66] It was already
leery of Cleage and GOAL, but when Cleage launched a personal attack
on Dr. Remus Robinson, the sole Black member of the School Board
since 1959, the battle lines were drawn. Cleage held Robinson personally responsible for segregation and discrimination and for what he saw
as Robinson's reluctance to act against them.[67] The NAACP rushed to
Robinson's defense, condemning Cleage as shortsighted.

While the suit was working its way through the legal system (it was
finally adjourned in 1965 due to "substantial" progress on desegregation), Cleage turned to what many saw as an outrageous mode of protest.
In the spring and fall elections of 1963, Cleage proceeded to drum up
opposition against a tax millage intended to increase school funding.
Why, Cleage asked, should Black parents vote to increase their property
taxes in order to fund and perpetuate a system that mistreated their children? "No Taxation for Discrimination" became the movement's slogan.
Cleage's antimillage campaign brought down a storm of criticism from
the liberal coalition. "We must decide whether we will follow in the paths

of destruction and chaos of Negro and white extremists," read an editorial in the *Michigan Chronicle*, which summarized the opposition to Cleage's crusade. "By voting against the millage, we are automatically casting our lot with the lunatic fringe. . . . We cannot afford to sacrifice the future of our young by following the foolish counsel of the radical elements in our midst."[68]

In the weeks leading up to the April 1 vote, Cleage debated his way through a good portion of the city's liberal coalition. He faced off, in person and print, against Horace Sheffield and the TULC, attorney (and future judge) Damon Keith of the Detroit Council for Political Education, the NAACP, the School Board itself, and Ofield Dukes and the other editorial writers at the *Michigan Chronicle*. Cleage faced Remus Robinson in a debate held at Fr. (by this time Canon) Malcolm Dade's St. Cyprian's Church and a representative of the Detroit Federation of Teachers at another debate staged by Detroit CORE.[69] Cleage held his ground throughout. While members of the liberal coalition did their best to neutralize him, his campaign did have an effect. After dozens of articles and speeches delivered at more than 250 meetings throughout the city, approximately fifty thousand Black voters changed their votes from yes to no. Ninety-eight percent of all Black voters had favored the millage in 1959, but in 1963 more than 40 percent opposed it.[70] The millage was in fact defeated in the spring (mostly by angry *white* voters), but it passed in the fall.

Cleage and GOAL were simultaneously at work on the related issue of urban renewal. Asking Blacks to finance schools that discriminated against their children was, for Cleage and the Henry brothers, no different from asking them to finance (again, with tax dollars) the destruction of Black neighborhoods and the displacement of their former inhabitants. "Urban Renewal," wrote Cleage and the Henrys time and time again in the *Illustrated News*, was "Negro Removal." GOAL had hoped that urban renewal, like school reform, would become a unifying issue for the city's civil rights community. It invited the NAACP, the TULC, the Cotillion Club, and others to join in the fight to keep Negro removal out of urban renewal. There was already widespread concern over the way the city's urban renewal policies were being carried out, and many in the liberal coalition were more than a little annoyed at being "invited" to the struggle by the GOAL arrivistes.

By 1962, almost ten thousand acres of "blighted" area, or 15 percent of the city, had been cleared under the urban renewal program. Roughly 57 percent of those personally affected by the clearance were Black. Although renewal programs were in principle racially open, most of the new housing projects were privately owned and rents were high, factors that worked against African American occupancy. What urban renewal really does, wrote the NAACP's Arthur Johnson, "is to relocate Negroes from one blighted area into one that is already overcrowded, thus eventually transforming it into a slum." "Increasingly," added councilman Mel Ravitz, "it has become an instrument primarily for the economic advantage of certain citizens and businesses who profit from investment, or who may benefit from residence in the city."[71]

Part of the problem came from the fact that it was unclear whether urban renewal was supposed to improve the quality of life for the city's present residents or whether its purpose was to attract suburbanized, white, middle-class families back to Detroit. "They're not going to return," said Black councilman William T. Patrick, insisting that the city focus more on low-income units. But it was not just access to new housing that was at issue; questions of equity also came into play when deciding which areas would be slated for clearance in the first place. Cleage and GOAL saw no reason why African Americans should be made to surrender their homes and neighborhoods disproportionately. Together with other organizations, GOAL launched a full frontal assault on the constitutionality of the Urban Renewal Redevelopment Program, filing a suit in federal court on the premise that the Urban Renewal Authority had no right to condemn and clear private properties for the benefit of private organizations.[72]

Actually, GOAL filed two lawsuits. One involved the Detroit Eight Mile Road Conservation site, one of many sites in the city that were judged to be viable but in need of conservation and improvement. The problem was that plans for the Eight Mile site (on the northwest border of Detroit) called for the destruction of an entire strip of Black businesses fronting Eight Mile Road and their replacement with a shopping center in which the displaced businesses were unlikely to be granted space. The second suit focused on the Medical Center, which was slated for the cleared land that was once Black Bottom. While GOAL was well aware of ongoing efforts by the Fellowship of Urban Renewal Churches, headed by Reverends Louis Johnson and Nicholas Hood, to oppose these same programs, Cleage and his fellow activists were unimpressed. Cleage was particularly exercised over the idea that Black churches had been selected for demolition while a number of white churches were to be left untouched. From his point of view Black ministers and congregations were caught in the absurd situation of being privately assured that everything was going to be worked out while at the same time being "maneuvered into a position of begging for our legal rights." The fellowship's negotiations, Cleage insisted in the pages of the *Illustrated News*, missed the real crux of the problem.[73]

Instead of negotiations, Cleage and GOAL turned to lawsuits to stop what they saw as a violation of rights destructive of Black churches and businesses and a threat to concentrations of Black political and economic power. They hoped to obtain a binding legal decision to correct a string of injustices committed through conservation and redevelopment programs. They demanded that conservation be rigorously pursued, that the process include the affected residents, and that displaced people and businesses be granted the right to return to redeveloped areas with assistance for their relocation or return. They also insisted on a broadly conceived antidiscrimination provision: "The government must guarantee through operable law and administrative measures, that no business, institution, apartment, person or persons in a conserved or redeveloped area may practice racial discrimination in any form, including its economic guise."[74]

The coalition that GOAL had joined was much more narrowly focused. The Medical Center urban renewal dispute centered not so much on the city's right to proceed with the project, although questions were certainly raised about the ethics of using public funds to subsidize private enterprise. Rather, in this case the major issues were the destruction of area Black (but not white) churches and racial discrimination in the hospitals that stood to benefit most from the project.[75] The Detroit Urban League provided well-documented evidence of systematic discrimination against African American health care professionals and patients. With prodding from Reverend Hood and his Fellowship of Urban Renewal Churches, area ministers banded together to protect as many Black churches as possible. It was a hard-fought battle, but it resulted, unlike the GOAL lawsuit, in significant concessions from the city.

Some of the Black churches that were threatened under the Medical Center plan, including Plymouth Congregational and Bethel AME, were granted a reprieve, allowing them to pool their funds in order to buy land and rebuild within the area. The coalition was unable to convince the city to build low-income public housing to allow for the return of displaced residents, but some churches, such as Friendship Baptist and Plymouth, sponsored their own low-income housing projects with assistance from city and federal agencies. Of equal significance, the coalition succeeded in gaining pledges of nondiscrimination from the hospitals. Monitored by the DUL, these pledges resulted in better treatment of

Black patients and an increase in employment opportunities for Black doctors, nurses, and orderlies.[76]

Although the coalition led by Reverend Hood's fellowship group would seem to have been more effective in the long run, Cleage and his GOAL colleagues felt that the very existence of the urban renewal controversy confirmed the necessity of meeting power with power—of not asking politely but demanding. It was neither the first nor the last time that GOAL would be accused of working at cross-purposes with the liberal coalition. The urban renewal and conservation controversies also reinforced Cleage's arguments about the ability of churches to improve the day-to-day lives of their communities. More important, at least for our purposes, these contests over housing and public education were instrumental in the genesis of a new civil rights community distinct from the liberal coalition.

Reverend Hood captured some of the underlying difference between these two groups when comparing himself to Reverend Cleage. Whereas Hood worked within the liberal coalition to get elected to the Common Council in 1965, Cleage aligned himself with efforts to build an all-Black political party; while Hood worked within the corridors of power, Cleage worked from the outside, seeking to fundamentally alter established power relations. But both men played an important role. "In the city, we've got to have the thrust of an Al Cleage," Hood opined in the 1970s, "because he scares people half to death and then they open the door to me."[77] Scaring people half to death was becoming a full-time job for Cleage, a prophetic burden that he carried in addition to his priestly duties at Central Congregational.

IN THE NAME OF SAINT CYNTHIA

Cleage's critique of the liberal-labor coalition and his efforts to mobilize the community on school reform and urban renewal increased his cachet among the city's young activists. Cleage took seemingly daring and confrontational positions, always well to the left of the NAACP, which made him attractive to those who questioned the viability of the established Black leadership and its white liberal allies. Cleage and the Henry brothers welcomed young activists into the ranks of GOAL and, along with the local Socialist Workers Party (SWP), supported young people's own attempts at organizing. A Detroit Commission on Community Relations report on one group of young Black radicals notes that "they have a great deal of respect for Reverend Cleage and the leadership of GOAL" and goes on to suggest that "only Cleage and the Henrys might be able to discipline them."[78] This last observation is inaccurate. Like Cleage, these young activists were searching for alternatives to the liberal coalition and were arriving at conclusions ideologically similar to his. Cleage may have offered encouragement but not discipline.

Many of the new organizations founded by these young radicals were small, and their activities were generally sporadic. Historian Sidney Fine may be right in describing them as "flyspecks in terms of posing a threat to the black leadership position occupied in Detroit by the NAACP."[79] But they were important as markers of slow but steady ideological shifts within the city's civil rights movement. By the late 1960s, this new generation of activists would have a decisive impact on the course of political mobilization in Detroit—in the labor struggles of the League of Revolutionary Black Workers and the wildcat strikes of 1968 and in the spheres of welfare rights, antipoverty work, and Black community empowerment.

One of the most important of these "flyspecks" was UHURU, which was organized in March 1963 by Luke Tripp (who was a twenty-two-year-old college senior at the time, majoring in mathematics and physics) with John Watson, Ken Cockrel, and General Baker, all of whom would later be active in the founding of the League of Revolutionary Black Workers, and a variety of other Wayne State students. Taking their name from the Swahili word for freedom, UHURU's stated purpose was to "seek the closest possible alliance of militant black groups from the broadest possible united black front to wage a tit-for-tat struggle against the anti-Negro machine that is America; to fight for 'uhuru quita' [freedom now] . . . and to affirm the principle of self-defense in the Negro freedom struggle."[80] As a group UHURU tended to reject the ethic of nonviolence and embrace the logic of anticolonial and third-world revolution. Although there were many such philosophical and political differences between UHURU and the liberal coalition, it was the hostility of the group's rhetoric that coalition members found most disturbing. "Their bitterness," wrote a field investigator for the Detroit Commission on Community Relations, is "totally destructive"; worse, it is a "complaint against capitalism."[81]

While UHURU was an exclusively Back organization—white people could help, but they could not join—it did maintain close ties to the SWP and the mostly white Young Socialist Alliance, which was based on the Wayne State campus. "We [UHURU] produced newsletters," recalled Baker. "We went to SWP's Militant Labor Forum and got introduced to people that was coming around the country on circuits."[82] The Detroit

Commission on Community Relations also noted this connection but did not see the ties between UHURU and the Young Socialist Alliance as indicative of a shared intellectual culture. Rather, the DCCR implied that (once again) well-meaning Blacks were being duped by a group of white subversives out to destroy the American way of life. The anxiety of the DCCR and others was completely out of proportion to UHURU's power. The organization functioned primarily as a discussion group for young, disaffected, Black university students, and none of its occasional forays into political activism was exactly revolutionary.

UHURU did some of its work in conjunction with GOAL, one of the "militant black groups" included in UHURU's vision of a "black united front." At other times its actions were entirely self-directed. That the group's activities tended toward symbolic forms of protest should not decrease their significance, and these actions often betrayed a lively sense of humor. The group first came to public attention in the fall of 1963, when it disrupted a ceremony and rally staged by the committee lobbying to make Detroit the host of the 1968 Olympic Games. It was UHURU's position that "Detroit wasn't deserving of the Olympics because it didn't have open occupancy." Since the rally, held in front of the City-County Building in downtown Detroit and featuring the Olympic torchbearer, was to be "broadcast all over the world," it was also an opportunity to exploit the media and make a big symbolic splash.[83] Whereas CORE and the NAACP's Housing Committee confined their protests on open housing to placards, UHURU took a more vocal approach. "We were singing and hissing," remembered Baker. When the police band began playing the national anthem, UHURU members increased the volume of their jeers and catcalls. They also "embarrassed" Hayes Jones, the Black runner bearing the Olympic torch, by taking great pains to "remind him of his second class citizenship."[84] The city administration and the civil rights establishment were outraged. CORE issued a statement denying any connection with UHURU and its protest; its members were already angry at UHURU members for showing up a week earlier at their picket outside of a local Kroger grocery store with signs that read "Cross at Your Own Risk."[85] The TULC was already cool toward the new organization. Shortly before the Olympic protest, UHURU had descended on the TULC's Freedom House to protest the appearance of Mayor Cavanagh, "the Man," and their "Uncle Tom elders." Reportedly, Sheffield, Battle, and other angry council members "took the little radicals out back and beat the shit out of them."[86]

Michigan Chronicle columnist Ofield Dukes, who was also director of the Young Adult Division of the NAACP, bemoaned UHURU's disrup-

tion of the "peaceful" demonstration planned by the NAACP's Housing
Committee. He was particularly upset that the NAACP's actions had
been upstaged by "the unruly mob," which jeered at "the National
Anthem, our Negro Councilman [William T. Patrick], and a Mayor who
put his neck on the political chopping block [in defense of open occu-
pancy]." In terms reminiscent of his rebuke of Cleage's antimillage campaign, Dukes characterized UHURU members as "irresponsible and
absurd in their approach to the race problem" and accused them of having a "subversive aim" to "wreck completely all Negroes relations with the
white community." Taking the assessment one step further, he drew a
parallel between UHURU's political orientation—"Mau Mau Maoist"—
and the supposedly "subversive" influence of the Communist Party
decades earlier.[87]

Finally, interjecting the generational aspect, Dukes wrote them off as
ungrateful youths: "Negroes in Detroit have too much at stake to sit by
quietly while the blind young beneficiaries of years of efforts by the
Negro-white coalition are methodically destroying the framework in
which these gains were made." It does not seem to have occurred to
Dukes that, for the members of UHURU, this framework was part of the
problem—that younger activists were in fact challenging the basic
assumptions guiding the liberal coalition. Indeed, Detroit's young radicals were probably gratified by the harsh reactions they received from
"liberals," as well as the support they received from Cleage, GOAL, and
other "militants." In any case, UHURU was unrepentant. When city
administrators, backed by law enforcement officials, identified the protesters and demanded a public apology, the group refused.[88]

Days later, warrants were issued for the arrest of UHURU president
Luke Tripp, John Watson, General Baker, John Williams, and Gwendolyn Kemp, one of the group's few female members. For most of them,
it was, as Baker put it, their "first real antagonism with the law," although
Watson and Kemp had been arrested in Charleston, Mississippi, during
a SNCC mobilization.[89] Incredibly, the case went to trial in November
with GOAL's Milton Henry serving as defense counsel. Henry created a
minor sensation, arguing that a true jury of his defendants' peers would
have to be all Black—a suggestion dismissed by the trial's African American judge as frivolous.[90] Years later Ken Cockrel and his white radical
partner Justin Ravitz would use similar tactics in defense of Black defendants in the city's courtrooms.[91]

The five members of UHURU were acquitted by mistrial in May
1964, but the entire experience did nothing to endear them to the city's
legal system and the police department, another favorite UHURU tar-

get. UHURU members protested in front of city police stations on a regular basis. The police force was amazingly restrained, probably thanks to the intercession of George Edwards, the liberal police commissioner and ex-UAW organizer; since Cavanagh's appointment of Edwards, police-community relations had shown signs of improvement. In one relatively minor scuffle, Luke Tripp and Gwendolyn Kemp were detained for making "inflammatory" statements, but both of them were soon released.[92]

But the event that probably radicalized the young militants the most was the police slaying of Cynthia Scott. "Saint Cynthia" as Scott was known, was a middle-aged Black prostitute who worked the streets of the Twelfth Street district not far from Cleage's Central Church. Six feet tall and 198 pounds, Scott was a raucous local fixture who had tallied up a string of confrontations with the law for "soliciting and accosting."[93] With her record, it probably did not seem too far out of the ordinary when Officer Theodore Spicher and his partner began to harass Scott in the early morning of July 5, 1964. But the encounter turned nasty, and Scott, who in a drunken state supposedly pulled a knife on the officer, ended up with two bullets in her back and one in her stomach. Saint Cynthia was no Rosa Parks (by this time Parks and her family had moved to Detroit to escape retaliatory southern violence), but the incident did touch off a storm of protests. The outrage felt by some segments of the Black community reached a climax when the officers were cleared of wrongful death charges on self-defense grounds.[94] The dead prostitute swiftly became a martyr. Several hundred people picketed police headquarters on July 13 as a part of street rallies organized by Reverend Cleage, GOAL, and UHURU. Cleage, James Boggs, and the Henrys were featured speakers at a number of these rallies, demanding that Officer Spicher be retried. GOAL attorneys, including Milton Henry, assisted Scott's mother with a five-million-dollar lawsuit against the officer and the police department. UHURU members also staged a sit-in in Mayor Cavanagh's office, demanding that a Black chief of police be appointed to replace Edwards.[95]

The Scott affair became an important point of reference for the city's activists and the Black community as a whole. When Cleage's brother Henry ran for Wayne County prosecutor on the all-Black Freedom Now Party ticket in 1964, he promised, "When I am elected, I will see to it that the case of Cynthia Scott is re-opened." The murder even made a literary appearance in Barbara Tinker's 1970 novel, *When the Fire Reaches Us,* as something "damned few black people" in the city had forgotten: "Self defense, he [the Man] said. Only how come she was shot in the back?" Finally, in his detailed study of the 1967 rebellion, Sidney Fine identifies the Scott killing as one of African Americans' many lingering grievances against the police and the city's administration.[96]

THE BLACK REVOLT OF 1963

Reverend Cleage was proud of his ability to cause trouble, once boasting of being the only "Negro leader in this labor-dominated city to defy labor leaders." In a later sermon, Cleage ridiculed Walter Reuther as "our great black leader," who had apparently forgotten that UAW organizers once fought, looted, and defied the law in order to establish their union. But that was before they got respectable, Cleage chided.[97] Increasingly, Cleage's brand of Black nationalism was presented as a viable alternative to "working within the system" of city administrators or labor union officials. Hence, Cleage and the growing group of Black nationalists arrayed around him at GOAL and Central Congregational were a constant source of tension during the civil rights mobilizations of the mid- to late 1960s. Indeed, one could argue that Black nationalism was as divisive in the 1960s activist community as anticommunism had been a decade earlier.

These tensions—over Black nationalism, the possibility of coalition politics, and, once again, the proper role of churches and clergymen— were becoming apparent in Black communities across the nation. In Detroit they came to a head immediately before, during, and after the Walk to Freedom march of Sunday, June 23, 1963. With a turnout of between 125,000 and 200,000 participants, the Detroit march, which preceded the March on Washington by two months, was until then "the largest civil rights march in the nation." It was dubbed a success by the media, both Black and white, but its planning and implementation created a rift within the local movement that would never be repaired and would later be amplified by the Cynthia Scott protests, UHURU's antics at the Olympic torch ceremony, and the creation of the Freedom Now Party. The initial idea for the Detroit march came from a segment of the city's activist community that considered itself well to the left of the NAACP. The need for an "unprecedented show of strength" to dramatize the frustrations of Black Detroiters was expressed by Cleage at the end of an otherwise "disappointing" NAACP-sponsored demonstration in sympathy with civil rights protesters in Birmingham ("Bombingham"), Alabama. James Boggs recalls that there were about 50 people present for the event, mostly trade union militants, and that toward the end of the demonstration he began to call for Cleage.[98]

The idea of holding a massive march in Detroit caught on, and plans began to take shape on May 17, when more than eight hundred Black Detroiters gathered to commemorate the ninth anniversary of the *Brown* decision at New Bethel Baptist Church, which was pastored by the Rev. C. L. Franklin. Born in 1915 in the heart of the Mississippi Delta, Franklin had grown up poor and nearly illiterate in a rural community sustained both by faith and by the Delta blues of fellow Mississippians such as B. B. King, Son House, and Charley Patton. To many, it seemed nothing short of miraculous that Franklin had managed to escape his early surroundings, obtain a decent education, and develop a captivating preaching style based on his rich and sonorous singing voice. Franklin had begun to develop this style even before he arrived in Detroit in 1943, interweaving the secular and the sacred, the blues and the Bible. It would eventually propel him to national prominence in the 1950s and 1960s as a preacher's preacher, a performer, and a recording artist.

In the pulpit and on the stage, Franklin lived a flashy and unconventional life studded with fine suits, ostentatious jewelry, and beautiful women. Perhaps to make himself look better by contrast, Franklin once used his very popular Sunday radio show to chastise the truly unconventional James "Prophet" Jones, of the Pentecostal Universal Triumph, the Dominion of God, Incorporated, who was known for his unorthodox interpretations of Christianity and for wearing full-length white minks coats, as a "threat" to "the very foundations of our religion."[99] Yet Franklin was often on the receiving end of similar charges. Deeply moved by the events that were rapidly transforming the social and political landscape of his childhood South, by the early 1960s Franklin had begun to play an active role in the city's civil rights movement.[100]

Franklin was soon thereafter named head of the newly organized Detroit Council for Human Rights (DCHR). Because he had only recently become politically active, various members questioned whether he had the sort of experience necessary to lead the group, but Franklin insisted that he could handle the responsibility. Cleage was also named to the board of directors. Some within the DCHR hoped that the group would eventually eclipse the NAACP as the city's leading civil rights group, but its first, more limited order of business was to coordinate the march, a goal that proved more difficult to achieve than anyone could have anticipated. Since the march was to double as a fund-raiser for the Southern Christian Leadership Conference, it was agreed that the Rev. Martin L. King Jr., a close friend of Franklin's, should be invited to lead the march and address a rally at Cobo Hall, the city's riverfront convention center. Consensus on which other dignitaries and speakers should be invited proved elusive, however. Cleage, for one, wanted to keep the march as militant and Black led as possible. But it was a losing battle. Mayor Cavanagh and the UAW's Reuther were added to the list, leading Cleage to accuse the march's organizers of attempting to "legitimize" the event (thus limiting its effect) by involving the white establishment.

The DCHR also found itself placating other factions of the Black clergy. The Rev. Charles W. Butler of New Calvary Baptist had just been designated as Detroit's new SCLC representative in part as a conciliation to the powerful Baptist Ministerial Alliance, of which Butler was a member. Soon afterward alliance ministers voiced their opinion that Butler, not Franklin, should play the lead role in the march and rally. As Franklin's biographer, Nick Salvatore, notes, Reverend Franklin had long been dismissed by influential Detroiters such as the Rev. A. A. Banks of Second Baptist and Edward Turner of the NAACP as "a mere preacher." "They abhorred his public style and denigrated his political analysis," Salvatore continues. "Yet, in this moment of crisis"—with the SCLC barely solvent after the costly Birmingham campaign—"King had reached out not for Arthur Johnson, his Morehouse College classmate, nor other close acquaintances among the black social elite, but for the Mississippi-born migrant."[101]

If Reverend Franklin's rise was disturbing to the alliance, Reverend Cleage's was truly horrifying; many worried about what the ascension of these two accomplished, yet very different, preachers might portend. Their opponents were reportedly disquieted by the pair's insistence on maintaining the march's "Negro character" and insisted that "local white churches wanted to have a share in raising funds . . . and to support future actions towards desegregation."[102] When he attempted to make peace with the alliance, Franklin, whose efforts to keep his distance from the group had already gotten him into trouble with its membership, was forced to purchase a membership before it would allow him to speak. Franklin went ahead and made his case but to no avail. The alliance not only declined to support the march, but it even organized an alternative program at King Solomon Baptist on the same day.[103]

The local NAACP's resentment toward Cleage, Franklin, and others within the DCHR was at least as strong as its feelings toward the alliance. Having been repeatedly denounced by the DCHR as "a bunch of Uncle Toms," the NAACP was in no mood to cooperate in the march. Looking back on the matter, the NAACP's Arthur Johnson diplomatically recalled that the planning for the march was initiated by "three or four men whose credentials were not as clear as we would have liked them to be." The NAACP hierarchy went so far as to threaten a boycott;

Cavanagh and Reuther's inclusion in the event was the price that the NAACP exacted for its support.[104]

In the end, the march was not all that Cleage and Franklin had hoped it would be. But it was nonetheless an impressive show of solidarity with the southern struggle. The turnout was larger than expected, perhaps in part because Cleage and others held "prerallies" at their churches, encouraging people to attend the march. And most of the city's other civil rights organizations eventually signed on, including CORE, GOAL, the UAW, and especially the TULC.

Even with all this support, no one—neither the organizers nor the participants nor the city's officials—was prepared for the thousands and thousands of marchers, mostly Black and dressed in their Sunday best, who formed a human sea washing down the streets of the city. During his address at Cobo Hall, King proclaimed the march "the largest and greatest demonstration for freedom ever held in the United States." It was, according to him, a "magnificent new militancy" that could be harnessed and magnified in an equally massive march on Washington in support of the civil rights legislation pending in Congress. At the close of his forty-eight-minute speech, King delivered a longer and richer version of the "Dream sequence" that famously highlighted his speech at the March on Washington.[105]

Reverend Cleage also addressed the crowd. As James Boggs recalled, "After King finished talking about conditions in the South, Reverend Cleage got up and said that we'd better start looking at conditions in Detroit."[106] Cleage's speech actually preceded King's that day, but Boggs's memory is otherwise accurate: for one brief moment, the tensions within the local civil rights movement appeared to have been smoothed over and contained.

But the moment passed quickly. Members of the DCHR felt the march had proved that they, not the NAACP, were truly "in touch with the masses." For James Del Rio, a successful Black real estate agent and DCHR member, the march "was a direct repudiation of the NAACP" and a personal rejection of NAACP president Edward Turner and executive secretary Arthur Johnson. Similarly, Reverend Franklin expressed "deep respect" for the NAACP in general but accused its leadership of being "too close" to whites and consequently losing contact with "the Negro man-in-the-streets." The NAACP responded by reminding Detroiters that it was the oldest and still the most viable civil rights organization in town—which it was.[107] The organization's ability to survive internal and external challenges, both locally and nationally, is noteworthy to this day.

The Detroit Council on Human Rights was attempting to occupy a position somewhere between the NAACP, on the one hand, and Cleage, UHURU, and GOAL on the other. It wanted to become the center of the city's new civil rights coalition, but it would not hold that position for long. Even as it was launching salvos in its war of words with the NAACP, the DCHR was experiencing internal problems of its own. Ideological differences between Cleage and Franklin finally broke the surface during the DCHR's effort to create a Northern Christian Leadership Conference (NCLC), as a counterpart to the SCLC.[108] The resulting eruption destroyed whatever unity had ever existed within the council and, perhaps more significantly, exposed even deeper tensions in the city's civil rights movement, particularly regarding Black nationalism.

The proposed three-day founding convention of the NCLC (November 8–10, 1963) was to be open to delegates from all of the northern civil rights organizations. Cleage was appointed chairman of the Conference Committee, but his plans to invite Conrad Lynn and William Worthy, founding members of the newly organized Freedom Now Party, were rejected by Reverend Franklin, who continued to serve as the organization's head. Worthy, a reporter for the *Baltimore Afro-American* and a committed pacifist, had been a special CBS News correspondent in Moscow during the 1950s and had defied the U.S. travel ban to Cuba, for which he lost his passport in 1962. Lynn was a radical attorney based in New York City and a veteran activist who faced angry mobs during the 1947 Journey of Reconciliation to test the Supreme Court ruling against segregation on buses in cases of interstate travel. Both men had ties to the Socialist Workers Party and Robert Williams (Lynn was his lawyer), who was living in exile in Cuba.[109] The idea for the Freedom Now Party had grown out of conversations among a group of New York-based radicals, including Lynn, Worthy, and Black intellectual Harold Cruse; its founding was announced in a *New York Times* story on August 24, 1963, four days before the March on Washington. Interested parties in New York, Detroit, and elsewhere had planned for weeks to meet at the march in Washington in order to hash out the party's platform—an arrangement that made them highly unpopular with their liberal colleagues.[110]

Even as plans for the NCLC gathering developed, Cleage still did not join the Freedom Now Party. But he clearly expressed his hopes of building an all-Black independent political party and invited the participation of GOAL and UHURU, as well as representatives of the Nation of Islam, including Minister Wilfred X, head of Temple #1 in Detroit, and his brother, Minister Malcolm X. Reverend Franklin forbade the invitation of "communists" (Lynn and Worthy) or "extremists" (Malcolm and Wilfred X), proclaiming that "mingling" with "communists, black nationalists and persons with criminal records" would only "destroy our image." "Ours is the Christian view and approach," added Del Rio. "Those who refuse to turn the other cheek are having their own conference." Frustrated, Cleage resigned from the DCHR in early November and began to make plans for a rival meeting, the Northern Negro Grass Roots Leadership Conference, whose very name was meant to symbolize the groups' differences.[111]

Cleage and GOAL scheduled the rival Grass Roots conference for the same weekend as the DCHR's event. There was no reason to do so other than spite, which was rewarded when the DCHR convention flopped. Even though Adam Clayton Powell addressed the DHCR's public rally at Cobo Hall, only "a disappointing 3,000 souls attended" (Cobo Hall seats fifteen thousand). Only a select group of one hundred had been invited to the weekend workshops and meetings, but less than half that number showed. And of those who did several, including Gloria Richardson, an accomplished organizer from Maryland, left the DCHR's convention for GOAL's.[112] Reverend Franklin and the DCHR were, as Nick Salvatore notes, caught between opposing forces: the NAACP, the Baptist Ministerial Alliance, and the liberal leadership of the city's civil rights movement on one side; and Cleage, GOAL, and the small but growing cadre of militants and nationalists on the other. In fact, it was not so much Cleage and GOAL's alternative conference that crippled the plans for an NCLC but a virtual boycott of the event by the ministerial alliance under the leadership of the Rev. A. L. Merritt. Trapped between warring parties, the would-be centrist NCLC quickly succumbed. Franklin, who rejected gradualism but insisted on nonviolence and opposed Black nationalism, found himself similarly squeezed.[113]

The Grass Roots Leadership Conference, while slightly better attended, was really only a small blip on Detroit's political radar. When it is remembered at all, it is generally for Malcolm X's appearance and his "Message to the Grass Roots" speech. It was one of Malcolm X's last public addresses before he broke with the Nation of Islam, and in it he struggled to articulate a position on "real" revolution in a national and international context. The speech was not terribly successful in this regard, although it did illuminate distinctions between the liberal and nationalist approaches to Black freedom. "Who ever heard of a revolution where they lock arms, as Rev. Cleage was pointing out beautifully, singing 'We Shall Overcome'?" Malcolm X asked. The ultimate goal of the Black struggle, he argued before an audience of three thousand gathered at the King Solomon Baptist Church, was not civil rights but rather land and a Black nation.

> When you want a nation, that's called nationalism. When the white man became involved in a revolution in this country against England, what was it for? He wanted this land so he could set up another white nation. . . . The American revolution was white nationalism. The French Revolution was white nationalism. The Russian Revolution too—yes, it was—white nationalism. You don't think so? . . . All the revolutions that are going on in Asia and Africa today are based on what?—black nationalism. A revolutionary is a black nationalist. He wants a nation.[114]

Reverend Cleage regarded Malcolm X as a political ally despite their religious and ideological differences. Religiously, Cleage and GOAL members went out of their way to unite Christians and Muslims, a unity they symbolized in the image of "a Christian Negro minister marrying an Islamic invocation into a Christian prayer."[115] Cleage's and Malcolm X's speeches were dotted with references to each other; but their positions on the revolution, while similar, were not exactly the same. Reverend Cleage never believed in the Black nation as a separate geographical entity. The Black nation was political, economic, cultural, and spiritual, not physical. His revolution did not seek land but power and self-determination. In fact, Cleage broke with Richard and Milton Henry over this distinction when the Henrys founded their separatist Republic of New Africa in the late 1960s. "Revolution—real revolution—is for power," Cleage told the crowd at King Solomon's. "Negroes must learn to refuse to accept anything less than complete freedom" here in the United States in their own communities. "And we must make it clear to white people that we will enjoy our freedom—all of it—or they won't enjoy theirs either."[116]

But, despite their differences, Cleage incorporated both the flavor and substance of Malcolm X's philosophy into his own thinking. After Malcolm X's assassination in 1965, Cleage debated Marxist and SWP member George Breitman over the true meaning of Malcolm X and his legacy. Breitman suggested that in the last year of his life Malcolm X was well on his way to becoming an international socialist, adopting some of the same conclusions about revolution and anticapitalism as the SWP. Cleage rejected the notion. "I am not a Marxist—I don't pretend to be, I don't even pretend to know anything about it," Cleage retorted, in what was at least his second speech to a SWP Friday Night Forum.[117] Insisting that Malcolm X "wasn't fooled in Mecca, he wasn't fooled in Africa," Cleage argued that Malcolm X's internationalism was of a different kind, one based on the fight against racial, rather than economic, oppression.

These differences over the relationship between land and power and about what role, if any, white radicals could play in the revolution continued to structure the evolution of a Black nationalist perspective in Detroit and elsewhere well after Malcolm X's assassination. The Grass-Roots Conference had helped to launch the Michigan chapter of the Freedom Now Party; a year or so later James Boggs founded the closely aligned Organization for Black Power. The FNP was hampered from the beginning by disagreements over which school of Black nationalism it would adhere to. Shortly after the founding of the national party, the disagreement manifested itself in a dispute over whether the FNP should pursue a separatist or integrationist strategy. "A shaky compromise was reached," explains Conrad Lynn, under which "all candidates for public office would be black, but individuals of whatever color were free to join. In this way we hoped to have a party primarily devoted to the interests of blacks."[118] The problem for many was with the insertion of that adverb, *primarily,* and the questions it posed about the political affinities of the party's white members.

These debates were somewhat reminiscent of the arguments that swirled around A. Philip Randolph's March on Washington movement in 1940 after Randolph broke with the National Negro Congress over the involvement of the Communist Party. A faint echo of Randolph can be heard in James Boggs's sharp missive to Conrad Lynn some twenty years later. "I wrote that I did not believe the party should be under any kind of umbrella," Boggs warned Lynn.

> If you want to know what I mean by an umbrella, I mean that it should not be under the auspices of any radical group. And if you want me to be more concrete I am under the impression that the people you have in Detroit and Cleveland are people whom you were given by the SWP. . . . If white radicals are saying that they must be in the party in order for it to be a party, then I am against the damn party. . . . For instance, Grace, my wife, hasn't got a damn bit of business in the black political party unless they label her a Negro in this country.[119]

Boggs was absolutely right. For well over a month the FNP's chief person in Detroit had been none other than George Breitman, William Worthy's close friend and frequent correspondent. It was Worthy who in many ways had been the Harlem-based party's progenitor; he used Breitman as a sounding board and a conduit for information on the situation in Detroit. In this capacity, Breitman was able, for instance, to supply information on James Boggs, whom Worthy had met only once, briefly; Breitman cautioned Worthy against involving Boggs too closely in his efforts. When Worthy asked about possible youth involvement, it was once again Breitman who was able to suggest Luke Tripp. But above all the two men discussed Reverend Cleage and whether he would actually join the FNP.[120] At one point an obviously frustrated Breitman complained about the extent to which it "has been and grows increasingly difficult for me to be your contact here," not only because of the "need to avoid leaks" but also because "I am not a Negro." While Breitman continued to support the Michigan FNP, he eventually found someone more suitable to head its forces in Detroit, a young, unemployed man by the name of LaMar Barrow. Barrow was neither experienced nor sophisticated, but he was, Breitman wrote, "responsible and reliable."[121]

The FNP generally stuck to its compromise on the question of race and membership. White radicals, particularly those associated with the SWP, did join or support the party, as Breitman's story makes clear. Grace Lee Boggs was the only non-Black member who ran for office on the FNP ticket. As a Chinese American, she apparently presented a problem for the party's efforts to enforce race-based membership categories. The Michigan FNP had a politically diverse constituency, however, attracting people who had been involved with GOAL and UHURU, as well as those who had worked with the TULC, CORE, and NAACP. At least one of the party's members, Christopher Alston, had been a Communist. The party ran a full slate in 1964, with Reverend Cleage as the gubernatorial candidate; Milton Henry running for Congress; and Ernest C. Smith, a teacher at Cody High School, running for Senate. The party also ran a full slate of eight candidates for the state Board of Education. One of the six women on the ticket, Helen Kelly, was a member of Teamsters Local 458 and had been active with both the TULC and the Sherrill School Parents Committee. Another candidate, Ella Mae Perryman, was a member of Cleage's church and the Harmony Neighborhood Civic Group, one of the city's numerous block club organizations. Attorney Henry Cleage ran for Wayne County prosecuting attorney in a campaign largely focused on the police slaying of Cynthia Scott. Grace Boggs stood for the Board of Trustees of Wayne State University.[122]

Although Cleage was slow to join the FNP, once he did so he showed absolute commitment. He became the Michigan Freedom Now Party's state chairman and wrote and spoke frequently on behalf of the party.

ELECT NEGRO CANDIDATES

By Voting
FREEDOM NOW
PARTY

VOTE for
MILTON R. HENRY

**U.S. CONGRESS
1st DISTRICT
BALLOT NO. 199**

ELECT NEGRO CANDIDATES

By Voting
FREEDOM NOW
PARTY

VOTE for

BALLOT NO. 204

CHRISTOPHER C. ALSTON
STATE REPRESENTATIVE 10th - DISTRICT

ELECT NEGRO CANDIDATES
VOTE FOR
DR. LOUIS J. CLEAGE
BOARD OF EDUCATION
NON-PARTISAN
ELECTION, SEPT. 1
ENDORSED BY

GOAL - GROUP ON ADVANCED LEADERSHIP
FREEDOM NOW PARTY
LEAGUE OF NEGRO WOMEN VOTERS

Freedom Now Party Voter Information Cards, 1964 (Ernest C. Smith Collection.
Courtesy of Walter P. Reuther Library, Wayne State University.)

On October 11, 1963, he gave a speech to an FNP rally that wove many of the year's political developments into an argument about why 1963 was the year of the Black revolt. Affirming that "we have come a long way in a short period of time," Cleage began by referencing the recent debate over an open occupancy ordinance proposed by Councilmen William T. Patrick and Mel Ravitz and about the role of "our white liberal friends" in helping to defeat the proposal. Cleage was especially hard on Philip Van Antwerp, who had defeated African American candidate Jackie Vaughn in a hard-fought election in 1962 for a seat on the Common Council. Cleage chided those who had felt that, since the two were both liberals and expressed practically no differences of political opinion, it was better to vote for the more experienced Van Antwerp than the newcomer Vaughn.[123]

When the council finally voted, the open occupancy ordinance was defeated seven to two. Van Antwerp voted with the majority, maintaining that unsegregated housing was a moral issue and therefore impossible to legislate—a position the *Michigan Chronicle* branded as an "absurd parade of stupidity and ignorance." Years later, Ravitz vividly recalled the intensity of the controversy. It was, he reflected, "the first time I became really aware of the virulence of hatred in this city, when I had to have my house guarded, [and when I had my] tires slashed." At the raucous public hearings, held at Ford Auditorium in order to accommodate the crowds, the councilmen had to be escorted by armed guards.

To make matters worse, not only was the Patrick-Ravitz ordinance voted down but a rival measure affirming the "freedom" to discriminate was brought before the council by the Greater Detroit Homeowners' Association and then directly to voters through an initiative petition of the same sort once used by leftists to force action on an FEPC ordinance. The association needed only four days to collect the signatures necessary to get this so-called Poindexter Ordinance (named after attorney and councilman Thomas Poindexter, who lost his reelection bid to Nicholas Hood in 1965) on the ballot. The NAACP's legal challenge to the ordinance's inclusion on the ballot was to no avail. In September 1964, the measure passed by a vote of 136,671 to 111,994.[124]

"The whole open occupancy situation," Cleage said to the audience gathered for the 1963 Freedom Now rally, "has done more for the Freedom Now Party in the city of Detroit than anything anybody could have said to anybody." Many, including Cleage, noted the "progressive" UAW's absence from the debate over open occupancy. He also referred to the Cynthia Scott slaying and its aftermath; the UHURU Olympic protest; that September's Birmingham church bombing, which had killed four African American girls; and the Kennedy administration and Congress's inability to secure the rights of Black citizens. What additional proof did anyone need, Cleage asked rhetorically, to prove that "the white man does not intend to give the Negro equality?"[125]

Instead of "accidentally" wasting votes by supporting fair-weather white liberals such as Kennedy and Cavanagh—"We took Cavanagh and we made a mayor out of a little lawyer who didn't have a chance. And we wasted our vote"—Cleage suggested that FNP voters might as well waste their votes on purpose. This was not just a protest vote or even a vote of conscience. Rather, it was part of what Cleage called "an organized and deliberate strategy of chaos." "I'm not talking about that natural ability that we have to tear up things," he explained. "I'm talking about a deliberately conceived plan to tear up those things from which we are excluded in these United States—it either accepts us in it, or we'll do everything possible to tear it up." The FNP was to become a thorn in the Democratic Party's side, an open rejection of the argument that Blacks ought to support Democrats as the lesser of two evils. It was a risky strategy, which reflected Cleage's campaign for a no vote on the 1963 school millage question seeking to hold Detroit's schools accountable for their failure to meet the needs of Black children and their communities.

When speaking publicly about the Freedom Now Party during late 1963 and 1964 Cleage never mentioned the SWP and tended not to speak in terms of full-scale nationalist or socialist revolution. Still, the bulk of the SWP membership continued to support the new political party. Not everyone in the Socialist camp was happy with this decision, but in internal party arguments George Breitman carried the day.[126] There were other ties as well. William Worthy was close to the SWP (he had been one of the featured speakers at the October 1963 rally in Detroit), and the SWP's 1964 national ticket included a number of FNP-friendly African Americans—particularly Clifton DeBerry, a New York state party organizer who ran for president with Edward Shaw, a former Detroit auto worker and party organizer. The SWP also ran a slate of candidates in Michigan's statewide races; not wanting to split the modest ranks of those willing to vote for candidates of either party, the SWP abstained from certain designated races.[127]

The FNP's stance on Black nationalism and its tacit endorsement from the SWP did nothing to endear the new party to the city's liberal coalition. An older generation of Black ministers, including the Rev. Charles A. Hill, was especially vocal in its opposition. "I don't want anything to do with organizations which want all-black," Hill told a meeting of Baptist ministers. "There are white people suffering and dying for civil

Freedom Now Party campaign poster, 1964 (Ernest C. Smith Collection. Courtesy of Walter P. Reuther Library, Wayne State University.)

rights, too." Believing in God power, not Black power, Hill urged, "We should close our churches to them [the FNP]."[128]

Hill attempted to do just that. The FNP, recognizing that Black churches were important sites for community organizing, sought to meet in as many area churches as possible. The petition drive to get the FNP on the ballot had also centered in African American churches and was part of Cleage's attempt to organize at the religious grass roots of Black Detroit. Hill believed that by shutting the FNP out of these community venues he and his colleagues could effectively shut the party down.

In one much-remarked instance, Hill was able to persuade a local minister, the Rev. W. R. Haney of Dexter Avenue Baptist, to reverse his decision to allow the Freedom Now Party to meet in his church by convincing him that the FNP stood for "Black nationalism and a separate state idea." The rest of the ministerial alliance followed Hill's lead. It was, to be sure, a complete reversal for a clergyman who had begun his political career by opening his church to dissidents. Milton Henry remarked on Hill's turnabout, which Henry saw as inconsistent. "It is difficult to understand how Rev. Hill could have allowed a dinner party to be held at his church . . . for the Communist Party's Benjamin Davis last May, and yet try to deny my church, Dexter Avenue Baptist, the right to hold a Freedom Now meeting." Perhaps, Henry added, Hill "feels that the Communist Party is okay since it is interracial."[129] In the course of over three decades of activism, Reverend Hill had gone from accusations that he was "commie" to suggestions that he was a "Tom." His political philosophy had not changed at all, but Detroit's political struggles had undergone a transformation around him.[130]

Actually, Reverend Hill avoided calling the FNP "communistic" on the basis of its ties to the SWP, as others had. Yet it is interesting to wonder whether Hill's affinity for the CP, with its long-standing hatred of the SWP, influenced his position in any way. The FNP's ties to the socialists were also a problem for Cleage and his fellow Black nationalists, given Cleage's (false) insistence that his party had no connection with the SWP or any other "white radicals."[131]

Although the SWP and the other groups associated with the Freedom Now Party campaigned hard, the state election results were less than edifying. Cleage received only 4,767 votes for governor; the only candidate who made a decent showing was Henry Cleage, who garnered 6,603 votes in his congressional race.[132] Disappointed, Cleage and Grace Lee Boggs both left the FNP shortly after the election.

The loss was, however, an important learning experience. Having made a shaky peace with the Democratic Party, candidate Cleage rose again, this time to run for the Common Council in 1965—twenty years after Reverend Hill's first campaign. It was a phenomenal campaign season. An unprecedented thirteen African American candidates entered the primaries that year, including Cleage, George Crockett, Jackie Vaughn, the UAW's Marc Stepp, and the still cantankerous Snow Grigsby, who was described as "a surprising dynamo on the speaker's circuit." The despised councilman Thomas Poindexter also joined the race. Cleage did not survive the primaries, but Reverend Hood, backed by a "Unity Slate" comprising the TULC, the Cotillion Club, and the Interdenominational Ministerial Alliance (of which Hill was a prominent member), went on to become the second African American ever elected to the council, edging out Poindexter for the ninth seat.[133]

For Cleage, the defeat carried yet another important lesson about the potential and limitations of the political arena. Thus, while 1963 may not have been the year of the Black revolt, as he had prophesied, the Freedom Now Party's efforts, coupled with the growing popularity of Black nationalism, were having a noticeable effect on the younger ranks of the city's civil rights community.

IN SEARCH OF ALTERNATIVES

Although young, self-styled militants had been involved in the Grass-Roots Conference and the Freedom Now Party (Luke Tripp and Gwen Kemp were on the FNP's Executive Committee), they did not wholeheartedly share Cleage's political objectives. These young activists did not give the work of organizing political parties and running candidates for public office equal weight with efforts to go "back to the ghetto" in a more direct and sustained fashion. At the same time that Lyndon Johnson was initiating the national War on Poverty, of which Detroit's Total Action against Poverty (TAP) was a major component, a large segment of the Left in Detroit and elsewhere was reorienting its activism almost exclusively toward community organizing.[134]

It was a national change that even the media felt compelled to comment on. Political power, noted an article in the *Detroit News,* was now defined in terms of creating "new pressure groups by organizing Detroit's slum dwellers into political units." As a spokesperson for Detroit CORE put it, "the whole civil rights movement shifted in a downward manner . . . [to] take into account the black nationalist movements and the separatists." While there were heated debates over Black nationalism within the ranks of Detroit CORE, the organization was not willing to renounce its efforts to promote integration. Instead, the idea was "to show people that by organizing, they can still participate in our integrated society."[135] Yet it was a Black nationalist perspective, variously defined, that was steadily becoming the basis for new coalition- and community-building efforts and the associated grassroots activism.

By the spring of 1964, Detroit CORE had begun organizing communities around issues important to their residents. The group opened a branch office in the Twelfth Street district and began organizing tenants' rights groups. It was also one of the first groups to organize Detroit's Aid to Dependent Children (ADC) mothers, although they were ultimately unable to sustain this campaign.[136]

This "ghetto program" prefigured the creation of a whole series of new community groups. By far the most active and successful of these, the West Central Organization, is illustrative. Headed by the Rev. Richard Venus of the Fourteenth Avenue Methodist Church, the WCO was an interracial group active in the city's Wayne State University district. Organized in 1965, the group was committed to organizing in the style of Saul Alinsky.[137] Because Alinsky's method involved integrating oneself and one's organization into neighborhood life without preconceived tactical or strategic notions, the WCO found it vastly superior to the "maximum feasible participation" approach of federally directed antipoverty programs. The WCO's idea was not to change people to fit institutions and programs imposed from outside but to modify institutions in ways that would allow the poor to represent themselves.[138]

Like Alinsky's Industrial Areas Foundation in Chicago, the WCO established ties to local religious organizations, including the Archdiocesan Solidarity Federation, the Detroit Catholic Worker, and individual parishes and churches. The WCO felt that church involvement, even if limited to financial support, was essential and that churches must begin "to relate to the people who make up the lower socio-economic levels in society." Echoing Cleage's attack on the Black middle-class clergy, the WCO insisted that the church must confront its own "class and cultural barriers" and establish a "meaningful relationship with people outside of the middle-class structure."[139] Rising to this challenge, various churches and religious bodies funneled thousands of dollars into the community-organizing efforts of groups such as the WCO.

The WCO was based in the older, interracial, and interethnic neighborhoods around the Wayne State University campus. Among the young activists, Sheila Murphy and her future husband, Ken Cockrel, were both members, as was Marian Kramer, who was married to fellow activist and WCO member General Baker. At its height, the group was a federation of over thirty organizations.[140] Like CORE, the WCO initially focused on such community problems as absentee landlords who exacted high rents for scant services and stores that inflated their prices. Like every rights-oriented group since the 1910s and 1920s, the WCO also worked in the area of police brutality, criticizing the police department's dismal record in responding to crime in poor and Black neighborhoods. In one instance, the group left Police Commissioner Ray Girardin a nightstick sheathed in foam rubber, with a bag of black and white jelly beans attached. "Only when the police force is as integrated as these jelly beans should the sheath come off the night stick," read the attached note.[141]

But, although the WCO claimed minor successes in these efforts, it was in the fight against discriminatory urban renewal polices that they had the greatest effect. The WCO, like GOAL and the liberal coalition working in the Medical Center area, was not opposed to urban renewal in principle. It simply argued that residents' right to self-determination had been repeatedly violated by city agencies and helped the aggrieved residents work out a confrontational action plan. It was not a revolutionary program, although some members of the group thought revolution might be necessary to achieve their goals. In 1966, for example, when the city moved to evict families in the Hobart Street area as part of the Wayne State redevelopment plan, some families, accompanied by WCO members, locked themselves in. The city turned off the water, then the electricity and gas, but the barricaded resisters managed to jerry-rig backup service. Police arrested two dozen protesters outside of the apartment building, and the city eventually negotiated a compromise.[142]

Within two years, however, tensions over race and ideology had severely hampered the WCO's effectiveness. Perhaps the tensions were in part a natural consequence of diversity within the WCO and the neighborhoods where it operated. "Black elements over on, say, Butternut Street might have been concerned about a son or a nephew getting his ass kicked . . . by the police," Ken Cockrel explained, "and that might not play well over on Commonwealth Avenue, where the concern might be, you know, street lights, garbage pickup, things of that kind." Cockrel maintains that the organization was also hampered by the strictures of the Alinsky method. Alinsky tended to caution against antagonizing organized labor—it simply created more problems than it solved—and radicals such as Cockrel weren't "too happy about being counseled not to take on discriminatory industries because of this policy," as they would soon prove with the Revolutionary Union Movement.[143]

Lorenzo ("Rennie") Freeman, a driving force in the WCO, resigned from the group in 1968 because he didn't believe that a racially integrated organization could be effective in Black ghettos. "What was radical two years ago," remarked Freeman, recalling the Hobart Street confrontation, "isn't radical today . . . and it takes radicals to bring about social change." Like other young Detroit militants, Freeman was enormously affected by the 1967 rebellion and the inability of established groups such as the WCO and CORE to prevent the uprising. Many came to wonder whether there might be a way to harness the power of Black Detroit's frustration. Concluding, perhaps with a tinge of regret, that "We're just going to have to take the gloves off," Freeman—like Reverend Cleage, the Henry brothers, the Boggses, and so many others alongside them—continued to search for alternatives.[144]

CONCLUSION

Motown Is Burning,
Jesus Is Black, and the
Struggle Continues

> Motown, if you don't come around, we're gonna burn you down.
> —Stokely Carmichael, Detroit, 1966

Neither the work of community organizations such as the WCO nor that of established civil rights organizations, from the NAACP and the Detroit Urban League to the Group on Advanced Leadership, nor the resources channeled into Detroit's War (some called it a skirmish) on Poverty was enough to prevent the outbreak of urban rebellion in the city. Several years after the uprisings in Watts and Harlem, and just weeks after one in Newark, Detroit was rocked by four days of fires, shooting (much of it done by the police and the National Guard), and looting. The rebellion left 43 dead and another 347 were injured. Over 7,000 people, the majority of them Black, had been arrested, and nearly 1,300 buildings lay in ruins. Detroit would never be the same.[1] Before the rebellion, city officials and some civil rights spokespersons were still clinging to the image of Detroit as a "model city." But image and reality were in obvious conflict.

Years later Mel Ravitz, who by 1967 had served six years on the Common Council and would go on to serve many more, opined that the city administration's problems began after the 1965 elections at the beginning of Cavanagh's second term. The incumbent faced raging debates over education, housing, and police-community relations, as well as heated disagreements with the council on budgetary issues. In the wake of the rebellion, Ravitz recalled, Cavanagh seemed "unable to comprehend what had happened. . . . I think he had begun to believe that some of the things that were being said about Detroit being a model city in regard to race relation were true. I think the riot stunned him and I don't think that he ever recovered thereafter."[2] Cavanagh's perplexity and paralysis can be seen as a metonym for the reaction of some segments of the liberal-labor coalition in general, and they were certainly characteristic of the reactions of many city leaders, who had never looked behind the thin veneer of progress.

The late 1960s found Detroit's economy in the midst of one of its longest boom cycles to date. Opportunities for Black industrial employment had been increasing steadily since 1963. Yet the unemployment rate for inner-city Black adults was stuck at 11 percent, more than triple the average for workers in the Detroit metropolitan region. Almost half of all Black public school students were dropping out before graduation, and unemployment among those twenty-five and under ranged from 30 to 40 percent. Even those who completed their high school education could expect to earn an average of sixteen hundred dollars less than their white counterparts. The economic inequality had a severe impact, with one of every three Black families living below the federal poverty line of three thousand dollars annual income. Detroit's War on Poverty was one of the largest local efforts in the nation, but of the 360,000 residents living in poverty only 70,000 were receiving direct aid.[3] The rebellion brought the connections between race and poverty into stark clarity. On the one hand, it spurred a mad scramble for more funding from public, private, and especially religious sources and for more community organizing around the concept of self-determination. On the other hand, it fueled efforts to combat racial and economic exploitation at the point of production in the Detroit area plants.

Attendance at Central Congregational/Shrine of the Black Madonna skyrocketed after the rebellion, and Reverend Cleage soon became "the titular head of the 700,000-member Detroit Black community."[4] Reverend Cleage had already launched an early version of his Black Christian nationalism movement by unveiling a large painting of the Black Madonna and child on Easter Sunday 1967. In this striking painting, which is eighteen feet high by nine feet wide, an imposing and very dark woman in a white headdress or veil and a white robe with a blue shawl cradles an equally dark infant swaddled in saffron cloth. The pair is posed before a blue sky standing defiantly on gray and rocky ground with a town barely visible along the horizon. The portrait hangs in the church's chancel, above the altar, covering an original stained-glass window (from the old days of Brewster-Pilgrim Congregational) depicting Governor Bradford landing at Plymouth Rock.[5]

According to the artist, Glanton Dowdell, the portrait was meant to symbolize the connections between the Madonna and "any Negro mother, an ADC mother whose child goes wrong, anyone."[6] The model for the Madonna is said to have been a young woman, Rose Walden, who lived in the neighborhood around the shrine. Because the infant is nestled against his mother, his face is not visible, but given Dowdell's troubled history, it is possible that he saw himself in the image of the Black Christ-child.[7] A native of Detroit, in 1949 Dowdell had been sentenced to a thirty- to forty-year sentence in the Jackson (Michigan) State Prison for second-degree murder. While in prison he honed his artistic ability and even assembled a one-man show of his "prison scenes" in Detroit before being paroled in 1962. He later became active in the Revolutionary Action Movement—a group that advocated armed self-defense and sponsored "gun clubs"—and worked in and around the developing radical Black Left. He also operated a small art gallery, which was destroyed during the rebellion, and helped to organize the 1966 Detroit Black Arts Conference. Dowdell was particularly close to General Baker, who helped him with the painting of the Black Madonna and Child.

Shortly after it was finished, Dowdell and Baker were convicted on concealed weapons charges.[8] Before Reverend Cleage began his sermon marking the occasion of the unveiling, he offered a prayer for Baker and Dowdell, "the artists of the Black Madonna," who were to be sentenced the next day in Recorder's Court. "No justice could be served by sending these men to jail," Cleage intoned; their predicament was merely "part of being Black in a white man's world." Cleage then wondered whether, instead of a sermon, the congregation would not be better served by simply sitting and admiring the new chancel painting, "marveling that we have come so far that we can conceive of the Son of God being born of a black woman."

"Now we have come to the place," he continued,

> where we not only can conceive of the possibility, but we are convinced, upon the basis of our knowledge and historic study of all the facts that Jesus was born to a black Mary, that Jesus, the Messiah, was a black man who came to save a black nation. It would have little significance if we unveiled a black Madonna and it had no more

Photograph of the Black Madonna and Child, Shrine (number 1) of the Black Madonna of the African Orthodox Christian Church, Detroit, Michigan. (Photograph by the author.)

meaning than just another picture in a church. Our unveiling of the Black Madonna is a statement of faith.[9]

Hoping to produce a cultural, political, and religious "awakening" of Black peoples, the painting harmonized with Cleage's theology of a Black revolutionary Christ dedicated to the salvation of a Black nation.

Cleage's view on the subject of the Blackness of Christ and the Holy Family was intensely controversial, primarily because his interpretation was so literal and genealogical. "When I say Jesus was black, that Jesus was the black Messiah," he explained, "I'm not saying 'Wouldn't it be nice if Jesus was black?' or 'Let's pretend that Jesus was black' or 'It's necessary psychologically for us to believe that Jesus was black.' I'm saying that Jesus WAS black."¹⁰ Adopting a position not unlike that advanced by the white Christian Marxist Claude C. Williams, Cleage claimed that the Apostle Paul had confused the revolutionary message of Christianity with obscure supernaturalism in his efforts to "integrate" Christianity into the world beyond. The belief that Jesus was white, along with the idea that a highly spiritualized Christ was resurrected from the dead, was for Cleage at best a mystification and at worst a lie.¹¹

Like Williams, in 1964 Cleage was put on ecclesiastical "trial" for his theological innovations. Undeterred by the Metropolitan Detroit Association of Congregational Churches or any other "church hierarchy," Cleage continued to trace the implications of his views, insisting that the original disciples were not primarily concerned with the bodily resurrection of Jesus but with the collective resurrection and salvation of the Black nation. Hence, he argued that Blacks—whether Christian, Muslim, or atheist—needed to get back to the original, and more authentic, message.¹²

In elaborating a Black Christian nationalism on the existence of an actual, flesh and blood, Black Messiah, Cleage was not working with a blank canvas. He drew, for example, on the legacy of Marcus Garvey and the UNIA's African Orthodox Church, which had also promoted the idea of a Black Christ. After 1924, Garveyites and members of the church had declared Jesus "the Black Man of Sorrow" and his mother "the Black Madonna." "Let us start our Negro painters getting busy," had proclaimed Archbishop George Alexander McGuire, "and supply a black Madonna and a black Christ for the training of our children." The vision of a Black Christ as one of the Prophets of Allah also featured in the theology of the Nation of Islam. While the NOI certainly taught that Christianity was a white man's religion, and while it denied that Jesus was the divine son of God and part of the Holy Trinity, Christ was nonetheless claimed as a prophet and a Black man. "Christ wasn't white," Malcolm X said in a 1963 interview in *Playboy*. "Christ was a black man." This view was also adopted by Cassius Clay when he converted to the NOI and took the name Muhammad Ali. Ali accepted as an article of his faith the idea that Christ was not white and that if Jesus had lived in Kentucky he "would be cooped up in the 'Jim Crow' cars.'"¹³

Cleage may also have drawn on a number of artistic sources for his belief in the Blackness of Jesus. Visual depictions of Jesus and Mary (and less often Joseph) as Black were not uncommon during and after the Harlem Renaissance. In Lawrence Jacobs's *Catholic New Orleans* (1941), an image of a Black Christ is included among the other icons in the religious store where a Black woman is shopping; while in William Johnson's *Jesus and Three Marys* (1939), a Black Jesus hangs on a large white cross, surrounded by three Black, horror-stricken Marys. These same four figures, accompanied by the two thieves who were crucified with Jesus on Calvary, also appear in Johnson's 1939 work, *Lamentations*.[14]

The poets Countee Cullen and Langston Hughes also contributed to the tradition. In poems such as "Christ Recrucified" (1922), and especially the dense and plodding epic "The Black Christ" (1929), Cullen explores the thorny question of theodicy and Black suffering, depicting a world in which "Christ's awful wrong is that he's dark of hue." Similarly, in Hughes's "Christ in Alabama," written as part of his *Scottsboro Limited* (1932) collection, the poet creates a Black and southern Jesus crucified/lynched.

> *Christ is a nigger,*
> *Beaten and black:*
> On, bare your back.
>
> *Mary is His mother:*
> Mammy of the South,
> Silence your Mouth.
>
> *God's His Father—*
> White Master above,
> Grant us your love.
>
> *Most holy bastard*
> *Of the bleeding mouth:*
> Nigger Christ
> On the cross of the South.

"Christ in Alabama" was composed at around the same time that Hughes said, in another poetic work, "Goodbye, Christ" to the "white man's" Jesus of hypocrisy, racism, and materialism.[15]

The effort to "blacken" Christ as a way of representing Black suffering and the search for justice was not limited to African Americans. In 1961, Black South African artist Ronald Harrison painted a Black Christ, who resembled anti-apartheid activist and African National Congress leader Albert Luthuli, being crucified by officials of the white South African government. The painting hung briefly in St. Luke's Anglican Church in Salt River before it was banned by the government and subsequently smuggled out of the country. (In 2004, the recently discovered painting was returned to the country and prominently displayed on the walls of St. George's Cathedral in Cape Town.)[16] And in 1964 the people of Cardiff, Wales (perhaps inspired by Paul Robeson's participation in a demonstration of striking Welsh miners in London in the late 1920s and by his subsequent visits to Wales),[17] donated the "Wales Window for Alabama" to the Sixteenth Street Baptist Church one year after the bombing that murdered four Black girls and damaged the church's original stained glass. The Cardiff window, designed by stained-glass artist John Petts, features a Black Christ with head bowed, one hand outstretched in protest, the other extended in a sacrificial posture. Etched around the feet of Jesus are the words "You do it to me" in reference to Matthew 25:40: "And the King will answer them, 'Truly, I say to you, as you did it to one of the least of these my brethren, you did it to me.'"[18]

Given all of these prior depictions of a Black Christ, one wonders why Cleage's theology and the painting at his shrine caused such a stir. The shrine's Black Madonna was not the only Black religious icon created in Detroit during those postriot days. Immediately after the rebellion subsided, a minor war broke out over the coloring of the statue of Jesus outside the Sacred Heart Seminary on West Chicago Boulevard and Linwood. It was painted black and then repainted white within a span of a few days, after which a group of seminary students painted it black again. Across town at St. Cecilia's Roman Catholic Church, in 1969, a dome painting, "Black Christ," by local artist DeVon Cunningham, was unveiled. The work depicts an obviously Black Jesus surrounded by a multicultural cadre of angels. It was subsequently featured on the cover of *Ebony* magazine, accompanying an article entitled "The Quest for a Black Christ." The parish's Lebanese American priest, Fr. Raymond Ellis, explained that he and his congregants wanted to "affirm that Christ today *is also black*" as opposed to Cleage's insistence on the actual, literal, and historical Blackness of Jesus.[19]

The distinction is an important one. Cleage believed that "Black people cannot build dignity on their knees worshiping a white Christ."[20] A Black theology imagined as the religious arm of Black power demanded something more. For Cleage and BCN, the Black Christian nation had both religious and secular manifestations to the extent that the two could be separated. Synthesizing theology and Black power politics, in 1966, Cleage, along with Rennie Freeman, Ken Cockrel, Grace Lee and James Boggs, and others, organized the Inner-City Organizing Committee (ICOC), a local organization dedicated to improving the living conditions of inner-city residents, protecting their rights and interests, and increasing the Black population's consciousness of its history through cultural activities. The group also sought to develop a program for the complete and humane reorganization of urban life, including housing, education, transportation, industry, welfare, health, recreation, justice, and government, in accordance with modern social and technological developments.[21] In short, it was yet another attempt by the Boggses to bring the revolution to Detroit.

In that same year, Cleage and Freeman also joined the Board of Directors of the Interfaith Foundation for Community Organizing. The IFCO described itself as "a unique coalition of Roman Catholic, Jewish, Protestant, Black and Methodist organizations" dedicated to "helping disadvantaged people to help themselves." Both the ICOC and IFCO were designed to take advantage of the millions of dollars being distributed to grassroots activists while maintaining community control of the programs those dollars supported.[22]

"We'll accept white money," Cleage remarked, "but not white leadership and dictation."[23] Insisting on self-determination for the poor, Reverend Cleage and others argued that past attempts to achieve residents' "maximum feasible participation" in antipoverty efforts had failed, chiefly because they failed to appreciate the distinction between Black participation and Black control or Black direction. With funding from organizations that were willing to abide by this position, such as the IFCO, Cleage transformed his church into a base of political, economic, religious, and cultural ferment. Of course, these ideas were not peculiar to Cleage or the political landscape of Detroit: the demands for community control and a political role for the Black church were part of larger national and historical trends.

In the late 1960s, Black religious scholars from different denominations and parts of the country began codifying a systematic Black theology. The writings of scholars such as James H. Cone, Gayraud Wilmore, Nathan Wright Jr., and Vincent Harding represented a concerted effort to separate African American Christianity from the theology of mainline white churches and seminaries.[24] Although Cleage was not a practicing theologian in the academic sense, he was a charter member of the National Committee of Black Churchmen—an interdenominational organization whose membership rolls included many of the new Black theologians. Cleage participated in the committee's first public theological discussions, which in essence launched Black theology as a religious and political movement.[25] The new movement shared a number of key features with liberation theology, which was growing out of the Latin American political and social struggles going on at the time. Like liberation theology, Black theology placed theology, religious practice, and the institutional resources of the church at the disposal of the oppressed.[26]

Cleage saw this as a very serious and practical enterprise that was aligned with other, more secular articulations of Black power—especially Charles V. Hamilton and Stokely Carmichael's 1967 volume *Black Power: The Politics of Liberation*. Cleage's quest for a revolutionary transformation of institutions and practices eventually motivated his defection from the National Committee of Black Churchmen, which he later denounced as a Black version of scholasticism "written for a white audience."[27]

Cleage's devotion to working with Black communities and organizations, along with his post-1965 aversion to electoral politics, explains the dizzying array of local and national organizations with which he collaborated after the 1967 rebellion. In addition to IFCO and the ICOC, he was a founder and cochairman with Glanton Dowdell of the City-Wide Citizens Action Committee. The committee was founded in August 1967 and immediately proclaimed itself the "New Black Establishment," committed to uniting the city's nationalists in an effort to "control everything." The funding it received from the Interfaith Emergency Council (nineteen thousand dollars) and IFCO (eighty-five thousand dollars) was used to establish the Black Star Coop and other community-based ventures. Horrified by the committee's nationalist bent, a group of Black liberals and moderates founded a rival group, the Detroit Council of Organizations, headed by the Rev. Roy Allen, which included the NAACP, the Cotillion Club, and the TULC among its members.[28]

In an effort to unify the two contingents, Cleage founded yet another organization, the Federation for Self-Determination, as a broad "popular front" uniting radicals and nationalists with moderates and liberals. He used his new column in the *Michigan Chronicle*—itself a sign of his newfound prominence—to issue repeated calls for unity.[29] Although Cleage's efforts produced some overlap in the two groups' membership, the Detroit Council of Organizations refused to be "united" out of existence. Toward the end of 1967 both the federation and the council sought comprehensive funding from the New Detroit Committee. This committee, whose purpose was to oversee efforts to repair the damage done by the rebellion, included Henry Ford II, Max Fisher, J. L. Hudson, and other powerful citizens, along with three Black militants—Rennie Freeman, Alvin Harrison, and Norvell Harrington of the ICOC—and six other, more moderate African Americans.[30]

Confronted with competing proposals from mutually hostile organizations, both of which claimed the exclusive right to speak for Black Detroiters, the New Detroit Committee granted each group one hundred thousand dollars for a one-year period. There were a number of conditions and strings attached. But Cleage was unwilling to compromise. In January 1968, the Federation for Self-Determination returned its share of the money and severed relations with New Detroit. Black members Rennie Freeman and Norvell Harrington resigned from the New Detroit Committee in protest. "As the news of the Federation's action spread," Cleage wrote in his column, "congratulations began to pour in from Chicago, New York, California and across the country. Everywhere black brothers and sisters were glad that a black organization had finally expressed in concrete terms of the meaning of the black revolution without the confusion of a hot summer night."[31] Looking past the author's exaggerations, the New Detroit affair led activists in Detroit and Black communities across the country to raise important questions about self-determination and community control.

While admirable in principle, the federation's decision left local nationalists with practical questions about how the revolution would be funded. Their search for practical solutions led to the publication of *The Black Manifesto,* a document delivered from the pulpit of the Riverside Church by James Forman, the international affairs director of SNCC, on May 1, 1969, demanding 500 million dollars ("$15 per nigger") from white Christian churches and Jewish synagogues. Since these religious bodies were "part and parcel of the system of capitalism," the payments were to be penance for their complicity in oppression, racism, and colonialism.[32] The *Manifesto* laid out ten major areas into which the money would be funneled, including a southern land bank; four major publishing and printing centers in Detroit, Atlanta, Los Angeles, and New York; a National Black Labor Strike and Defense Fund; and an educational and fund-raising body, the International Black Appeal.

Although Forman and his coauthors targeted white churches and synagogues, they were cognizant of walking a fine line religiously. Complicity with the *Manifesto*'s demands was characterized as the "true test of their faith and belief in the Cross and the words of the prophets." But the authors were far more forgiving when it came to Black Christians, insisting that "we do not intend to abuse our black brothers and sisters in black churches who have uncritically accepted Christianity."

> We want them to understand how the racist white Christian church
> with its hypocritical declarations and doctrines of brotherhood has
> abused our trust and faith. An attack on the religious beliefs of black

people is not our major objective, even though we know that we were not Christians when we were brought to this country, but that Christianity was used to help enslave us.

For Black Christians such as the Rev. Charles A. Hill, who had devoted a lifetime to Christian principles, striving to realize the brotherhood of all mankind, the *Manifesto* was an assault on their most fundamental beliefs. But the *Black Manifesto,* perhaps more than any other artifact of those troubled and heady times, demonstrates how far local activists had moved from the ethic of interracial unity, King's "beloved community," and the political theology of the social gospel. The generational chasm—symbolized to some degree by the political and theological differences between Hill and Cleage—would never really be closed, and the Black church's role in local and national politics would never be quite the same.

For all of its faults, the *Manifesto* was a remarkable document. Uniting a critique of organized religion with a call for economic self-determination, it was drafted in Detroit during the 1968 National Black Economic Development Conference. The conference, organized in part with IFCO funds, was held at Wayne State University on April 25–27 of that year and was attended by over six hundred delegates from organizations across the country. The conference situated local activists within a larger national trend, but the fact that it took place in Detroit was not without significance. The body heard from James Boggs and Milton Henry, who, along with his brother Richard, had just organized the separatist Republic of New Africa. In several resolutions, many proposed by local activists, conference participants rejected the definition of Black power as Black capitalism and minority entrepreneurship and emphasized the importance of landownership and control of ghetto institutions, especially schools.

Many of the resolutions reflected the Marxist position on Black nationalism being developed by James and Grace Lee Boggs, Ken Cockrel, General Baker, John Watson, James Forman, and others. While there is some question about whether the *Manifesto* was directly influenced by Cleage, it is known that Watson, Cockrel, Luke Tripp, and Mike Hamlin—all of whom were nominated to the Steering Committee assigned to implement the *Manifesto*'s programs—assisted Forman in drafting the document.[33] The reaction of most white churches and nearly all of the synagogues that weighed in was negative if not out-and-out hostile. But this, too, was indicative of changes in the local movement culture. White churches and clergymen were no longer seen as valuable allies. Instead, they had become mere funding sources. Blacks and whites alike were growing deaf to calls for interracial brotherhood.[34]

At the same time, younger activists, who were more inclined to think in Marxist terms, turned toward the factory as the prime site for organizing Black power. Organizers were welcome at the Shrine of the Black Madonna, but many of them felt that Cleage's approach did not go far enough. Many of these younger radicals came to understand religion (particularly Black theology) as just one of many cultural—and I would say ethical—dimensions in their evolving philosophy. Those who had belonged to groups such as UHURU and the WCO felt that what was now needed was a Marxist-Leninist movement linking the community, churches, and the shop floor.

In particular they seemed to feel that the strictures of the Alinsky model had led them to ignore the unions for too long. "I think that in order to have been effective in Detroit in the late '60s," observed Sheila Murphy Cockrel, "organizations like WCO would have had to take on organized labor, given the nature of racism in the unions."[35] There was also a sense that older Black unionists, from A. Philip Randolph down to Horace Sheffield and the TULC, had "sold out": no longer part of the solution, they were now viewed as part of the problem. Having gotten valuable training in groups such as the WCO, younger activists were moving in a different direction. "At that time SNCC was moving towards Black Power," recalled Mike Hamlin. "White radicals were moving toward mysticism and saying that the working class was too corrupt, could not be organized, wasn't a revolutionary force. Part of our effort was to prove that wasn't true."[36] But the fact that activists could no longer rely on the labor movement—and had in fact become antagonistic toward it—is surely one of the biggest changes from the 1930s to the 1960s.

Nearly a year before the rebellion, Mike Hamlin, General Baker, and John Watson started their own independent newspaper, the *Inner-City Voice*. This paper, and later Wayne State's student newspaper, *The South End* (which had been "liberated" by John Watson), served as forums for the new ideological debate; the first issue of the *Inner-City Voice* included writings by Ché Guevara, even though he was "white." The paper was also, like the *Illustrated News* had been years before, a vehicle for propaganda and organizing. Several members of the *Voice* group worked in the Dodge Main plant and decided to use the shop floor as their point of entry into the class struggle. "We took the paper, which called for revolution, out to the plants," explained Hamlin, "and distributed it and were prepared to fight to the end with any worker, Black or white, or anybody else who tried to stop us from distributing it." At the same time,

their offices became a gathering place, attracting nationalists with "nothing else to do," students, and others "just off the streets," what James
Boggs called "the street force."[37]

This loosely organized vanguard led a series of wildcat strikes in the
spring of 1968 that spread throughout other city plants. The strike led to
the formation of the Dodge Revolutionary Union Movement, of similar
Revolutionary Union Movements in other plants, and in 1969 to the
emergence of the League of Revolutionary Black Workers. For many, the
wildcat strikes called to mind the sit-downs in the 1930s with the addition of bongo drums and other forms of Black cultural expression.
Edward Lee, a worker at Dodge Main and the brother of Grace Lee
Boggs, described the scene he observed from a factory window as someone on the street began to beat a bongo drum and was joined by another
"until a line of perhaps twenty bongo players rent the air with the curi-
ous, alien and slightly frightening noise."

> On the streets a group of young blacks began to dance. Dressed in
> Afro robes, they complement the drums and draw the interest of the
> bystanders. Some of the workers at the windows mutter "Obscene sav-
> ages" but there are also some who watch intently, apparently studying
> the action. Old photographs and antidotes of the sitdown strikes of
> 1937 come to my mind. The spontaneity and fellowship of those days
> seem related to what is taking place. . . . It seems to me that here, as
> in the sitdowns of a generation ago, there is a superb job of organi-
> zation and leadership.[38]

There seems to have been a general feeling that the strikes, familiar
as they may have seemed to some older activists, were at the same time
something new and different. Still, with the establishment of DRUM and
the league, the patterns of political radicalism in Detroit did in a sense
come full circle—back to labor if not to the organized labor movement.
Many of the trends seen in Detroit's political radicalism from the early
1960s onward now coalesced in the league. League members attempted
to create an almost entirely comprehensive revolutionary political and
cultural center, and before the group broke apart in the early 1970s,
wrenched by internal and external pressures, it was well on its way to
establishing a multilevel strategy for revolution that, like the initiatives
outlined in the *Black Manifesto,* connected labor, education, the media,
and the political process.

The multifaceted network that the league managed to establish during its short life span included a publishing company, a bookstore, a film

production unit, and a well-funded nonprofit organization.[39] Afraid that the romantic appeal of the California-based Black Panther Party, which they considered to be politically uninformed, would challenge the league's preeminence, Luke Tripp and John Watson preemptively organized a Detroit chapter of the Panthers and attempted to induce its members to join their own "street force."[40] They also worked with young people, supporting school walkouts, protests, and efforts to create independent "freedom schools." Throughout the late 1960s and early 1970s, they maintained their relationship with Reverend Cleage's Black Christian nationalism and the various efforts stimulated by the publication of *The Black Manifesto*. League members also kept in personal and ideological contact with Grace Lee and James Boggs and the Socialist Workers Party (particularly in opposition to the Vietnam War), as well as with the Henry brothers.

The antiwar effort was led, in part, by the ICOC, which worked with the Cambridge, Massachusetts-based RESIST to assist young Black men in either avoiding or resisting the draft. Along with groups such as the Detroit chapter of the Northern Student Movement and People against Racism, the league also engaged in antiwar demonstrations and educational programs. Detroit once again found itself in the vanguard of political radicalism.

The league was eventually destroyed, to some extent, by its own success. The process was emblematic of the overall decline in the fortunes of the city's second civil rights community. Having spread itself thin, organizationally and ideologically, the league, like so many groups before it, dissolved into a loose army of factions whose differences proved irreconcilable.[41] Like the rest of the civil rights community, the league also attracted a formidable array of hostile adversaries. The old liberal-labor coalition was never very accepting of what it characterized as a group of young, communistic upstarts, and the UAW hierarchy more or less closed ranks against it.

Historian Heather Thompson recounts a story that exemplifies the terrible relationship between the league and the UAW. In August of 1973 a wildcat strike broke out at Chrysler's Mack Avenue stamping plant in Detroit. Although the action was not actually lead by the league, the group was blamed for the strike by the enraged UAW hierarchy. When negotiations to end the walkout broke down, the UAW International decided to take matters into its own hands. Union officials from across the city were contacted to assist in ending the strike. "The next morning, at 4:30 a.m., one thousand union officials met at the Local 212 union hall and began to map out their strategy for ending the wildcat,"

Thompson writes, "With baseball bats, pipes, and an assortment of other weapons in hand . . . the assembled union officials marched in groups of 250 to each of the four Mack gates and began to attack picketing workers." By early morning the UAW had violently and successfully ended the action, which not coincidentally proved to be the last of its kind. The best that can be said of this shocking turn of events is that the attackers were an interracial group—an unforeseen spin on the old labor slogan "Black and White, Unite and Fight."[42]

Many white rank-and-file workers—particularly those who cast their lot with George Wallace's racist 1968 presidential campaign—greeted the upsurge in Black labor radicalism with fear, suspicion, and at times open hostility.[43] Adding insult to injury, the league, along with other Black radical groups in Detroit and across the nation, was subjected to investigations by COINTELPRO, the FBI's notorious counterintelligence program, which had already targeted organizations such as the Communist Party and the Socialist Workers Party.

COINTELPRO's policy with regard to Black nationalist groups, which the bureau labeled "Black Hate" organizations, was to "expose, disrupt, misdirect, discredit, or otherwise neutralize . . . their leadership, spokesmen, membership, and supporters" in order to prevent the groups from developing coalitions and establishing a level of respectability.[44] Its efforts and the white backlash against Black radicalism were at least as instrumental in the destruction of the league and its fellow radical groups of the late 1960s and early 1970s as HUAC and anticommunist hysteria had been in the destruction of Detroit's earlier civil rights community. As one activist put it: "There were political forces opposed to us and they knew what they were for and against. They prevailed, and we didn't."[45] Still, the federal government's efforts to hinder individual and organizational action on behalf of civil rights, social justice, and African American liberation were matched blow for blow by the activists' own efforts to transform society.

Many of the groups active in the late 1960s did not weather these internal and external pressures. With a few exceptions—notably the Shrine of the Black Madonna—the vast majority of organizations from the later civil rights community have long since dissolved. The league carried all of its ancillary groups, including the International Black Appeal, with it to the grave; the ICOC ceased operations, as did the Boggses' various groups, including the Organization of Black Power. And the Henry brothers' Republic of New Africa was killed in a rain of bullets through the windows and doors of C. L. Franklin's New Bethel Baptist Church. On March 29, 1968, shortly before midnight, police raided the church, where a Republic of New Africa meeting of 250 adults and children was just breaking up. The reasons for the use of deadly force remain unclear, but the police's aggressive action resulted in major damage to the church, the death of 1 officer, and the wounding of 3 of the meeting's participants. Mass arrests immediately followed, with a total of 142 men, women, and children dragged to Detroit's downtown jail—an action that prompted George Crockett, by then a Recorder's Court judge, to hold an all-night marathon of bond hearings.

The speed with which Crockett moved to allow the defendants to post bond did not endear him to the police or the city's angry reactionaries. He nevertheless survived subsequent attempts to unseat him and indeed went on, in 1980 (at age seventy-one), to win the congressional seat vacated by Charles C. Diggs Jr.

The New Bethel incident was just one of a string of violent confrontations with overzealous police. The New Bethel defendants were tried in two separate trials, with Ken Cockrel serving as the lead defense counsel. His belligerent yet brilliant defense led to acquittals in both cases. The city's Black radicals declared a major victory, but the Republic of New Africa never really recovered.[46]

Detroit's civil rights community was always more than the sum of its component organizations and institutions, however. Many of its members entered the city's administration, especially after the 1973 election of Mayor Coleman A. Young, who remained in the office until 1992; others managed to achieve positions within the UAW hierarchy or continued to work in radical and grassroots associations. Grace Boggs, a loyal Detroiter and committed activist, still lives in the city and runs the Boggs Center, a progressive nonprofit organization dedicated to nurturing community leadership, especially among young people. The SWP's ranks have been greatly diminished over the years thanks to a series of internal purges, but Solidarity, an organization founded in part by ex-SWP members, still supports rank-and-file labor activism in the city. As both role models and contemporary activists, its members serve as a living legacy for future generations.

The churches are also still there, still struggling to meet the needs of their congregants and the city's residents. Hartford Avenue (now Memorial) Baptist has gone from humble beginnings in 1920, as a thirty-five-member congregation on the city's old west side, to a massive church in terms of both membership and its stately stone structure on the city's northwest side. The Rev. Charles G. Adams, who has pastored the congregation since Hill's retirement in April 1968 at age seventy-five, has managed in many ways to combine the legacies of Reverends Hill and

Cleage. Hartford currently runs the AGAPE House, which offers medical and legal referrals, clothing, a daily senior citizens program, a hunger task force, and the REACH program for AIDS awareness, among its other efforts. While maintaining an array of outreach programs for young people and families, the Hartford Economic Development Foundation has also worked with national chains such as Kmart and Home Depot to help spark the much-needed return of investment to the city. "The church needs to concentrate on the business of creating economic institutions," suggests Adams, who has just entered his fifty-first year in the ministry. Given the problem of corporate downsizing and plant closures, Reverend Adams continues, the Black church "finds itself in a situation where it is the best continuing, organized entity in the black community for the acquisition and redevelopment of land, the building of business enterprises and the employment of people."[47]

Plymouth Congregational (now UCC), too, remains true to the activist heritage of the Rev. Horace White and his successor, the Rev. Nicholas Hood Sr. The church has been pastored by the Rev. Nicholas Hood Jr. since his father's retirement in 1985. Like his father, Reverend Hood Jr. has also served on the Common Council and currently oversees the creation of the Medical Center Court Apartments, renamed in honor of Reverend Hood Sr., as well as the newer Medical Center Village Apartments and the Housing Ministry at Plymouth. The church also continues to deliver services to developmentally disabled and mentally retarded adults through the Cyprian Center (named in honor of Hood's daughter, Sarah Cyprian Hood) and a variety of assisted-living and independent-living residences. Reverend Hood Jr. also founded the Plymouth Education Center, the first charter school in Michigan to build a new building (at a cost of twelve million dollars) from the ground up. The school currently has an enrollment of more than eight hundred students.[48]

Fr. Canon Malcolm Dade remained active in the church and the community even after his 1972 retirement from St. Cyprian's, right up until his death in 1991. Much like Reverend Hill, Father Dade never lost faith in the possibilities of an enlightened liberalism. He helped to establish new churches in predominately African American communities in Inkster (St. Clement's) and Ecorse (Church of the Resurrection) and was also the founder and first president of the Michigan Chapter of the Union of Black Episcopalians. In 1961, Father Dade was appointed the first Black honorary canon of the Cathedral Church of St. Paul in Detroit. He served by appointment on various City Commissions under five different mayoral administrations from 1942 to 1976. Unlike many old west-side churches, St. Cyprian's has remained firmly rooted in the neighborhood where it grew up.[49]

One wonders what Father Dade really thought of Albert Cleage's Black Christian nationalism and the Black power movement in general. "My father might have endorsed some of the values in Black nationalism," his son, Malcolm C. Dade Jr., conjectures, "but, let's put it this way, he was no disciple of Malcolm X." When asked what the Black church should be doing "in these troubled times," Father Dade's reply, published in a volume of essays on the Black gospel within white churches, was: "Do what we have been doing for the past thirty years! Identify with our people; be where they are; be willing to be hurt, to be misunderstood, to be denounced and falsely judged. . . . The Gospel can speak through us in Detroit!"[50]

In 1968 Reverend Cleage stunned Detroiters by giving back the hundred thousand dollars granted to the Federation for Self-Determination by the New Detroit Committee because the money "brought interference from whites and bickering among Blacks." He called a national press conference to announce his decision, which seems in hindsight to have signaled a turning point. In the years since, the shrine has continued to grow and evolve. In the early 1970s, Cleage, who took the name Jaramogi Abebe Ageyman, turned his back on the public world of predominately white funding agencies, organizational rivalries, and rhetorical grandstanding and turned inward toward the shrine and the Black Christian nationalism movement. In his book, *Black Christian Nationalism,* he writes, "I am not convinced that Black theologians cannot move beyond the basic theological statements outlined in *The Black Messiah.* Therefore I feel compelled to move on to the essential restructuring of the Black church implicit in that theology."[51]

Guided by the desire to create a separate nation within a nation—the long, hard dream of Black nationalists since the eighteenth century—Cleage/Ageyman strove to erect a series of counterinstitutions and methods of consciousness-raising to meet the political and spiritual needs of African Americans. In this way, the shrine would point the way toward a new promised land of Black power, dignity, and control. "I have been running around the country for some time now trying to *talk* Black people into power," Cleage/Ageyman said on another occasion. "I no longer believe this approach can work. . . . I'm going to have to function differently from now on."[52]

Black Christian Nationalism lays out the concrete program for nation building and begins to specify qualifications for membership (e.g., a twelve-month training program before full initiation, followed by two additional years of advanced leadership training), an educational and training schema comprised of three levels (i.e., the act of beginning or Kunanza, the process of growing or Kua, and the initiation into full membership or Kuanzisha), and a more elaborate political theology. It was a turn not only toward building the institutions necessary to sustain the nation but also toward the cultivation of an inner divinity and a new, much more collective sense of self. As the BCN Creed, which is still recited in the various shrines in Detroit, Atlanta, and Houston, puts it:

> I believe that both my survival and my salvation depend upon my will-
> ingness to reject INDIVIDUALISM and so I commit my life to the lib-
> eration struggle of Black people, and accept the values, ethics,
> morals and program of the Black Nation, defined by that struggle
> and taught by the Pan African Orthodox Christian Church.

In essence, *Black Christian Nationalism* codifies a set of beliefs that Cleage and his associates had loosely articulated for years. By 1969, the concept of a nation within a nation was adopted in the church's *Black Christian Manifesto,* the document that sparked a restructuring of the rituals, orga-nizations, and programs of the church. Central Congregational was officially renamed the Shrine of the Black Madonna in 1970. This was followed soon after by the institution of African naming ceremonies and new holy days; the establishment of a food cooperative program; and the inauguration of a training center, bookstore, and cultural center on Liv-ernois Avenue (where the store still stands today, doing a brisk business in the community).

Even as they began to establish new shrines (two in Detroit that were subsequently consolidated into Shrine #1 at the original Linwood loca-tion and others in Atlanta and Houston), Abebe Ageyman continued to search for ways to make critical interventions in local politics. One vehi-cle, the Black Slate, Inc., was inaugurated in 1973 in order to support the election of Mayor Coleman A. Young. Schooled early on by his associa-tion with Reverend Hill, Young always understood the power of religion and the church in political mobilization. "Mayor Young always felt the Shrine's early endorsement of his campaign was a critical piece of his success," recalled a former adviser, "and he never forgot that."[53] The Black Slate, which incorporated earlier tactics such as plunking and the lessons learned from the ill-fated Freedom Now Party, is also widely cred-ited with the elections of Atlanta mayors Maynard Jackson and Shirley Franklin and a long roster of Black candidates in Detroit, including

Councilwoman JoAnn Watson, U.S. Representatives Barbara Rose-Collins and Carolyn Cheek Kilpatrick, and Representative Kilpatrick's son, Detroit's current mayor, Kwame Kilpatrick.

In 1978 the shrine also renamed the "Black Christian Nationalist Church" the "Pan African Orthodox Church," signaling the advent of yet another phase in its theological and institutional evolution. The change was followed three years later by the establishment of the Beulah Land Farm Project, the goal of which was to acquire and run a fully mechanized, self-sustaining farm on five thousand acres in Abbeville, South Carolina. The farm opened in 1999 and is still operating. The Beulah Land Farm Project may have been inspired by the Cleage family farm in Belleville, Michigan, which was purchased by Dr. Albert B. Cleage Sr. and used by his family for many years to nourish body and soul. The Beulah Land Farm at Abbeville and all that it represents—self-sufficiency and self-determination, the building of skills, a communal approach to life and work, the dream, perhaps, of a Promised Land here on earth—were Jaramogi Abebe Ageyman's last great achievements. He died there in February 2000. Today the church and movement that he built claim a combined membership of some fifty thousand, including approximately seven thousand active, core members. Abebe Ageyman's legacy is still alive, even as the city that he loved continues to struggle.[54] Indeed, one of the things that distinguishes churches and religious congregations such as the shrines or Hartford Memorial Baptist is precisely the kind of intergenerational, living legacy of pastoral care and prophetic commitment that its founders instilled and their progeny carry on.

Cultural theorist Jerry Herron begins his book *AfterCulture: Detroit and the Humiliation of History* by noting that "Detroit is the most representative city in America": where Detroit once stood for success, it now stands for failure. "This is the place," Herron continues, "where bad times get sent to make them belong to somebody else." But the city, which has surely suffered from the painful postwar transformation of America and the rise of a global economy, is sustained by the unrelenting activism of new generations. I have tried to tell their story in a way that reflects both changes and continuities over the course of three troubling, exhilarating, inspirational, and enraging decades. Like every historian wise and honest enough to admit it, I am humbled to contemplate the innumerable words, ideas, and actions that have been unsaid, unrecorded, or misunderstood. At best, this book offers one story about religion and political radicalism in Detroit; but it is far from the *only* story that could be written. Detroit is still, as Reverend Franklin once remarked, a "city of good preachers." It is also a city in which many continue to keep the faith.

NOTES

INTRODUCTION

1. Ofield Dukes, "Clergy Integral Part of Leadership Growth," Michigan *Chronicle,* October 5, 1963.

2. Morris, *The Origins of the Civil Rights Movement: Black Communities Organizing for Change* (New York: Free Press, 1984).

3. Among the clearest and most persuasive presentations of this argument are Nelson Lichtenstein and Robert Korstad, "Opportunities Found and Lost: Labor, Radicals, and the Early Civil Rights Movement," *Journal of American History* 75 (1988): 786–811; more recently Korstad's *Civil Rights Unionism: Tobacco Workers and the Struggle for Democracy in the Mid–Twentieth Century South* (Chapel Hill: University of North Carolina Press, 2003); and Rick Halpern, "The CIO and the Limits of Labor-Based Civil Rights Activism: The Case of Louisiana's Sugar Workers, 1947–1966," in *Southern Labor in Transition,* ed. Robert H. Zieger (Knoxville: University of Tennessee Press, 1997): 86–112.

4. Battle quoted in Steve Babson with Ron Alpern, Dave Elsila, and John Revitte, *Working Detroit: The Making of a Union Town* (New York: Adama Books, 1984), 165.

5. King, *Civil Rights and the Idea of Freedom* (New York: Oxford University Press, 1992), 4.

6. See, for example, Theoharis and Woodard, eds., *Freedom North: Black Freedom Struggles Outside the South, 1940–1980* (New York: Palgrave, 2003), which has essays by Self (on Oakland), Bates (on Detroit), Theoharis (on Boston), and Woodard (on Newark). See also Matthew Countryman's *Up South: Civil Rights and Black Power in Philadelphia* (Philadelphia: University of Pennsylvania Press, 2006); and Biondi's excellent *To Stand and Fight: The Struggle for Civil Rights in Postwar New York City* (Cambridge: Harvard University Press, 2003). Although the story I want to tell begins well before World War II and the immediate postwar period, these studies have greatly enriched my own thinking and approach in the years since I finished my dissertation in 1995.

7. Hood, interview with author, Detroit, June 2, 2005. The Web site for Plymouth Congregational provides a brief biography of Hood.

8. See, for instance, August Meier and Elliot Rudwick, *Black Detroit and the Rise of the UAW* (New York: Oxford University Press, 1979; rpt., Ann Arbor: University of Michigan Press, 2007); Richard W. Thomas, *Life for Us Is What We Make It: Building Black Community in Detroit, 1915–1945* (Bloomington: Indiana University Press, 1992); Christopher H. Johnson, *Maurice Sugar: Law, Labor, and the Left in Detroit, 1912–1950* (Detroit: Wayne State University Press, 1988); Heather Ann Thompson, *Whose Detroit? Politics, Labor, and Race in a Modern American City* (Ithaca: Cornell University Press, 2001); and Suzanne E. Smith, *Dancing in the Streets: Motown and the Cultural Politics of Detroit* (Cambridge: Harvard University Press, 1999).

9. Franklin quoted in *Give Me This Mountain: Life History and Selected Sermons of C. L. Franklin,* ed. Jeff Todd Titon (Urbana: University of Illinois Press, 1989), 19. Also on Franklin see Nick Salvatore, *Singing in a Strange Land: C. L. Franklin, the Black Church, and the Transformation of America* (New York: Little Brown, 2005).

10. Among the best studies of the significance of the Black church historically and in the present is C. Eric Lincoln and Lawrence H. Mamiya's *The Black Church in the African American Experience* (Durham: Duke University Press, 1990). Equally useful sources include Gayraud S. Wilmore, *Black Religion and Black Radicalism: An Interpretation of the Religious History of Afro-American People,* 2d ed. (Maryknoll, NY: Orbis, 1991); Fredrick C. Harris, *Something Within: Religion in African American Political Activism* (New York: Oxford University Press, 1999), which has a good overview of the debate over whether Black churches and African American Christianity encourages or hampers political participation; and Albert J. Raboteau, *A Fire in the Bones: Reflections on African-American Religious History* (Boston: Beacon, 1995).

11. Evelyn Brooks Higginbotham, *Righteous Discontent: The Women's Movement in the Black Baptist Church, 1880–1920* (Cambridge: Harvard University Press, 1993); Elsa Barkley Brown, "Negotiating and Transforming the Public Sphere: African American Political Life in the Transition from Slavery to Freedom," *Public Culture* 7 (1994): 107–46; Victoria W. Walcott, *Remaking Respectability: African American Women in Interwar Detroit* (Chapel Hill: University of North Carolina Press, 2001), esp. chap. 2.

12. White, "Who Owns the Negro Church?" *Christian Century,* February 9, 1938, 177.

13. Coleman A. Young with Lonnie Wheeler, *Hard Stuff: The Autobiography of Coleman Young* (New York: Viking, 1994), 45.

14. Niebuhr, "The Detroit Microcosm in the American Microcosm," draft in the Niebuhr Papers, Box 56, Folder 7, Library of Congress. See also June Bingham, "Reinhold Niebuhr in Detroit," *Christian Century,* March 8, 1961, 296–99. For more on his years in Detroit and how they shaped his later activism, see Charles C. Brown, *Niebuhr and His Age: Reinhold Niebuhr's Prophetic Role in the Twentieth Century* (Philadelphia: Trinity Press International, 1992), chap. 2.

15. Lloyd H. Bailer, "Negro Labor in the Automotive Industry," PhD diss., University of Michigan, 1943. See also Joyce Shaw Peterson, "Black Automobile Workers in Detroit, 1910–1930," *Journal of Negro History* 64 (summer 1979): 177–90.

16. Dade, Oral History Interview with Jim Keeney and Roberta McBride, September 17, 1969, Archives of Labor History and Urban Affairs [cited hereafter as ALHUA], Wayne State University, Detroit, Michigan, 4. As I argue in chapter 2, the relationship between Black ministers and the Ford Motor Company was always complex.

17. Pope, *Millhands and Preachers: A Study of Gastonia* (New Haven: Yale University Press, 1942). See also Dwight B. Billings, "Religion as Opposition: A Gramscian Analysis," *American Journal of Sociology* 96:1 (July 1990): 1–31, which uses Pope's data on the "conservative" uses of religion and contrasts them with more "progressive" applications.

18. Hill, Oral History Interview with Roberta McBride, May 8, 1967, ALHUA, 5.

19. Evans and Boyte, *Free Spaces: The Sources of Democratic Change in America* (New York: Harper and Row, 1986), chap. 1.

20. Maki, Oral History Interview with Norman McRae, March 26, 1970, ALHUA, 7.

21. Nowak, *Two Who Were There: A Biography of Stanley Nowak* (Detroit: Wayne State University Press, 1989), 69.

22. Ibid.,176–77; Sugrue, *The Origins of the Urban Crisis: Race and Inequality in Postwar Detroit* (Princeton: Princeton University Press, 1996), 73. On the housing conflict, see Dominic J. Capeci Jr., *Race Relations in Wartime Detroit: The Sojourner Truth Housing Controversy of 1942* (Philadelphia: Temple University Press, 1984).

23. Ward, *Our Economic Morality and the Ethic of Jesus* (New York: Macmillan, 1929), 30.

24. For a good overview on Coughlin, see Alan Brinkley's *Huey Long, Father Coughlin, and the Great Depression* (New York: Vintage, 1983), esp. chap. 4, "The Radio Priest." On Smith, see Glen Jeansonne, *Gerald L. K. Smith: Minister of Hate* (New Haven: Yale University Press, 1988); and Leo P. Ribuffo, *The Old Christian Right: The Protestant Far Right from the Great Depression to the Cold War* (Philadelphia: Temple University Press, 1983).

25. Williams, "Hell-Brewers of Detroit," *The Protestant*, April–May 1943. On Williams's background and career, see Anthony Dunbar, *Against the Grain: Southern Radicals and Prophets, 1929–1959* (Charleston: University Press of Virginia, 1981); and Cedric Belfrage, *A Faith to Free the People* (New York: Dryden Press, 1944), which focuses more on Williams's political theology. See also Belfrage's earlier biography of Williams, *South of God* (New York: Modern Age Books, 1941).

26. The best single source on the riot is Dominic Capeci and Martha Wilkerson, *Layered Violence: The Detroit Rioters of 1943* (Jackson: University Press of Mississippi, 1991); see also Harvard Sitkoff, "Detroit Race Riot of 1943," *Michigan History* 53 (fall 1969): 183–206.

27. Stanley and Margaret Nowak to Dr. Leslie Bechtel, December 5, 1944, Nowak Collection, Box 4, ALHUA.

28. Hill to Reverend Burnett Magruder, February 4, 1943, Williams Collection, Box 18, ALHUA.

29. See Erdmann D. Benyon, "The Southern White Laborer Migrates to Michigan," *American Sociological Review* 3 (June 1939): 333–43; Alan Clive, *State of War: Michigan in World War II* (Ann Arbor: University of Michigan Press, 1979), chap. 5, "Tennessee and Kentucky Are Now in Michigan"; and especially Chad Berry, *Southern Migrants, Northern Exiles* (Urbana: University of Illinois Press, 2000).

30. A good overview of Williams's theology can be found in Bill Troy, with Claude Williams, "People's Institute of Applied Religion," copy in Williams Collection, Box 18, ALHUA. See also, Belfrage, *A Faith to Free the People*, esp. 221–81.

31. Johnson in *Detroit Lives*, ed. Robert Mast (Philadelphia: Temple University Press, 1994), 50.

32. Tripp quoted in Ofield Dukes, "UHURU Leader Says: 'Must Crush White Man,'" *Michigan Chronicle*, October 19, 1963, 1, 4.

33. Detroit Commission on Community Relations, "Inter-office Correspondence, Re: UHURU," September 15, 1963, DCCR Papers, III, Box 21, ALHUA.

34. Georgakas in Mast, *Detroit Lives*, 292. In addition to Georgakas and Surkin's *Detroit: I Do Mind Dying* (New York: St. Martin's, 1974), see James A. Geschwender, *Class, Race, and Worker Insurgency: The League of Revolutionary Black Workers* (Cambridge: Cambridge University Press, 1977); and Thompson, *Whose Detroit?* 84–86.

35. Cleage, "An Epistle to Stokely," in *The Black Messiah* (New York: Sheed and Ward, 1968), 35–36.

36. On the *Black Manifesto* and the IFCO see Wilmore, *Black Religion and Black Radicalism*, 202–10.

37. West, "Religion and the Left," *Monthly Review*, July–August 1984, 14. See also Billings, "Religion as Opposition."

38. Lasch, "Religious Contributions to Social Movements," *Journal of Religious Ethics* 18 (spring 1990): 101. David Chappell stresses the importance of "old time" religion with its belief in "irrational" practices in his brilliant study of religion and the southern civil rights movement, *Prophetic Religion and the Death of Jim Crow* (Chapel Hill: University of North Carolina Press, 2004). See also Jasper M. James, *The Art of Moral Protest: Culture, Biography, and Creativity in Social Movements* (Chicago: University of Chicago Press, 1997); and James, "The Emotions of Protest: Affective and Reactive Emotions in and around Social Movements," *Sociological Forum* 13 (1998): 397–424.

39. Rauschenbusch, *A Theology for the Social Gospel* (Louisville: Westminster John Knox Press, [1917] 1997), 131.

40. Ibid., 142.

41. Peter W. Williams, *America's Religions: From Their Origins to the Twenty-first Century* (Urbana: University of Illinois Press, 2002), chap. 32; and Sydney E. Ahlstrom, *A Religious History of the American People* (New Haven: Yale University Press, 1972), chap. 47. Both of these works have good, though basic, overviews of the social gospel and the various debates regarding dating and influence.

42. Ralph E. Luker, *The Social Gospel in Black and White: American Racial Reform, 1885–1912* (Chapel Hill: University of North Carolina Press, 1991), 4. Luker also does a wonderful job of characterizing the racial ambiguity, and at times the racism, within the writings and speeches of advocates of the social gospel.

43. Ibid.; Susan Lindley, "Neglected Voices and Praxis in the Social Gospel," *Journal of Religious Ethics* 18 (spring 1990): 75–103; Philip S. Foner, ed., *Black Socialist Preacher: The Teachings of Reverend George Washington Woodbey, and his Disciple, Reverend G. W. Slater, Jr.* (San Francisco: Synthesis Publications, 1983); Raboteau, *A Fire in the Bones;* Clarence Taylor, *Black Religious Intellectuals: The Fight for Equality from Jim Crow to the 21st Century* (New York: Routledge, 2002).

44. Drake and Cayton, *Black Metropolis* (Chicago: University of Chicago Press, 1945), 736. In a similar vein see Mark Naison, *Communists in Harlem during the Depression* (Urbana: University of Illinois Press, 1983); and Kelley, *Hammer and Hoe: Alabama Communists during the Great Depression* (Chapel Hill: University of North Carolina Press, 1990).

45. Young, *Hard Stuff*, 44.

46. Detroit NNC File, Labadie Collection, University of Michigan; and NNC

Records, Microfilm, Reel 6. On the CRF, see "Constitution of the Conference for the Protection of Civil Rights (1935)," Civil Rights Congress [CRC] Papers, Box 1, ALHUA; and John Bollens, "Why a Civil Rights Federation?" *Civil Rights Federation News,* November 8, 1938, copy in CRC Papers, Box 1, ALHUA.

47. Marx, "Toward the Critique of Hegel's *Philosophy of Right*," in *Marx and Engels: Basic Writings on Politics and Philosophy,* ed. Louis S. Feuer (London: Fontana, 1969), 304, emphasis mine. On the "double-edged" nature of Marx's understanding of religion, and on the ways in which religion has been handled by a number of Marxist theorists, see Michael Löwy's excellent *The War of the Gods: Religion and Politics in Latin America* (London: Verso, 1996).

48. *Daily Worker,* September 19, 1954. Thanks to Alan Wald for bringing this cartoon to my attention.

49. Congress of Industrial Organizations, Department of Research and Education, *Labor and Religion* (Washington, DC: CIO, 1944), 10–11.

50. Lichtenstein and Korstad, "Opportunities Found and Lost," 811. A similar argument is put forth in Johnson's *Maurice Sugar,* 302: "In looking at the Left and labor before the victory of Reuther and his conception of trade unionism we are dealing with a sharply defined era in U.S. labor history, one that began with the Depression and ended with the Cold War."

51. Cleage, *The Black Messiah,* 211. On Cleage's contributions to Black theology, see James Cone, *Black Theology and Black Power* (San Francisco: Harper, [1969] 1989); and Wilmore, *Black Religion and Black Radicalism;* as well as Cleage's own *Black Christian Nationalism: New Directions for the Black Church* (New York: William Morrow, 1972). The only full-length biography of Cleage is Hiley Ward, *Prophet of a Black Nation* (Philadelphia: Pilgrim Press, 1969).

52. The commentator is *Detroit Free Press* reporter William Serrin, quoted in Georgakas and Surkin, *Detroit: I Do Mind Dying,* 33. The Georgakas quote is at p. 5. See also Thompson, *Whose Detroit?*

53. Cleage, "The Next Step," *Illustrated News,* November 1963.

54. Cleage quoted in Ward, *Prophet of a Black Nation,* 42.

55. Cleage, "A Sense of Urgency," in Cleage, *The Black Messiah,* 22.

56. On Breitman and the SWP in Detroit, see Naomi Allen and Sarah Lovell, eds., *A Tribute to George Breitman: Writer, Organizer, Revolutionary* (New York: Fourth International Tendency, 1987). Breitman's papers, at the Tamiment Library at New York University, are also a rich source for materials. Also interesting on this question is "Questions of the American Revolution: Conversations in Detroit between James Boggs and Xavier Nicholas" (spring 1973) in the Labadie Collection, University of Michigan; and the autobiography of Grace Lee Boggs, *Living for Change* (Minneapolis: University of Minnesota Press, 1998). On the SWP and the Black freedom movement in general, see Conrad Lynn, *There Is a Fountain: The Autobiography of Conrad Lynn* (Westport, CT: Lawrence Hill, 1979); Van Gosse, *Where the Boys Are: Cuba, Cold War America, and the Making of a New Left* (London: Verso, 1993); and Timothy Tyson, *Radio Free Dixie: Robert F. Williams and the Roots of Black Power* (Chapel Hill: University of North Carolina Press, 1999); as well as Van Gosse, "More Than Just a Politician: Notes on the Life and Times of Harold Cruse," in *Harold Cruse's* The Crisis of the Negro Intellectual *Reconsidered,* ed. Jerry Watts (New York: Routledge, 2004), 17–40.

57. Brooks Higginbotham, *Righteous Discontent,* 49.

CHAPTER ONE

1. Wright, *Uncle Tom's Children* (New York: Harper and Row, 1940), 130.

2. Ibid., 130–31.

3. Ibid., 178.

4. Ibid., 180.

5. Young, *Hard Stuff,* 42.

6. Bermecia (Hill) Morrow McCoy, interview with author, Detroit, January 13, 1992; Charles A. Hill Jr., interview with author, Detroit, June 10, 2005.

7. David Katzman, *Before the Ghetto: Black Detroit in the Nineteenth Century* (Urbana: University of Illinois Press, 1973), 91–92; Olivier Zunz, *The Changing Face of Inequality: Urbanization, Industrial Development, and Immigrants in Detroit, 1880–1920* (Chicago: University of Chicago Press, 1982), 247–48. Zunz's 1900 sample found only three mixed marriages between Blacks and Germans.

8. Hill's birth certificate, Hill Papers, Box 1, Michigan Historical Collections, Bentley Historical Library, University of Michigan (cited hereafter as MHC).

9. Katzman, *Before the Ghetto,* 79.

10. Webster to Forrester, June 9, 1916, DUL Papers, Box 1, MHC.

11. Bermecia (Hill) Morrow McCoy, interview with author.

12. David G. Morrow, "Charles Andrew Hill—Family," transcript of remarks for a 1968 retirement celebration, Hill Papers, Box 1, MHC.

13. Katzman, *Before the Ghetto,* 56–59.

14. Ibid., 59–71.

15. Francis H. Warren, *Michigan Manual of Freedmen's Progress* (Detroit: John M. Green, [1915] 1985); Thomas, *Life for Us,* chap. 2; Katzman, *Before the Ghetto,* 59–61.

16. On the challenges to and relative success of the urban church in this period, see Lincoln and Mamiya, *The Black Church in the African American Experience,* chap. 6.

17. Katzman, *Before the Ghetto,* 138; Everard W. Daniel, "St. Matthew's Need—a Challenge," *Michigan Churchman* 28 (December 1923): 22. St. Matthew's Episcopal Church Centennial Celebration, 1846–1946," St. Matthew's/St. Joseph Collection, Box 1, MHC.

18. "A Brief History of St. Matthew's Church," n.d., St. Matthew's/St. Joseph's Collection, Box 1, MHC.

19. Marshall F. Stevenson, "Points of Departure, Acts of Resolve: Black-Jewish Relations in Detroit, 1937–1962," PhD diss., University of Michigan, 1988, 41; Katzman, *Before the Ghetto,* 146–48.

20. Katzman, *Before the Ghetto,* 140–41; Bethel AME Papers, Box 1, MHC.

21. William H. Myers, *God's Yes Was Louder Than My No: Rethinking the African-American Call to Ministry* (Trenton NJ: Africa World Press, 1994), 44–45; Raboteau, *Fire in the Bones,* chap. 8.

22. Bermecia (Hill) Morrow McCoy, interview with author.

23. A copy of Hill's transcript was supplied courtesy of the Records Department at Cleary; his diploma is included in the Hill Papers, Box 1, MHC.

24. James F. Findlay Jr., *Dwight L. Moody: American Evangelist, 1837–1899* (Chicago: University of Chicago Press, 1969), chap. 5; see also Ahlstrom, *A Religious History of the American People,* 743–46, n. 812. There is also a brief section on Moody and the school in George M. Marsden, *Understanding Fundamentalism and Evangelicalism* (Grand Rapids, MI: Eerdmans, 1991), 21–22.

25. Wayne J. Urban, *Black Scholar: Horace Mann Bond, 1904–1972* (Athens: University of Georgia Press, 1992), 15.

26. Gaines, *Uplifting the Race: Black Leadership, Politics, and Culture in the Twentieth Century* (Chapel Hill: University of North Carolina Press, 1996), 2–3.

27. Urban, *Black Scholar*, 14.

28. Ibid., chap. 2; Horace Mann Bond, *An Education for Freedom: A History of Lincoln University, Pennsylvania* (Chester, PA: Lincoln University, 1976); Bond, *The Education of the Negro in the American Social Order* (New York: Prentice Hall, 1934). Also of interest are the sections on Lincoln in Kwame Nkrumah, *The Autobiography of Kwame Nkrumah* (Edinburgh, NY: Nelson, 1957). Nkrumah was at Lincoln from 1935 to 1939, however, much later than the time of Hill's tenure.

29. Bond, *History and New Design of Lincoln University, 1854–1954* (Princeton: Princeton University Press, 1954), 31. See also Bond, *An Education for Freedom*.

30. Adams quoted in Mast, *Detroit Lives,* 248; Adams, interview with author, Detroit, July 12, 1993; Charles Hill Jr., interview with author.

31. Seminary course catalogs for 1915 and 1918, copies supplied courtesy of the Archives Department, Lincoln University. See also Department of the Interior, Bureau of Education, *Survey of Negro College and Universities* (Washington, DC: Government Printing Office, 1929; rpt., New York: Negro Universities Press, 1969).

32. Charles Adams in Mast, *Detroit Lives,* 248.

33. For a more sustained discussion of evangelical liberalism, especially in relation to the social gospel, see Ronald C. White Jr. and C. Howard Hopkins, *The Social Gospel: Religion and Reform in Changing America* (Philadelphia: Temple University Press, 1976), 246–58.

34. Certificates from the teacher training course (1919) and the National War Work Council (1919) in the Hill Papers, Box 1, MHC; on the Sunday school movement in America, see Marsden, *Understanding Fundamentalism and Evangelicalism,* 23–25.

35. DuBois, "Returning Soldiers" (1919), in *The Oxford W. E. B. DuBois Reader,* ed. Eric J. Sunquist (New York: Oxford University Press, 1996), 381.

36. Randolph quoted in Jervis Anderson, *This Was Harlem, 1900–1950* (New York: Farrar Straus Giroux, 1981), 187–88. On the other movements during this period, see Christopher Lasch, *The New Radicalism in America, 1889–1963* (New York: Knopf, 1965).

37. Locke, "The New Negro," in *The New Negro: An Interpretation,* ed. Alain Locke (New York: Atheneum, [1925] 1992), 3. Whether Locke's New Negro was the same as Randolph's is the source of some debate. Barbara Foley argues that by the time Locke's 1925 volume was published the movement had been taken over and essentially deradicalized and that the postwar New Negro Movement had been co-opted and replaced with the Harlem Renaissance. See Foley, *Spectres of 1919: Class and Nation in the Making of the New Negro* (Urbana: University of Illinois Press, 2003).

38. The literature on these anti-Black race riots is extensive. See, for instance, William M. Tuttle Jr., *Race Riot: Chicago in the Red Summer of 1919* (New York: Atheneum, 1970); Elliott Rudwick, *Race Riot at East St. Louis, July 12, 1917* (Carbondale: Southern Illinois University Press, 1964); Scott Ellsworth, *Death in the Promised Land: The Tulsa Riot of 1921* (Baton Rouge: Louisiana State University Press, 1982); and Roberta Senechal, *The Sociogenesis of a Race Riot: Springfield, Illinois, in 1908* (Urbana: University of Illinois Press, 1990).

39. Hill, Oral History, ALHUA, 1.

40. Forrester B. Washington, "The Negro in Detroit: A Survey of the Conditions of a Negro Group in a Northern Industrial Center during the World Prosperity Period" (Detroit, 1920), copy in the Labadie Collection, University of Michigan. See especially chapter 5, "The Negro in the Industries of Detroit." See also David Allan Levine, *Internal Combustion: The Races in Detroit, 1915–1926* (Westport, CT: Greenwood, 1976), 72, 130–31.

41. "Population" section, in Washington, "The Negro in Detroit," 6; Thomas, *Life for Us,* 6–28; Sidney Glazer, *Detroit: A Study in Urban Development* (New York: Bookman Associates, 1965).

42. Walcott, *Remaking Respectability,* 65; Cara L. Shelly, "Bradby's Baptists: Second Baptist Church of Detroit, 1910–1946," *Michigan Historical Review* 17:1 (spring 1991): 1–33.

43. On Bradby's background see "Subject of a Sketch," n.d., Second Baptist Papers, Reel 3, "Pastor's Papers," MHC; and *Second Baptist Church of Detroit Eyewitness History* (Detroit, 1976), copy in author's possession.

44. Bermecia (Hill) McCoy Interview; the quotation is from "Mrs. Georgia Hill: Mother of the Week," *Michigan Chronicle,* n.d., Hill Papers, Box 2, MHC.

45. *A Brief History of Hartford Avenue Baptist Church* (Detroit, 1945), Burton Historical Collection, Detroit Public Library (cited hereafter as BHC).

46. Hill quoted in *1917–1962: 45th Anniversary of Hartford Avenue Baptist Church* (1962 program), Hill Papers, Box 1, MHC.

47. Georgia Hill's obituary, *Detroit Free Press,* September 24, 1983; Georgia Hill Red Squad File, copy in author's possession; "Mrs. Georgia Hill: Mother of the Week," *Michigan Chronicle,* n.d., Hill Papers, Box 2, MHC.

48. Letter to Hill from the Board of Deacons, n.d., Hill Papers, Box 2, MHC; Hill, Oral History, ALHUA, 8.

49. Charles A. Hill Jr., interview with author.

50. On Murphy's remarkable career, see Sidney Fine, *Frank Murphy: The Detroit Years* (Ann Arbor: University of Michigan Press, 1975); and *Frank Murphy: The Washington Years* (Ann Arbor: University of Michigan Press, 1984).

51. Georgia Hill, Oral History with Charles A. Hill, ALHUA, 23.

52. The close observer here is Coleman A. Young, who would prove to be very successful in courting the political loyalties of Black ministers during his successive campaigns for mayor of Detroit. See Young, *Hard Stuff,* 38.

53. Hill, Oral History, ALHUA, 2.

54. Michigan branch report, *Crisis,* 8 (July 1914); Katzman, *Before the Ghetto,* 98–99.

55. On the Sweet case, see Levine, *Internal Combustion,* 3–4, 167–90; and Kevin Boyle, *Arc of Justice: A Saga of Race, Civil Rights, and Murder in the Jazz Age* (New York: Henry Holt, 2004).

56. Bermecia (Hill) Morrow McCoy Interview; Hill Oral History, ALHUA, 15.

57. This information is scattered throughout the Detroit Urban League Papers, MHC, Boxes 1 and 11; see also Martin, *Detroit and the Great Migration,* 55–56.

58. J. H. Porter to Detroit Board of Commerce, March 11, 1918, DUL Papers, Box 1, MHC.

59. Good Citizenship League pamphlet, "To Colored Men and Women Voters of Michigan" (1922), DUL Papers, Box 1, MHC; "Annual Report of the Good Citizen-

ship League" (1921), also in Box 1. On the GCL in general, see Levine, *Internal Combustion*, 122–24.

60. Levine, *Internal Combustion,* 124.

61. Garvey quoted in ibid., 102.

62. On Garveyism in Detroit, see Thomas, *Life for Us,* 194–201; Judith Stein, *The World of Marcus Garvey: Race and Class in Modern Society* (Baton Rouge: Louisiana State University Press, 1986), 228–34; Levine, *Internal Combustion,* 100–103, 112–13; and Walcott, *Remaking Respectability,* 125–27, which is particularly sensitive to the gender dynamics of the movement.

63. Smith Interview, January 9–10, 1987, in Jeannette Smith-Irvin, *Footsoldiers of the Universal Negro Improvement Association* (Trenton, NJ: Africa World Press, 1989), 46–47.

64. The exact numbers are difficult to ascertain. For instance, in a 1924 address at a UNIA convention in New York, J. A. Craigen and F. E. Johnson claimed a membership "7,000 strong," which made the Detroit division "a power in Detroit" that local politicians "were now courting." See "Convention Report [New York, 5 August 1924]," in *The Marcus Garvey and Universal Negro Improvement Association Papers,* ed. Robert A. Hill (Berkeley: University of California Press, 1986), 5:661–62.

65. Stein, *The World of Marcus Garvey,* 230–31. On Lowe, see Hill, *Marcus Garvey and UNIA Papers,* 5:510, n. 1.

66. Bagnall, "The Madness of Marcus Garvey," *Messenger* (March 1923): 638–48; "2,000 Negroes Hear Garvey Denounced," *New York Times,* August 21, 1922, reprinted in Hill, *Marcus Garvey and UNIA Papers,* 4:932–33.

67. Tony Martin, *Race First: The Ideological and Organizational Struggles of Marcus Garvey and the Universal Negro Improvement Association* (Westport, CT: Greenwood, 1976), 75–77, includes a discussion of Muhammad's relationship with the UNIA, as well as the possible interrelationships between the UNIA and Islamist groups such as the Moorish-American Science Temples, which also had a presence in Detroit.

68. Garvey quoted in Randall K. Burkett, *Garveyism as a Religious Movement: The Institutionalization of Black Civil Religion* (Metuchen, NJ: Scarecrow Press, 1978), 47.

69. McGuire quoted in Wilmore, *Black Religion and Black Radicalism,* 149, 150–51. See also A. C. Terry-Thompson, *The History of the African Orthodox Church* (New York: AOC, 1956).

70. Harris, *Something Within,* 140–41; Wilmore, *Black Religion and Black Radicalism,* 149–51. See also Burkett, *Garveyism as a Religious Movement* (Metuchen, NJ: Scarecrow Press, 1978); and Martin, *Race First,* chap. 4, "Religion."

71. Smith Interview in Smith-Irvin, *Marcus Garvey's Footsoldiers,* 60.

72. Richard T. Ortquist, "Unemployment and Relief: Michigan's Response to the Depression and the Hoover Years," *Michigan History* 57 (fall 1973): 209–36.

73. Charles Lawrence, "Negro Organizations in Crisis: Depression, New Deal, World War II," PhD diss., Columbia University, 1952; June Woodson, "A Century of Negroes in Detroit," MA thesis, Wayne State University, 1954; Beth Tompkins Bates, "A New Crowd Challenges the Agenda of the Old Guard in the NAACP, 1933–1941," *American Historical Review* 102:2 (April 1997): 340–77.

74. Baltimore *Afro-American,* July 22, 1933; Gary Jerome Hunter, "'Don't Buy Where You Can't Work': Black Urban Boycott Movements during the Depression," PhD diss., University of Michigan, 1977, 45.

75. On the BTWTA and the Housewives League, see Walcott, *Remaking*

mith, *Dancing in the Streets,* 60–62, 67–68; and Thomas, *Life for*

l By-Laws of Housewives League of Detroit and *Declaration of Prin-*
nd By-Laws of the Booker T. Washington Trade Association 1937,
gue of Detroit Papers, Box 1, BHC.
History Interview with Roberta McBride, March 12, 1967,

78. Walcott, *Remaking Respectability,* 295, n. 15.

79. Grigsby, "Christianity and Race Relations," in *White Hypocrisy and Black Lethargy* (Detroit: Snow Grigsby, 1935), 14.

80. Ibid., 20.

81. Detroit Civic Rights Committee, "Open Letter to the Councilmen of the City of Detroit," Maurice Sugar Collection, Box 10, ALHUA; Hunter, "Don't Buy Where You Can't Work," 148–50.

82. Grigsby, *An X-Ray Picture of Detroit* (Detroit: Snow Grigsby, 1933), copy in MHC; see also "Grigsby Goes Gunning," *Detroit Tribune,* December 19, 1933.

83. Thomas, *Life for Us,* 241–43; *Detroit Tribune,* May 27, 1939, June 10, 1939, September 23, 1939, and October 14, 1939.

84. Roger Keeran, *The Communist Party and the Auto Workers Union* (Bloomington: Indiana University Press, 1980), chaps. 5 and 6; *Auto Workers News,* July, September, and October 1927, copies in ALHUA.

85. On the resolution introduced during the Sixth World Congress of the Communist International, see Philip S. Foner and James S. Allen, eds., *American Communism and Black Americans: A Documentary History, 1919–1929* (Philadelphia: Temple University Press, 1987), chap. 6 and chap. 7, "Party Work among Blacks, 1929." On the relationship between Blacks to the CP in general during this period, see Mark Solomon, *The Cry Was Unity: Communists and African Americans, 1917–1936* (Jackson: University Press of Mississippi, 1998).

86. James R. Prickett, "Communists and the Automobile Industry in Detroit before 1935," *Michigan History* 57 (fall 1973): 190.

87. On the LSNR, see Robin Kelley, "Communist Party USA, African Americans and the," for Africana.com Web site; Solomon, *The Cry Was Unity,* esp. 190–96.

88. Prickett, "Communists and the Automobile Industry," 193–94. Among the evidence cited are one, reports from the *Worker* that the largest membership was in Detroit, two, a report to the party's Political Committee by Earl Browder claiming that the "struggle against eviction" was more advanced in Detroit than elsewhere, and three, the sheer size of hunger marches in the city in the early 1930s.

89. Oral History Interview with Joseph Billups (and Rose Billups) by Herbert Hill, Shelton Tappes, and Roberta McBride, October 27, 1967, Detroit, ALHUA, 6. Used by permission of Herbert Hill.

90. Babson et al., *Working Detroit,* 57. On the Unemployed Councils in general, see Babson et al., *Working Detroit,* 54–57; Daniel J. Leab, "'United We Eat': The Creation and Organization of the Unemployed Councils in the 1930s," *Labor History* 8 (1967): 300–315; and Herbert Benjamin, *A Manual for Hunger Fighters: How to Organize and Conduct United Action for the Right to Live* (New York: Worker's Library Publishers, 1933).

91. Billups (and Rose Billups) Interview, ALHUA, 8. Billups himself was a frequent speaker at these outdoor forums.

92. Gomon quoted in Prickett, "Communists and the Automobile Industry," 196–97.

93. "Ford Hunger March File," Labadie Collection, University of Michigan; Maurice Sugar, *The Ford Hunger March* (Berkeley, CA: Meiklejohn Civil Liberties Institute, 1980); Alex Baskin, "The Ford Hunger March—1932," *Labor History* 13 (summer 1971): 331–61; *50 Years, 1932–1982, in the Struggle for Jobs: 50th Anniversary Ford Hunger March Commemoration* (Detroit, 1982).

94. Baldwin quoted in Sugar, *The Ford Hunger March*, 73; Detroit ACLU Collection, Box 1, ALHUA.

95. Baskin, "The Ford Hunger March," 350; Prickett, "Communists and the Automobile Industry," 196; "After the Dearborn Massacre," *New Republic*, March 30, 1932, 172; Sugar, "Bullets—Not—for Ford Workers," *Nation*, March 23, 1932, 333–35.

96. Moore quoted in Babson et al., *Working Detroit*, 60.

97. Biography, Chris and Mart Alston Collection, ALHUA.

98. Billups, Oral History, ALHUA, 10; Baskin, "The Ford Hunger March," 357; "Ford Victim to Be Buried Today," *Daily Worker*, August 13, 1932. Mayor Frank Murphy received dozens of telegrams from residents over the Williams affair (Mayor's Office Papers, 1932, Box 4, BHC).

99. Tappes, Oral History, ALHUA, 17.

100. Wilson Record, *Race and Radicalism: The NAACP and the Communist Party in Conflict* (Ithaca: Cornell University Press, 1964), 76–77. For a broader perspective on the CP's race work, see also Naison, *Communists in Harlem during the Depression;* and Kelley, *Hammer and Hoe.*

101. Joseph (and Rose) Billups, Oral History, ALHUA, 7.

102. Harry Haywood, "The Scottsboro Decision," *Communist* 11 (December 1932); *Daily Worker*, April 10, 11, 12, 17, 18, 25, 1931; *Daily Worker*, November 26, 1934; James W. Ford, "The United Front in the Field of Negro Work," *Communist* 14 (April 1935).

103. Hill and Dade's involvement with the Scottsboro Defense Clubs is mentioned in Scott Craig, "Automobiles and Labor: The Transformation of Detroit's Black Working Class, 1917–1941," MA thesis, Wayne State University, 1986, 70. See also Letter from the Scottsboro Defense Committee to Mayor Frank Murphy, Mayor's Office Papers, 1935, Box 6, BHC.

104. Jim Jacobs, "Sugar, Maurice," in *Encyclopedia of the American Left,* ed. Mari Jo Buhle, Paul Buhle, and Dan Georgakas, 2d ed. (New York: Oxford University Press, 1998), 806.

105. The campaign literature is in the Sugar Collection, Box 11, ALHUA. In 1961 Hill was the designated honoree at the Buck Dinner. The poster, with the signatures and best wishes of those in attendance, became a highly prized possession. The Hill family keeps it prominently displayed at its summer home in Harbor Beach. See "The Fiftieth Anniversary of the Buck Dinner" (1979), brochure in Supplement, Sugar Collection, AHLUA.

106. Johnson, *Maurice Sugar*, 152–53.

CHAPTER TWO

1. Eugene P. Link, *Labor-Religion Prophet: The Times and Life of Harry F. Ward* (Boulder: Westview, 1984), 160.

2. Meier and Rudwick, *Black Detroit,* 10. The original source for this story about the lunch meeting is an unpublished term paper (for a class at the University of Michigan) by David Lewis, "History of Negro Employment in Detroit Area Plants of Ford Motor Company, 1914–1941," 17–18, which is, in turn, based on interviews and materials subsequently removed from the Ford archives.

3. Bradby to Marshall, October 18, 1926, Second Baptist Papers, Reel 3, "Pastor's Papers," MHC.

4. Bradby to Mr. Weston, August 10, 1926, Second Baptist Papers, Reel 3, "Pastor's Papers," MHC.

5. Bradby to Whom It May Concern, April 21, 1931: "This is to certify that the bearer, Mrs. Myrtle Jackson, is a member of the Second Baptist Church of which I am the minister, and has been for a great number of years. It is our understanding that she is now seeking a position with the Welfare Department of the City of Detroit, and we are very happy to add our word of recommendation to her character and worthiness"; Bradby to Miss Velma McDonald, September 25, 1926. Both letters are in Second Baptist Papers, Reel 3, "Pastor's Papers," MHC.

6. Thomas, *Life for Us,* 272. In his dissertation, however, Thomas adopts a much harsher and more negative view of the entente. See Thomas, "From Peasant to Proletarian: The Formation and Organization of the Black Industrial Working Class in Detroit, 1915–1941," PhD diss., University of Michigan, 1976.

7. Claude and Martha Fisher to Daniel, October 12, 1929, St. Matthew's/St. Joseph's Papers, Box 1, MHC; see also Vestry Minutes, December 5, 1927, Box 1.

8. Hill, Oral History, ALHUA, 2.

9. Alston, *Henry Ford and the Negro People* (Washington, DC: National Negro Congress and Michigan Negro Congress, 1940), 5–6.

10. Norma Kenneth Miles, "Home at Last: Urbanization of Black Migrants in Detroit, 1916–1929," PhD diss., University of Michigan, 1978, 80–81. Ford's visits to St. Matthew's are also recorded in Meier and Rudwick, *Black Detroit,* 17.

11. Adams in Mast, *Detroit Lives,* 248–49.

12. Meier and Rudwick, *Black Detroit,* 10–11. For more details on Bennett and the Service Department, see Stephen H. Norwood, *Strikebreaking and Intimidation: Mercenaries and Masculinities in Twentieth-Century America* (Chapel Hill: University of North Carolina Press, 2002), chap. 5.

13. Bates, "A New Crowd Challenges the Agenda of the Old Guard in the NAACP, 1933–1941," *American Historical Review,* 102:2 (April 1997): 340–41.

14. On the priestly and the prophetic dimensions of African American Christianity, see Lincoln and Mamiya, *The Black Church in the African American Experience,* 10–16. On a more cautionary note Evelyn Brooks Higginbotham observes: "Arguments over the accommodationist versus liberating thrust of the Black church misses the range as well as the fluid interaction of political and ideological meanings represented within the church's domain" (*Righteous Discontent,* 18).

15. Dade, Oral History, ALHUA, 4.

16. Ibid.,15.

17. Hill, Oral History, ALHUA, 4; Thomas, *Life for Us,* 293–96.

18. White quoted in Meier and Rudwick, *Black Detroit,* 37.

19. White's obituary, *Detroit Free Press,* February 11, 1958; *Detroit Tribune,* November 4, 1940; NAACP Files, Gloster Current Papers, Box 1, ALHUA.

20. Thomas, *Life for Us,* 256–57.

21. Ibid., 265–70; Diggs's obituary, *Detroit Free Press*, April 26, 1967; Thomas S. Solomon, "Participation of Negroes in Detroit Elections," PhD diss., University of Michigan, 1937.

22. *Journal of the Senate of the State of Michigan: 1937 Regular Session*, 388, 2226; Daniel B. Neusom, "The Michigan Civil Rights Law and Its Enforcement," MA thesis, Wayne State University, 1952; "Statement on Diggs Law Violation" (March 27, 1940), CRC Collection, Box 80, ALHUA.

23. The Proletarian Party was one of the most militantly Marxist groups associated with the Socialist Party in Michigan. As a supporter of the Bolshevik revolution, it was among the first of many left-wing groups expelled (in May 1919) from the SP. While it took part in the founding of the Communist Party, disagreements soon caused a breech and the Proletarian Party remained independent, forming the Proletarian University in Detroit and specializing in educational communism. Its members were active in the 1933 Briggs Auto Body strike and in the sit-downs in Flint and elsewhere. Several, such as Emil Mazey and Frank Marquart, went on to become top officials in the UAW. See Allen Ruff, "A Path Not Taken: The Proletarian Party and the Early History of Communism in the United States," in *Culture, Gender, Race, and U.S. Labor History*, ed. Ronald C. Kent, Sara Markham, David Roediger, and Herbert Shapiro (Westport, CT: Greenwood, 1993); as well as the entry in Buhle, Buhle, and Georgakas, *Encyclopedia of the American Left*, 641–42.

24. Stanley Nowak, Oral History, ALHUA; Nowak, *Two Who Were There*, 148.

25. Crockett in Mast, *Detroit Lives*, 168.

26. Goodman in *Untold Tales, Unsung Heroes: An Oral History of Detroit's African American Community, 1918–1967*, ed. Elaine Latzman Moon (Detroit: Wayne State University Press, 1994), 61–63.

27. Ibid., 63.

28. Georg Schrode, "Mary Zuk and the Detroit Meat Strike of 1935," *Polish American Studies* 43 (autumn 1986): 3–24; Thaddeus C. Radzilowski, "Ethnic Conflict and the Polish Americans of Detroit," in *The Polish Presence in Canada and America*, ed. F. Renkiewicz (Toronto: Multicultural History Society of Ontario, 1982): 196–207; *Daily Worker*, April 10, 1936. On Zuk, see also Nowak, *Two Who Were There*, 17–21, 32–38.

29. Harvard Sitkoff, *A New Deal for Blacks: The Emergence of Civil Rights as a National Issue: The Depression Decade* (New York: Oxford University Press, 1978), chap. 3; Anthony Badger, *The New Deal: The Depression Years, 1933–1940* (New York: Noonday Press, 1989). On the more problematic nature of the New Deal and the question of race, see Ira Katznelson, *When Affirmative Action Was White: An Untold History of Racial Inequality in Twentieth-Century America* (New York: Norton, 2005).

30. On the early strike wave, see Sidney Fine, *The Automobile under The Blue Eagle* (Ann Arbor: University of Michigan Press, 1963); Keeran, *The Communist Party and the Auto Workers Union*, chap. 4; and Phil Raymond, "The Briggs Strike," *Labor Unity* 8 (March 1933): 21–23.

31. *NLRB v. Jones and Laughlin* 301 U.S. 1 (1937), 33; Staughton Lynd, "The Right to Engage in Concerted Activity after Union Recognition: A Study of Legislative History," *Indiana Law Journal* 50 (1975): 720–56.

32. Mark Naison, "Remaking America: Communists and Liberals in the Popular Front," in *New Studies on the Politics and Culture of U.S. Communism*, ed. Michael E. Brown, Randy Martin, Frank Rosengarten, and George Snedeker (New York:

Monthly Review Press, 1993), 45–73. While Naison acknowledges some of the internal tensions and contradictions of the policy, he has comparatively little to say about the negative effects of the CP's reversal of policy following the Hitler-Stalin pact of 1939. For a more critical reading, see Frank A. Warren, "A Flawed History of the Popular Front," *New Politics* 7:2 (winter 1999): 112–25. On the various shifts and changes, see the entry on the Popular Front in Buhle, Buhle, and Georgakas, *Encyclopedia of the American Left*, 627–30. It is difficult to chart the effects of the post-1939 switch in particular, but two good and interesting sources are Art Preis, *Labor's Giant Step* (New York: Pioneer, 1964); and Bert Cochran, *Labor and Communism: The Conflict That Shaped America's Unions* (Princeton: Princeton University Press, 1977).

33. Browder, "The United Front—The Key to Our Tactics and Organization," *Communist* 14 (December 1935): 1075–129; *Daily Worker*, August 5, 1935.

34. Prickett, "Communism and Factionalism in the United Automobile Workers Union, 1939–1947," *Science and Society* 32:3 (summer 1968): 257–77; Nelson Lichtenstein, *Labor's War at Home: The CIO in World War II* (New York: Cambridge University Press, 1982).

35. Naison, "Remaking America," 45.

36. Haywood, *Black Bolshevik: Autobiography of an Afro-American Communist* (Chicago: Liberator Press, 1978), 533; 554.

37. James, *C. L. R. James on the "Negro Question"* (Jackson: University Press of Mississippi, 1996), 5. This argument is nicely formulated in Ted McTaggart, "Black Self-Determination: Robert F. Williams, Harry Haywood, and the League of Revolutionary Black Workers," a seminar paper written for my class on Williams and the legacy of Black radicalism, University of Michigan, winter 2005. Critical assessments of the Popular Front are also incorporated into Kelley's pro–Third Period history *Hammer and Hoe*.

38. Johnson, *Maurice Sugar*, 152. Sugar's campaign notebooks detail the range of his support within the city's Left. They can be found in the Sugar Collection, Box 10, ALHUA. See also "Maurice Sugar, Labor Candidate vs. W. P. Lovett's City League," *Detroit Labor News*, March 1, 1935.

39. Haywood, *Black Bolshevik*, 436–38. For a broader perspective on the ILD, see Charles H. Martin, "The International Labor Defense and Black America," *Labor History* 26 (1985): 165–94.

40. *A Negro on Trial for His Life: The Frame-Up of James Victory Exposed—Speech to Jury by Counsel for Defense, Maurice Sugar* (Detroit: Candidates for Judge of Recorder's Court, 1935), in Sugar Papers, Box 2, ALHUA. On Darrow's performance during the Sweet trial, see Boyle, *Arc of Justice*, 292–96, 330–34.

41. The pamphlet is in the Sugar Papers, Box 2, ALHUA; see also Johnson, *Maurice Sugar*, 151–52.

42. Scott Craig, "Black Workers and the Communists in Detroit, 1929–1941," MA thesis, Wayne State University, 1986.

43. Murphy quoted in Babson et al., *Working Detroit*, 82. On Murphy's role during the GM strike and his views on the sit-downs, see J. Woodford Howard Jr., "Frank Murphy and the Sit-Down Strikes," *Labor History* 1:2 (spring 1960): 103–40. Murphy would go on to serve on the U.S. Supreme Court and played a role in the Thornhill decision, which established the constitutionality of picketing. See Sidney Fine, "Frank Murphy, The Thornhill Decision and Picketing as Free Speech," *Labor History* 6:2 (spring 1965): 99–120.

44. Sugar, "Is the Sit-Down Legal?" *New Masses*, May 4, 1937; Russell B. Porter, "The Broad Challenge of the Sit-Down Strike," *New York Times Magazine*, April 4, 1937. On the use of the tactic during the 1936 GM strike, see Sidney Fine, *Sit-Down: The General Motors Strike of 1936–1937* (Ann Arbor: University of Michigan Press, 1969).

45. "Constitution of the Conference for the Protection of Civil Rights" (1935), CRC Collection, Box 1, "CFPRC Files," ALHUA.

46. Bollens, "Why a Civil Rights Federation?" *Civil Rights News*, November 8, 1938, 1.

47. For a good overview of the ideology and activism of the Liberty League, see Frederick Rudolph, "The American Liberty League, 1934–1950," *American Historical Review* 56 (October 1950): 19–33.

48. Bollens, "Why a Civil Rights Federation?" 2–3; on the bill see Johnson, *Maurice Sugar*, 168, 172.

49. "Speakers Outline, Civil Rights Federation Organizational Approach," [n.d.,] CRC Collection, Box 1, ALHUA.

50. Ibid.

51. *Detroit Labor News*, March 30 and May 3, 11, and 17, 1935.

52. CRC Collection, Box 1; Ernest Goodman Collection, Box 3; National Lawyers Guild Collection, Box 1, all in ALHUA.

53. Maki, Oral History Interview by Norman McRae, March 26, 1970, ALHUA, 2.

54. McPhaul, Oral History Interview with Norman McRae, April 5, 1970, ALHUA, 9; interview with author, April 9, 1994, Detroit.

55. Ralph J. Bunche, "The Programs, Ideologies, Tactics, and Achievements of Negro Betterment and Interracial Organizations" (1940), memorandum prepared for the Carnegie-Myrdal study for *An American Dilemma*, copy at the Schomburg Center, New York Public Library; James W. Ford, "The National Negro Congress," *Communist* 15 (April 1936); Lawrence S. Wittner, "The National Negro Congress: A Reassessment," *American Quarterly* 22 (winter 1970): 883–901. On the convention movement historically, see Meier and Rudwick, *From Plantation to Ghetto*, 3d ed. (New York: Hill and Wang, 1976), 124–28.

56. Davis, *Let Us Build a National Negro Congress*," in *Black Protest: History, Documents, and Analysis*, ed. Joanne Grant (New York: Fawcett, 1968), 242.

57. *Official Proceedings of the National Negro Congress, February 14, 15, 16, 1936*. Copy in the Labadie Collection, University of Michigan.

58. Naison, *Communists in Harlem*, 138–40; Robin D. G. Kelley, "'This Ain't Ethiopia, but It'll Do': African-Americans and the Spanish Civil War," in *Race Rebels: Culture, Politics, and the Black Working Class* (New York: Free Press, 1994).

59. Randolph to White, April 8, 1936, and White to Davis, March 3, 1939, both in NAACP Collection, Library of Congress, I, C, Box 383, "NNC Folder."

60. "Church Leaders in Opposition to the Program of the National Negro Congress," (1936) in NAACP Collection, Library of Congress, I, C, Box 383, "NNC Folder." See *Official Proceedings of the National Negro Congress*, 30–31, for the original resolution about the role of churches.

61. NNC File, Labadie Collection, University of Michigan. The "Detroit Files" of the FBI file on the NNC lists Stanley Nowak; Reverends Hill, White, and John Miles; and unionists Chris Alston, Hodges Mason, John Conyers, Luke Fennel, and Senator Diggs as among those who sponsored the Michigan section of the NNC. C. LeBron

Simmons also attended the founding convention and served for a time as president of the Detroit chapter (Simmons, Oral History Interview with Norman McRae, ca. 1969, ALHUA, 1, 5–6.

62. See also Link, *Labor-Religion Prophet;* Ralph Lord Roy, *Communism and the Churches* (Ithaca: Cornell University Press, 1965), chap. 5; and Dunbar, *Against the Grain,* 39–40.

63. Roy, in *Communism and the Churches,* 159–60, also reports that Knox became disillusioned with the various "Communist fronts" that he had worked with and that he remained a bitter opponent of the CP. See also Jack Raskin, Oral History, ALHUA, 2, 20.

64. Hill quoted in "The NAACP Convention's Statement to the Nation," *Michigan Chronicle,* June 12, 1943.

65. Young, *Hard Stuff,* 112–13.

66. On Zuk and class tensions within the Polish American community see Schrode, "Mary Zuk and the Detroit Meat Strike"; Stevenson, "Points of Departure, Acts of Resolve," 136–37; and Raskin, Oral History Interview, ALHUA. On this as a general phenomenon, see Lizabeth Cohen, *Making a New Deal: Industrial Workers in Chicago, 1919–1939* (New York: Cambridge University Press).

67. Peter H. Amann, "Vigilante Fascism: The Black Legion as an American Hybrid," *Comparative Studies in Society and History* 25 (1983): 490–524.

68. *Civil Rights Bulletin,* July 27, 1938, in CRC Collection, Box 2, ALHUA.

69. *New Republic,* June 17, 1936; B. J. Widick, *Detroit: City of Race and Class Violence,* Rev. ed. (Detroit: Wayne State University Press, 1989), chap. 1; "The True Story of the Black Legion Plot to Murder Maurice Sugar," Sugar Papers, Box 1, ALHUA.

70. *Civil Rights News,* March 1939; *Detroit News,* June 21, 1936; "Report upon the Black Legion and Other Vigilante Organizations," CRC Collection, Box 12, ALHUA; James Basil Jacobs, "The Conduct of Local Police Intelligence," PhD diss., Princeton University, 1977, 114–16.

71. *Civil Liberties in American Cities: A Survey Based on 332 American Cities of over 10,000 Population* (New York: ACLU, 1939).

72. "Report on the Activities of the Civil Rights Federation, 1938–1939," CRC Collection, Box 1, "CRF Files," ALHUA. See also *Report of the Mayor's Committee on Race Relations* (Detroit: Bureau of Governmental Research, 1926); and Thomas, *Life for Us,* 164–66. In 1939, the ACLU ranked Detroit as one of the worst major cities in the area of rights violation by police (*Civil Liberties in American Cities,* 3).

73. *United Automobile Worker,* December 24, 1938; Thomas, *Life for Us,* 282.

74. Hill, Oral History, ALHUA, 18.

75. "Police Will Continue Illegal Arrests, Pickert Tells Our Delegation," *Civil Rights News,* November 1938.

76. Bollens to La Follette Committee, March 23, 1937, Record Group 46, Box 86, National Archives. The committee, organized in 1936, grew out of a series of National Labor Relations Board hearings and limited itself mainly to company abuses. See Jerold S. Auerbach, *Labor and Liberty: The La Follette Committee and the New Deal* (Indianapolis: Bobbs-Merrill, 1966).

77. U.S. House Resolution 282.

78. Bollens to Martin Dies, July 16, 1938, CRC Papers, Box 31, ALHUA.

79. U.S. House of Representatives, *Hearings before a Special Committee on Un-American Activities,* 75th Cong., 3d sess., vol. 2, October 11, 12, 13, at Detroit, Michigan

(Washington DC: Government Printing Office, 1938), 1239–486. There is an extensive clippings file from the hearings in the Sugar Collection, Box 49, ALHUA.

80. Ibid., 1356–57.

81. Ibid., 1334–35.

82. Young, *Hard Stuff,* 112.

83. Flyer, CRC Collection, Box 11, ALHUA.

84. Coughlin quoted in Forrest Davis, "Father Coughlin," *Atlantic Monthly* 156:6 (December 1935): 660; also *Detroit Free Press,* July 26, 1930. On his career in general see Charles J. Tull, *Father Coughlin and the New Deal* (Syracuse: Syracuse University Press, 1965); Shelton Marcus, *Father Coughlin: The Tumultuous Life of the Priest of the Little Flower* (Boston: Little Brown, 1973); and Alan Brinkley, *Voices of Protest: Huey Long, Father Coughlin, and the Great Depression* (New York: Vintage, 1983).

85. The full text of the encyclical, issued on May 15, 1891, can be found at http://www.osjspm.org/cst/rn.htm.

86. Frankensteen quoted in Babson et al., *Working Detroit,* 56, 100–101.

87. Brinkley, *Voices of Protest,* chap. 4; Leslie Tentler, *Seasons of Grace: A History of the Catholic Archdiocese of Detroit* (Detroit: Wayne State University Press, 1990), 324–44.

88. *Civil Rights News,* December 1939; Tentler, *Seasons of Grace,* 340–41.

89. Though short-lived, *Equality* was a fascinating magazine. Many of the issues have been collected and reprinted in *Equality* (Westport, CT: Greenwood, 1970), with an introduction by Jack Salzman.

90. Albert Lee, *Henry Ford and the Jews* (New York: Stein and Day, 1980). See also Neil Baldwin, *Henry Ford and the Jews: The Mass Production of Hate* (New York: Public Affairs, 2001).

91. Meier and Rudwick, *Black Detroit,* 6–8. In general this is still the best source on efforts to unionize Ford and involve the Black community; see also Thomas, *Life for Us,* chap. 8.

92. Meier and Rudwick, *Black Detroit,* 86–87.

93. Mason, Oral History Interview with Herbert Hill, November 28, 1967, Detroit, ALHUA, 9 (used by permission of Herbert Hill); interview with author, Detroit, January 16, 1994.

94. "Tentative Draft of Suggested Resolutions for Consideration by the Detroit Conference, June 29–July 4, 1937," NAACP Papers, I, B, Box 14, Library of Congress; Homer Martin, "Address to the Convention of the National Association for the Advancement of Colored People" (June 1930), Martin Papers, ALHUA; "Resolutions Adopted by the Twenty-eighth Annual Conference of the N.A.A.C.P. in Detroit, Michigan, July 4, 1937," NAACP Papers, I, B, Box 4, Library of Congress; Meier and Rudwick, *Black Detroit,* 56–59.

95. "Editorial," *Crisis* 44 (August 1937): 241; Daniel quoted in *Pittsburgh Courier,* August 28, 1937; Meier and Rudwick, *Black Detroit,* 58.

96. Bradford quoted in Alston, *Henry Ford and the Negro People,* 11–12. See also Thomas, *Life for Us,* 258–59.

97. Babson et al., *Working Detroit,* 103.

98. Tappes, quoted in Babson et al., *Working Detroit,* 104.

99. "Ford Motor Company Ordered to Cease Unfair Labor Practices," National Labor Relations Board press release, August 1940, ACTU Papers, Box 19, ALHUA; Allen Nevins and Frank Ernest Hill, *Decline and Rebirth, 1933–1941* (New York: Scribner's, 1963), 150–51.

100. CRC Collection, Box 1 ("CFPCR Files"), ALHUA.

101. Mason, Oral History, ALHUA, 12. On the exposition, see Thomas, *Life for Us*, 223–27.

102. Rose Billups with Joseph Billups, Oral History, ALHUA, 6.

103. Copy in Nowak Papers, Box 8, ALHUA; Radzilowski, "Ethnic Conflict and the Polish American of Detroit," 67–69; Nowak, *Two Who Were There*, chap. 13, "The Ford Organizing Committee"; Roger Keeran, "The International Workers Order and the Origins of the CIO," *Labor History* 30 (summer 1989): 385–408.

104. The narrative of the Ford strike has been told and retold many times by historians. See, for example, Meier and Rudwick, *Black Detroit,* esp. chap. 2; Thomas, *Life for Us,* chap. 8; Irving Howe and B. J. Widick, *The UAW and Walter Reuther* (New York: Random House, 1949); Robert H. Zieger, *The CIO, 1933–1935* (Chapel Hill: University of North Carolina Press, 1995), chap. 6; and Nelson Lichtenstein, *The Most Dangerous Man in Detroit: Walter Reuther and the Fate of American Labor* (New York: Basic Books, 1995), chap. 9.

105. Thomas, *Life for Us,* 228–30; Meier and Rudwick, *Black Detroit,* 67–72.

106. Marshall quoted in Meier and Rudwick, *Black Detroit,* 71.

107. Quoted in Philip Bonosky, *Brother Bill McKie: Building the Union at Ford* (New York: International, 1953), 178.

108. Meier and Rudwick, *Black Detroit,* 106–7.

CHAPTER THREE

1. Martin, "Detroit—Still Dynamite," *Crisis* 51 (January 1944): 8.

2. Lichtenstein and Korstad, "Opportunities Found and Lost," 794–96; Meier and Rudwick, *Black Detroit,* chap. 4.

3. Crockett in Mast, *Detroit Lives,* 167.

4. Lichtenstein and Korstad, "Opportunities Found and Lost," 796–97.

5. Keeran, *The Communist Party and the Auto Workers Union,* 218, 231–35; U.S. Congress, House Committee on Un-American Activities, *Communism in the Detroit Area.* 82d Cong., 2d sess., March 10–11, 1952, 3036–45, 3117–35; William D. Andrew, "Factionalism and Anti-communism: Ford Local 600," *Labor History* 20 (spring 1979): 227–55; James R. Prickett, "Communism and Factionalism in the United Automobile Workers, 1939–1941," *Science and Society* 32:3 (summer 1968): 257–77. Overall, the CP's record of support for Black demands during the war was mixed, incorporating both the submerging of civil rights work in the name of winning the war and a continuation of the party's prewar antiracist positions, though not as consistently or as forcefully.

6. Peter J. Kellogg, "Civil Rights Consciousness in the 1940's," *Historian* 42 (1979): 18–41. The importance of World War II in the history of the Black freedom struggle has been given renewed prominence by contemporary historians. See, for instance, Steven Lawson, *Running for Freedom: Civil Rights and Black Politics in America since 1941* (New York: McGraw-Hill, 1996); Harvard Sitkoff, "African American Militancy in the World War II South," in *Remaking Dixie: The Impact of World War II on the American South,* ed. Neil McMillen (Jackson: University Press of Mississippi, 1997), 70–92; and Megan Taylor Shockley, *We, Too, Are Americans: African American Women in Detroit and Richmond, 1940–54* (Urbana: University of Illinois Press, 2004).

7. See, for example, "Hill, McClendon Supporters in Clash," *Michigan Chronicle,*

December 5, 1942; "The NAACP Elections" (editorial) and "NAACP Candidates Make Ready for Showdown," *Michigan Chronicle*, December 12, 1942.

8. "Rev. C. A. Hill Announces His Candidacy," *Michigan Chronicle*, December 5, 1942. On the paper's pro-Hill bias, see a "We Honor" segment featuring Hill and highlighting his accomplishments as an activist and organizer on December 5, the same day that Hill officially announced his candidacy, as well as the paper's decision to print a scathing letter by Shelton Tappes on the front page criticizing the conduct of the elections (December 19, 1942).

9. The December 19 issue of the *Michigan Chronicle* carried extensive coverage of the elections and the aftermath under the banner headline "McClendon Wins Election in Stormy NAACP Elections."

10. "Reserve Officer Told to Resign or Face Quiz," *Detroit Free Press*, January 30, 1951. As I detail in the next chapter, Hill's son faced difficulties because of his father's involvement in supposedly "un-American" activities.

11. Hill, Oral History, ALHUA, 6.

12. Jack Raskin, Oral History Interview with Norman McRae, ca. 1970, ALHUA, 8; Dominic Capeci, *Race Relations in Wartime Detroit* (Philadelphia: Temple University Press, 1984), 13.

13. Maki, Oral History, AHLUA, 8.

14. Ibid., 7.

15. Knox to Bollens, Letter of Resignation, Civil Rights Congress Collection, Box 1, ALHUA; Ralph Lord Roy, *Communism and the Churches* (New York: Harcourt, Brace, 1960), 159–60; Raskin, Oral History, ALHUA, 15.

16. The speculation on the membership numbers and composition of the CRF comes from an interview with Shelton Tappes conducted by Marshall Fields Stevenson. See his "Points of Departure, Acts of Resolve," 136, n. 25.

17. Raskin, Oral History, ALHUA, 1–2. A similar version of this story is told in Detroit Urban League, *7th Annual "Salute to Distinguished Warriors,"* program, March 20, 1986 (Detroit: DUL, 1986).

18. "Program of the Civil Rights Federation," Box 4, CRC Papers, ALHUA. On the complications of Black and Jewish relations in Detroit, especially the question of Jewish anti-Black racism and Black anti-Semitism, see Stevenson, "Points of Departure, Acts of Resolve"; and "African Americans and Jews in Organized Labor: A Case Study of Detroit, 1920–1950," in *African Americans and Jews in the Twentieth Century: Studies in Convergence and Conflict*, ed. V. P. Franklin, Nancy Grant, Harold M. Kletnick, and Genna Rae McNeil (Columbia: University of Missouri Press, 1998), 237–63.

19. Raskin, Oral History, ALHUA, 21–22.

20. Randolph, "Why I Would Not Stand for Re-election as President of the National Negro Congress," *American Federationist* (July 1940): 24–25; Lawrence S. Wittner, "The National Negro Congress: A Reassessment," *American Quarterly* 22 (winter 1970): 899–901. See also Mark Solomon, *The Cry Was Unity: Communists and African Americans, 1917–1936* (Jackson: University Press of Mississippi, 1998), for a broad overview of how the controversy fits into the evolution of the relationship between Blacks and the CP.

21. Theodore R. Bassett, "The Third National Negro Congress," *Communist* 19 (June 1940): 547–49. For a good overview of Randolph's relationship with the NNC, see John B. Kirby, *Black Americans in the Roosevelt Era: Liberalism and Race* (Knoxville: University of Tennessee Press, 1980), 164–70. Also helpful are Jervis Anderson,

A. Philip Randolph: A Biographical Sketch (Berkeley: University of California Press, [1972] 1986), chap. 16; and Beth Tompkins Bates, *Pullman Porters and the Rise of Protest Politics in Black America, 1925–1945* (Chapel Hill: University of North Carolina Press, 2001), 144–47.

22. The national office of the NAACP was worried that the Detroit branch and the movement there were in danger of being taken over by communists. In a typical correspondence, Walter White writes: "Does [state senator] Diggs know of the widespread belief that John Davis and the NNC are reputed to be Communist? . . . I wish you would write me confidentially about Diggs' knowledge of the political implications of this whole situation and his affiliations." White to McClendon, May 5, 1941, NAACP Papers, II, C, Box 86, Library of Congress.

23. The best spin on the CP's opposition to the MOWM after the United States entered World War II is that the party believed that the MOWM's attacks on Roosevelt and its all-Black composition would "lead to the isolation of the Negro people from their most important allies" (Keeran, *The Communist Party and the Auto Workers Union,* 231). A less rosy picture is provided by Albert Parker in "Why Communist Party Attacks 'Double V,'" *Militant,* April 4, 1942, which is also an example of the types of critiques mounted by the Socialist Workers Party during the war. On the complicated question of whether the CP abandoned the struggle for Black rights during the war, see Maurice Isserman, *Which Side Were You On?* (Middletown: Wesleyan University Press, 1982), in which he challenges the perspective of total abandonment yet recognizes that the CP argued that "a too militant defense of black rights at home would interfere with the war effort" (119). On the MOWM in general, the best source remains Herbert Garfinkel, *When Negroes March* (New York: Atheneum, 1969).

24. Martin, "Detroit—Still Dynamite," 10.

25. Randolph, "Let the Negro Masses Speak," *Black Worker,* March 1941, 4–5.

26. *Baltimore Afro-American,* June 23, 1941; *Detroit Tribune,* June 25 and July 12, 1941; Hunter, "Don't Buy Where You Can't Work," 294–95; and Beth T. Bates, "'Double V for Victory' Mobilizes Black Detroit, 1941–1946," in Theoharis and Woodard, *Freedom North,* 17–39.

27. On the FEPC, see Louis Ruchames, *Race, Jobs, and Politics: The Story of the FEPC* (New York: Columbia University Press, 1953).

28. Anderson, *A. Philip Randolph,* 243; Brooks, *Walls Come Tumbling Down: A History of the Civil Rights Movement, 1940–1970* (Englewood Cliffs, NJ: Prentice-Hall, 1974), 27. On the tensions raised within the Roosevelt administration by the MOWM and its demands, see Daniel Kryder, "The American State and the Management of Race Conflict in the Workplace and in the Army, 1941–1945," *Polity* 26 (summer 1994): 603–34; as well as his *Divided Arsenal: Race and the American State during World War II* (New York: Cambridge University Press, 2000), 53–67.

29. "Call to Negro Americans to March on Washington for Jobs and Equal Participation in National Defense," May 1, 1941, quoted in Brooks, *Walls Come Tumbling Down,* 27–28.

30. Niebuhr, *Moral Man and Immoral Society* (New York: Scribner's, 1932); also Richard H. Pells, *Radical Visions and American Dreams: Culture and Social Thought in the Depression Years* (Urbana: University of Illinois Press, 1998), 141–50. For more on the idea of mediating structures, see Peter L. Berger and Richard John Neuhaus, *The Role of Mediating Structures in Public Policy* (Washington, DC: American Enterprise Institute, 1997).

31. On the centrality of FEPC legislation, see Sidney Fine's exhaustive *Expanding the Frontiers of Civil Rights: Michigan, 1948–1968* (Detroit: Wayne State University Press, 2000). See also Biondi, *To Stand and Fight,* chap. 1, on the role of FEPC campaigns on mass mobilizations in New York; and Bates, *Pullman Porters,* chap. 8.

32. "Randolph to Adopt Gandhi Technique, Nonviolent Disobedience May Be Used," *Chicago Defender,* January 9, 1943. On the dissemination of Gandhism among Black Americans in the 1940s, see Kapur Sudarshan, *Raising up a Prophet: The African-American Encounter with Gandhi* (Boston: Beacon, 1992).

33. *Pittsburgh Courier,* February 14, 1942; *Chicago Defender,* March 14, 1942; Ralph N. Davis, "The Negro Newspapers and the War," *Sociology and Social Research* 27 (May–June 1943): 373–80.

34. *Michigan Chronicle,* July 3, 1943. See also Clive, *State of War,* 131–34.

35. Hill quoted in *Detroit Tribune,* January 22, 1940.

36. Martin, "Detroit—Still Dynamite," 10.

37. Detroit Urban League, "Negroes Beginning to Get Jobs Now: Sixteen Points on How to Make Good" (1942), DUL Papers, Box 4, MHC; Clive, *State of War,* 136–38; Thomas, *Life for Us,* 153–55; Meier and Rudwick, *Black Detroit,* 136–37.

38. Bledsoe, Oral History Interview with Norman McRae, ca. 1970, ALHUA, 6. On the question of class bias in civil rights organizations, see Charles Denby, *Indignant Heart: A Black Worker's Journal* (Detroit: Wayne State University Press, 1989), 98–99.

39. A brief history of the founding of the organization is given in "Who's Who on the Executive Board of the Metropolitan Detroit Fair Employment Practice Council," December 10, 1945, in ACTU Papers, Box 18, ALHUA.

40. Metropolitan Detroit Council on Fair Employment Practices, "Membership List" (August 1943), "Constitution and By-Laws," in CRC Collection, Box 49, ALHUA; Clarence Anderson, "Metropolitan Detroit FEPC: A History of the Organization and Operation of a Citizen's Action Group to Encourage Equal Opportunity in Employment Practice without Regard to Race, Creed, or National Origins," MA thesis, Wayne State University, 1947; Meier and Rudwick, *Black Detroit,* 113–14, 130, 138.

41. Fine, *Expanding the Frontiers,* 13–14; Anderson, "Metropolitan Detroit FEPC," 86–98.

42. *Michigan Chronicle,* November 21 and December 5, 1942; Minutes of Detroit NAACP Executive Board, November 9, 1942 and February 1, 2, 1943, in Gloster Current Papers, Box 1, ALHUA; Meier and Rudwick, *Black Detroit,* 114–16.

43. "The Social Dynamics of Detroit" (December 3, 1942), report for the Bureau of Intelligence, Office of War Information, Record Group 44, Box 1814, National Archives.

44. "Citizen's Committee Gathers Cases for F.E.P.C. Hearing," press release, January 6, 1943, ACTU Papers, Box 29, ALHUA.

45. FEPC, "Complaints Based on Religious Discrimination" (n.d.), Record Group 228, Box 404, National Archives.

46. Rev. George Higgins, "Catholics and the F.E.P.C. Case: An Analysis of Catholic Teaching and Discrimination in Railroad Employment against Negroes," *Catholic Action,* January 1944, in CRC Collection, Box 51, ALHUA. On Catholics and the ACTU in Detroit in general, see Steve Rosswurm, "The Catholic Church and the Left-Led Unions: Labor Priests, Labor Schools, and the ACTU," in *The CIO's Left-Led Unions,* ed. Steve Rosswurm (New Brunswick, NJ: Rutgers University Press, 1992),

120–37. Rosswurm nicely chronicles the changes in the Catholic Church's position after 1945 from a previously "positive" approach to anticommunism that allowed it to align itself with progressive labor unions and groups to "an entirely negative one as its CIO activity became synonymous with the effort to destroy communism" (120).

47. John A. Davis, "Summary of War Production Board Report on Detroit" (September 29, 1943), Record Group 44, Box 1817, National Archives; "Urgent Need for Unskilled Labor in the Forge and Foundry Industries in this Area, 199," report, Detroit-Willow Run, Committee for Congested Production Areas, Record Group 212, Box 52, National Archives; Robert C. Weaver, "Detroit and Negro Skill," *Phylon* 4 (April–June 1943): 33–136; Thomas, *Life for Us,* 162–64.

48. Jones, *Labor of Love, Labor of Sorrow: Black Women, Work, and the Family from Slavery to the Present* (New York: Vintage, 1985), 235–40 (Hatcher quoted on 236); Paddy Quick, "Rosie the Riveter: Myths and Realities," *Radical America* 9 (1975): 115–21.

49. Gabin, *Feminism in the Labor Movement: Women and the UAW, 1935–1975* (Ithaca: Cornell University Press, 1990), 88–89; Shockley, *We, Too, Are Americans,* 2–3; *Michigan Chronicle,* November 14 and 21 and December 5, 1942; *Ford Facts,* December 1, 1942. For a good summary, see Meier and Rudwick, *Black Detroit,* 151–53.

50. Jones estimates that as many as twenty-five thousand Black women may have remained unemployed (*Labor of Love, Labor of Sorrow,* 240).

51. Current to White, July 24, 1943, NAACP Papers, II, C, Box 86, Library of Congress; Meier and Rudwick, *Black Detroit,* 116–17; Minutes of Detroit NAACP Executive Board, February 1–2, 1943, Current Papers, Box 1, ALHUA.

52. Wendell R. Harrison and Donald Walden, "Discussion on Life and Music," in Moon, *Untold Tales, Unsung Heroes,* 318–22; Babson et al., *Working Detroit,* 164–65.

53. Roy Brooks quoted in Moon, *Untold Tales, Unsung Heroes,* 280; also Lars Bjorn, with Jim Gallert, *Before Motown: A History of Jazz in Detroit, 1920–1960* (Ann Arbor: University of Michigan Press, 2001).

54. Young, *Hard Stuff,* 112.

55. Wendell Harrison in Moon, *Untold Tales, Unsung Heroes,* 321. On Current, see "We Honor," *Michigan Chronicle,* November 14, 1942. On Cleage, see Hiley H. Ward, *Prophet of the Black Nation* (Philadelphia: Pilgrim Press, 1969), 45.

56. Chad Berry, *Southern Migrants, Northern Exiles* (Urbana: University of Illinois Press, 2000), 1–9, 33–34; Neil Fligstein, *Going North: Migration of Blacks and Whites from the South, 1900–1950* (New York: Academic Books, 1981). On the migration to the West, see James N. Gregory, *American Exodus: The Dust Bowl Migration and Okie Culture in California* (New York: Oxford University Press, 1989). See also Gregory's impressive recent volume, *The Southern Diaspora: How the Great Migrations of Black and White Southerners Transformed America* (Chapel Hill: University of North Carolina Press, 2005).

57. Adamic, "The Hill-Billies Come to Detroit," *Nation,* February 13, 1935, 177–78.

58. Friedlander, *The Emergence of a UAW Local, 1936–1939: A Study in Class and Culture* (Pittsburgh: University of Pittsburgh Press, 1975), 121–31. Friedlander pays close attention to the problem of White southern racism and anticommunism, insisting that both dynamics led southern Whites to support Homer Martin and his rival UAW-AFL union in the elections to the National Labor Relations Board in 1940. See also Berry, *Southern Migrants, Northern Exiles,* chap. 2.

59. Clive, *State of War,* chap. 5, "Tennessee and Kentucky Are Now in Michigan";

Erdmann D. Beynon, "The Southern White Laborer Migrates to Michigan," *American Sociological Review* 3 (1938): 338–48; Sugure, *Origins of the Racial Crisis,* chap. 2.

60. Jon C. Teaford, *Cities of the Heartland: The Rise and Fall of the Industrial Midwest* (Bloomington: Indiana University Press, 1993), 193.

61. Gregory, *American Exodus,* 193–94; Berry, *Southern Migrants, Northern Exiles,* chap. 6; Clive, *State of War,* chaps. 4 and 5.

62. Berry, *Southern Migrants, Northern Exiles,* 155–66; James C. Cobb, "From Rocky Top to Detroit City: Country Music and the Economic Transformation of the South," in *You Wrote My Life: Lyrical Themes in Country Music,* ed. Melton A. McLaurin and Richard A. Peterson (Philadelphia: Gordon and Breach, 1993), 63–79; D. K. Wilgus, "Country-Western Music and the Urban Hillbilly," *Journal of American Folklore* 83 (April–June 1970): 157–79.

63. Ahlstrom, *A Religious History of the American People,* pt. 8; Robert Wuthnow, *The Restructuring of American Religion: Society and Faith since World War II* (Princeton: Princeton University Press, 1988).

64. Berry, *Southern Migrants, Northern Exiles,* 90–92, 144–55.

65. Brewster Campbell and James Pooler, "Hallelujah in Boom Town," *Collier's,* April 1, 1944, 18–19, 52–53; Clive, *State of War,* 178–80.

66. Howard Hill et al., "Survey of Religious and Racial Conflict Forces in Detroit" (September 30, 1943), Jewish Community Council [JCC] Papers, Box 685, 6–7. According to the key provided, Howard Hill conducted most of the interviews. The other research team members were: Dr. Gertrude Duncan, Judge Herefried Dugan, A. L. Campbell, and Barbara Krenger. The document is typeset but unbound. Another copy is located in the papers of the Civil Rights Congress, Box 71, ALHUA.

67. Robert Coles, *Migrants, Sharecroppers, Mountaineers,* vol. 1 of *Children of Crisis* (Boston: Little Brown, 1967); *The South Goes North,* vol. 3 of *Children of Crisis* (Boston: Little Brown, 1972). On the very similar situation among African American migrants, see Walcott, *Remaking Respectability,* 113–26, 194–204.

68. Hill et al., "Survey of Religious and Racial Conflict Forces in Detroit," 37–39.

69. Smith, Oral History, in Studs Terkel, *Hard Times: An Oral History of the Great Depression* (New York: Random House, 1970), 324. Smith told the same story, almost verbatim, in an interview with J. Fraser Cocks III on March 26–30, 1968, in Los Angles (Smith Papers, BHC, 15–16).

70. Hill quoted in Hill et al., "Survey of Religious and Racial Conflict Forces in Detroit," 55.

71. The split between evangelicals and fundamentalists, who began as the conservative wing of the evangelical community, took place between 1870 and 1920 and continued to develop and harden throughout the twentieth century. For an admirably clear summary of these developments, see Marsden, *Understanding Fundamentalism and Evangelicalism.* On Norris, see Barry Hankins, *God's Rascal: J. Frank Norris and the Beginnings of Southern Fundamentalism* (Lexington: University of Kentucky Press, 1996).

72. Dispensational premillennialism is a belief that we are living in an age, or dispensation, of decline and decay for Christian civilization, which is manifested in the spread of secularization and apostasy. In each age, human beings are tested and fail. Each age, we are now living in the sixth, thus ends with a catastrophic divine judgment. Our age will follow this pattern; after seven years of war, destruction, and calamity, Jesus will return to establish a literal kingdom in Jerusalem from which he

will reign for a thousand years. See Marsden, *Understanding Fundamentalism and Evangelicalism,* 39–41.

73. Hankins, *God's Rascal,* 91.

74. Ibid., 104–5. Both the CRF and the JCC kept extensive clipping files on Norris.

75. Hill et al., "Survey of Religious and Racial Conflict Forces in Detroit," 4.

76. On Smith's background, see Glen Jeansonne, *Gerald L. K. Smith: Minister of Hate* (New Haven: Yale University Press, 1988); and Ribuffo, *The Old Christian Right.*

77. Smith Oral History, BHC, 13.

78. Ribuffo, *The Old Christian Right,* 136–37.

79. Jeansonne, *Gerald L. K. Smith,* 68–71.

80. Smith quoted in Widick, *Detroit: City of Race and Class Violence,* 89. Copies of *The Cross and the Flag* may be found in the Smith Papers, Box 5, MHC, Bentley Library, University of Michigan.

81. Ralph Lord Roy, *Communism and the Churches,* 256.

82. Tappes, "Detroit's Negro Housing Problem" (March 31, 1944), "Miscellaneous Publications," ALHUA.

83. Quoted in Bette Smith Jenkins, "The Racial Policies of the Detroit Housing Commission and Their Administration," MA thesis, Wayne State University, 1950, 30.

84. Hill, Oral History, ALHUA, 12–13.

85. The fullest treatment of the controversy can be found in Capeci, *Race Relations in Wartime Detroit.*

86. Young, *Hard Stuff,* 48–49; also Sugrue, *Origins of the Urban Crisis,* 73–77.

87. Dzink quoted in Hill et al., "Survey of Religious and Racial Conflict Forces in Detroit," 35–36.

88. Dzink to C. F. Palmer of the U.S. Housing Authority (n.d.), quoted in Charles S. Johnson and Fisk University Social Science Institute, *To Stem This Tide: A Survey of Racial Tension Areas in the United States* (Boston: Pilgrim Press, 1943), 51; Capeci, *Race Relations in Wartime Detroit,* 78–79.

89. Hill Papers, Box 1, ALHUA; Jenkins, "The Racial Policies of the Detroit Housing Commission," 54–57; *Detroit Tribune,* February 24, 1942; CRC Collection, Box 26, ALHUA; Meier and Rudwick, *Black Detroit,* 176–81.

90. *Detroit News,* March 3, 17, 18, 1942; Capeci, *Race Relations in Wartime Detroit,* 132–35; Meier and Rudwick, *Black Detroit,* 185–87; Hill Papers, Box 1, ALHUA.

91. Bledsoe, Oral History, ALHUA, 6.

92. Martin, *Michigan Chronicle,* February 14, 1942; telegrams in Mayor's Office Papers, 1942, BHC.

93. C. E. LaReau to Hill, March 20, 1942, and Hill to LaReau, March 24, 1942, Hill Papers, Box 1, ALHUA.

94. "To Loyal and Patriotic Polish Americans Living Near Sojourner Truth Homes" (1942), in Hill Papers, Box 1, ALHUA.

95. Williams, "Hell-Brewers of Detroit," 6.

96. Belfrage, *A Faith to Free the People,* 260–61; Stanley and Margaret Nowak to Dr. Leslie Bechtel, December 5, 1944, Nowak Collection, Box 4, ALHUA. Fr. Malcolm Dade was also a supporter. He invited Williams to give the annual Labor Sunday address at St. Cyprian's in 1943. See Dade to Williams, July 5, 1943, as well as Dade to Williams, January 26, 1945, Williams Papers, Box 4, ALHUA.

97. Hill to Reverend Burnett Magruder, February 4, 1943, in Williams Collection, Box 18, ALHUA.

98. On the reordination ceremony, see *Detroit News,* May 2, 1965. For their correspondence, see, for example, Hill to Williams, January 7, 1948, and October 17, 1965, and Williams to Hill, April 1, 1965, all in Williams Papers, Box 10, ALHUA.

99. Williams and Bill Troy, "People's Institute of Applied Religion," copy in Williams Collection, Box 18, ALHUA; as well as Mark Naison's two-part series, "Claude and Joyce Williams: Pilgrims of Justice," which was published in *Southern Exposure* 1:3–4 (1974), copies in Williams Papers, Box 22. More complete biographies include Anthony Dunbar, *Against the Grain: Southern Radicals and Prophets, 1929–1959* (Charlottesville: University Press of Virginia, 1981); and Cedric Belfrage's biography, *A Faith to Free the People.*

100. Naison, "Claude and Joyce Williams," 2–3; Dunbar, *Against the Grain,* 29–33.

101. Dunbar's *Against the Grain* provides a collective biographical portrait of these southern radicals and their impact on labor, especially the STFU, and civil rights, especially the Highlander Folk School.

102. Adams, interview with author, Detroit, July 12, 1993. The best explication of Williams's theology is probably Belfrage, *A Faith to Free the People;* and his *South of God.* See also Robert Elwood Wenger, "Social Aspects of American Christianity, 1930–1960," MA thesis, Southern Methodist University, 1962.

103. Dunbar, *Against the Grain,* chaps. 4 and 5; Naison, "Claude and Joyce Williams," 4–5. On the STFU and southern radicalism in general, see Kelley, *Hammer and Hoe,* chap. 9.

104. Niebuhr to Ward Rogers of the STFU, September 5, 1934; Ward to Niebuhr, September 15, 1934; Niebuhr to Williams, January 17, 1935; Williams to Niebuhr, January 2, 1935, all in Williams Papers, Box 1, ALHUA. See also Naison, "Claude and Joyce Williams," 4–7.

105. Naison, "Claude and Joyce Williams," 6–7; Williams and Troy, "People's Institute of Applied Religion," 48–50. Copies of many of the charts developed during this period and later are collected in Williams Papers, Box 18, ALHUA. In subsequent years, the charts were produced by Visual Education Press (VEP) in New York City. VEP to Williams, April 9, 1943, Williams Papers, Box 2, ALHUA.

106. Williams and Troy, "People's Institute of Applied Religion," 50–51; Naison, "Claude and Joyce Williams," 9–11. The correspondence between Uphaus and Williams is extensive and scattered throughout the Williams Papers. Pope is listed as a PIAR sponsor on letterhead from 1941; see Pope to Williams, n.d. (ca. 1943), Box 2, Williams Papers, ALHUA.

107. Williams and Troy, "People's Institute of Applied Religion," 48.

108. Naison, "Claude and Joyce Williams," 8–10.

109. Williams to Henry D. Jones, April 3, 1942, in Williams Papers, Box 2, ALHUA.

110. Hill et al., "Survey of Religious and Racial Conflict Forces in Detroit," 116–17. One of the survey's authors, A. L. Campbell, had joined the PIAR in the South and come to Detroit with Williams during the war.

111. "Speech by Virgil Vanderburg—Shop Preacher, Brotherhood Squadron," n.d., Williams Papers, Box 23, ALHUA; "Workers at Worship," *Detroit News,* April 25, 1942; *Daily Worker,* July 5, 1943; Williams and Troy, "People's Institute of Applied Religion," 52.

112. Babson et al., *Working Detroit,* 118.

113. Smith Oral History, MHC, 28.

114. *Wage Earner,* June 11, 1943; "Detroit Is Dynamite," *Life,* August 17, 1942; Walter White quoted in *Detroit Free Press,* June 4, 1943.

115. There have been many fine accounts of the Detroit riot. Among the best are Harvard Sitkoff, "The Detroit Race Riot of 1943," *Michigan History* 53 (fall 1968): 29–48; Robert Shogun and Tom Craig, *The Detroit Race Riot: A Study in Violence* (Philadelphia: Temple University Press, 1964); and the very thorough Dominic J. Capeci, Jr. and Martha Wilkerson, *Layered Violence: The Detroit Rioters of 1943* (Jackson: University Press of Mississippi, 1991).

116. On Nakane/Takahashi and the Development of Our Own, see Robert A. Hill, ed., *The FBI's RACON: Racial Conditions in the United States during World War II* (Boston: Northeastern University Press, 1995), 111–12. The quotation is from "Midsummer Madness," *Detroit News,* June 22, 1943.

117. Hill, Oral History, ALHUA, 16.

118. Williams, "Someday, I'm Going Back South," *The Worker,* April 3, 1949, 3. Williams is identified simply as a "Detroit Auto Worker." On his experiences in Detroit, see Timothy Tyson, *Radio Free Dixie: Robert F. Williams and the Roots of Black Power* (Chapel Hill: University of North Carolina Press, 1999), 37–42.

119. Martin, "Detroit—Still Dynamite," *Crisis* 51 (January 1944): 10.

120. Jeffries quoted in Carol O. Smith and Stephen B. Sarasohn, "Hate Propaganda in Detroit," *Public Opinion Quarterly* 10 (spring 1946): 30.

121. Ibid.

CHAPTER FOUR

1. Peter J. Kellogg, "Civil Rights Consciousness in the 1940s," *Historian* 42 (1979): 18–41; Donald R. McCoy and Richard T. Ruetten, *Quest and Response: Minority Rights and the Truman Administration* (Lawrence: University of Kansas Press, 1973); Alonzo L. Hamby, *Beyond the New Deal: Harry S. Truman and American Liberalism* (New York: Columbia University Press, 1973).

2. "Proceedings of the Fourth Congress of the Detroit Council of the National Negro Congress," June 30, 1945, NNC Vertical File, ALHUA; Thomas, *Life for Us,* 251–52.

3. Hill, campaign radio address transcript (1945), Hill Papers, Box 1, ALHUA.

4. Mary S. McAuliffe, *Crisis on the Left: Cold War Politics and American Liberals, 1947–1954* (Amherst: University of Massachusetts Press, 1978), provides a good overview of this split nationally and its role in the creation of a "new" (anticommunist) liberalism.

5. Nowak, "Address to the Members of the Michigan Committee of the American Slav Congress" (n.d.), Nowak Papers, Box 4, ALHUA. On the deportation hearings against Nowak, see Nowak, *Two Who Were There,* 193–98, 234–37.

6. Among the fullest discussions of anticommunism inside and outside the CIO is Harvey Levenstein, *Communism, Anticommunism, and the CIO* (Westport, CT: Greenwood, 1981); see also Zieger, *The CIO.* For the political implications of domestic anticommunism, see also Rosswurm, *The CIO's Left-Led Unions;* Michal Belknap, *Cold War Political Justice: The Smith Act, the Communist Party, and American Civil Liberties* (Westport, CT: Greenwood, 1977); Philip S. Foner, *Organized Labor and the Black Worker, 1619–1981* (New York: International Publishers, 1981), chap. 19, "The Cold War

Witch Hunts and the Black Worker"; and Kevin Boyle, *The UAW and the Heyday of American Liberalism, 1945–1968* (Ithaca: Cornell University Press, 1995).

7. Milton Kaufman to Jack Raskin, May 12, 1946, CRC Collection, Box 7, ALHUA; "Merger of NNC into CRC," November 21–23, 1947, CRC Collection, Box 7, ALHUA; Louis Harp, "The Case of the Detroit Congress Chapter," *Jewish Life*, August 1947, 3–4; Gerald Horne, *Communist Front? The Civil Rights Congress, 1946–1956* (London: Associated University Presses, 1988).

8. "The Next Step," *Michigan Chronicle*, March 31, 1945; Henry Lee Moon, "Political Action—City Level 1945," Michigan AFL-CIO Collection, Box 8, ALHUA. See also Moon, *Balance of Power: The Negro Vote* (New York: Doubleday, 1948), which extends the analysis into the national arena.

9. Biondi, *To Stand and Fight*, 18–21, 44–47. J. O. Holly of the Cleveland, Ohio, Outlook League came to Detroit to explain the techniques used in the Cleveland campaign (*Michigan Chronicle*, October 13, 1945). On the Outlook League in general, see Kimberley L. Phillips, *AlabamaNorth: African-American Migrants, Community, and Working-Class Activism in Cleveland, 1915–1945* (Urbana: University of Illinois Press, 1999).

10. Hill, Oral History, ALHUA, 35; Grigsby, Oral History, ALHUA, 7.

11. Gloster B. Current, "Negro Participation in August 7, 1945 Primary in Detroit," MA thesis, Wayne State University, 1949, 25–26. Current, then the executive secretary of the Detroit NAACP, was able to write his thesis from the perspective of a participant-observer in the Hill campaign.

12. Widick, *Detroit*, 3–4.

13. Current, "The Detroit Elections: Problem in Reconversion," *Crisis* 52 (November, 1945): 319.

14. Current took copious notes at the meeting. See his "Negro Participation in August 7 Primary," chap. 4 (the quotes are from an anonymous source cited on p. 32). See also "Charles C. Diggs Indicted in 1941 Race Track Plot" and "Hill Named to Run for Council," which appeared on the same page of the *Michigan Chronicle*, March 31, 1945.

15. Simmons's letter was printed in the *Michigan Chronicle*, May 5, 1945; the editorial is from the issue of May 12, 1945. See also Current, "The Detroit Elections," 320–21.

16. See, for example, "Interracial Committee Backs Hill," *Michigan Chronicle*, April 21, 1945; and "Marshall Shepard [of the CRF] Urges Support for Chas. Hill," *Michigan Chronicle*, September 15, 1945.

17. Hill's campaign literature, quoted here, is spread throughout his Red Squad File; and Hill Papers, Box 1, ALHUA. See also Hill Papers, Box 2, MHC, which has photocopies of some of the Red Squad file.

18. Davis's measure did become part of New York City's Administrative Code. See Current, "Negro Participation in August 7 Primary," 27–28.

19. Groundbreaking ceremony at Hartford, *Michigan Chronicle*, April 1, 1945; Herman Glass, a former deacon at Hartford, interview with author, Detroit, June 7, 1993; Dorothy Johnson, interview with author, Detroit, April 13, 1993. For a broader perspective, see Charles V. Hamilton, *The Black Preacher in America* (New York: Morrow, 1972), esp. chap. 5.

20. Anonymous minister quoted in Current, "Negro Participation in August 7 Primary," 48.

21. George W. Crockett, "Labor Looks Ahead," column, *Michigan Chronicle,* May 5, 1945. Crockett gives ten reasons why such a deal would be disastrous, from Jeffries's race and labor baiting to his mishandling of the affairs of the police department.

22. "CIO Picks UAW Leader in Campaign to Defeat Anti-labor Jeffries," *United Automobile Worker,* June 1, 1945; Current, "The Detroit Elections," 321; Current, "Negro Participation in August 7 Primary," 48–50; James Caldwell Foster, *The Union Politic: The CIO Political Action Committee* (Columbia: University of Missouri Press, 1975), 58–61.

23. Current, "Negro Participation in August 7 Primary," 51; "Walter Ruch, "Detroit Campaign Stirs Labor Hopes," *New York Times,* October 21, 1945; *Detroit News,* October 24, 1945; *Michigan Chronicle,* October 15, 1945; *Daily Worker,* September 17, 1945; Smith and Sarasohn, "Hate Propaganda," 32–34; Henry Lee Moon, "Detroit in Danger," *Crisis* 52 (January 1946): 12–13; Martin Halpern, *UAW Politics in the Cold War Era* (Albany: State University of New York Press, 1988), 41–44.

24. Current, "Negro Participation in August 7 Primary," 34–36; "Interracial Committee Backs Hill in Campaign," *Michigan Chronicle,* April 22, 1945; Horace White, "Facts in Our News" column, *Michigan Chronicle,* April 28, 1945.

25. Hill, Oral History, ALHUA, 18.

26. Wilbur H. Baldinger, "The UAW: Detroit's Most Dynamic Force," *PM,* September 10, 1945, 9. In a similar vein see Martin Harvey, "Frankensteen Differs Little from Jeffries," *Labor Action,* September 24, 1945.

27. *Michigan CIO News,* August 10, 1945; *Detroit News,* August 6, 8, 1945; Current, "Negro Participation in August 7 Primary," 50; Halpern, *UAW Politics,* 4.

28. Smith and Sarasohn, "Hate Propaganda," 42–43; Jeffries, drafts of radio address, Mayor's Office Papers, 1945, Box 6, BHC. A similar sentiment is expressed in a Jeffries campaign letter, on official mayoral stationery, October 10, 1945, Frankensteen Papers, Box 2, ALHUA.

29. *Detroit News,* November 5, 1945; *Home Gazette,* October 31, 1945; Smith and Sarasohn, "Hate Propaganda," 38–39; Moon, "Danger in Detroit," 12–13.

30. *Home Gazette,* October 31, 1945, in Hill Papers, "Clippings," Box 1, ALHUA.

31. "Frankensteen Says Mayor Stirs Hate," *Detroit News,* October 23, 1945. On the housing crisis and how the issues influenced local politics, see Sugrue, *Origins of the Urban Crisis,* chap. 2; the 1945 campaign is discussed on pages 80–81. See also Gary Gerstle, "Working-Class Racism: Broaden the Focus," *International Labor and Working-Class History* 44 (fall 1993): 35–37.

32. "Frankensteen and Father Coughlin: Facts Every Jewish Citizen Should Know," *North Detroiter,* October 31, 1945, copy in Frankensteen Papers, Box 3, ALHUA; Smith and Sarasohn, "Hate Propaganda," 40–42. There was, however, some justification since the two men had at one point been allies. *First Year Book and History of the A.I.W.A.* (December 1935), the program for an event held on December 14, was dedicated "To our advisor and supporter Father Charles E. Coughlin, the friend and educator of the masses." Copy in Frankensteen Papers, Box 1, ALHUA.

33. There are numerous slightly different versions of "Goodbye Christ." The one reproduced in part here is from Arnold Rampersad, *The Life of Langston Hughes,* vol. 1: *1902–1941: I, Too, Sing America* (New York: Oxford University Press, 1986), 252–53. The aftershocks of the poem are discussed on pages 390–95.

34. "Gerald Smith, Rev. Hill Debate Langston Hughes Issue," *Michigan Chronicle,* May 8, 1943.

35. Sarasohn and Smith, "Hate Propaganda," 48–51; Editorial, *Wage Earner* (n.d.), Frankensteen Papers, Box 3, ALHUA. On the election results, see Halpern, *UAW Politics,* 42–43.

36. Horace White had seen it as more of a clash of personalities, a view he presented in his *Michigan Chronicle* column, December 26, 1942. This time around, McClendon declined to run for reelection and Hill was easily elected. See *Michigan Chronicle,* December 22, 1945.

37. "Branch News," *Crisis,* December 1947; "Test for Covenants," editorial, *Crisis,* November 1947; "Branch News," *Crisis,* April 1946; Sugrue, *Origins of the Urban Crisis,* 181–83; Clement Vose, *Caucasians Only: The Supreme Court, the NAACP, and Restrictive Covenant Cases* (Berkeley: University of California Press, 1959).

38. "Detroit NAACP Cuts Left Link," *Wage Earner,* December 20, 1946. That same year Gloster Current left Detroit to become director of branches and Edward Swan took over his job as executive secretary. By 1947, apparently, the "communist threat" had dissipated. See "Detroit NAACP Swan Has the Commies Mad" (1946), Michigan AFL-CIO Collection, Box 185, ALHUA; and Wilson Record, *The NAACP and the Communist Party* (Ithaca: Cornell University Press, 1964), chap. 5.

39. "Rev. Hill Urges Unity against Cop Brutality," *Michigan Worker,* August 21, 1949; campaign literature, Red Squad File.

40. Campaign literature, Hill Red Squad File; and Hill Papers, Box 1, ALHUA. Hill's various campaigns also got ample coverage in the *Daily Worker,* whose local correspondent, William Allen, was a friend and a political ally. See, for example, the issues of August 29, 1948; June 2 and 6, 1949; and August 11 and September 12, 1949.

41. "Hill Tells Tigers: Sign Negro Players," *Michigan Worker,* September 11, 1949. Hill sent an open letter to Tiger manager Billy Evans demanding that the team desist in its unsportsmanlike behavior. See Frank Rashid Interview, in Mast, *Detroit Lives,* 147; "Virgil Gets Five Hits," *New York Times,* June 18, 1958.

42. Campaign Literature, Hill Red Squad File; "Copy of the Post Ordinance to Establish a Loyalty Investigating Committee," October 17, 1949, Michigan Committee on Civil Rights Papers, Part 3, Box 15, ALHUA. The list of individuals and organizations opposing the so-called Loyalty Amendment was long. It included members of the CRC and the Lawyers Guild, as well as the Michigan Federation of Teachers and the ADA. See the flyer "We Urge You to Vote No on 144 City Charter 'Loyalty' Amendment," Michigan Committee on Civil Rights Papers, Part 3, Box 15, ALHUA.

43. Hill was one of the signers of a national petition urging a ban on the use of atomic weapons and the control of atomic power by the United Nations, where its use would be subject to vetoes by the United States and the Soviet Union. The measure was advocated by the Soviet Union and supported by the American Communist Party. See "23 From Michigan Sign A-Bomb Plea," *Detroit Times,* December 14, 1949.

44. "Open Letter to U.S. Senator Homer Ferguson: What the Rearmament of Western Germany Means to the American People" (1951), signed by Hill, Stanley Nowak, and Isadore Starr, a local attorney. Copy in Hill's Red Square File. The letter was more than likely part of Hill's support of the leftist American Peace Crusade, an organization that opposed the Marshall Plan and the Korean War. Hill was one of the sixty-five initial sponsors of the group. See *Michigan Worker,* February 1, 1951; and "City Wide Conference Sets Program for Peace," *Detroit Times,* February 4, 1951. On

the movement in general, see Robbie Lieberman, *The Strangest Dream: Communism, Anticommunism, and the U.S. Peace Movement, 1945–1963* (Syracuse: Syracuse University Press, 2000).

45. For a more extensive analysis of the relationship between the MDCP and the Michigan CRC, see Edward Pintzuk, "Going Down Fighting: The Michigan Communist Party after World War II," PhD diss., Wayne State University, 1992, 91–96. My operative definition of a "front group" is one initiated and/or guided, though not necessarily "controlled," by the CP. The term need not have a negative connotation. In fact, as Pintzuk demonstrates, there is ample evidence that the Michigan CRC and the older Civil Rights Federation were also arms of the MDCP.

46. "Stanley Nowak to Dear Sir" (n.d.), Nowak Collection, Box 4, ALHUA; Jack Raskin to Milton Kaufman and Milton Kemnitz, August 21, 1946, CRC Collection, Box 7, ALHUA; *The Issues* (newsletter of the Michigan CRC), September 14, 1946, and "Press Release," September 4, 1946, CRC, Box 50, ALHUA; *Daily Worker,* December 23, 1946; "Draft Memorandum for Campaign for Michigan State FEPC" (n.d.), CRC Papers, Part II, Reel 26, ALHUA.

47. "Current Notes," *Michigan Chronicle,* December 14, 1946.

48. *Plymouth Beacon,* October 23, 1946.

49. Hill, "Press Release," September 14, 1946, CRC Collection, Box 50, ALHUA.

50. Hill, "Red-Baiting the FEPC to Death," *Jewish Life,* August 1947, 16.

51. Dorothy Johnson Interview; "Progress Report, Initiative Petition Campaign" (n.d.), CRC Collection, Box 50, ALHUA.

52. Committee for a State FEPC, "Press Release," November 24, 1946, CRC Collection, Box 50, ALHUA. For a similarly worded statement made by clergymen, see *Detroit News,* October 12, 1946.

53. Anne Shore to Jeffries, "Draft of the Proclamation for FEPC Day," November 9, 1946, CRC Collection, Box 50, ALHUA; Mayor's Office Papers, 1946, Box 7, BHC. The proclamation was issued on April 17, 1946, and declared a Fair Employment Practice Week from April 22–29, 1946. Jeffries also joined the National Committee to Abolish Poll-Tax and issued a proclamation declaring March 24–29, 1946, Abolish the Poll-Tax Week.

54. *Wage Earner,* October 18, 1946.

55. Bledsoe, Oral History, ALHUA, 7, 9.

56. On the lobbying efforts of the Michigan Manufacturers' Association see Fine, *Expanding the Frontiers,* chap. 1, which has a good overview of the entire campaign.

57. Hill, "Red-Baiting," 16–17; "Factional Fight Hampers FEPC," *Michigan Chronicle,* January 4, 1947; "Michigan Council for Fair Employment Legislation, Meeting of Sponsors," January 3, 1947, UAW Fair Practices Papers, Box 8, ALHUA; Stevenson, "Points of Departure," 408–12; "Michigan High Court Bars FEPC from April 7 Ballot," *UAW Fair Relations Fact Sheet,* 1:1 (March 1947); Fine, *Expanding the Frontiers,* 17–21.

58. *To Secure These Rights: The Report of the President's Committee on Civil Rights* (New York: Simon and Schuster, 1947); Schermer, "Proposals for Action," November 27, 1947, and "To Secure These Rights" (n.d.), UAW Fair Practices Papers, Box 8, ALHUA; Fine, *Expanding the Frontiers,* 20–22.

59. Wallace Campaign Letter to UAW, quoted in Norman D. Markowitz, *The Rise and Fall of the People's Century: Henry A. Wallace and American Liberalism, 1941–1948* (New York: Free Press, 1973), 271.

60. Athan Theoharis, "The Rhetoric of Politics: Foreign Policy, Internal Security, and Domestic Politics in the Truman Era, 1945–1950," in *Politics and Policies of the Truman Administration,* ed. Barton J. Bernstein (Chicago: Quadrangle, 1970), 242–68; Peter H. Irons, "American Business and the Origins of McCarthyism: The Cold War Crusade of the United States Chamber of Commerce," in *The Specter: Original Essays on the Cold War and the Origins of McCarthyism,* ed. Robert Griffith and Athan Theoharis (New York: New Viewpoint, 1974), 172–89.

61. Barton Bernstein, "Walter Reuther and the General Motors Strike of 1945–1946," *Michigan History* 49 (September 1965): 260–65; David M. Oshinsky, "Labor's Cold War: The CIO and the Communists," in Griffith and Theoharis, *The Specter,* 116–51; Halpern, *UAW Politics in the Cold War Era,* chap. 4; Lichtenstein, *The Most Dangerous Man in America,* 228–46.

62. Among the best studies of the postwar strike wave is George Lipsitz, *A Rainbow at Midnight: Labor and Culture in the 1940s* (Urbana: University of Illinois Press, 1994), chaps. 5, 6, and 7.

63. Public Laws, Ch120, 80th Cong., 1st sess., 1947, 144; U.S. Congress, House, Committee on Education and Labor, *Amendments to the National Labor Relations Act, Hearings,* 80th Cong., 1st sess., 1947, 2129–39.

64. Halpern, *UAW Politics in the Era of the Cold War,* chap. 6; Keeran, *The Communist Party and the Auto Workers Union,* chap. 6.

65. On Reuther's relationship with the Left, see Kevin Boyle, "Building the Vanguard: Walter Reuther and Radical Politics in 1936," *Labor History* 30 (summer 1989): 433–48; and Lichtenstein, *The Most Dangerous Man in America,* chap. 3.

66. "Ernest Goodman and the National Lawyers Guild" and Ernest Goodman, "Reflections on the Dismissal of the Attica Indictments," in *A Tribute to Ernest Goodman, Saturday, December 13, 1980,* Norman McRea Collection, Box 16, ALHUA.

67. Prickett, "Communism and Factionalism," 257–77; Lichtenstein, *The Most Dangerous Man in America,* 251–54, 317–23.

68. Horace Sheffield, Oral History Interview by Herbert Hill and Roberta McBride, Detroit, July 24, 1968, ALHUA, 8–9, 10.

69. Hill, Red Squad File; "60 Leading Ministers Join Campaign for Wallace-Taylor," *Michigan Worker,* August 14, 1948, and October 3, 1948. On the religious aspects of the campaign and the involvement of clergy, see Roy, *Communism and the Churches,* 206–9.

70. *Daily Worker,* August 15, 1948.

71. Graham J. White, *Henry A. Wallace: His Search for a New World Order* (Chapel Hill: University of North Carolina Press, 1995), 274. On Wallace and the Progressive Party, see also Curtis Daniel MacDougall, *Gideon's Army* (New York: Marzani and Munsell, 1965); and Markowitz, *The Rise and Fall of the People's Century.*

72. White and Maze's *Henry A. Wallace* does a better job than most with the religious and spiritual dimensions of Wallace's life. Henry A. Wallace, *Statesmanship and Religion* (New York: Round Table Press, 1934), is a fascinating volume that reveals the extent of Wallace's engagement with Old Testament prophets, especially Amos and Isaiah.

73. "Sadowski, Hill and Nowak Together in Primary," *Daily Worker,* September 12, 1948. George Sadowski was running for reelection to Congress. Hill's slogan was "End Jim Crow in the Common Council." Crockett served as his campaign manager. See "Hill States Issues Facing Council Hopefuls," *Michigan Chronicle,* September 4, 1948; and *Michigan Chronicle,* August 21, 1948.

74. Rank and File Committee for Wallace, Ford Local 406, "Read It for Yourself!" Nat Ganley Collection, Box 2, ALHUA; Halpern, *UAW Politics in the Cold War Era,* 243–45.

75. "No Third Party in '48: Text of a Radio Address by CIO President Philip Murray over the National Broadcasting Company, January 30, 1948," CRC Collection, Box 97; CIO-PAC, press release, January 22, 1948, and Jack Kroll to Dear Sir and Brother, January 30, 1948, UAW-Political Action Division Papers, Box 1; Reuther et al., To All Members of UAW-CIO Local Unions 453, October 22, 1948, UAW-Political Action Division Papers, Box 2, all in ALHUA. The letter from Reuther and his colleagues is representative of many that were sent out, stating: "Because we are advised that some of the officers of your Local Union refuse to cooperate 100% with UAW-CIO and CIO-PAC in this election campaign, we are taking this opportunity of coming directly to you to ask your personal participation in the International Union's political action program."

76. UAW-CIO Public Relations Department, Political Action Resolution Adopted by International Executive Board, March 3, 1948, UAW-Political Action Division Papers, Box 2, ALHUA; "Detroit ADA Organizing Committee" (n.d.), and ADA, "General Purposes," March 18, 1947, ACTU Papers, Box 9, ALHUA; *ADA Review* 1:5 (November 1947), Michigan AFL-CIO, Box 185, ALHUA; "The A.D.A. and the Liberal-Democratic Movement in the Past Decade," Reinhold Niebuhr Papers, Box 1, Library of Congress; Record, *Race and Radicalism,* 156–58.

77. Young, *Hard Stuff,* 110–11.

78. Hill ran for Congress in 1951 but did not get beyond the primary. See *Michigan Worker,* July 22 and 29, September 9, 1951. Hill did have the support of Ford Local 600. See *Detroit Tribune,* September 9, 1951.

79. Wallace quoted in Nowak, *Two Who Were There,* 222–23; see also "Nowak Faces Party Ouster," *Detroit News,* September 2, 1948.

80. Patterson to Wilkins, November 14, 1949; Wilkins to Patterson, November 22, 1949; Patterson to Wilkins, November 29, 1949, all in NAACP Papers, II, A, Box 195, Library of Congress; Record, *Race and Radicalism,* 180–81.

81. Quoted in Hershel Hartman, "FEPC Crusaders in Washington," *Jewish Life,* March 1950, 7. See also Biondi, *To Stand and Fight,* 165–68; Record, *Race and Radicalism,* 153–56.

82. "Publicity" (n.d.), NAACP Papers, II, A, Box 193, Library of Congress.

83. Hartman, "FEPC Crusaders," 7.

84. Patterson to Raskin, November 9, 1949, National CRC Papers, Part II, Reel 27, ALHUA.

85. Pintzuk, "Going Down Fighting," 93–94, 135–37. Pintzuk was able to interview Raskin about the relationship between the CP and the CRC and quotes from it extensively. See Shore to Aubrey Grossman, July 10, 1950, CRC Papers, Reel 47; and Horne, *Communist Front?* 289–93.

86. Arthur McPhaul, Oral History, ALHUA, 7–8; Interview with author, Detroit, April 9, 1994.

87. Bledsoe, Oral History, ALHUA, 5–6; McPhaul, Oral History, ALHUA, 18–19.

88. "Minutes and Correspondence, Executive Board Meeting," September 15, 1950, CRC Collection, Box 95, ALHUA.

89. Schrecker, "McCarthyism and the Decline of American Communism,

1945–1960," in Brown et al., *New Studies on the Politics and Culture of U.S. Communism,* 132.

90. Pintzuk, "Going Down Fighting," 98–104; N-CRC Papers, Boxes 81 and 82, microfilm, Michigan CRC Collection, Box 62, ALHUA.

91. "Coroner's Jury to Sift Shooting," *Detroit News,* June 12, 1948. The same edition carried a picture from Mosely's funeral under the banner "Communist Leaders at Boy's Funeral" with an arrow denoting the MDCP's Carl Winter. Detroit Chapter, Michigan Committee on Civil Rights, "Leon Mosely Case," *Bulletin,* January 5, 1949, in JCC Papers, Box 418, ALHUA; "Report on Leon Mosely Case by Edward Swann, Executive Secretary NAACP" (n.d.), in JCC Papers, Box 418, ALHUA; Pintzuk, "Going Down Fighting," 105–9.

92. Hill quoted in Pintzuk, "Going Down Fighting," 107.

93. Starobin quoted in Schrecker, *New Studies in the Politics and Culture of U.S. Communism,* 133; see also Starobin, *American Communism in Crisis* (Cambridge: Harvard University Press, 1972). He had been the foreign editor of the *Daily Worker.* The Michigan Six were Saul Wellman, a Spanish Civil War vet; Thomas Dennis; Nat Ganley; Philip Schatz; Helen Winter, the wife of Carl Winter, who was jailed as a result of the first Smith Act trial in New York; and William ("Billy") Allen, editor of the *Michigan Worker* and Michigan correspondent for the *Daily Worker.* See press releases, October 19 [1953] and October 27, 1953, CRC Collection, Box 36, ALHUA; and Goodman, Crockett, Eden, and Robb to Anne Shore, November 10, 1953, on payment, or lack thereof, for legal services, CRC Collection, Box 36, ALHUA.

94. McPhaul, "HUAC in Detroit" (n.d.), CRC Collection, Box 75, ALHUA.

95. "Fact Sheet on the McPhaul Case" (n.d.), CRC Collection, Box 94, ALHUA.

96. "6 Subpoenaed for Red Quiz," *Detroit News,* February 19, 1955; "Women Hunted in Red Quiz after Fleeing Subpoena," *Detroit News,* February 26, 1952; "Missing Woman Teacher Makes Surprise Appearance at Inquiry,"*Detroit News,* February 27, 1952.

97. HUAC, *Hearings on Communism in Detroit,* I, 2891; "Congressman Rakes Rev. Hill as Red," *Detroit Free Press,* February 27, 1952; "Red Inquiry Widened to 6 Michigan Cities, Rev. Hill Also Heard," *Detroit News,* February 27, 1952; "Negro Minister Linked to Party," *Detroit News,* February 28, 1952.

98. "Majority of Ministers Backing Rev. Hill's Position," *Detroit Courier,* March 8, 1952.

99. "The Rev. Hill Answers Rev. White," *Michigan Chronicle,* December 1, 1951; "Rev. Hill Too Hot to Handle," *Detroit Courier,* March 1, 1952.

100. Dade's statement was reprinted in "Colored Pastor Assails Reds," *Detroit Times,* February 29, 1952; and "Negro Pastor Defends Race," *Detroit News,* February 29, 1952. A longer version, "The Detroit Negro Spurns Communism," was submitted to (and rejected by) the *Christian Century.* A copy is in Dade's Papers, Box 5, BHC. Dade was named to the city's Loyalty Commission in 1949. *Detroit Free Press,* February 1, 1949.

101. On the Turner testimony, see *Detroit News,* February 27, 1952; and "A Warrior for Civil Rights," *Detroit Free Press,* March 9, 1983.

102. Dorothy Johnson, interview with author. Johnson was a longtime member of Hartford and served as Hill's personal secretary during the 1950s. Hill's Red Squad File does, however, include a few flyers posted near his church asking people to stay

away from his "Red Church," as well as letters asking for a full investigation of his activities. The source of these flyers and letters, none of which was signed, was never ascertained. Young discusses the circulation of recordings of his testimony in *Hard Stuff,* 130–31; see also Smith, *Dancing in the Streets,* 242–43.

103. "Five 'Pro Commies' Fired from Local 600," *Detroit News,* March 22, 1952; "Background of Senator Nowak Case" (n.d.), ACTU Papers, Box 29, ALHUA.

104. Simmons, Oral History, ALHUA, 10.

105. Crockett in Mast, *Detroit Lives,* 168.

106. *Labor Action,* March 4 and 17, 1952.

107. *Labor Action,* March 12, 1951; Widick, *Detroit,* chap. 8.

108. Irving Richter, "How a Young Pilot Beat a Disloyalty Charge," *Detroit Courier,* May 5, 1951. The magazine section carried a full spread on the case (Hill, interview with author).

109. Goodman in Moon, *Untold Tales, Unsung Heroes,* 266.

110. Young, *Hard Stuff,* 110–14; "The Buck Dinner: 50 Years of Dedication to the Causes of Equality, Peace, and Justice, 1919 to 1979," commemorative pamphlet, Norman McRae Collection, Box 16, ALHUA.

111. "Rev. Williams, Reordained, Vows Continued Rights Fight," *Daily Worker,* May 1965; "Taint of Heresy Fades on the Way to Triumph," *Detroit News,* May 2, 1965. Joyce and Claude Williams greeted another generation of southern civil rights activists with open arms. See, for example, "A White Man's View of Black Power: Claude Williams Calls the Concept a Positive Development," *National Guardian,* December 3, 1966; and Naison, "Claude and Joyce Williams," 7–9.

112. Hill to Members of Hartford (n.d.), Hill Papers, Box 1, ALHUA.

113. Bledsoe, Oral History, ALHUA, 2; "Robeson Sings and Speaks to 6000 in Detroit," *Freedomways,* May 1953; "Robeson at Rev. Hill Fete, Blasts People's Enemies," *Michigan Worker,* November 29, 1953. As late as 1963, Hill's church was open to communists. See, for example, "Ben Davis Fights for Negro Rights as Red Leader," *Detroit Free Press,* May 3, 1963, about Davis's appearance at Hartford. This observation finds its way into most conversations about Hill. In recent years, Hartford has honored Hill's willingness to stand by Robeson. Until it was destroyed by a fire, a large and beautiful portrait of Robeson was prominently displayed in the Charles A. Hill Chapel at the church's new facilities on the northwest side of Detroit.

114. Wynn, *The NAACP versus Negro Revolutionary Protest: A Comparative Study of the Effectiveness of Each Movement* (New York: Exposition Press, 1955), 47, n. 56.

115. This wonderful description of Hill is from Abner W. Berry, "Behind Detroit's Elections," *New Masses,* November 6, 1945, 5. On the American Committee for Protection of Foreign Born, see John W. Sherman's *A Communist Front at Mid-Century: The American Committee for Protection of Foreign Born, 1933–1959* (Westport, CT: Praeger, 2001).

116. Babson et al., *Working Detroit,* 156–65.

117. Young quoted in Mindy Thompson, "The National Negro Labor Council: A History," Occasional Paper no. 27 (New York: American Institute for Marxist Studies, 1978), 13; see also Foner, *Organized Labor and the Black Worker,* chap. 20.

118. Brown quoted in Thompson, "The National Negro Labor Council," 25; "Call to the Founding Convention of the National Negro Labor Council," CRC Collection, Box 2, ALHUA.

119. "Brownell Adds to Our Country's Shame: Statement by National Negro Labor Council" (New York: NNLC, 1956), Ernest Thompson Collection, Schomburg Center, New York Public Library.

120. Thompson, "The National Negro Labor Council," 35–40; Jones, *Labor of Love, Labor of Sorrow*, 266–68; Hill, Oral History, ALHUA, 7–8.

121. "Special FEPC Bulletin: To All Members and Friends of the Civil Rights Congress, and the Michigan Committee for Protection of Foreign Born" (fund-raising letter), July 28, 1951, CRC Collection, Box 49, ALHUA; *Detroit Courier*, May 5, 1951.

122. "25 Groups Back FEPC," *Detroit Courier*, June 6, 1951; "FEPC Urged to Foil Reds," *Detroit News*, June 27, 1951.

123. *Detroit Tribune*, August 14, 1951; *Detroit Courier*, August 4, 1951; *Michigan Chronicle*, July 28, 1951; Reuther quoted in Foner, *Organized Labor and the Black Worker*, 295.

124. "FEPC Petition Kept off Ballot," *Detroit News*, October 6, 1951.

125. Fine, *Expanding the Frontiers*, chap. 2, provides a good overview of how the act was finally enacted.

126. Young quoted in Thompson, "The National Negro Labor Council," 73–75.

CHAPTER FIVE

1. Young quoted in Thompson, "National Negro Labor Council," 79–80.

2. In 1956 there were no more than twenty thousand party members in the United States. By 1958, in the wake of Nikita Khrushchev's 1956 revelations of Stalin's crimes and the invasion of Hungary, party membership dropped to only three thousand. See Maurice Isserman, *If I Had a Hammer . . .: The Death of the Old Left and Birth of the New Left* (New York: Basic Books, 1987).

3. See, for example, Loren Miller, "Farewell to Liberals: A Negro View," *Nation*, October 20, 1962, 235–38.

4. For a broader perspective see Eva Mueller, *Location Decisions and Industrial Mobility in Michigan* (Ann Arbor: Institute for Social Research, University of Michigan, 1982); and Barry Bluestone and Bennett Harrison, *The Deindustrialization of America: Plant Closings, Community Abandonment, and the Dismantling of Basic Industry* (New York: Basic Books, 1982).

5. Babson et al., *Working Detroit*, 160–63.

6. Joe T. Darden, Richard Child Hill, June Thomas, and Richard Thomas, *Detroit: Race and Uneven Development* (Philadelphia: Temple University Press, 1987), 100–103.

7. Nancy Gabin, "Women Workers and the UAW in the Post–World War II Period, 1945–1954," *Labor History* 21 (winter 1979–80): 5–30.

8. Allen quoted in Babson et al., *Working Detroit*, 114; Foner, *Organized Labor and the Black Worker*, 309–11; Jones, *Labor of Love, Labor of Sorrow*, chap. 7.

9. When government economists assessed these conditions, they did so in terms of the Metropolitan Detroit region, which presented a rosier picture and tended to obscure the actual conditions in the city proper. See Widick, *Detroit*, chap. 9; and Darden et al., *Detroit*, chap. 2.

10. DCCR, "The Negro in Detroit" (1961), DCCR Collection, Series III, Box 12, ALHUA; Joel D. Aberbach and J. L. Walker, *Race in the City: Political Trust and Public*

Policy in the New Urban System (Boston: Little, Brown 1973), 7–17. See also Amy Maria Kenyon, *Dreaming Suburbia: Detroit and the Production of Postwar Space and Culture* (Detroit: Wayne State University Press, 2004).

11. Darden et al., *Detroit*, 202–13. Crockett had been in danger of losing his practice because of his defense of communists and suspected communists in the 1950s. He managed to overcome the negative associations and was elected to Recorder's Court in 1966. William T. Patrick Jr. was the son of the attorney for whom Reverend Hill had apprenticed back in the 1910s before deciding to devote his life to the ministry.

12. "Biography of Rev. Dr. Nicholas Hood, Sr.," copy in author's possession; Hood, interview with author, Detroit, June 2, 2005.

13. Herb Boyd in Mast, *Detroit Lives*, 78; Berry Gordy, *To Be Loved: The Music, the Magic, the Memories of Motown* (New York: Warner Books, 1994), 169; Smith, *Dancing in the Streets*, 6–8.

14. DCCR, "The Negro in Detroit"; Darden et al., *Detroit*, 151–200. See also George Lipsitz, *The Possessive Investment in Whiteness: How White People Benefit from Identity Politics* (Philadelphia: Temple University Press, 1998).

15. Sugrue, *Origins of the Urban Crisis*, 49–50. Jeffries served from 1940 to 1948, followed by Eugene Van Antwerp, 1948–50; Albert Cobo, 1950–57; Louis Miriani, 1957–62; and Jerome P. Cavanagh, 1962–70.

16. Harold Black, "Urban Renewal: A Program Involving a Multiplicity of Participants," PhD diss., University of Michigan, 1973; Sugrue, *Origins of the Urban Crisis*, chap. 7; Darden et al., *Detroit*, 166–70.

17. Young, *Hard Stuff*, 144.

18. "Twelfth Street Study" (1961), Jerome P. Cavanagh Papers, Box A–8, ALHUA; George Henderson, "Twelfth Street: An Analysis of a Change Neighborhood," *Phylon* 25 (1964): 91–96. On the often tense relationship between Blacks and Jews in the area, see Stevenson, "Points of Departure," chap. 8; and Sugrue, *Origins of the Urban Crisis*, 242–45.

19. Hood, interview with author.

20. Ibid.; Darden et al., *Detroit*, 172–73; "Plymouth Congregation Meets Community Needs," *Michigan Chronicle*, August 4, 1962. See also *Michigan Chronicle*, February 3 and June 16, 1962.

21. Hood, interview with author. Details on the church's housing ministry can be found on the Plymouth Web site: http://www.puccdetroit.org.

22. Lemann, *The Promised Land: The Great Black Migration and How it Changed America* (New York: Vintage, 1992), 109–222.

23. Hood, e-mail to author, May 29, 2005, in my possession.

24. Morris, *Origins of the Civil Rights Movement*, chap. 2; Steven M. Miller, "The Montgomery Bus Boycott: A Case Study in the Emergence and Career of a Social Movement," in *The Walking City: The Montgomery Bus Boycott, 1955–1956*, ed. David J. Garrow (Brooklyn: Carlson, 1989), 381–605; Douglas Brinkley, *Rosa Parks* (New York: Penguin, 2000).

25. NNLC, "An Open Letter to the AFL-CIO: The Only Road to Labor Unity Is Equality and Democracy for All" (1955), CRC Collection Box 2, ALHUA.

26. "Meany Vows Fight on Bias When Labor's Ranks Unite," *New York Times*, February 27, 1955; "Report of the Resolutions Committee on Civil Rights, 1955," in *Proceedings of the First Constitutional Convention of the AFL-CIO* (New York: AFL-CIO, 1955),

109–13; "AFL-CIO Seats Two Negroes," *Pittsburgh Courier,* December 5, 1955. All of these are reprinted in Philip S. Foner and R. L. Lewis, eds., *Black Workers: A Documentary History from Colonial Times to the Present* (Philadelphia: Temple University Press, 1989).

27. "AFL-CIO Civil Rights Committee," CIO Secretary-Treasurer's Collection, Box 195, ALHUA; James Gross, "NAACP, AFL-CIO and the Negro Worker," PhD diss., University of Wisconsin, 1962; Foner, *Organized Labor and the Black Worker,* 312–22; Bruce Nelson *Divided We Stand: American Workers and the Struggle for Black Equality* (Princeton: Princeton University Press, 2001), 232–43, 294. The AFL-CIO and certain member unions, including the UAW, did contribute funds to civil rights organizations, although the relationship between labor and the New Left was often strained at points. See Peter B. Levy, *The New Left and Labor in the 1960s* (Urbana: University of Illinois Press, 1994).

28. King, *Stride toward Freedom,* in *A Testament of Hope: The Essential Writings of Martin Luther King Jr.,* ed. James M. Washington (San Francisco: Harper and Row, 1986), 476.

29. This critique of the southern movement has been put forth in a number of studies, most notably, Frances Fox Piven and Richard A. Cloward, *Poor People's Movements: Why They Succeed, How They Fail* (New York: Vintage, 1979). For a general summary of this argument, see James MacGregor Burns and Stewart Burns, *A People's Charter: The Pursuit of Rights in America* (New York: Knopf, 1991), 325–38.

30. On the early involvement of Nixon, Rustin, and Parks, see Taylor Branch, *Parting the Waters: America in the King Years, 1954–63* (New York: Simon and Schuster, 1988), chap. 5; and John D'emilio, *Lost Prophet: The Life and Times of Bayard Rustin* (New York: Free Press, 2003).

31. Flyer for "Freedom and Justice Rally," November 13, 1955, and "Lecture Notes—Till," Dillard Collection, Box 3, ALHUA; Stephen J. Whitefield, *Death in the Delta: The Story of Emmett Till* (Baltimore: Johns Hopkins University Press, 1991).

32. Denby, *Indignant Heart* (Detroit: Wayne State University Press, 1989), 184–85.

33. Dillard in Moon, *Untold Tales, Unsung Heroes,* 157–60; Dillard interview with author, Detroit, August 21, 1993.

34. "An Open Letter to the White People of Mississippi" (1956), "Records of the Citizen Committee" (1955–56), and "Lecture Notes," all in Dillard Papers, Box 2, ALHUA. On the anti-Stalinist Left in general, see Alan Wald, *The New York Intellectuals: The Rise and Decline of the Anti-Stalinist Left from the 1930 to the 1960s* (Chapel Hill: University of North Carolina Press, 1987), chap. 10; and Robert J. Alexander, *International Trotskyism, 1929–1985: A Documented Analysis of the Movement* (Durham: Duke University Press, 1991), 834–42.

35. "A Black official," quoted in Sidney Fine, *Violence in the Model City: The Cavanagh Administration, Race Relations, and the Detroit Riot of 1967* (Ann Arbor: University of Michigan Press, 1989), 37.

36. Arthur L. Johnson, "A Brief Account of the Detroit Branch of the NAACP" (1958), NAACP Papers, III, Box C64, Library of Congress; Detroit Branch Annual Report, 1952, NAACP Papers, II, Box A90, Library of Congress.

37. On the NALC see Foner, *Organized Labor and the Black Worker,* chap. 22; and Nelson, *Divided We Stand,* 272–75. Copies of the NALC founding program, as well as its constitution, are in Dillard Papers, Box 2, ALHUA.

38. Horace Sheffield, Oral History Interview with Hebert Hill and Roberta McBride, Detroit, July 24, 1968, 7–8, 10 (used by permission of Herbert Hill). Sheffield was reportedly recruited into the SWP by Edward Keemer, a Black Trotskyist and well-known doctor in Detroit who performed abortions. See his autobiography, *Confessions of a Pro-Life Abortionist* (Detroit: Vinco Press, 1980). See also Erwin Baur to Alan Wald, August 18, 2000 (used by permission of Alan Wald).

39. On the TULC in general, see Thompson, *Whose Detroit?* 49–59. It is also the case, as Thompson notes on page 51, that "some TULC leaders hailed from the historically combative and left-wing Local 600."

40. *Vanguard,* September 1961. The *Vanguard* was the official paper of the TULC.

41. Dillard in Moon, *Untold Tales, Unsung Heroes,* 158; Sheffield quoted in Babson et al., *Working Detroit,* 170. There was an exchange of charges of countercharges in the pages of the *Michigan Chronicle,* August 4 and 11, 1962.

42. "Trade Union Leadership Council: Experiment in Community Action—Interviews with Robert Battle III and Horace Sheffield," *New University Thought,* October 1962, 25.

43. Dillard, interview with author. This lack of public discussion was confirmed by Marilynn Adams (interview with author, Detroit, February 21, 1995). White labor activist and Shachtmanite (yet another group that split from the SWP) B. J. Widick was also active in the TULC and served a stint on its Executive Board (Widick, interview with author, Ann Arbor, Michigan, November 5, 1993).

44. Foner, *Organized Labor and the Black Worker,* 330–37; also Cornelius C. Thomas, "The Trade Union Leadership Council: Black Workers Respond to the United Automobile Workers, 1957–1967," *New Politics* 38 (winter 2005): 124–37.

45. Dillard, "Negro Report," July 4, 1954, Dillard Papers, Box 3, "SWP" Folder, ALHUA; "Questions of the American Revolution: Conversations in Detroit between James Boggs and Xavier Nicholas" (spring 1973), 9–10, copy in the Labadie Collection, University of Michigan.

46. "Discrimination Action Committee" (n.d.) and Records of the Committee, Dillard Papers, Box 1, ALHUA.

47. Johnson in Mast, *Detroit Lives,* 199.

48. Oscar and Dolores Paskal, interview with author, Detroit, March 19, 1994; Dillard, interview with author. See also Boggs in Moon, *Untold Tales, Unsung Heroes,* 154–55.

49. Kimberly Thomas, "Hunger for Justice Helped Integrate Restaurants," *Detroit News,* February 20, 1995.

50. Marilynn Adams, interview with author, Detroit, February 12, 1994. Adams, whose married name is Dillard, is the author's mother. She is not related to Ernie and Jessie Dillard, who were nonetheless close friends and mentors.

51. United States Commission on Civil Rights, *Hearings on Housing and Job Discrimination against Negroes,* December 14, 1960, 86–89; "US Rights Unit Gets Full Report on Job Bias in the City," *Michigan Chronicle,* October 24, 1960; *Detroit News,* October 15, 1960; Thompson, *Whose Detroit?* 49–51.

52. Hill, "AFL-CIO and the Black Worker: Twenty-Five Years after the Merger," *Journal of Intergroup Relations* (spring 1982): 15–17; "Meany Must Go," *Michigan Chronicle,* November 11, 1962; Stevenson, "Points of Departure," chap. 8.

53. *Vanguard*, quoted in Babson et al., *Working Detroit*, 165–66.

54. The TULC's Willie Baxter issued a stinging rebuke to Meany ("Black Workers Answers Meany on Civil Rights"), and Chris Alston spoke at a Friday Night Labor Forum on Meany and civil rights. See *Michigan Militant*, November 14, 1959; and Foner, *Organized Labor and the Black Worker*, 235.

55. The complex relationship between the UAW and the civil rights movement is slightly beyond the scope of this present study, and the debate about it continues to be waged, especially between historians Nelson Lichtenstein and Herbert Hill. See Lichtenstein, *The Most Dangerous Man in Detroit*, esp. ch. 16; Hill, "Lichtenstein's Fictions: Meany, Reuther, and the 1964 Civil Rights Act," *New Politics* 7 (summer 1998): 83–102; "Lichtenstein's Fictions Revisited: Race and the New Labor History," *New Politics* 7 (winter 1999): 148–63; and Lichtenstein, "Walter Reuther in Black and White: A Rejoinder to Herbert Hill," *New Politics* 7 (winter 1999): 133–47.

56. "Cavanagh Campaign," *Vanguard*, November 1, 1961; *Detroit News*, October 16, 1961; "TULC in '5 Plus 1' Campaign," *Michigan Chronicle*, October 21, 1961; City Election Committee, "Official Canvas of Votes Cast, September 12, 1961 Primary," in Dillard Papers, Box 2, ALHUA; Fine, *Violence in the Model City*, 12–16; Widick, *Detroit*, 151–56; Babson et al., *Working Detroit*, 165–66; Thompson, *Whose Detroit?* 30–32.

57. On Sheffield and Spottswood, see "It Began with a Conversation," *Michigan Chronicle*, January 6, 1961; see also *Michigan Chronicle*, November 11, 18, 1961.

58. Tom Nicholson, "Detroit's Surprising Mayor," *Harper's*, December 1963; Fine, *Frank Murphy;* Fine, *Violence in the Model City*.

59. Edwards quoted in *Kerner Report: The 1968 Report of the National Advisory Commission on Civil Disorders* (New York: Pantheon, [1968] 1988), 85.

60. Thompson, *Whose Detroit?* 24; Dorothy B. Kaufman, *The First Freedom Ride: The Walter Bergman Story* (Detroit: ACLU Fund Press, 1989); "A Deserved Tribute to Dr. Bergman," *Michigan Chronicle*, March 17, 1962. On Liuzzo, see Babson et al., *Working Detroit*, 165.

61. *Michigan Militant*, March 13, 1960; Thompson, *Whose Detroit?* chap. 2. The *Michigan Militant* was the local SWP newspaper.

62. TULC flyer and TULC to "Dear Freedom Fighter," November 1, 1961, Dillard Papers, Box 2, ALHUA; Babson et al., *Working Detroit*, 162; Thompson, *Whose Detroit?* chap. 2.

63. Young, *Hard Stuff*, 168–69.

64. Watson in Mast, *Detroit Lives*, 88; Smith, *Dancing in the Streets*, chap. 1; Gerald Early, *One Nation under a Groove: Motown and American Culture* (Hopewell, NJ: Ecco Press, 1995).

65. Stanley H. Brown, "Slow Healing of a City," *Fortune*, June 1965; Widick, *Detroit*, chap. 10.

66. Hamlin in "BWC [Black Workers Congress] Leader Looks at Past, Sees New Strategy," *Guardian*, February 28, 1973; also Geschwender, *Class, Race, and Worker Insurgency*, chap. 4; Georgakas and Surkin, *Detroit: I Do Mind Dying*, chap. 1; Thompson, *Whose Detroit?*

67. Georgakas in Mast, *Detroit Lives*, 292; Baker in Mast, *Detroit Lives*, 305.

68. Hamlin in Mast, *Detroit Lives*, 85.

69. "Ken Cockrel: Revolutionary Black Attorney," *Michigan Chronicle*, September 20, 1967; Rod Bush, "Victory of a Black Radical: Interview with Ken Cockrel," in *The*

New Black Vote: Politics and Power in Four American Cities, ed. Rod Bush (San Francisco: Synthesis Press, 1984), 181–98; Georgakas and Surkin, *Detroit: I Do Mind Dying,* 73–77.

70. Tripp quoted in *Michigan Chronicle,* October 19, 1963.

71. Johnson in Mast, *Detroit Lives,* 50.

72. Robert D. Sherad, "The Social Responsibility of the Negro Church," *Freedomways,* spring 1962, 134. Cleage's critique of the Black church is discussed in more detail in the next chapter.

73. Josaitis in Mast, *Detroit Lives,* 41.

74. Shelia Murphy Cockrel in Mast, *Detroit Lives,* 181; Kenneth Cockrel, Interview with Sidney Fine, Detroit Riot Oral History Project, August 26, 1985, transcript in BHC.

75. Posa in Mast, *Detroit Lives,* 55–56.

76. Biography of Ravitz in Mel Ravitz Collection, ALHUA.

77. "The Block Club Movement within the Detroit Tenth Police Precinct," May 1962, DUL Papers, Box 36, MHC; Charles E. West, "The Role of the Block Clubs in the Detroit Civil Disorder of July 1967," MA thesis, Wayne State University, 1970.

78. DCCR, "Some Comments regarding the West Central Organization" (n.d.), DCCR Papers, III, Box 21, ALHUA; *Michigan Chronicle,* November 6 and 13, December 5 and 12, 1965; *Detroit News,* August 15 and 17, December 15, 1965; *Detroit Free Press,* December 11, 1965.

79. Information on block clubs, including their newspapers and meeting minutes, are scattered throughout the papers of the DUL at the Bentley Library, in the papers of the NAACP and the Ernest and Jessie Dillard Papers in ALHUA, and in the pages of the *Michigan Chronicle* and *Detroit Courier,* both of which tended to focus on the social aspects of the clubs.

80. Sims in Mast, *Detroit Lives,* 34.

81. Cockrel in Mast, *Detroit Lives,* 181–82. On Alinsky and his methods, see Alinsky, *Reveille for Radicals* (New York: Vintage, 1969); Alinsky, *Rules for Radicals: A Practical Primer for Realistic Radicals* (New York: Vintage, 1971); and P. David Finks, *The Radical Vision of Saul Alinsky* (New York: Paulist Press, 1984).

82. Baker in Mast, *Detroit Lives,* 99.

83. Kramer in Mast, *Detroit Lives,* 103.

84. Ibid.,103–4. On gender and the league in general, see Thompson, *Whose Detroit?* 168–69, 171–72.

85. Baker quoted in Darrell Dawsey, "An American Revolutionary," *Detroit News,* April 21, 1992; Hamlin in Mast, *Detroit Lives,* 86. On the influence of James and Grace Lee Boggs in general, see Georgakas and Surkin, *Detroit: I Do Mind Dying,* 15–16; and Geschwender, *Class, Race, and Worker Insurgency,* 80, 83–84, 88.

86. Dawsey, "An American Revolutionary"; "Biographical Information—James Boggs," James and Grace Lee Boggs Papers, Box 3, ALHUA; Grace Lee Boggs, *Living for Change: An Autobiography* (Minneapolis: University of Minnesota Press, 1998), chap. 4.

87. Boggs, *Living for Change,* chap. 1; "Biographical Information—Grace Lee Boggs," James and Grace Lee Boggs Papers, Box 4, ALHUA.

88. The very complicated history of the SWP and Trotskyism in general can be told through a series of factions, tendencies, and splits. At the time when James and

Dunayevskaya formed their own tendency there were two other major factions within the party, which eventually split over the question of the Soviet Union after the signing of the Hitler-Stalin pact. The first group, led by James P. Cannon ("Cannonites"), an ex-CP member and one of the founders of American Trotskyism, agreed that while the Soviet Union was a degenerate workers state it still merited defense in the face of Western imperialist aggression. The second group, led by Max Shachtman ("Shachtmanites") viewed the Soviet Union not as a workers' state of any kind but as a new form of class society that had developed a system of bureaucratic collectivism. The latter refused to defend the Soviets and adopted a "third-camp" perspective in opposition to both the Soviet Union and the United States. In 1940, the Shachtmanites left the SWP and formed the Workers Party. The Johnson-Forest tendency belonged to this faction until it reentered the SWP in 1947. See Wald, *The New York Intellectuals;* James P. Cannon, *The History of American Trotskyism* (New York: Pioneer, 1944); and Buhle, *Marxism in the United States,* chap. 6.

89. However, their critique of the Soviet Union and Stalinism did not prevent the U.S. government from attacking them as a subversive organization. SWP members were among the first to be tried under the Smith Act, and the failure of the CP to come to their defense increased the bitterness between the two groups. See Cannon, *The History of American Trotskyism,* chap. 4. On the persecution of the SWP by the government, see Nelson Blackstock, *COINTELPRO: The FBI's Secret War on Political Freedom* (New York: Pathfinder, 1988).

90. James, Dunayevskaya, and Lee, *State Capitalism and World Revolution* (Chicago: Charles H. Kerr, [1950] 1989).

91. James, "Philosophy of History and Necessity" (1943), quoted in Paul Le Blanc, "Introduction: C. L. R. James and Revolutionary Marxism," in *C. L. R. James and Revolutionary Marxism: Selected Writings of C. L. R. James, 1939–1949,* ed. Scott McLemee and Le Blanc (Atlantic Highlands, NJ: Humanities Press, 1994), 20.

92. James, "The Revolutionary Answer to the Negro Problem in the United States" (1948), reprinted in McLemee and Le Blanc, *C. L. R. James and Revolutionary Marxism.*

93. James, "Three Black Women Writers: Toni Morrison, Alice Walker, Ntozake Shange" (1981), reprinted in *The C. L. R. James Reader,* ed. Anna Grimshaw (Oxford: Blackwell, 1992), 414–15. The Boggses were for a time very supportive of Cleage and his attempts to build a Black Christian nationalist movement. See, for example, their "Detroit: Birth of a Nation," *National Guardian,* October 7, 1967; and Grace Lee Boggs, *Living for Change,* 121–23.

94. James et al., *Report and Discussion on Break with S. W. P.* (1951), quoted in Le Blanc, "Introduction: C. L. R. James and Revolutionary Marxism," 17. The Johnson-Forrest tendency left the Workers Party in 1947 and rejoined the SWP only to leave the Trotskyist movement entirely in 1950. In 1953 the SWP suffered a further split led by Bert Cochran, who rejected Trotskyism as unrealistic in cold war America and rejected the SWP as an overly sectarian defender of a sterile orthodoxy. Like the group led by Max Shachtman, the Cochranites moved closer to the Socialist Party and then to a more diffuse social democratic position. See Wald, *The New York Intellectuals,* 298–304.

95. A number of works note the influence of *Correspondence* and Dunayevskaya's *Notes and Letters* group in introducing young radicals to some of James's ideas. See, for

example, Dan Georgakas, "Young Detroit Radicals, 1955–1965," in a special issue of *Urgent Task* dedicated to James (summer 1981); Geschwender, *Class, Race, and Worker Insurgency,* 83–84; and Grace Lee Boggs, *Living for Change,* 99–109.

96. For a good discussion of this phase of James's life see Scott McLemee, "Afterword: American Civilization and World Revolution—C. L. R. James in the United States, 1938–1953 and Beyond," in McLemee and Le Blanc, *C. L. R. James and Revolutionary Marxism,* 221–32; and Paul Buhle, *C. L. R. James: The Artist as Revolutionary* (Verso: London), chaps. 3 and 4.

97. On Dunayevskaya's career, see Richard Greeman, "Raya Dunayevskaya: Thinker, Fighter, Revolutionary," *Against the Current* 12–13 (January–February and March–April 1988): 55–57. See also Dunayevskaya's *Philosophy and Revolution* (New York: Dell, 1973).

98. Once the Boggses left, Martin Glaberman led what remained of the group (twenty-five members nationally with about half in Detroit) until he dissolved it in 1970. Glaberman was himself another important conduit of cross-generational influence. He taught classes on Marx's *Capital,* for instance, that were attended by a number of young radicals. See his "C. L. R. James: A Recollection," in McLemee and Le Blanc, *C. L. R. James and Revolutionary Marxism,* 45–52.

99. James Boggs's "The American Revolution: Pages from a Negro Worker's Notebook" first appeared in *Monthly Review* (July–August 1963) and was widely read in Detroit at the time. See also James Boggs, *Racism and the Class Struggle: Further Pages from a Black Worker's Notebook* (New York: Monthly Review, 1970); and James Boggs and Grace Lee Boggs with Freddy Paine and Lyman Paine, *Conversations in Maine: Exploring Our Nation's Future* (Boston: South End Press, 1978).

100. James, *Marxism and the Intellectuals* (Detroit: Facing Reality, 1962), 25; Le Blanc, "Introduction: C. L. R. James and Revolutionary Marxism," 18–19. On her break with James, see Grace Lee Boggs, *Living for Change,* 107–13.

101. James was the primary author of the SWP's first resolution, "Negro Work," which grew out of a series of discussions he had with Trotsky. Both are included in *Leon Trotsky on Black Nationalism and Self-Determination,* ed. George Breitman (New York: Pathfinder Press, 1967).

102. See, for example, Breitman's *Marxism and the Negro Struggle* (New York: Merit, 1965); and *How a Minority Can Change Society: The Real Potential of the Afro-American Struggle* (New York: Merit, 1965).

103. Naomi Allen and Sarah Lovell, eds., *A Tribute to George Breitman: Writer, Organizer, Revolutionary* (New York: Fourth Internationalist Tendency, 1987), especially the reminiscence of Evelyn Sell, 20–24.

104. Hill's Red Squad File cites his attendance at four forums throughout the late 1950s.

105. Robert Williams, *Negroes with Guns* (New York: Marzani and Munsell, 1962), 12; Charles Jones, "SNCC: Nonviolence and Revolution," *New University Thought* 3 (September–October 1963): 8–19; Tyson, *Radio Free Dixie,* 214–17 on the King-Williams debate and the ways in which King essentially invents a Williams to criticize. On armed self-defense in general, see Lance Hill, *The Deacons for Defense: Armed Resistance and the Civil Rights Movement* (Chapel Hill: University of North Carolina Press, 2004).

106. Van Gosse, *Where the Boys Are: Cuba, Cold War America, and the Making of a New Left* (London: Verso, 1993), 152–53. Gosse credits Williams with being in the fore-

front of the Black-Cuban connection, which began to receive a good deal of attention in the wake of Castro's weeklong stay in Harlem's Theresa Hotel. Castro was warmly received in Harlem and was able to meet with a number of Black political figures, including Malcolm X and Robert F. Williams. Rosemary Mealy, *Fidel and Malcolm X: Memories of a Meeting* (New York: Ocean Press, 1993); Tyson, *Radio Free Dixie,* 220–25.

107. Robert Himmel [then the SWP candidate for mayor], "Freedom Rides Hailed, but Pacifism Won't Stop Terror," *Michigan Militant,* June 1961; Gosse, *Where the Boys Are,* 153–54.

108. Lynn, *There Is a Fountain: The Autobiography of Conrad Lynn* (Brooklyn: Lawrence Hill, 1979), 185 and chap. 13; also the exchange of letters between Lynn and Williams in the Williams Papers, Box 3, MHC.

109. Baker in Mast, *Detroit Lives,* 307.

110. Lynn, *There Is a Fountain,* 185 and chap. 16.

111. Boyd in Mast, *Detroit Lives,* 78–79.

112. Baker in Mast, *Detroit Lives,* 307.

113. See, for example, *Michigan Militant,* March 6 and 14, April 15, and June 10, 1960, and May 5, 1961. Gosse has an extensive discussion of the Fair Play for Cuba Committee and the role of the SWP in its development in his *Where the Boys Are,* chap. 5.

114. Baker in Mast, *Detroit Lives,* 307; "75 Students Defy Cuba Travel Ban," *Militant,* June 22, 1964. In the wake of the trip they were all investigated by the House Un-American Activities Committee. *I. F. Stone's Weekly,* September 14, 1964.

115. House in Mast, *Detroit Lives,* 83. On the influence of Cuba on young Black activists in SNCC, especially Stokely Carmichael, see Clayborne Carson, *In Struggle: SNCC and the Black Awakening of the 1960s* (Cambridge: Harvard University Press, 1985), 272–77; see also Tony Martin, "Rescuing Fanon from the Critics," *The Pan-African Connection: From Slavery to Garvey and Beyond* (Dover, MA: Majority Press, 1983), chap. 12.

CHAPTER SIX

1. Cone, *Black Theology and Black Power.*

2. Cleage, *Black Christian Nationalism,* 16.

3. Boggs, *Living for Change,* 119; Ward, *Prophet of a Black Nation,* 34–35.

4. Ward, *Prophet of a Black Nation,* 38, 43. The story of the Cleage children not being allowed to play with darker children was related by Bermecia (Hill) Morrow, interview with author. The two families lived within blocks of each other.

5. Barbara (Cleage) Martin, phone interview with author, June 23, 2005; "The Early Outreach Ministry of Jaramogi Abebe Ageyman (Rev. Albert B. Cleage, Jr.), 1928–1950," in *The Shrines of the Black Madonna Jubilee Celebration, August 1–3, 2003* (Detroit: PAOCC, 2003), 29; Jaramogi Menelik Kimathi, interview with author, June 23, 2005, Detroit.

6. Cleage, "Message to the Black Nation," *Michigan Chronicle,* July 20, 1968. On the declaration of Black inferiority, see Cleage, *Black Christian Nationalism,* xxv–xxviii. As early as 1952, Cleage preached a sermon condemning the evils of intraracial color prejudice as a practice that comes from mimicking white society. "Rev. A. B. Cleage Condemns Evil," *Michigan Chronicle,* February 23, 1952.

7. Cleage, "An Epistle to Stokely," 42–43. Cone and Cleage developed very dif-

ferent theological ideas about the Blackness of God. For Cone, the concept became highly abstracted and metaphysical, so much so that everyone is invited to "become Black with God" through an acknowledgment of solidarity with the exploited and dispossessed of the world. This is what it means to be like God since, as Cone put it, "Either God is identified with the oppressed to the point that their experiences become his, or he is the god of racism." Cone, *A Black Theology of Liberation* (New York: Lippincott, 1970), 120–21.

8. Ward, *Prophet of a Black Nation*, 30–31; Barbara (Cleage) Martin, phone interview.

9. On Dunbar, which was originally located on St. Antoine Street and Frederick, see Elizabeth Anne Martin, *Detroit and the Great Migration, 1916–1929* (Ann Arbor: Bentley Historical Library, University of Michigan, 1993), 42–45; Grigsby quoted in Thomas, *Life for Us*, 183.

10. Bowles was also regarded as incompetent and corrupt. In July 1930, voters decided to recall him, facilitating the election of Frank Murphy. Sidney Fine, *Frank Murphy: The Detroit Years* (Ann Arbor: University of Michigan Press, 1975), 206–11. After the change of administrations, Dr. Cleage retained his position. Cleage's account of being beat up because of Bowles is in Ward, *Prophet of a Black Nation*, 40.

11. Ward, *Prophet of a Black Nation*, 40–41.

12. Barbara (Cleage) Martin, phone interview; Cleage, "What's Wrong with Our Schools," *Illustrated News*, February 12, 1962; Ward, *Prophet of a Black Nation*, chap. 5, "The Monster Schools."

13. Ward, *Prophet of a Black Nation*, 47.

14. Ibid., 42; "The Early Outreach Ministry," 29. Dade's early admiration for Hill surely helps to account for his strong defense of Hill during the 1952 HUAC hearings. Many others also had fond memories of St. Cyprian's youth ministry, including future judge Damon Keith. Keith to Dade, February 25, 1983, in Dade Family Private Collection. Especially memorable was the fact that Dade allowed dances at his church at a time when this was rare for African American churches. Margaret Dade, interview with author, Detroit, June 25, 2005.

15. Ward, *Prophet of a Black Nation*, 49–50; Reverend White's obituary, *Detroit Free Press*, February 11, 1958; Dukes, "Clergy Integral Part of Leadership Growth."

16. Ward, *Prophet of a Black Nation*, 48–51.

17. Cleage, *Black Christian Nationalism*, 109.

18. Jaramogi Kimathi, interview with author.

19. On neo-orthodox theology in general, see Williams, *America's Religions*, 348–51.

20. Ward discusses Cleage's interest in neo-orthodox theology on pages 102–10 of *Prophet of a Black Nation*. On Niebuhr's influence on King and others involved in the civil rights movement, see Chappell, *A Stone of Hope*, esp. chap. 2.

21. Cleage quoted in Ward, *Prophet of a Black Nation*, 103.

22. Ibid., 42.

23. Cleage quoted in ibid., 102–3. The critique of King by Black theologians on these grounds was prevalent during the late 1960s and early 1970s. More recently, James H. Cone, among others, has begun to reevaluate their previous assessments. See, for example, Cone, *Malcolm and Martin and America* (New York: Orbis, 1994).

24. Cleage, "Dr. King and Black Power," in *The Black Messiah*, 210–11.

25. Thurman, *Footprints of a Dream: The Story of the Church for the Fellowship of All Peoples* (New York: Harper and Brothers, 1959).

26. Cleage, "New-Time Religion," in *The Black Messiah,* 110.

27. Cleage's assessment of Fisk might be unfair given Fisk's civil rights work among African Americans and Japanese Americans, not to mention Thurman's high regard for his colleague. On Fisk, see Ward, *Prophet of a Black Nation,* 54–55.

28. For Thurman's description of Tagore, see his autobiography, *With Head and Heart* (New York: Harcourt Brace Jovanovich, 1979), 129. That this might also be a good description of Thurman himself is suggested by Vincent Harding in his introduction to *For the Inward Journey: The Writings of Howard Thurman,* ed. Anne Spencer Thurman (New York: Harcourt Brace Jovanovich, 1984), ix.

29. Thurman, "Mysticism and Social Change" (1939), reprinted in *A Strange Freedom: The Best if Howard Thurman on Religious Experience and Public Life,* ed. Walter Earl Fluker and Catherine Tumber (Boston: Beacon, 1998), 108–23; also Thurman, *Search for Common Ground: An Inquiry into the Basics of Man's Experience of Community* (Richmond, IN: Friends United Press, 1986).

30. Along with Thurman's autobiography, see the brief biographical sketch in Fluker and Tumber, *A Strange Freedom,* 1–17.

31. Thurman, "The Fellowship Church of All Peoples" (1945), reprinted in Fluker and Tumber, *A Strange Freedom,* 221–22.

32. Thurman, *Jesus and the Disinherited,* in *For the Inward Journey,* 124–25.

33. Ibid.; Cleage, "New-Time Religion," 110–11. On his use of Exodus symbolism, see "We Are God's Chosen People," "But God Hardened Pharaoh's Heart," "The Promised Land," and "Coming in out of the Wilderness," all in *The Black Messiah.* On the tendency to equate Jesus and Moses and the stress on the Exodus in African American Christianity, see Albert Raboteau, *Slave Religion: The "Invisible Institution" in the Antebellum South* (New York: Oxford University Press, 1978); Raboteau, *Fire in the Bones;* and Eugene Genovese, *Roll, Jordan, Roll: The World the Slaves Made* (New York: Pantheon, 1974), 254–55, 272–27. On the problem with Paul in Black religious thought, see Amos Jones Jr., "In Defense of the Apostle Paul: A Discussion with Albert Cleage and James Cone," DD thesis, Vanderbilt University, 1975, 1–42.

34. "The BCN Message and Mission: Revolutionary Transformation," and "Messiah," in *10th Anniversary of Shrine #10: National Tribute to Jaramogi Abebe Agyeman* (N.p., June 1987).

35. Ward, *Prophet of a Black Nation,* 56; "The Early Outreach Ministry;" 31. Filmmaking seems to have been the road not taken for Cleage, but once he made his decision to pursue other avenues for reaching the Black masses he apparently never looked back. Years later, in the 1980s, some camera equipment arrived for Cleage and he simply let it sit untouched. Jaramogi Kimathi, interview with author.

36. Ward, *Prophet of a Black Nation,* chap. 4

37. Quotes from interviews conducted by Ward and reproduced in his *Prophet of a Black Nation,* 62–64; "Early Outreach Ministry,"31–32.

38. "Rev. A. B. Cleage Condemns Evils," *Michigan Chronicle,* February 23, 1952.

39. Cleage quoted in "Early Outreach Ministry," 37. This phase in Cleage's career is discussed on pages 36–38.

40. Cleage quoted in the *Michigan Chronicle,* February 3, 1962. Ward also found a great deal of evidence pointing to Cleage's continued interest in youth during his time in Springfield.

41. Cockrel Interview with Fine, BHC, 12.

42. "Early Outreach Ministry," 38.

43. On the Henry brothers, see Ernest Dunbar, "The Making of a Black Militant," *Saturday Review of the Society*, December 16, 1972, 25–32, copy in Norman McRae Collection, Box 18, ALHUA; Grace Lee Boggs, *Living for Change*, 119–20; and Salvatore, *Singing in a Strange Land*, 232–35, 274–76.

44. Evans, quoted in Ward, *Prophet of a Black Nation*, 47; "Early Outreach Ministry," 39. On the overall importance of the Black press, see Roland E. Wolseley, *The Black Press, U.S.A.*, 2d ed. (Ames: Iowa State University Press, 1990).

45. Cleage, "The Negro in Detroit" (Chapter Four), *Illustrated News*, December 18, 1961. He was obviously influenced by the work of the Black sociologist E. Franklin Frazier, *Black Bourgeoisie: The Rise of a New Middle Class in the United States* (New York: Collier, [1957] 1962). Many of his ideas are also closely aligned with the early writings of Black theologian and historian Joseph Washington. See, for example, Washington's *Black Religion* (Boston: Beacon, 1964), in which he argues for the distinctiveness of African American Christianity while also casting aspersions on the "inauthenticity" of the idea of Black theology—a view he would come to soften in his second book, *The Politics of God* (Boston: Beacon, 1967). Wilmore, *Black Religion and Black Radicalism*, 246, n. 49, 210–11.

46. Cleage, *Black Christian Nationalism*, 75.

47. Cleage, "The Negro in Detroit" (Chapter Five), *Illustrated News*, January 1, 1962.

48. Cleage was responding to a letter from a White man who insisted that his church was happily interracial. "Reverend Cleage Tells You about Negro Separatism," *Detroit Free Press*, September 16, 1968.

49. Symposium, "Race Prejudice in Jazz: It Works Both Ways," *Down Beat*, March 15 and 29, 1962; Frank Kofsky, *Black Nationalism and the Revolution in Music* (New York: Pathfinder, 1970). For a good discussion of Roach and Lincoln's politics, see Eric Porter, *What Is This Thing Called Jazz? African Americans as Artists, Musicians, and Activists* (Berkeley: University of California Press, 2002), 169–76, 181–89; as well as Penny M. Von Eschen, *Satchmo Blows up the World: Jazz Ambassadors Play the Cold War* (Cambridge: Harvard University Press, 170–71, 188–89).

50. "Abbey Lincoln and Black Nationalism," *Illustrated News*, December 3, 1962.

51. Cleage, "Message to the Black Nation" (column), *Michigan Chronicle*, August 3, 1968.

52. On the conventions and the Black arts movement in Detroit and elsewhere in general, see James Edward Smethurst's wonderfully informative and engaging study *The Black Arts Movement: Literary Nationalism in the 1960s and 1970s* (Chapel Hill: University of North Carolina Press, 2005), 226–28, 334; Julius E. Thompson, *Dudley Randall, Broadside Press, and the Black Arts Movement in Detroit, 1960–1995* (Jefferson, NC: McFarland, 1999); and Melba Joyce Boyd, *Wrestling with the Muse: Dudley Randall and the Broadside Press* (New York: Columbia University Press, 2003). On the Revolutionary Action Movement, see Hill, *The Deacons for Defense*, 221–24; Boggs, *Living for Change*, 125, 134; and Cockrel Interview with Fine, 30–31.

53. *Illustrated News*, January 22, 1962.

54. "Cleage Cites 'Apathy' of Civic Groups," *Michigan Chronicle*, February 10, 1962. The selective-buying campaign was conducted by the Negro Preachers of Detroit and Vicinity. Initiated in August 1961, the group claimed success in gaining Black employment at the Taystee Bread Company, Wonder Bread, Ward Baking Company, Sealtest Dairy, Borden's, Standard Oil, Mobil Oil, and the *Detroit News*. See *Michigan Chronicle*, April 28, 1962, and January 19, 1963.

55. "Didn't Cavanagh Get the Message?" *Illustrated News,* January 8, 1962; "Our New Mayor Bears Watching," *Illustrated News,* January 15, 1962; "Open Letter to Cavanagh," *Illustrated News,* November 20, 1961.

56. "Council Assails Racism," and "Racism Defended by Cleage," *Michigan Chronicle,* August 4, 1962; "Commission Censors 'Illustrated News,'" *Michigan Chronicle,* August 11, 1962.

57. "What's Wrong with Our Schools?" *Illustrated News,* December 18, 1961; "Little Rock Comes to Detroit, *Illustrated News,* January 15, 1962; "Teacher Continues a Northwestern Exposé," *Illustrated News,* February 29 and March 5, 1962.

58. Cleage quoted in "Rev. A. B. Cleage, Center of Controversy," *Michigan Chronicle,* February 3, 1962.

59. Marilyn Gittell and T. E. Hollander, *Six Urban School Districts* (New York: Praeger, 1968); National Commission on Professional Rights and Responsibilities of the National Education Association of the United States, *Detroit, Michigan: A Study of Barriers to Equal Opportunity in a Large City* (Washington, DC: National Education Association, 1967).

60. See, for example, William R. Grant, "Community Control vs. School Integration: The Case of Detroit," *Public Interest* 24 (summer 1971); and especially Derek Edgell, *Class Wars: The Movement for Community Control of New York City's Schools, 1966–1970* (Lewiston, NY: Edward Mellen, 1998).

61. Fine, *Violence in the Model City,* 42–45.

62. "Rev. A. B. Cleage, Center of Controversy"; Richard Henry quoted in the *Illustrated News,* November 13, 1991. The group had its first informal meetings in October 1961 and was incorporated as a nonprofit educational organization in April 1962. "GOAL," in Rosa Parks Papers, Box 2, ALHUA; *Michigan Chronicle,* June 16 and 23 and July 14, 1962. A pamphlet from 1963 lists Richard Henry as president, Henry King as first vice president, Edward Broom as second vice president, Henry Leon as treasurer, James Hurst as financial secretary, O. Lee Molette as general counsel, Constance Molette as recording secretary, and Vivian Broom as corresponding secretary, with an Executive Board rounded out by William Bell, Milton Henry, Octavia Vivian Henry, Alphonso Wells, and the Rev. Albert Cleage Jr. George Breitman Papers, Box 47:1, Robert F. Wagner Archives, Tamiment Library, New York University (cited hereafter as RFW-NYU).

63. "Cleage Cites 'Apathy' of Civic Groups," *Michigan Chronicle,* February 10, 1962.

64. Cleage, "Parents Protest Segregation—Court Action Threatened," *Illustrated News,* January 15, 1962; *Detroit News,* January 21 and 23, 1962; *Michigan Chronicle,* January 20 and 27, February 3, and March 10, 1962. On Hill and the Northwestern strike in general, see *Michigan Chronicle,* October 20 and 27 and November 3, 1962.

65. Dunbar, "The Making of a Militant," 29.

66. "School Report Supports Sherrill Parents Bias Suit," *Illustrated News,* March 19, 1962; "Race Bias Breeds Hate," *Illustrated News,* April 14, 1962; *Michigan Chronicle,* January 27, July 7, and August 18, 1962; Fine, *Violence in the Model City,* 47–49.

67. Cleage, "The Strange Role of Dr. Remus Robinson on the School Board," *Illustrated News,* April 2, 1962; "School Boycott Shaping Up for Fall," *Illustrated News,* August 27, 1962.

68. The quotation is actually from the fall of 1963, when the millage was again up for a vote, but it is wholly representative of the editorials produced earlier that year. "Millage Extremists Follow Path of Chaos," *Michigan Chronicle,* November 2,

1963. The attacks on Cleage and GOAL grew worse leading up to the November vote, especially after the paper ran articles on massive layoffs of teachers and crumbling facilities.

69. "Rev. Cleage, Horace Sheffield Debate Millage," *Michigan Chronicle*, March 30, 1963; as well as his column on March 23, 1963. On the DCPE, see *Michigan Chronicle*, January 26 and February 23, 1963. On Robinson, see "Speakers Urge Millage Support," *Michigan Chronicle*, March 2, 1963; and Ofield Dukes, "Mich. Chronicle to Analyze School Millage Proposal," *Michigan Chronicle*, March 9, 1963 and related stories on March 16 and 23, 1963. On the CORE debate, see *Michigan Chronicle*, March 16, 1963; "Cotillions Caught in Millage Hassle," *Michigan Chronicle*, March 23, 1963 (the group was criticized for not taking a position); and *Michigan Chronicle*, February 2 and 23 and March 2, 1963.

70. "We Defeated the Millage," *Illustrated News*, April 8, 1963; *Detroit Free Press*, April 7, 1963. Seeing the glass as half full, the *Michigan Chronicle* was insistent on the fact that most African Americans seemed to have supported the millage. "Center District Votes 60% for Millage," *Michigan Chronicle*, April 6, 1963. It also ran a series of stories and editorials warning of the dire consequences of the millage being voted down by extremists and racists. See, for example, "1,000 Local Negro Teachers Face Loss of Jobs in 1964," *Michigan Chronicle*, May 25, 1963; as well as the lead editorial on the same day and on November 2, 1963.

71. "Is Urban Renewal Blight or Boon to the Negro?" *Detroit Courier*, September 15, 1962, and September 29, 1962.

72. Patrick quoted in *Detroit Courier*, September 15, 1962.

73. Cleage, "Negro Churches Can Not Be Forced out of Medical Center," *Illustrated News*, February 12, 1962.

74. "GOAL Defines Position on Urban Renewal," *Illustrated News*, March 5, 1962; "Urban Renewal: Patrick and the Real Issues," *Illustrated News*, April 2, 1962.

75. "Negro Churches Cannot Be Forced," *Illustrated News*, February 12 and September 17, 1962; Henry Cleage, "Can They Place the Negro out of the Near Inner City?" *Illustrated News*, November 27, 1961; Harold Black, "Urban Renewal: A Program Involving a Multiplicity of Participants," PhD diss., University of Michigan, 1973, 39–42; Darden et al., *Detroit*, 167–73.

76. Clarence C. White, "Community Organization, Participation, and Interaction in Renewal Areas of Detroit," MA thesis, Wayne State University, 1964, 51–69; "Detroit Fellowship Aids Churches," *Michigan Chronicle*, June 29, 1963; "Groups Merge in Fight against 'Negro Removal,'" *Michigan Chronicle*, June 8, 1962.

77. Hood's statement from 1970 quoted in Phil Corner, "Years Moderate Cleage's Fury," *Detroit News*, April 13, 1976; Hood, interview with author.

78. Detroit Commission on Community Relations, "Inter-office Correspondence, Re: UHURU" (September 15, 1963), DCCR Papers, III, Box 21, ALHUA.

79. Fine, *Violence in the Model City*, 27.

80. Luke Tripp quoted in Dukes, "UHURU Leader Says: 'Must Crush White Man,'" *Michigan Chronicle*, October 19, 1963; "UHURU Says US Has 'Racist, Savage Society,'" *Detroit Courier*, October 19, 1963; Thompson, *Whose Detroit?* 109; Boggs, *Living for Change*, 125, 140, 175.

81. Detroit Commission on Community Relations, "Inter-office Correspondence, Re: UHURU," July 15, 1963, DCCR Papers, III, Box 21, ALHUA.

82. Ibid.; Baker in Mast, *Detroit Lives*, 306.

83. Baker in Mast, *Detroit Lives,* 306.

84. Ibid., 306; *Detroit News,* October 15 and 16, 1963; *Detroit Free Press,* October 12 and 15, 1963.

85. *Detroit Courier,* November 30, 1963; *Michigan Chronicle,* October 26, 1963. On the dispute at the Kroger picket between Detroit CORE and UHURU, see "CORE Moves Out," *Detroit Courier,* October 19, 1963.

86. B. J. Widick, TULC member and independent socialist, interview with author, April 15, 1995, Detroit. The pickets at TULC are also mentioned in Dukes, "UHURU Leader Says: 'Must Crush White Man.'"

87. The "Mau Mau Maoist" reference did not originate with Dukes. It is a quote from an unidentified UHURU member: "On the international scene our orientation is Mau Mau Maoist . . . and we support the Cuban Revolution 100 percent" (*Michigan Chronicle,* October 19, 1963). See also "Citizens React against Booing at Ceremonies," which was published in the *Michigan Chronicle* on the same day. Dukes revisits the parallel subversive elements today and the CP in previous struggles in a November 16, 1963, column.

88. "GOAL Supports Jailed Pickets," *Michigan Chronicle,* October 19, 1963. GOAL president Richard Henry did, however, express his opposition to booing the National Anthem.

89. Detroit Supporters of SNCC, "Fund-raising Letter" (September, 1962), Detroit NAACP Papers, Box 19, ALHUA. The group was attempting to raise bail for Watson, Kemp, and two other young Detroiters.

90. Baker, *Detroit Lives,* 306; "UHURU On Trial!" flyer for prehearing rally at Woodward and Fort Street, November 15, 1963, Breitman Papers, Box 47:1, RFW-NYU; *Detroit Courier,* November 30, 1963; *Detroit News,* April 28, 1964; "Mistrial Is Ruled in Booing Case," *Detroit Free Press,* May 3, 1964.

91. On Cockrel and Ravitz's legal strategies, see Thompson, *Whose Detroit?* esp. chap. 6; as well as Georgakas and Surkin, *Detroit: I Do Mind Dying,* chap. 9.

92. DCCR, "Inter-office Correspondence: UHURU" (August 13, 1963), DCCR Papers, III, Box 21, ALHUA.

93. Fine, *Violence in the Model City,* 105–7. As Fine points out (105), before the Scott affair the police department's Community Relations Board had not received a single brutality complaint in nearly six months.

94. *Illustrated News,* July 22, 1963; *Detroit Free Press,* July 6, 9, and 14 and August 8, 1963; *Michigan Chronicle,* July 13, 20, and 27 and August 3, 1963.

95. These and other protests are summarized in Fine, *Violence in the Model City,* 106–7. On the protest at police headquarters, at 1300 Beaubien, see Boggs, *Living for Change,* 126; Salvatore, *Singing in a Strange Land,* 256–59; and *Michigan Chronicle,* July 13, 20, and 27 and August 3, 1963.

96. Fine, *Violence in the Model City,* 107, 150; Tinker, *When the Fire Reaches Us* (New York: William Morrow, 1970), 142. The novel is filled with negative depictions of the relations between Blacks and the police.

97. Cleage, "The Detroit NAACP Is a Joke to People Everywhere," *Illustrated News,* March 4, 1963; Cleage, "Grapes of Wrath," in *The Black Messiah,* 139.

98. "Questions of the American Revolution," 10–11.

99. "Rev. C. L. Franklin Continues Attack on Prophet Jones," *Michigan Chronicle,* June 18, 1955. Prophet Jones was a fascinating and very popular presence in Detroit. Before his ministry was destroyed by his arrest on charges of homosexual solicitation,

his church had thousands of members and received a good deal of media coverage. See, for example, "Prophet Jones: Bizarre Detroit Evangelist Builds Himself a $2 Million Kingdom in the Slums, *Ebony*, April 1950, 67–72; "Preview for the Prophet," *Time*, March 2, 1953, 2; "The Prophet Jones," *Newsweek*, January 12, 1953, 7; and John Kobler, "Prophet Jones: Messiah in Mink," *Saturday Evening Post*, March 2, 1955, 20–21, 74–77. Horace White had raised questions about Jones as early as 1944 ("Prophet Jones—Not a Strange Phenomenon," *Michigan Chronicle*, December 9, 1944).

100. On Franklin, see Salvatore, *Singing in a Strange Land;* as well as my review, "A Preacher in Motown," *New York Times*, February 9, 2005.

101. Salvatore, *Singing in a Strange Land*, 249. His account of the preparations, negotiations, and difficulties leading up to the march is the best currently available. See also Smith, *Dancing in the Streets*, chap. 1.

102. "Negro Ministers Vote 'Hands Off,'" *Detroit Free Press*, June 12, 1963. To a large extent, much of the dispute over the march was reported on in the press, both Black and white.

103. "Ministers Row over March," *Michigan Chronicle*, June 1, 1963. Jose Rames, in "Racial Anatomy of a City," *New University Thought*, September–October 1963, which includes a section on the dispute over the march, notes that there were also questions raised about the DCHR's handling of funds. Word of the dispute also reached King and the SCLC, and there was a suggestion that he "gracefully withdraw" from leading the Detroit march. Branch, *Parting the Waters*, 842–43.

104. The march was postponed once because of the NAACP, and the dispute was taking on the character of an open feud. *Michigan Chronicle*, May 25 and June 22, 1963; *Detroit News*, June 25, 1963. Arthur Johnson, Interview with Sidney Fine, July 23, 1984, Detroit Riot Oral History Project, BHC, 11–12.

105. A recording of King's speech was released by Gordy Records (#906), and distributed by Motown as part of its Black Forum series. Gordy, *To Be Loved*, 248–50; Branch, *Parting the Waters*, 843.

106. "Conversations in Detroit between James Boggs and Xavier Nicholas," 10; "Early Outreach Ministry," 40.

107. While Johnson admitted "sharp personal differences" on "programs and tactics," he denied evidence of a split "of any consequence among the responsible leaders of the community." Johnson and Del Rio quoted in *Detroit News*, July 22, 1963.

108. "Plan Rights Group Patterned on King's," *Detroit News*, November 6, 1963.

109. Worthy was also close to Robert Williams. "ACLU Challenges Government in Conviction of Worthy," *Militant*, February 10, 1964, and March 3, 1964. Williams, Lynn, and Worthy were all active in the Fair Play for Cuba Committee and supportive of Castro and other Cuban revolutionaries. See Gosse, *Where the Boys Are*, esp. chap. 5.

110. The history of the short-lived FNP has not been well documented, and there is some discrepancy about the details of its founding. The best account is in Van Gosse, "More Than Just a Politician: Notes on the Life and Times of Harold Cruse," in *Harold Cruse's* The Crisis of the Negro Intellectual *Reconsidered*, ed. Jerry Watts (New York: Routledge, 2004): 17–40.

111. Franklin quoted in *Detroit Courier*, November 16, 1963; Del Rio quoted in *Detroit News*, November 10, 1963. Sidney Fine gives a brief overview of the rival conferences in *Violence in the Model City*, 28–29; see also Smith, *Dancing in the Streets*, 54–59. Salvatore (*Singing in a Strange Land*, 260) contends that Cleage's decision to

resign from the DCHR was sudden, but contemporary sources suggest that the break had a longer gestation period. See "Cleage-Franklin Split Brewing for Long Time," *Michigan Chronicle*, November 2, 1963.

112. Reverend Franklin blamed the low turnout on confusion about times and locations. "Northern Negro Leadership Conference 'a Failure,'" *Detroit Courier*, November 16, 1963; *Detroit News*, November 10 and 11, 1963; "Conversations in Detroit between James Boggs and Xavier Nicholas," 10–11.

113. Salvatore, *Singing in a Strange Land*, 261. On Merritt and the alliance, see "Leaders 'Withdrew Support from Two 'Splinter' Groups," *Michigan Chronicle*, November 16, 1963; and "Franklin Tiffs with Merritt at Alliance," *Michigan Chronicle*, November 2, 1964.

114. "Message to the Grass Roots," in *Malcolm X Speaks*, ed. George Breitman (New York: Grove Weidenfeld, 1965): 3–17, quote on page 10. On the conference, see also GOAL, "Call to the Northern Negro Grass-Roots Leadership Conference to be held in Detroit, November 9–10," October 30, 1963; as well as "Resolutions Passed at the Northern Negro Grass Roots Leadership Conference, Detroit, Michigan, November 9–10, 1963," both in Breitman Papers, Box 48:2, RFW-NYU. For coverage of the conference, see "Malcolm X Blasts 'Big Six,'" *Michigan Chronicle*, November 16, 1963.

115. Sterling Gray, "Man of the Year: Reverend Albert B. Cleage, Jr., Architect of a Revolution," *Liberator*, December 1963, 8. Dan Watts and Gray of the *Liberator* staff attended the conference and reported on it. Recordings of the proceedings are available in the Audio and Visual Division of ALHUA.

116. Cleage quoted in ibid., 9. Gray attempts to smooth over the distinction between land and power: "Power or land, power AND land, the Northern revolution was on." On Cleage's rejection of the RNA, see "Reverend Cleage Tells You about Negro Separatism," *Detroit Free Press*, September 1, 1968. See also Milton R. Henry, "An Independent Black Republic in North America," in *Black Separatism and Social Reality: Rhetoric and Reason*, ed. Raymond L. Hall (New York: Pergamon, 1977), 33–40.

117. The debate between Breitman and Cleage took place on February 24, 1967, and was reprinted as, "Myths about Malcolm X: Two Views," *International Socialist Review*, September–October 1967, 33–60. Also see Breitman's *The Last Year of Malcolm X: The Evolution of a Revolutionary* (New York: Pathfinder, 1967). On Cleage's previous appearance, see "Rev. Cleage Speaks at Socialist Forum," *Michigan Chronicle*, September 15, 1962.

118. Lynn quoted in Van Gosse, "More than Just a Politician," 29.

119. Boggs's letter to Lynn quoted in Lynn *There Is a Fountain*, 185. This was also the critique that Harold Cruse presented, a critique based on the relationship to white leftists and the essentially "integrationist" outlook of the party's founders. Cruse, *Crisis of the Negro Intellectual: A Historical Analysis of the Failure of Black Leadership* (New York: Quill, [1967] 1984), 414–16.

120. The correspondence between Breitman [GB] and Worthy [WW] about Cleage begins in July with a letter in which Breitman notes the swift change in Cleage's stature over the previous year and mentions that Cleage is a good FNP candidate because "he doesn't give a damn about the Democratic Party." GB to WW, July 27, 1963. The meaning of an all-Black party is discussed in GB to WW, August 30, 1963. On Boggs, see WW to GB, August 4, 1963; on Tripp and others from UHURU,

GB to WW, August 19, 1963; on the difficulty with being Worthy's representative, GB to WW, August 19, 1963; and on problems with getting Cleage to commit to the FNP, GB to WW, September 19 and 20, 1963. All these letters are in Breitman Papers, Box 47, RFW-NYU.

121. GB to WW, August 19, 1963, Breitman Papers, Box 47, RFW-NYU.

122. "Fact Sheet on the Freedom Now Party Candidates, Nov. 3, 1964 Elections," Ernest C. Smith Collection, Box 1, ALHUA.

123. Vaughn was still angry about his defeat as well. See, for example, "Jackie Vaughn Takes Potshot at Van Antwerp," *Michigan Chronicle*, October 5, 1963.

124. Editorial, *Michigan Chronicle*, September 28, 1963; "Van Antwerp's 'No' on Housing Bill Hit," *Michigan Chronicle*, October 5, 1963; "NAACP Asks Court to Halt Racists," *Michigan Chronicle*, September 14, 1963; Fine, *Violence in the Model City*, 59–61; Sugrue, *Origins of the Urban Crisis*, 227–29; Ravitz, Interview with Sidney Fine, Detroit Riot Oral History Project, July 26, 1985, BHC, 19–20.

125. There is a written copy of Cleage's text in Ernest C. Smith Papers, Box 1, ALHUA, but the audio recording is much richer and Cleage strays from his text. The audio version, available at ALHUA as part of the James and Grace Lee Boggs Collection, is also good for getting a sense of how humorous Cleage could be when addressing a crowd.

126. SWP (Resolution), *Freedom Now: New Stage in the Struggle for Negro Emancipation* (New York: Pioneer, 1964). On the internal debate between Breitman and fellow party member A. Philips (Art Fox), see "Breitman's Ballistics: Comments in the Michigan Freedom Now Party" (n.d.), Breitman Papers, Box 47:14, RFW-NYU.

127. "The DeBerry-Shaw Ticket Stands for Freedom Now," *Militant*, June 13, 1964. The SWP also backed Black Marxist Paul Boutelle for New York's City Council. "Freedom Now Enters Race in Harlem," *Militant*, August 10, 1964; "Vote Socialist," *Michigan Militant*, November 6, 1964.

128. "Negro Ministers Here Hit Rights Move Violence," *Michigan Chronicle*, April 15, 1964.

129. "GOAL Members Asked to Join 'Freedom Now' Petition Drive," *Michigan Chronicle*, March 28, 1964; "Dexter Baptist Turns Down Freedom Now Meeting," *Michigan Chronicle*, March 21, 1964; *Detroit News*, March 16, 1964.

130. "Rev. Charles A. Hill Stands on His Record," *Michigan Chronicle*, November 18, 1967.

131. At the same time, Cleage often spoke at SWP Forums in Detroit and New York. "Rev. Cleage to Speak on FNP at Two New York Meetings," *Militant*, May 11 and 21, 1964.

132. County of Wayne, State of Michigan, "Official Statement of Votes Cast at the General Election, November 3, 1964," in Ernest Smith Collection, Box 1, ALHUA.

133. "Results Reveal a New Negro Vote," *Michigan Chronicle*, September 18, 1965; *Michigan Chronicle*, July 3, September 4 and 11, August 14 and 28, October 2 and 30, and November 6, 1965.

134. The particulars of Detroit's TAP program are beyond the scope of my narrative. For a detailed study of its structure, see Sidney Fine, *Violence in the Model City*, chap. 4; Mayor's Committee for Community Renewal, *Total Action against Poverty* (Detroit, 1964); and Special Committee to Investigate Irregularities in the Total Action against Poverty Program in the City of Detroit, *Examination of the War on*

Poverty, 74th Cong., regular sess., 1968 (Washington, DC: Government Printing Office, 1968).

135. "Detroit's Militant Rights Groups Aim for Political Power," *Detroit News,* February 28, 1965; Grace Lee Boggs, "New Direction for CORE," *Michigan Chronicle,* August 7, 1965.

136. August Meier and Elliott Rudwick, *CORE: Study in the Civil Rights Movement, 1942–1968* (New York: Oxford University Press, 1973), 205–6, 305. This change of direction was not peculiar to Detroit but was part of a national trend, which Meier and Rudwick discuss at some length. Moreover, community work was the hallmark of SNCC. See Doug McAdam, *Freedom Summer* (New York: Oxford University Press, 1988); and Clayborne Carson, *In Struggle: SNCC and the Black Awakening of the 1960s* (Cambridge: Harvard University Press, 1981).

137. The WCO had sent representatives to Chicago to observe Alinsky's method. In the fall of 1965, the WCO was engaged in raising funds to bring Alinsky to Detroit for five days to serve as a consultant. *Michigan Chronicle,* October 2, 1965.

138. Jessie R. Baclis, "Minority Report regarding West Central Organizing Committee" (n.d.), DCCR, III, Box 21, ALHUA; Alinsky, *Reveille for Radicals;* Finks, *The Radical Vision of Saul Alinsky.*

139. Baclis, "Minority Report." See also James F. Findley, *Church People in the Struggle: The National Council of Churches and the Black Freedom Movement* (New York: Oxford University Press, 1993).

140. WCO, *A People's Union: The Self-Determination of Neighborhood Groups* (Detroit: WCO, 1966); *Detroit News,* August 15, 1965.

141. "WCO Pickets Police," *Michigan Chronicle,* December 6, 1965.

142. "House on Hobart Street," *West Central Action News,* November 24, 1966; *Detroit Free Press,* November 16, 1966; DCCR, "Inter-office Correspondence—WCO" (August 10, 1966), DCCR Collection, Box 21, ALHUA; Fine, *Violence in the Model City,* 63–64, 171–72.

143. Cockrel Interview with Fine, BHC, 6.

144. Freeman quoted in *Detroit Free Press,* September 8, 1968.

CONCLUSION

The opening quotation is from the *Detroit Free Press,* September 28, 1966. Carmichael, then head of SNCC, spoke at Cleage's Shrine of the Black Madonna on September 27, 1966, to a crowd of more then a thousand. See also the *Detroit News,* September 28, 1966.

1. I have no intention of adding to the volumes of literature on Detroit's rebellion. The best comprehensive study is Sidney Fine, *Violence in the Model City;* see also *The Kerner Report: The 1968 Report of the National Advisory Commission on Civil Disorders* (New York: Pantheon, [1968] 1988).

2. Ravitz Interview with Fine, BHC, 6–7.

3. Fine, *Violence in the Model City,* chaps. 3 and 4; Darden et. al., *Detroit,* chap. 3.

4. "Early Outreach Ministry," 41–42.

5. Materials on the original chancel stained glass window were supplied by Paul Lee, the unofficial historian of the shrines and the Pan African Orthodox Christian Church, in an e-mail exchange, April 9, 2005, in my possession. When members of

the departing church, Brewster-Pilgrim, asked to take the stained glass window with them, Cleage offered to sell it to them. The glass remained. Kimathi, interview with author.

6. Dowdell quoted in *Detroit Free Press,* March 25, 1967.

7. Paul Lee to author, e-mail exchange, April 4, 2005.

8. The following year, in 1968, Dowdell was indicted on charges of forging twenty thousand-dollar savings bonds and attempting to pass them. In 1970 he fled to Sweden, where he successfully fought extradition efforts by the U.S. government. While in Sweden he kept in contact with members of the League of Revolutionary Black Workers and established its Solidarity Committee. Ken Cockrel and Luke Tripp visited Dowdell in Sweden in 1970. Georgakas and Surkin, *Detroit: I Do Mind Dying,* 121–22; "Sweden Refuses to Return Detroit Artist for Trial," *Detroit News,* June 16, 1971, and related stories on March 16 and 22, 1971; *Detroit Free Press,* March 17, 1971.

9. Cleage, "The Resurrection of the Nation," in *The Black Messiah,* 85. The prayer for Dowdell and Baker is not included in the published version of the sermon, but it is in the original recording, "'Resurrection' (Unveiling of the Black Madonna), March 26, 1967," copy supplied courtesy of James W. Ribbron, a longtime member of the shrine.

10. Cleage quoted in Alex Poinsett, "The Quest for a Black Messiah," *Ebony,* March 1969, 176. In various sections of the sermons collected in *The Black Messiah,* Cleage gives detailed historical reasoning to support his claim. Other Black theologians, such as James Cone and J. Deotis Roberts, were less convinced of the literal Blackness of Christ and took a more symbolic approach. See Kelly Brown Douglas's discussion of this debate in *The Black Christ* (Maryknoll, NY: Orbis, 1994), chap. 3; as well as Theo Witvliet, *The Way of the Black Messiah: The Hermeneutical Challenge of Black Theology as Black Liberation* (Oak Park, IL: Meyer Stone, 1987). As Kelly Brown Douglas notes, there is no ample evidence to suggest that Cleage was on the right track, that Jesus was dark skinned, or that the early Israelite tribes to which Jesus was ancestrally linked were "a mixed group of people with African connections" (*The Black Christ,* 79). See also Cain Felder, *Troubling Biblical Waters: Race, Class, and Family* (Maryknoll, NY: Orbis, 1989).

11. Cleage, *The Black Messiah,* 92–94; also Hubert Maultsby, "Paul, Black Theology, and Hermeneutics," *Journal of the Interdenominational Theological Center* 32 (spring 1976): 49–64. Similarly, Williams held Paul responsible for distorting the revolutionary message of the historical Jesus. On Williams's theology, see Belfrage, *A Faith to Free the People.*

12. On the 1964 hearings about Cleage's political and theological views, see Ward, *Prophet of a Black Nation,* 146–55.

13. On Garveyism and the African Orthodox Church, see Burkett, *Garveyism as a Religious Movement;* Wilmore, *Black Religion and Black Radicalism,* 145–52; "Negroes Acclaim a Black Christ," *New York Times,* August 6, 1924; and Elijah Muhammad, *The True History of Jesus* (Chicago: Coalition for the Remembrance of Elijah Muhammad, 1992). Muhammad Ali quoted in Stephen Prothero, *American Jesus: How the Son of God Became a National Icon* (New York: Farrar Straus Giroux, 2003), 214; Malcolm X's statement to *Playboy* (March 1963) quoted in Prothero, *American Jesus,* 215.

14. On Johnson, see Samella Lewis, *African America Art and Artists* (Berkeley: University of California Press, 1990), 88–95; a photo reproduction of *Lamentations,* which is now part of the National Collection of Fine Arts at the Smithsonian, appears on page 93.

15. On Cullen's poetry, especially "The Black Christ," see Qiana Whitted, "In My Flesh I See God: Ritual Violence and Racial Redemption in 'The Black Christ,'" *African American Review* 38:3 (fall 2004): 379–94. See also Prothero, *American Jesus,* 220–22; Gerald Early's introduction to *My Soul's High Song: The Collected Writings of Countee Cullen,* ed. Gerald Early (New York: Anchor Books, 1991), which includes "The Black Christ"; and Alan R. Shucard, *Countee Cullen* (Boston: Twayne, 1984). On Hughes, see Rampersad, *The Life of Langston Hughes,* 224–26; the poem itself appears on page 224.

16. "Black Christ Returns to Church," *Africa News Service,* October 25, 2004; "Black Christ Painting Found in a Basement," *Electronic Mail and Guardian,* July 31, 1997, http://www.chico.mweb.co.za/mg/art/reviews/97; "Painting That Depicts a Black Christ Returned to South Africa," *Jet,* November 24, 1997, 25.

17. Robeson's identification with the Welsh is discussed in Martin Bauml Duberman, *Paul Robeson: A Biography* (New York: Ballantine, 1989), 191, 227–28, 414.

18. The description of the Cardiff window is taken from Whitted, "In My Flesh I See God," 10.

19. Alex Poinsett, "The Quest for the Black Christ," *Ebony,* March 1969, 170–78; also "Artists Portray a Black Christ," *Ebony,* April 1971, 177–80. A picture of the Black Christ was published on the front page of the *Michigan Chronicle* on August 5, 1967.

20. Cleage, *Black Christian Nationalism,* xxxiv.

21. "Constitution of the Inner-City Organizing Committee," October 2, 1966, Boggs Collection, Box 5:7, ALHUA; also "Detroit: Birth of a Nation," *National Guardian,* October 7, 1967, in which the Boggses also discuss the importance of Cleage as "the first Christian minister who has become a leading black nationalist spokesperson."

22. Murray Kempton, "The Black Manifesto," *New York Review of Books,* July 10, 1969, electronic version, http://www.nybooks.com/articles/11266. On Cleage and Rennie Freeman's role in IFCO, see Ward, *Prophet of a Black Nation,* 192–95.

23. "Militants Go It Alone," *Detroit Daily Press* [issued during a *Free Press* strike in 1968], January 6, 1968.

24. The writings of these and other Black theologians have been collected in *Black Theology: A Documentary History, 1966–1979,* ed. Gayraud S. Wilmore and James Cone (Maryknoll, NY: Orbis, 1979); see also Wilmore, *Black Religion and Black Radicalism,* chap. 8.

25. Leon W. Watts, "The National Committee of Black Churchmen," *Christianity and Crisis,* November 2, 1970, 237–43. As Wilmore and Cone note, Cleage was active in the beginning but later renounced the committee for its "Black schoolmen's" approach to theology "written for a white audience." Cleage quoted in Wilmore and Cone, *Black Theology,* 67.

26. See, for example, Herbert O. Edwards, "Black Theology and Liberation Theology," in Wilmore and Cone, *Black Theology,* 516–30; and George Cummings, *A Common Journey: Black Theology (USA) and Latin American Liberation Theology* (Maryknoll, NY: Orbis, 1993).

27. Cleage, *Black Christian Nationalism,* xvii. See also Kelly Brown Douglas's interesting comparison of the figure of the Black Christ in the theologies of Cleage, Cone, and J. Deotis Roberts (*The Black Christ,* chaps. 3 and 4).

28. "Detroit Courting Negro Militant," *New York Times,* August 13, 1967; "New Black Establishment Insists It Gives the Order," *Michigan Chronicle,* August 19, 1967; see also *Michigan Chronicle,* August 26, 1967. On the City-Wide Citizens Action Com-

mittee as part of a larger national trend, see "Negroes See Riots Giving Way to Black Activism in the Ghetto," *New York Times*, October 21, 1968; see also Fine, *Violence in the Model City*, chap. 16.

29. See, for example, Cleage, "What Kind of Unity," August 19, 1967; and his first column, "We Must Control Our Community," *Michigan Chronicle*, August 12, 1967.

30. On the New Detroit Committee see Fine, *Violence in the Model City*, chaps. 13 and 14; and Thompson, *Whose Detroit?* 73–88.

31. Cleage, "Self-Determination and Accountability," *Michigan Chronicle*, January 13, 1968. See also "Traditional Leadership, Corporations Get a Slap," *Michigan Chronicle*, January 13, 1968 and January 4, 1968; and Cleage's column, January 6, 1969.

32. *The Black Manifesto*, reprinted in Wilmore and Cone, *Black Theology*, 80–89. See also Robert S. Lecky and H. Elliott, eds., *The Black Manifesto* (New York: Sheed and Ward, 1969); Arnold Schuster, *Reparations: The Black Manifesto and Its Challenge to White America* (Philadelphia: Lippincott, 1970); and *The Political Thought of James Forman*, ed. Black Star Publishing Staff (Detroit: Black Star, 1970).

33. Freeman to James Boggs, NBEDC [National Black Economic Development Conference] Materials, August 4, 1969, Boggs Papers, Box 3, ALHUA. Dan Georgakas and Marvin Surkin discuss the conference and the connections between the resulting organization and the League of Revolutionary Black Workers in *Detroit: I Do Mind Dying*, 94–99. See also Wilmore, *Black Religion and Black Radicalism*, 202–9; and Thompson, *Whose Detroit?* 89–90, 97.

34. On the reaction of white churches to *The Black Manifesto*, see Murray Kempton, "The Black Manifesto;" Gayraud S. Wilmore, "The Church's Reaction to the Black Manifesto," in Georgakas Collection, Box 1, ALHUA; and Thomas A. Johnson, "Blacks Press Reparations Demands," *New York Times*, June 10, 1970.

35. Sheila Murphy Cockrel in Mast, *Detroit Lives*, 182.

36. Hamlin in Mast, *Detroit Lives*, 86–87; also Thompson, *Whose Detroit?* chaps. 6 and 7.

37. "BWC Leader Looks at Past, Sees New Strategy," *Guardian*, February 28, 1973. In Marxist-Leninist terms, the "street force" is comparable to the Black lumpen proletariat, a potential revolutionary force. Boggs, who continued to define Black power in strictly anticapitalist terms, continued to exert an influence on Black radicalism in Detroit. Boggs, "Black Power: A Scientific Concept," *Liberator*, April 1967; Boggs, John Williams, and Charles Johnson, "The Myth and Irrationality of Black Capitalism" (n.d.), position paper prepared for the Black Economic Development Conference, James and Grace Lee Boggs Papers, Box 4, ALHUA.

38. Edward Lee, "Whoever Heard of Bongo Drums on the Picket Line?" (n.d.), James and Grace Lee Boggs Papers, Box 5, ALHUA.

39. For a history of the league's "outreach" work, as well as its labor activism, see James A. Geschwender, *Class, Race, and Worker Insurgency*, esp. chap. 7; Georgakas and Surkin, *Detroit: I Do Mind Dying;* and Thompson, *Whose Detroit?*

40. For the league's derogatory view of the Panthers and their preemptive organizing, see Geschwender, *Class, Race, and Worker Insurgency*, 140–43.

41. Ernie Allen, "Dying from the Inside: The Decline of the League of Revolutionary Black Workers," in *They Should Have Served That Cup of Coffee*, ed. Dick Cluster (Boston: South End Press, 1979), 71–111.

42. Thompson, *Whose Detroit?* 201–3; *Detroit News* August 18, 1973.

43. On the relationship between the league, and other New Left groups, and the UAW, see Levy, *The New Left and Labor in the 1960s,* 75–78. Levy also includes a discussion of the Wallace campaign (182, 191–92). Wallace managed to obtain nearly 10 percent of the votes cast in Michigan, even after the UAW, the state AFL-CIO, and the Michigan Teamsters carried out a massive anti-Wallace campaign to combat pro-Wallace sympathies among workers. Babson et al., *Working Detroit,* 172–73.

44. Kenneth O'Reilly, *"Racial Matters:" The Secret File on Black America, 1960–1972* (New York: Free Press, 1989), 280. See also, Nelson Blackstock, *COINTELPRO: The FBI's Secret War on Political Freedom* (NewYork: Anchor Foundation, 1988), which focuses on the efforts to destroy the SWP.

45. Frank Joyce in Mast, *Detroit Lives,* 278.

46. "Congressman George W. Crockett, Jr., A Biographical Sketch," Norman McRae Collection, Box 16, ALHUA; also Crockett's statement on the incident, August 3, 1969, Norman McRae Collection, Box 16, ALHUA. Georgakas and Surkin, *Detroit: I Do Mind Dying,* has a lively account of the New Bethel incident, the trials, and the aftermath; see also Thompson, *Whose Detroit?* which is particularly interesting in terms of its focus on the legal strategy employed.

47. Adams quoted in Lloyd Gite, "The New Agenda of the Black Church: Economic Development for Black America," *Black Enterprise* 24:5 (December 1993), 55; Adams, interview with author.

48. Hood, interview with author; for a more detailed account of the efforts and successes of programs at Plymouth, see the church's Web site: http://puccdetroit.org/pages/8/page8.html.

49. "A Warrior for Civil Rights," *Detroit Free Press,* March 9, 1983; Margaret Dade, interview with author; Dade's obituary, *Detroit Free Press,* January 29, 1991.

50. Dade, "St. Cyprian's Looks Back and Looks Ahead," in *Black Gospel/White Church,* ed. John M. Burgess (New York: Seabury Press, 1982, 42); Malcolm G. Dade Jr., phone interview with author, July 6, 2005.

51. Cleage, *Black Christian Nationalism,* xvi–xvii.

52. Cleage quoted in "Early Outreach Ministries," 43.

53. "Detroit Shrine Celebrates 50th Anniversary," *Detroit News,* July 29, 2003; Young, *Hard Stuff,* 199; also "Young Relies on Preachers, and Draws on Their Style," *Detroit Free Press,* October 17, 1991.

54. Barbara (Cleage) Martin, interview with author; Jaramogi Menelik Kimathi, interview with author; "History of the Shrines of the Black Madonna of the Pan African Orthodox Christian Church," in *Jubilee Celebration, August 1–3, 2003,* 48–53; "Albert Cleage Is Dead at 88; Led Black Nationalist Church," *New York Times,* February 27, 2000.

INDEX